OLD EDITION

Rights of Light

Second edition

Rights of Light

Second edition

Stephen Bickford-Smith MA (Oxon), FCIArb
Barrister and Chartered Arbitrator,
A Master of the Bench of the Inner Temple
Landmark Chambers, London

and

Andrew Francis MA (Oxon)
Barrister of Lincoln's Inn
Serle Court, 6 New Square, London

with

Elizabeth de Burgh Sidley BA, FRICS
Chartered Surveyor
Drivers Jonas, London

David Blundell MA, M.Phil (Cantab)
Barrister of the Inner Temple
Landmark Chambers, London

JORDANS

Published by
Jordan Publishing Limited
21 St Thomas Street
Bristol BS1 6JS

British Library Cataloguing-in-Publication Data

A catalogue record for this book is available from the British Library.

ISBN 978 1 84661 024 0 $100516807 8$

Typeset by Letterpart Ltd, Reigate, Surrey

Printed in Great Britain by Antony Rowe Limited

ACKNOWLEDGMENTS

Our thanks are due to the staff of Jordans, particularly Tony Hawitt, whose patience and encouragement have lightened the load of preparing this new edition.

As in the case of the first edition, we have to thank our respective wives for putting up with the toll on our energy and time due to the long task of revising the text to take in the developments of the last 7 years. Our thanks also go to Andrew's son Hugo for providing the line drawings in Chapter 16.

Professional colleagues, too numerous to name, both lawyers and surveyors, have continued to be a valuable source of suggestions and opinions and help us to keep our feet on the ground. The first edition raised appreciative interest, and has prompted a steady flow of contact from members of the public with problems and questions. We have learned much from this contact, not least the need to make the subject comprehensible and accessible to ordinary people.

STEPHEN BICKFORD-SMITH

ANDREW FRANCIS
April 2007

FOREWORD

I am pleased to be invited to write a foreword to this new work on rights of light. It promises to become the standard practitioners' handbook on this important subject. As the authors point out in their preface, it is a subject which can have a profound impact on the development potential of land. They point to the fact that there may be no physical evidence of the existence of such rights other than the presence of windows in buildings which receive light over other land. Rights to light may be acquired by 20 years' user without any requirement of registration, and qualify as 'overriding interests'. Such considerations make it of the first importance that lawyers advising their clients on potential developments should be fully aware of the principles involved.

This book offers a comprehensive treatment of the subject. It covers the definition and extent of rights to light, their acquisition, their extinguishment, and their regulation by deed. There is also an extensive treatment of litigation relating to rights of light, brought fully up to date to take into account the Woolf reforms. The section on the measurement and valuation of light contains a clear exposition of the difficult technical issues. I particularly welcome the practical approach to explaining the interaction of rights to light with planning law. Finally, the conveyancing issues arising in relation to rights to light are fully examined.

In its Seventh Programme, approved in 1999, the Law Commission announced a new project for the examination of easements and analogous rights, with a view to their reform and rationalisation. This will be a major undertaking, and it is unlikely that it will yield legislative change for some years. In the meantime, the practitioner could have no better guide than this book. It will also provide a valuable starting point for our own work on this aspect of the law of easements. I strongly commend it to the legal world.

ROBERT CARNWATH
The Law Commission
21 January 2000

PREFACE TO THE SECOND EDITION

When we wrote the preface to the first edition, we set out our objective as to give a full account of the modern law relating to rights to light. This we believe we succeeded in doing. We also expressed our belief that the time was right for a book dedicated solely to rights to light. This has been borne out by events. The law relating to rights of light remains of great practical importance to many development projects. The case *of Regan v Paul Properties Ltd*, decided in September 2006, represents the first time the Court of Appeal has reviewed the law in this area for over 20 years, and testifies to the continued relevance of the subject.

In this new edition we have taken account of this decision, and other cases of relevance since 2000. We have also incorporated legislative changes, including provisions as diverse as the Land Registration Act 2002, the Anti-Social Behaviour Act 2003 and the Planning and Compensation Act 2004.

As we pointed out in the preface to the first edition, many common law countries have abolished prescriptive rights of light by statute even where, as in Australia, they gained an initial toehold as part of the law brought over from the mother country. Their durability in England is something of an anomaly. The Law Commission has recently launched a project to review the law of easements and covenants. It states that 'the law has never been subject to a comprehensive review and is now outdated and a cause of difficulty'. Time will tell whether any suggested cure is better or worse than the disease. The Prescription Act 1832, itself the source of much confusion and obscurity, was intended to reform the law. It seems unlikely that any change in the law is imminent.

The law is stated as at 1 March 2007 save where it has been possible to incorporate later material at proof stage.

STEPHEN BICKFORD-SMITH

ANDREW FRANCIS

June 2007

PREFACE TO THE FIRST EDITION

The purpose of this book is to give a full account of the modern law relating to rights to light. The authors believe that this has not been attempted since the appearance in 1911 of the now long-forgotten *Treatise upon the Law of Light* by R Nicholson Combe.

For many reasons, the time is right for a book dedicated solely to rights to light. At a time when the pace of economic and social change is accelerating and the world is increasingly seen as a single market-place, redevelopment of the built environment is becoming more necessary and more time-constrained to accommodate the exigencies of business and residential occupiers and their financial backers. Rights to light issues often arise in the redevelopment context. The raison d'être of rights to light is to protect the light received through windows in existing buildings from unreasonable interference by new buildings.

At this point, two peculiarities of rights to light as easements are important. First, there may be no physical evidence of their existence other than the presence of windows in buildings which receive light over other land. This is in contrast, for example, to a right of way, where it would normally be possible to discern the existence of the way both from its physical presence and from its use. Secondly, rights to light (like other easements) can be acquired in various ways. But rights to light, unlike other rights, can come into existence through 20 years' actual user, whether or not as of right, unless they are exercised by written permission. Such rights are, for land registration purposes, overriding interests, and hence are valid whether or not they are registered on the titles of dominant and servient owners.

For developers, the emergence of claims for rights to light over their land in favour of nearby buildings can, indeed, come as an unwelcome surprise, particularly if the project is already under way. There are, therefore, sound practical reasons for lawyers concerned with conveyancing and development to be aware of the problems of rights to light; this alone justifies a book dedicated to the subject.

A further reason for a fresh look at the law in this area is that it is in a state of constant development and change. Rights to light are affected directly by few Acts of Parliament: they form part of that body of the common law going back for many hundreds of years which recognises, as legal interests in land, not only complete ownership and leases but a diverse collection of other rights. This apparent antiquity, however, can be deceptive. The interface between the right to light and other areas of the law, often of more recent origin, raises important issues. For example, the relationship between rights to light and the law relating to town and country planning poses interesting riddles for lawyers and planners. Light obstruction notices, under the Rights of Light Act 1959, can involve judicial review issues. The remedies available to a person whose rights to light have allegedly been infringed involve issues on the grant of equitable remedies by way of injunctions and damages, which depend heavily on recent and ongoing developments in other legal contexts.

There is, therefore, a need to synthesise a number of diverse elements to cover the area satisfactorily. This we have sought to do.

Practitioners will be well aware that, both in negotiations and legal proceedings, issues of valuation of loss of light are of great importance. Detailed treatment of them is, therefore, essential and so a chapter on valuation has been contributed by a chartered surveyor with experience of both the legal and valuation issues which arise.

It is perhaps reasonable to ask whether rights to light ought to continue to exist, or at least be capable of being acquired (as at present) by prescription. There are two objections to the present law, neither of which is wholly unjustified. The first is that it skews the law too far in favour of the owners and occupiers of existing buildings, a kind of common law 'nimbyism'. A narrower objection is that by allowing rights to light to be acquired by 20 years' user, without any requirement of registration at the Land Registry, since they qualify as 'overriding interests', both the uncertainty of titles and difficulty of developing sites in urban areas are unnecessarily increased.

As to the latter point, the Law Commission and the Land Registry have recently reviewed the land registration system. The results of their investigations have been published in a document whose grandiose title *Land Registration for the Twenty-First Century* (Law Com 254) belies the thoroughness of its analysis of the existing land registration system. However, whilst its authors acknowledge the criticism of the existing system that easements acquired by prescription (as overriding interests) may be undiscoverable from searching the registering title, they reject significant changes to the present system in this regard, although there are suggestions governing the extinguishment of easements, and for registration of those which are expressly granted or contracted to be granted. It seems, therefore, that the present law can safely be regarded as unlikely to be changed soon.

By contrast, in other countries where common law applies, more radical solutions have been adopted. In the USA, there is no general recognition of a right to light in State law or Federal law. The courts there have taken the view that rights to light and air ought not to be recognised because they would inhibit building and expansion, although, in practice, light and views may be protected in various ways. For instance, the written grant of an easement of light may be recognised or local statute may restrict buildings in various ways, and where an area of land is sub-divided, or forms part of a planned unit development, there may be covenants, conditions and restrictions ('CC and Rs') embodied in a document which is issued to each owner providing for restrictions on the use of their properties. In practice, light issues relating to the construction of major buildings in down-town locations are governed by local ordinances which include provisions for protecting light received by existing buildings.

In New Zealand and Australia, the law has been changed by statute to restrict the acquisition of rights to light. In New Zealand, Part IX of the Property Law Act 1952 prohibits the acquisition of a right to light or air except as provided by that Act. The only rights to light or air which are recognised are those made by deed (or in appropriate statutory form), and which are duly registered within 12 months from the date of execution by the grantor, and which limit and define accurately 'the area or parcel of land on, to, or over which the uninterrupted access of light or air, or light and air, is intended to be provided for'. This system, which has been in force in various forms since 1894, addresses the twin problems of unreasonable restriction on development which may result from prescriptive rights to light and uncertainty as to the existence of such rights.

Likewise, in Australia the creation of easements of light arising by way of prescription has been abolished by legislation, and thus such rights can be acquired only by express or implied grant. Generally, local statutory provisions require that the existence of easements be registered in relation to the dominant and servient land. New South Wales requires that land benefited and burdened be identified in the instrument creating the easement if it is to be enforceable against an owner of the burdened land other than the original party to the arrangement.

Further, in some States in Australia, jurisdiction is conferred on the relevant Supreme Court, upon the application of any person interested in the land, to modify, or extinguish easements on certain specified grounds. These grounds include:

(a)   where the easement ought to be deemed obsolete, or its continued existence would impede the reasonable use of the servient land without securing a practical benefit to the persons entitled to the easement;

(b)   where those entitled to the easement have agreed to the easement being wholly or partly extinguished, or may reasonably be considered to have abandoned the easement wholly or partly; and

(c)   where the extinguishment would not substantially injure those entitled to the easement.

The provisions find an echo in those of s 84 of the (English) Law of Property Act 1925 relating to the variation and discharge of restrictive covenants, although, once again, there is no equivalent provision in English law.

Possibly, the time may have arisen for some fresh thought to be given as to whether some changes are needed to the English law on rights to light to meet modern needs and avoid the uncertainty and expensive disputes which are endemic in the law as it stands at present.

A more fundamental issue may be whether rights to light serve any useful purpose at a time when the development of land is so closely controlled by town and country planning legislation. Given, or so the argument runs, that planning is carried out in the public interest by democratically elected local bodies, what need is there of private rights which may conflict with the public interest? The authors would not accept this suggestion: those who are closely involved in planning law are conscious that its practical application does not always live up to its aspirations in terms of securing a consistent pattern of decision-making. More fundamentally, it is precisely because planning law operates in the public interest that there needs to be independent protection of private rights. These rights should not be expropriated by stealth, and any such attempt could raise issues under the Human Rights Act 1998.

The appearance of a Consultation Paper from the Department of the Environment, Transport and the Regions on the problems posed by high hedges and their detrimental effects on light to buildings and gardens, suggests that the law relating to rights to light may be on the move, although any new legislation seems some way off. The Consultation Paper is covered in Chapter 2.

We have endeavoured to state the law as at 1 February 2000, save where it has been possible to incorporate late material at proof stage.

STEPHEN BICKFORD-SMITH

ANDREW FRANCIS
February 2000

TABLE OF ABBREVIATIONS

A1P1	Article 1 of the First Protocol
BRE	Building Research Establishment
CCR	County Court Rules 1981
CPR	Civil Procedure Rules 1998
DCLG	Department of Communities and Local Government
DoE	Department of the Environment, Transport and the Regions
ECHR	European Court of Human Rights
EFZ	equivalent first zone
HCCCJO	High Court and County Courts Jurisdiction Order 1991
HRA 1998	Human Rights Act 1998
LDD	local development document
Lord Cairn's Act	Chancery Amendment Act 1858
LPA	local planning authority
LRA 1925	Land registration Act 1925
LRA 2002	Land Registration Act 2002
LRR 1925	Land Registration Rules 1925
PPGs	Planning Policy Guidance notes
PPSs	Planning Policy Statements
RPB	regional planning bodies
RSC	Rules of the Supreme Court 1965
RSS	regional spatial strategies
the 1832 Act	Prescription Act 1832
the 1959 Act	Rights of Light Act 1959
the 1990 Act	Town and Country Planning Act 1990
the Commission	European Commission of Human Rights
the Convention	the European Convention on Human Rights
the Secretary of State	the Secretary of State for the Environment, Transport and the Regions
the Strasbourg Court	the European Court of Human Rights
UDP	Unitary Development Plan
YP	Years' Purchase

TABLE OF ABBREVIATIONS

CONTENTS

TABLE OF STATUTES

References are to paragraph numbers.

TABLE OF STATUTORY INSTRUMENTS

References are to paragraph numbers.

TABLE OF CASES

References are to paragraph numbers.

Chapter 1

THE PROPERTY LAW CONTEXT

EASEMENTS IN PROPERTY LAW

1.1   Rights to light are an example of those rights known to the law as easements. An easement is defined in *Halsbury's Laws of England* as:[1]

> ' . . . a right annexed to land to utilise other land of different ownership in a particular manner (not involving the taking of any part of the natural produce of that land or any part of its soil) or to prevent the owner of the other land from utilising his land in a particular manner.'

An easement has been said judicially to be 'a familiar creature of English land law'.[2]

1.2   This definition applies to an easement of light as to others. One point of importance should, however, be stressed at the outset. A right to light can exist *only* in favour of *defined apertures* in *buildings*. There is no right recognised by law to receive light falling on unbuilt land. This distinguishes rights to light from many other easements such as, for example, rights of way, which can exist for the benefit of land whether or not it is built on.

> 'The principle . . . I conceive to be that, until defined and confined, there is . . . as in light . . . in its natural state, no subject matter capable of being the subject of a lawful grant, nor from the very nature of the thing can there be any definite occupation or enjoyment.'[3]

The reason for the rule is that an easement is a property right which must be sufficiently definite to be capable of being the subject of a grant, and:[4]

> 'Although the general access of light from the heavens to the earth is indefinite, the light which enters a building by a particular aperture does and may pass over the adjoining land in a course which, though not visibly defined is really certain and, in that sense, definite.'

1.3   The essential idea behind the concept of a right to light, as with other easements, is a *right over land belonging to another*, falling short of full ownership or possession. In Roman (and Scots) law the analogous concept is that of the *servitude*, a burden imposed on the land of one owner in favour of land belonging to another. The English law relating to easements is 'perhaps the most Roman part of English law'.[5] This results from extensive borrowings from Roman law to fill out the rather undeveloped native law during the early part of the nineteenth century, when England was increasing rapidly in

---

[1]   (4th edn) vol 14, para 1.
[2]   Per Hoffmann LJ in *Willies-Williams v National Trust* (1993) 65 P&CR 359 at 361, CA.
[3]   *Dalton v Angus* (1881) 6 App Cas 740 at 759 per Beld J. See Chapter 2 at **2.3–2.13**. But see Chapter 16 for the different law which applies under the High Hedges legislation.
[4]   Ibid, at 794 per Lord Selborne LC.
[5]   B Nicholas *An Introduction to Roman Law* (Oxford University Press, 1975) at p 148.

population, urbanisation, and wealth, and the need for a developed system of rights over land belonging to others became acute. The same historical process also accounts for the fact that most of the important decisions of the courts in this field date from the late nineteenth and early twentieth centuries. From the Roman law derive the English expressions *dominant land* (or *tenement*) (*praedium dominans*, from *dominus* = master), the land benefiting from the easement, and *servient land* (or *tenement*) (*praedium serviens*, from *servus* = slave, servant), the land which is subject to the easement. The Roman law divided easements (*servitutes*) into rural and urban categories. Rights of light were recognised as an urban servitude.[6] Also, the rule that an easement can only exist to benefit the dominant land probably derives from the Roman law.[7]

1.4   The theoretical legal basis of easements (including that of light) is therefore based on legal concepts of considerable antiquity whose relevance it is sometimes tempting to question. However, the law of easements in general, and rights of light in particular, is of considerable practical importance and difficulty. The practical importance of the law of easements is self-evident given the density of population and level of development activity particularly in the South East of England. The difficulties arise not only in determining the extent of the rights in any particular case but often as to whether they exist at all. Despite some recent changes in the law, notably by the Land Registration Act 2002 (see Chapter 14) and impetus for further reform,[8] easements remain a category of legal rights over land which enjoys two characteristics which are a recipe both for survival and for the ability to cause mischief. They can be acquired by prescription based on long use, and can exist outside the land registration system. In relation to rights of light, for example, any building with windows over 20 years old is likely to enjoy rights of light over nearby land[9] which only a physical inspection of the locus in quo coupled with an informed knowledge of architectural styles (to date the building) can discover. Issues relating to the existence, creation and transmission of rights to light do frequently turn on general concepts of real property law. No apology, therefore, is made for the following brief summary of the relevant salient features of the area.

1.5   Easements are a species of what the law terms 'incorporeal hereditaments'. In *Re Christmas*,[10] Cotton LJ, citing Blackstone's classic *Commentaries on the Law of England*, defined an incorporeal hereditament in the following words:

> ' . . . a right issuing out of a thing corporate, whether real or personal, or concerning or annexed to, or exercisable within, the same. It is not the thing corporate itself, which may consist in lands, houses, jewels, or the like; but something collateral thereto, as a rent issuing out of these lands or houses, or an office relating to those jewels.'

In another passage, Blackstone then said:

> 'Their existence is merely in idea and abstracted contemplation; though their effects and profits may be frequently objects of our bodily senses.'

---

[6]   *Ne altius tollat quis aedes suas, ne luminibus vicini officiatur* Justinian's Institutes, 2.3.1.

[7]   *Ideo autem hae servitudes praediorum appellantur, quoniam sine praediis constitui non possunt* Justinian's Institutes, 2.3.3.

[8]   The Law Commission is engaged in a project to 'examine easements, covenants and similar land law rights with a view to their reform and rationalisation'. It observes on its website (www.lawcom.gov.uk) as at 5 October 2005 that 'the law has never been subject to a comprehensive review, and many aspects are now outdated and a cause of difficulty'.

[9]   Prescription Act 1832, s 3.

[10]   *Re Christmas* (1886) 33 ChD 332.

1.6 The term 'hereditament' (from late Latin *haereditas* = inheritance) refers to property which devolved to the heirs at law of the owner, ie real property as opposed to personal property which could be disposed of by will. For present purposes, it may be equated to an interest in land.

1.7 Incorporeal hereditaments are, in law, contrasted with 'corporeal' hereditaments; medieval lawyers drew a distinction between interests in land giving rights to full possession which were said to be 'corporeal' and other such interests. Ownership of a 'corporeal' hereditament gave control over the corpus (body) of the land. An incorporeal hereditament gave lesser, intangible, rights over land. Modern technology would use the term 'proprietary interest' to describe a corporeal hereditament.[11]

1.8 Incorporeal hereditaments include both easements and profits. Easements are traditionally divided between positive and negative. Positive easements are those which entitle the dominant owner either to do some act on the servient land, such as exercise a right of way over it, or an act elsewhere than on the servient land, but which affects its enjoyment, for example, to carry on activities which would otherwise amount to a nuisance.[12] Negative easements require the servient owner to abstain from certain activities or uses on his land. A right of light is a negative easement, since it obliges the servient owner to restrain from erecting buildings on his land which obstruct the light received by the dominant tenement.

1.9 The category of rights over land which are capable in law of constituting easements is wide, and still growing and adapting to changes in economic and social conditions affecting land use.[13] However, as will be seen below this does not mean that the incidents of established types of easements will be extended by the courts simply because it is reasonable or desirable to do so. Further, the courts have declined to recognise certain proposed species of easement on various grounds, either because they lack precedent or because they are insufficiently clear or too widely restrictive of the servient owners' rights to be accepted:[14]

> 'Incidents of a novel kind cannot be devised, and attached to property, at the fancy or caprice of any owner.'

1.10 A right to light, like other easements, is said to be an 'appurtenant' incorporeal hereditament. This means simply that, however created, it is annexed to land. One cannot enjoy a right to light in gross, except as an incident of ownership of an interest in the land to which the right to light belongs.[15]

1.11 Although easements are of ancient origin, the importance of such matters as rights to light and rights of way to modern property transactions is obvious. Rights to light remain essentially an area of judge-made law. No statutory definition of a 'right to light' exists, and it is therefore necessary to consider the decided cases to establish the

---

[11] For a recent case on the distinction between corporeal and incorporeal rights, see *Brackenbank Lodge Ltd v Peart and Others* (1993) 67 P&CR 249, CA (concerned with whether stint holdings were corporeal or incorporeal hereditaments).

[12] *Sturges v Bridgman* (1879) 11 ChD 852.

[13] In *London & Blenheim Estates v Ladbroke Retail Parks Ltd* [1993] 1 All ER 307, a right to park vehicles was recognised as an easement. The issue was not considered on appeal (see [1993] 4 All ER 157, CA).

[14] See *Ackroyd v Smith* (1850) 10 CB 164 at 188 per Cresswell J citing Lord Bingham CJ in *Keppell v Bailey* (1834) 2 My&K 517 at 535.

[15] *Rangeley v Midland Railway Co* (1868) LR 3 Ch App 306 at 310–311; *King v David Allen & Sons Billposting Ltd* [1916] 2 AC 54; *London & Blenheim Estates Ltd v Ladbroke Retail Parks Ltd* [1993] 4 All ER 157, CA; see also **1.7**.

nature, extent and limitation of such rights. Recognition of the fact that easements are interests in land is provided by the Law of Property Act 1925 and the Land Registration Act 2002. By s 205(1)(ix) of the Law of Property Act 1925, 'land' is defined as including easements. By s 1(2)(a) of the same Act, as an interest in land, an easement is required to be:

> ' . . . for an interest equivalent to an estate in fee simple absolute in possession or a term of years absolute.'

The Land Registration Act 2002, s 132(1) which contains a definition of 'land' does not repeat the provision of the Land Registration Act 1925, s 3(viii) which expressly included easements as 'land' but there can be no doubt that under that statute easements are treated as interests in land. By s 187(1) of the Law of Property Act 1925:

> 'Where an easement, right or privilege for a legal estate is created, it shall enure for the benefit of the land to which it is intended to be annexed.'

The effect of this is that, once a legal easement is created, it attaches to the dominant land even if the actual interest benefiting from the easement at any time is equitable only.[16]

1.12   The express grant of a legal easement requires and can be effected only by deed.[17] In the case of registered land, when both dominant and servient titles are registered, an easement takes effect in equity only until registered.[18] Where the servient title alone is registered, the existence of the easement requires protection by entry of a notice against the servient title. A legal easement passes on transfer of the land to which it is appurtenant, without any express words, and irrespective of the provisions of s 62 of the Law of Property Act 1925.[19] A legal easement cannot be overreached, and does not require registration under the Land Charges Act 1972.

1.13   Registration of easements has been affected by the Land Registration Act 2002. Under the Land Registration Act 1925, s 70(1)(a) legal easements constituted overriding interests and hence did not require registration. Equitable easements required registration. This was subject to an exception where the easement was 'demised, occupied or enjoyed' with land.[20] In practice many expressly granted easements are not registered. Under the 2002 Act the basic principle is that title is created by registration, and in due course by e-conveyances. The basic rule is that the express grant or reservation of a legal easement is a registrable disposition.[21] An effort has been made to curtail unregistered easements by limiting 'interests which override'. The 2002 Act distinguishes between interests overriding first registration (Sch 1) and registered dispositions (Sch 3).[22] The basic idea is that first registration should neither improve nor worsen the registered proprietor's situation. Equitable interests which have not been registered are excluded from both Schedules (reversing *Celsteel v Alton House Holdings*)[23] and the effect of this is that:

---

[16]   See Barnsley 'Equitable Easements – Sixty Years On' (1999) 115 LQR 84.
[17]   Law of Property Act 1925, s 52(1).
[18]   Land Registration Act 1925, ss 19(2) and 22(2). For the position after 13 October 2003 see **1.13** and **1.14**.
[19]   See *Godwin v Schweppes Ltd* [1902] 1 Ch 926. For creation of rights of light under s 62 of the Law of Property Act 1925, see Chapter 5 at **5.22**.
[20]   Land Registration Rules 1925, SI 1925/1093, r 258; *Celsteel v Alton House Holdings* [1985] 1 WLR 204.
[21]   Land Registration Act 2002, s 27(2)(d).
[22]   Land Registration Act 2002, ss 11(4)(b), 12(4)(c), 29(2)(a)(ii) and 30(2)(a)(ii).
[23]   [1987] 1 WLR 291.

(1)   impliedly created equitable easements of necessity, common intention or under the
        rule in *Wheeldon v Burrows*[24] will no longer be overriding;

(2)   easements arising by virtue of proprietary estoppel will no longer be interests,
        which override. Quaere whether the dominant owner could be in actual
        occupation of an easement;[25]

(3)   on registered dispositions a legal easement will in principle be an overriding
        interest, but only if:
        (a)   it is registered under the Commons Registration Act 1965 (which has its own
                system of registration);
        (b)   it is actually known of by the purchaser;
        (c)   it is obvious on a reasonably careful inspection of the land over which the
                easement is exercisable; or
        (d)   it has been exercised within one year prior to the relevant disposition.[26] This
                is intended to cover such matters as easements of drainage through pipes,
                which may not be visible or known to either vendor or purchaser.

For a period of 3 years beginning on 13 October 2003 these provisions were disapplied
by virtue of Sch 12, para 10 to the 2002 Act so that any legal easement is an overriding
interest. This was to protect the continued existence of potential prescriptive easements
which ripened to the full prescriptive period during this time.

1.14   These provisions should bring about a curtailment of unregistered easements. In
the case of negative easements, including rights of light, it is not clear what exercise of
the easement requires for the purpose of these provisions. It is suggested that it most
likely involves the dominant tenement being in a physical state to use the right.
Therefore, if windows are blocked up the right of light is not being exercised.[27] How far
the provisions of the 2002 Act may be circumvented by proprietary estoppel is not yet
established, but the 2002 Act (s 116) recognises that estoppel-based rights are inherently
proprietary even before being made binding by the court.[28]

1.15   A legal estate is not capable of existing or being created in an undivided share of
land.[29] However, s 187(2) of the Law of Property Act 1925 provides that:

> 'Nothing in the Act affects the right of a person to acquire, hold or exercise an easement . . .
> over or in relation to land for a legal estate in common with any other person, or the power
> of creating or carrying such an easement.'

There is therefore no problem about several different dominant tenements, or the union
of separate interests in the dominant tenement, enjoying and being granted legal
easements of light over the same servient tenement.

---

[24]   (1879) 12 ChD 31.
[25]   See *Saeed v Plustrade* [2001] EWCA Civ 2011.
[26]   Land Registration Act 2002, Sch 3, para 3.
[27]   For the issue of abandonment generally see Chapter 8.
[28]   Rights of persons in actual occupation arising in this way have been held to bind purchasers under the
        previous regime of the Land Registration Act 1925, s 70. See *Lloyd v Dugdale* [2001] 1 EWCA Civ 1754. The
        same probably applies under the 2002 Act.
[29]   Law of Property Act 1925, s 1(6); Land Registration Act 1925, s 3(viii), (ix).

1.16   In many situations, the grant of an easement may arise by implication, for example, under the rule in *Wheeldon v Burrows*,[30] or by virtue of s 62 of the Law of Property Act 1925.[31] By the 2002 Act, s 27(7) the second type of implied grant is not a registrable disposition. Presumably the view was taken that the former rule is effectively subsumed in the latter. By the Land Registration Rules 2003,[32] r 33(1) where at the time of first registration the registrar is satisfied that an appurtenant right subsists as a legal estate for the benefit of the registered estate he may enter it in the register. The applicant for first registration must enter the details in the application. Under r 35 the registrar must enter a notice on the register of the burden of any interest which appears from his examination of title to affect the registered estate. This may include rights of light where information about them is available. Finally, on first registration where there is an agreement which prevents the acquisition of rights of light and air for the benefit of the registered estate, the registrar may make an entry on the property register of that estate. The purpose of this provision is to enable the existence of any agreement under s 3 of the Prescription Act 1832 to be noted against the title benefiting from it.[33]

THE ESSENTIALS OF EASEMENTS

1.17   We have seen that rights to light are a species of negative easement, appurtenant to the dominant tenement over the servient tenement. The courts have evolved a number of tests for establishing whether the rights claimed in a particular case contain the necessary ingredients of an easement.

1.18   There are four requirements to be satisfied before an easement (including a right to light) can be shown to exist:

(1)   there must be a dominant and a servient tenement;

(2)   the easement must accommodate the dominant tenement;

(3)   the dominant and servient tenements must be in separate ownership; and

(4)   the easement must be capable of forming the subject matter of a grant.

Each requirement will now be considered in detail.

1. There must be a dominant and a servient tenement

1.19   The first requirement means that there must be separate pieces of land which respectively benefit from the easement and over which the easement is enjoyed. It is not therefore possible for the same piece of land both to enjoy and be burdened by the same easement, although it is of course possible, and indeed not uncommon, for two separate parcels of land each to enjoy easements over the other. For example, two houses may share a driveway one half of which lies within the curtilage of each property, each property enjoying an easement of way over the half belonging to the other.

---

[30]   (1879) 12 ChD 31.
[31]   See Chapter 5 at **5.10–5.22**.
[32]   SI 2003/1417.
[33]   See Chapter 6.

2. The easement must accommodate the dominant tenement

1.20 Easements are rights appurtenant to land, and hence cannot exist unless they benefit a particular area of land. It is, therefore, not possible to create an easement recognised by the law in gross, ie as a freestanding right, not appurtenant to land. For example, it would not be possible to create an easement of light, nor a right of way, which did not benefit any particular land (where there is no servient tenement). It is therefore said that:[34]

'It is trite law that there could be no easement in gross.'

1.21 This principle is illustrated by *London and Blenheim Estates v Ladbroke Retail Parks Ltd*,[35] a case concerning the purported grant of a right to park vehicles. In that case a transfer of land to the plaintiff contained the grant of an easement entitling the plaintiff to park on certain land retained by the transferor. The transfer further provided that if the plaintiff purchased other land and gave notice to the transferor within 5 years of the original transfer, such other land would (provided the plaintiff was the owner of the originally transferred land at the date of the notice) also benefit from the same easement. The plaintiff purchased additional land. The transferor then sold the retained land (the servient tenement), and it subsequently vested in the defendants. Subsequent to the sale of the servient land by the transferor, the plaintiff gave notice under the terms of the original transfer to it that the other land it had purchased subsequent to the original transfer should benefit from the easement of parking on the land retained by the transferor. The plaintiff sought to establish that it had an enforceable easement against the defendants. The claim was rejected on the ground that at the date of the original transfer to the plaintiff there was no identified dominant tenement (apart from the original land transferred to the plaintiff), and, therefore, the terms of the original transfer did not create an enforceable option to create an easement. Since the servient land had been disposed of by the transferor before the dominant tenement had been created, the terms of the original transfer had not created an enforceable option. The court rejected a further argument that an easement was created when the plaintiff gave notice of acquisition of the further land, on the ground that by the time such notice was given the grantor had disposed of the servient land.

1.22 Although an easement must benefit the dominant tenement, the dominant and servient tenements need not be contiguous. In the case of rights to light, frequently the dominant and servient tenements are separated by land belonging to a third party, or a public or private road. The importance of the requirement is that the easement must directly benefit the dominant tenement. So, for example, if in the case of a right to light the dominant tenement in fact receives no light over the servient tenement the purported creation of an easement in favour of the dominant tenement will be invalid. There must be some connection between the existence of the easement and normal enjoyment of the dominant tenement.[36]

---

[34] See *London and Blenheim Estates Ltd v Ladbroke Retail Parks Ltd* [1993] 4 All ER 157 at 162h per Peter Gibson LJ, citing *Rangeley v Midland Railway Co* (1868) LR 3 Ch App 306 at 310–311; see also **1.10**. See further *Voice v Bell* [1993] 68 P&CR 441.

[35] [1993] 4 All ER 157, CA.

[36] *Re Ellenborough Park* [1956] Ch 131 at 153.

3. The dominant and servient tenements must be in separate ownership

1.23   It is well established that an easement cannot exist in circumstances where the same person both owns and occupies the 'dominant' and 'servient' tenements, on the ground that no person can have a right against himself.[37]

1.24   However, where the owner of a piece of land disposes of part of it and retains the remainder himself, or disposes of the whole to different owners by simultaneous or near-simultaneous conveyances, rights to light may arise by implication of law, or under s 62 of the Law of Property Act 1925, in favour of the purchaser of a piece of land having buildings on it, against the vendor. Thus if a vendor owns land with buildings on it, and divides the land into two plots, A and B, and sells plot A, on which there are buildings with windows receiving light across plot B, the purchaser may acquire a right to light in favour of these windows.

1.25   Acquisition in this way may also occur under the rule in *Wheeldon v Burrows*,[38] whose application to rights to light is well established.[39] All these methods of acquiring rights to light are reviewed in Chapter 5.

1.26   It should, of course, be noted that a right to light cannot arise in this way unless either the vendor retains the land *over which* the windows receive light or disposes of his entire land simultaneously. Thus, if in the example above the vendor sells plot B before plot A, the windows on plot A's buildings will enjoy no right to light over plot B. The position where simultaneous dispositions of both plots take place is considered in Chapter 3.

1.27   It is sometimes said that although a person has no easement over his own land, there can exist quasi-easements. If, whilst plots A and B are owned by the common owner in the above example, the buildings on plot A actually enjoy light through the windows of the buildings on plot A over plot B (albeit that plots A and B have not yet been conceived of or marked out) this enjoyment is capable of ripening into a true easement when plot A is laid out and sold.

1.28   It can sometimes be difficult to distinguish between quasi-easements and the enjoyment by a landowner of the totality of his land arising simply from the fact that he owns and has access to all of it, which does not create rights when part is sold off. If, for example, a vendor sells part of his garden, in which he was accustomed to walk for recreation, the purchaser will obviously not have the right to wander round the part retained by the vendor. There must be some actual enjoyment of the part subsequently sold off, to which the quasi-easement relates.[40]

1.29   Thus, in the case of rights to light, if in the example given at **1.24** the windows in the buildings on plot A had been at the time of sale permanently bricked up, or obscured by a high hedge or wall from plot B, no quasi-easement would exist, and hence no easement of light could arise on sale.

---

[37]   *Metropolitan Railway Co v Fowler* (1892) 1 QB 165; *Attorney General of Southern Nigeria v John Holt & Co (Liverpool) Ltd* [1915] AC 599 at 617–618, PC. But note the effect of occupation by tenants; see Chapter 6 at **6.30**.

[38]   (1879) 12 ChD 31. See Chapter 5 at **5.10–5.20**.

[39]   *Swansborough v Coventry* (1832) 9 Bing 305; *Leech v Schweder* (1874) 9 Ch App 463 at 472 per Mellish LJ.

[40]   *Long v Gowlett* [1923] 2 Ch 177; *Sovmots Investments Ltd v Secretary of State for the Environment* [1979] AC 144; *Payne v Inwood* (1997) 74 P&CR 42.

1.30   Where a building is occupied by a tenant of the owner, there is an important difference between an easement of light and other easements, by virtue of s 3 of the Prescription Act 1832.[41] In cases other than rights to light, a tenant of a landowner cannot by long-use enjoyment acquire an easement against his own landlord or another tenant of his landlord, since the law considers the occupation of the tenant to be that of the landlord.[42] It is a principle of common law prescription that the user must be by or on behalf of the owner of a fee simple interest in land against another fee simple owner.[43] However, this rule does *not* apply to the acquisition of easements of light. Section 3 of the Prescription Act 1832 provides for the acquisition of a right to light by 20 years' *actual* enjoyment. It follows from this that a tenant can acquire an easement of light by prescription against both his landlord and another tenant of the same landlord.

1.31   This constitutes an important exception to the general rule that easements cannot be acquired except where the dominant and servient tenements are owned and occupied by different persons.[44] Leases frequently make provision to avoid the consequence.[45]

4. The easement must be capable of forming the subject matter of a grant

1.32   The fourth requirement derives from the fact that the basis of the law of easements is a grant by one landowner to another of a recognised right over land capable of substituting as a legal estate.[46] Some doubt was expressed in the past as to whether a right to light, being a negative easement,[47] can properly be regarded as the subject of a grant. In *Birmingham Dudley and District Banking Co v Ross*,[48] Lindley LJ regarded a right to light as more in the nature of a restrictive covenant.[49] However, the position now seems to be well established that a right to light does satisfy this requirement. This was expressly recognised by Lord Selborne LC in *Dalton v Angus*.[50]

OTHER CATEGORISATIONS OF EASEMENTS

1.33   Easements are divided into *continuous* and *non-continuous* easements depending on whether the easement confers a right to do something of a continuous and constant nature. A non-continuous easement is one where enjoyment is of its nature only possible from time to time, by a series of acts. Easements of light come into the category of continuous easements, as do easements of the right to receive water through a water course, and (perhaps anomalously) a right of way if exercised over a formed road.[51]

---

41   See Appendix 1.
42   *Kilgour v Gaddes* [1904] 1 KB 457.
43   *Simmons v Dobson* [1991] 4 All ER 25, CA.
44   See *Frewen v Philipps* (1861) 11 CBNS 449; *Mitchell v Cantrill* [1887] 37 ChD 56; *Morgan v Fear* [1907] AC 425; *Mallam v Rose* [1915] 2 Ch 222. See Chapter 6 at **6.17**.
45   See Chapter 7 at **7.4–7.6**.
46   See **1.11**.
47   See **1.36**.
48   (1888) 38 ChD 295.
49   Cf *Hall v Litchfield Brewery Co* (1880) 49 LJ Ch 665 per Fry J.
50   (1881) 6 App Cas 740 at 794.
51   *Watts v Kelson* (1870) LR 6 Ch App 166 at 174 per Mellish LJ. See also *Brown v Alabaster* (1887) 37 ChD 490.

1.34   The distinction was at one time of importance in conveyancing, since upon severance of tenements easements used as a necessity, or in their nature continuous, would pass by implication of law without any words of grant, but easements which were discontinuous did not pass unless the owner by appropriate language showed an intention that they should pass.[52] However, the importance of the distinction has been lessened by s 62 of the Law of Property Act 1925.[53]

1.35   It remains of importance to the question whether an easement may be acquired under the rule in *Wheeldon v Burrows*,[54] but since it is well established that an easement of light can be so acquired the point is not generally relevant to rights to light. It is possible to conceive of circumstances where a claimed easement of light might fail to be 'continuous', for example, in the case of a temporary window aperture formed in a building or the intermittent use of a doorway for admission of light.[55] In *Harris v De Pinna*,[56] for example, the Court of Appeal rejected a claim for a right to light to an open-sided timber shed on the ground that:[57]

> ' . . . it will not do in order to establish a right, to show that though at some time light did not come in through a particular access, at other times it did, and that sometimes it came in through one and sometimes through another opening, which was there in the structure of the building, which would admit light.'

The position as regards which apertures in buildings may enjoy rights to light, and how the enjoyment of light may be inferred to have been abandoned, are considered elsewhere in this book.[58]

1.36   A further division of easements is into *positive* and *negative* easements. As has been seen, an easement must be capable of being the subject matter of a grant.[59] The right to do any positive act (unless illegal or contrary to public policy) can be granted. There is no reason why such a grant may not by implication allow the grantee to damage the servient land. For example, the grant of a right to mine under land may allow the grantee to let down the surface.[60] On the other hand, negative rights (in strict analysis immunities) are not a concept the law regards as often capable of being granted. Considered from the point of view of whether it can be granted, a right to light is conceptually different. For what the servient owner is granting in effect is not a positive right, but an immunity against further actions by him on his own land. Hence, in many cases, it has been suggested that a right to light, being such a negative easement, cannot derive from a grant, actual or notional.[61] On the other hand, there are many authoritative pronouncements to the contrary, the most authoritative being that of Lord Selborne in the House of Lords in *Dalton v Angus*, where he said:[62]

---

52   *Polden v Bastard* (1865) LR 1 QB 156 at 161 per Erle CJ.
53   Considered in Chapter 5 at **5.23**. See also Appendix 1.
54   (1879) 12 ChD 31.
55   See, further, Chapter 4 at **4.13**.
56   (1886) 33 ChD 238.
57   Per Cotton LJ at 257.
58   See Chapter 4.
59   See **1.18**.
60   *Rowbotham v Wilson* (1860) 8 HLC 348.
61   *Moore v Rawson* (1824) 3 B&C 332; *Rowbotham v Wilson* (1860) 8 HLC 348; *Scott v Pape* (1886) 31 ChD 554 at 571 per Bowen LJ; *Birmingham, Dudley and District Banking Co v Ross* (1888) 38 ChD 295; *Hall v Lichfield Brewery Co* (1880) 49 LJ Ch 565.
62   (1881) 6 App Cas 760 at 794. For other cases to the same effect, see *Booth v Alcock* (1873) 8 Ch App 663; *Leech v Schweder* (1874) 9 Ch App 463; *Philips v Low* [1892] 1 Ch 47.

'Some of the learned judges [ie those who were summoned to give their opinion] appear to think otherwise, and to doubt whether it could be the subject of grant. For that doubt I am unable to perceive any sufficient foundation. Littledale J., in *Moore v Rawson*, spoke of the right to *light* as being properly the subject, not of grant, but of covenant. If he had said (which he did not), that a right to light could not be granted, in the sense of the word "grant" necessary for prescription, I should have doubted the correctness of the opinion, notwithstanding the great learning of that eminent Judge . . . the light which enters a building by particular apertures does and must pass over the adjoining land in a course which, though not visibly defined, is really certain and, in that sense, definite. Why should it be impossible for the owner of the adjoining land to grant a right of unobstructed passage over it for that light in that course?'

1.37   The issue is, in any event, of less practical importance since s 3 of the Prescription Act 1832 came into force.[63] This enables a prescriptive right to light to be established by 20 years' actual user. Formerly, to establish an easement by prescription, it was necessary to establish either common law prescription, involving (at least in theory) use from 1189, or prescription under the doctrine of lost modern grant, including a (fictional) grant of the right in question. Under the regime, the question of whether or not a right to light was capable of being the subject of a grant was vital to attempts to establish prescription rights.[64] The law should now, in any event, be regarded in favour of the view that a right to light, though negative in character, is capable of being the subject of a grant as a negative easement.

---

[63]   See Appendix 1.

[64]   For common law prescription and lost modern grant as ways of acquiring rights to light, see Chapter 6.

Chapter 2

RIGHTS TO LIGHT DEFINED AND CONTRASTED

THE RIGHT DEFINED

2.1   A right to light is an easement, a right in property, which carries with it in favour of the dominant land the entitlement to receive sufficient natural illumination from the sky over the servient land through defined apertures in a building to enable use of the interior areas receiving light through such apertures for ordinary purposes to which the building is or may normally be expected to be put. The extent of natural illumination to which the dominant land is entitled is dealt with in Chapter 3.

2.2   Three general points are worth noting:

(1)   the right can only be enjoyed in respect of a *building*. What constitutes a building for these purposes and when the building is first taken to be sufficiently complete to give rise to enjoyment of such rights are questions addressed in Chapter 4;

(2)   the right can only be enjoyed in respect of defined apertures in a building *intended to admit light*. What apertures fall within the category of qualifying apertures is a matter also considered in Chapter 4. Where a building is demolished or altered, in the process destroying or altering the size or position of apertures which previously enjoyed rights of light, issues may arise as to whether, and if so for how long, the right to light previously received through these apertures survives their demolition or alteration. These topics are examined in Chapter 8;

(3)   the right is not one which confers on the dominant owner a right to receive the light previously enjoyed to its full extent. Rather, the test is whether, after considering the loss of light caused by a particular obstruction, the standard of illumination remains sufficient for the ordinary and normal use of the dominant land. As Farwell J said in *Higgins v Betts*:[1]

> 'The dominant owner was never entitled either by prescription or under the Act [i e the Prescription Act 1832] to all the lights that came through his windows. It was not enough to show that some light had been taken, but the question always was whether so much had been taken as to cause a nuisance . . .'

These words apply with as much force to rights of light obtained by grant as to those acquired by prescription, at least where the deed of grant does not show an intent to grant a right to light of unusual extent.[2]

---

[1]   [1905] 2 Ch 210.
[2]   *Frogmore Developments Ltd v Shirayama Shokusan Co Ltd* [2000] 1 EGLR 121 at 123M–124B.

These aspects of the law, and their practical effect, are considered in Chapter 3.

THE LIMITS OF PROTECTION

2.3   Rights to light do not, therefore, concern all the possible amenities which may be conceived to be enjoyed by the absence of other buildings in proximity to one's own windows. There are ten situations in which the law relating to light offers the dominant owner no protection.

2.4   As has been already noted, there is no right to receive natural light falling on land which has no buildings on it.[3] The reason for this is that such a right is too indefinite to form the subject of a grant. This limitation has the effect of depriving new buildings, unless they benefit from rights of light transferred from pre-existing buildings,[4] of rights of light unless and until they have been in place for a sufficient period to acquire such rights by prescription, or unless they benefit from some express grant.[5] It also means that areas used for sunbathing or other open-air recreation are not protected, nor are swimming pools (unless enclosed) or areas of land used for growing plants which may suffer from loss of light (unless they are in greenhouses).

2.5   As a corollary of the foregoing, the protection afforded is in respect not of particular building(s) but in respect of defined apertures in buildings designed for the receipt of light. Apertures intended to be closed by opaque doors are, therefore, excluded.[6]

2.6   The law relating to rights to light does not protect the right to a particular view. Thus, it cannot be invoked by reason of a building being erected which deprives a window of a pleasant prospect, or even of a direct view of the sky, if light is not interfered with to an actionable extent.

> 'But . . . for prospect, which is a matter only of delight and not of necessity, no action lies for stopping thereof, and yet it is a great commendation of a house if it has a long and large prospect . . . But the law does not give an action for such things of delight.'[7]

2.7   By inversion of the principle stated in the previous paragraph, law does not confer a right to *be viewed*, for example, so that commercial premises or a billboard or illuminated sign may attract customers, or so that the prominence of the premises in question may otherwise benefit the owner.[8] However, where the act causing the interference with the view is a public nuisance, any special damage sustained by an

---

3   *Robert v Macord* (1832) 1 Mood & R 230; *Potts v Smith* (1868) LR 6 Eq 311; *Dalton v Angus* (1881) 6 App Cas 740; *Harris v De Pinna* (1886) 33 ChD 238. See **1.2** and **2.16**. See **2.14** and Chapter 16 for the law relating to high hedges which is different.
4   See Chapter 8.
5   The grant of a right of light over undeveloped land may infringe the rule against perpetuities unless a perpetuity period is specified under the Perpetuities and Accumulations Act 1964: *Newham v Lawson* (1971) 22 P & CR 852; and see **9.58**.
6   *Levet v Gas Light & Coke Co* [1919] 1 Ch 24.
7   *Bland v Moseley Trinity 29 Gl12,* cited in *Aldred's case* (1616) 9 Co Rep 57(6); *Dalton v Angus* (1881) 6 App Cas 740 at 824; *Browne v Flower* [1911] 1 Ch 219 at 225; *Phipps v Pears* [1965] QB 76 at 83 per Lord Denning MR.
8   *Butt v Imperial Gas Co* (1866) 2 Ch App 158.

individual as a result may, subject to issues of foreseeability, be actionable.[9] Views may be protected by restrictive covenants or by planning law.[10]

2.8 Just as the view out cannot be guaranteed, neither can the *absence* of the view in. The law does not protect from prying eyes. Thus in *Browne v Flower*,[11] a landlord let a flat on three floors of a mansion block to Mrs Lightbody. Subsequently, a flat on the ground floor was let to the plaintiffs. Both flats had windows overlooking a communal garden. Subtenants of Mrs Lightbody's flat, with the landlord's consent, erected an open-work iron staircase leading from the garden to the first floor, between the windows of two of the bedrooms in the plaintiffs' flat, seriously affecting their privacy. The plaintiffs' claim against the landlord based on breach of an implied covenant for quiet enjoyment in their lease, and derogation from grant, to have the staircase removed, failed, on the ground that the staircase did not impair the user of the flat for the purposes for which it was demised. The actual decision does not deal directly with the question of a possible easement enjoyed by a freeholder as opposed to the implied obligation of a landlord. But Parker J said at p 225:

> 'In as much as our law does not recognise any easement or prospect of privacy, and (as I have already held) the Plaintiffs' light is not interfered with, it is difficult to find any easement which can have been interfered with by the erection of the staircase in question.'

This has not been questioned as a correct statement of the law, and is supported by the earlier case of *Chandler v Thomson*.[12] It seems consistent with principle, and with the well-established rule that it is not unlawful to open windows overlooking neighbouring land which may in due course acquire rights to light.[13] Further, a right to protection from overlooking would, like a right to a view, inhibit development of land to an unacceptably great extent.

2.9 The law recognises no right to air percolating generally over land. Thus in *Harris v De Pinna*[14] it was held that there was no right in favour of the owners of a timber yard in which timber was stacked for drying in open-sided sheds, to a flow of air from neighbouring land. The position is thus analogous to that of light, which can only be the subject of an easement if received through a defined aperture. However, it seems that where air is received through a defined aperture it may form the subject of an easement.[15] For example, in *Gale v Abbott*,[16] an injunction was granted to restrain the erection of a skylight over a yard which would interfere with air received to the plaintiff's window. Thus the same obstruction may interfere with both easements. This will be disappointing to those who see the salvation of the planet in small windmills for the generation of electricity on every house.

---

[9] *Campbell v Paddington Corporation* [1911] 1 KB 869.
[10] For restrictive covenants generally, see A Francis *Restrictive Covenants and Freehold Land: A Practitioner's Guide* (Jordans, 2nd edn, 2005); see also **2.26–2.32**. For planning law, see Chapter 14.
[11] [1911] 1 Ch 219.
[12] (1811) 3 Camp 81, 170 ER 1313.
[13] *Dalton v Angus* (1881) 6 App Cas 740 at 797 per Lord Selborne LC.
[14] (1886) 33 ChD 238. See also Chapter 4 at **4.11**.
[15] *Gale v Abbott* (1862) 8 Jur NS 987; *Dent v Auction Mart Co* (1866) LR 2 Eq 238; *Bass v Gregory* (1870) 25 QBD 481; *Aldin v Latimer Clark, Muirhead & Co* [1894] 2 Ch 437 at 446; *Chastey v Ackland* [1895] 2 Ch 389; *Cable v Bryant* [1908] 1 Ch 259. Dicta to the contrary of Littledale J in *Moore v Rawson* (1824) 3 B & C 332 are probably to be regarded as relating to the natural passage of air over land – see *Dalton v Angus* (1881) 6 App Cas 740 at 797 per Lord Selborne LC. For a case where an easement of ventilation was held to exist, see *Wong v Beaumont Property Trust* [1964] 2 All ER 119, CA.
[16] (1862) 8 Jur NS 987.

2.10   The law recognises no right to uninterrupted television reception as an easement.[17] Presumably, the same applies to telecommunications, radio, telephone and data transmission by airwaves.[18] Thus it is not unlawful to erect a building whose structure interferes with the receipt of such electronic waves, of whatever frequency.[19]

2.11   The law recognises no easement to prevent building by a neighbour which would interfere with the visibility of one's own premises to others; such visibility may benefit commercial premises by, for example, attracting passing trade or by providing a suitable surface for advertisements.[20]

2.12   The right to light is a right for illumination sufficient for the human eye, not a right to direct solar radiation for energy purposes.[21] It seems, therefore, that there is no protection of solar panels used for heating buildings or swimming pools, even if these are mounted on buildings and have been in place for a period which in the case of light through windows would be sufficient to establish prescriptive enjoyment. The law has yet to recognise a solar easement of the kind covered by legislation in some other jurisdictions.[22]

2.13   English law does not prohibit erection of 'spite fences', that is to say, fences which by reason of their height encroach upon the light of neighbouring buildings and which are higher than reasonably needed. Indeed, prior to the Rights of Light Act 1959, such fences were often used as a method of preventing the acquisition of prescriptive rights of light. By contrast laws in some states of the United States provide that fences unnecessarily exceeding certain heights erected maliciously and with the intent to cause annoyance are private nuisances. Heights above which the presumption applies vary from state to state.[23] In England the direct regulation of fence heights is a matter of planning law rather than the law of nuisance. However, legislation does now regulate the height of hedges in certain circumstances and this is considered in the next section.

REGULATION OF HIGH HEDGES[24]

2.14   In December 1999, the Department of the Environment, Transport and the Regions published a Consultation Paper[25] seeking views on the problem of hedges which obstruct light to buildings and gardens. The specific problem which has arisen is

---

[17]   *Hunter v Canary Wharf Ltd* [1997] 2 AC 655, HL. See Chapter 10 at **10.4**.

[18]   Cf *Bridlington Relay Ltd v Yorkshire Electricity Board* [1965] Ch 436.

[19]   But this does not necessarily mean that the emission of electrical interference cannot be a nuisance: *Network Rail Infrastructure Ltd v Morris (t/a Soundstar Studio)* [2004] EWCA Civ 172, [2004] Env LR 41

[20]   *Butt v Imperial Gas Co* (1866) 2 Ch App 158.

[21]   Although, in some circumstances, the standard of light for a particular building to which the dominant owner is entitled may be such as to imply sunlight to some extent. See Chapter 3 at **3.14–3.21**.

[22]   See, eg, Massachusetts General Laws, Part II, Ch 1871A and s 801 of the California Civil Code, with the latter defining a solar easement as 'the right of receiving sunlight across real property of another for a solar energy system'. Solar energy systems include solar collectors and structural and design features whose primary purpose is to provide for the collection, storage and distribution of solar energy.

[23]   See, eg, Massachusetts General Laws, Part I, Title VII, Ch 49, s 21 (fence unnecessarily exceeding 6 ft in height) and s 841.4 of the California Civil Code (fence unnecessarily exceeding 10 ft in height).

[24]   The detailed treatment of this subject is at Chapter 16.

[25]   'High Hedges'.

that caused by the fast-growing species of conifer, *X Cupressocyparis leylandii* (Leyland Cypress) and *Chamaecyparis Lawsoniana* (Lawson Cypress), commonly known as 'leylandii'.[26]

2.15 The Consultation Paper considered whether the existing law of light should be extended so that an easement of light could be granted or acquired over land generally rather than just in relation to buildings.[27]

2.16 Having reviewed various options the solution the Department favoured involved a system whereby those suffering from the effects of 'high hedges' (tentatively defined as those unduly interfering with the enjoyment or amenity of property or those hedges not in compliance with certain height and location restrictions) may lodge a formal complaint with their local authority. That authority would be empowered to hear both sides to the complaint and direct remedial action.

2.17 In due course these proposals were further developed and a methodology was devised by the Building Research Establishment ('BRE') under the aegis of the Office of the Deputy Prime Minister ('ODPM') for establishing when remedial action would be appropriate.[28] There followed after some vicissitudes the enactment of the proposals as Part 8 of the Anti-Social Behaviour Act 2003 ('the 2003 Act'), which are supported by regulations, guidelines issued by the BRE, and a 114-page guidance document published by the ODPM in 2005. These are fully discussed in Chapter 16.

2.18 In essence the scheme of the 2003 Act entitles an aggrieved occupier of domestic property (basically houses and flats and gardens and yards appurtenant to them) to complain to the local authority if the height of a hedge on the land of another interferes with the reasonable enjoyment of his property. The hedge must be over 2 m high and mostly evergreen or semi-evergreen, and must act as a barrier to light or access. If the council considers the complaint valid (ie as falling within the 2003 Act) and finds it justified, and if informal steps fail to produce a solution, a remedial notice may be served requiring work to the hedge. Failure to comply may lead to prosecution. There is a right of appeal against remedial notices to the Secretary of State. Appeals are in practice heard by a planning inspector. There is, however, no right of appeal against decisions to reject a complaint as invalid, so any challenge to such a decision can only be made by way of judicial review.

2.19 This brief review of the scheme of the 2003 Act is sufficient to show that the scheme it establishes differs substantially from rights to light. In particular, (i) those protected by the 2003 Act are limited to residential occupiers, (ii) the protection is against evergreen hedges only, not, for example, buildings or fences, and (iii) the 2003 Act operates by means of administrative machinery rather than court proceedings. It seems unlikely to offer a blueprint for future development of the common law. To be welcomed, however, is the recognition that protection of reasonable enjoyment of property should extend beyond the mere functional ability to carry out tasks involving visual discrimination within the buildings without artificial light and the statutory adoption of guidelines for determining whether reasonable enjoyment has been impaired (though, in practice, rights of light surveyors use similar tools when assessing

---

[26] The scale of the problem was shown at Part 3 of the Paper, where it is suggested that there may be as many as 17,000 problem hedges in England and Wales.

[27] Ibid, at para 5.17.

[28] 'High hedges, daylight and sunlight: a final report' (ODPM, July 2001).

common law claims). Whether the 2003 Act works in practice will depend to a great extent on whether local authorities provide and train the necessary personnel to operate their machinery.

2.20   The 2003 Act does not purport to supplant the common law or prevent parties who wish to do so from bringing court proceedings, even where the 2003 Act could be invoked. This raises two issues. First, assuming a potential claimant may alternatively bring a claim under the 2003 Act, what factors should he take into account in deciding whether to do so? Secondly, to what extent would the evidence and decision in a complaint under the 2003 Act bind the parties in any subsequent proceedings, and vice versa?

2.21   On the first point, the advantages of the 2003 Act procedure to a potential claimant are likely to include substantially lower costs (since the procedure is administered by the local authority) and the possibility of a claim for general loss of amenity. The disadvantages would seem to include: (i) the absence of any right to claim damages; (ii) the absence of any power to award an injunction; and (iii) dependence on the local authority taking action on the complaint, subject to an appeal under the 2003 Act or judicial review proceedings if appropriate.

2.22   As to the second point, the procedure under the 2003 Act requires the local authority to consider and decide complaints. These functions are essentially administrative and do not involve litigation of any 'cause of action' between the complainant and the alleged wrongdoer. The criteria applied in determining complaints are not the same as those which apply at common law. These differences are sufficient to prevent any decision based on a complaint under the 2003 Act creating a binding estoppel under the principle of res judicata[29] or because no cause of action (in any sense of the phrase) between parties has been litigated and no judgment given. The same must be true of the wider principle in *Henderson v Henderson*[30] which precludes a party from bringing proceedings in respect of a matter which could and should have been litigated in earlier proceedings. In the converse situation the position is the same. The local authority is not bound by the outcome of court proceedings even if the subject matter is the same, but must deal with the complaint on its merits and form its own decision on whether to entertain a complaint and if so what action should be taken. A challenge to this may be made by appeal under the 2003 Act, or judicial review where appropriate. It is thought, however, that it would be possible for the parties to a potential dispute to be estopped from pursuing successive remedies in the two venues[31] if they proceeded on a common assumption that the matter would be dealt with in one venue exclusively, or if one party so conducted himself as to lead the other to believe this would be the case, and the other party altered his position in reliance on this.[32]

2.23   It is possible to envisage situations where the availability of recourse to the other venue and/or previous recourse to it may have practical implications in subsequent proceedings or complaint under the 2003 Act. A court might well take the view, applying the analogy of mediation, that if a complaint could have been brought under the 2003 Act by the successful claimant he should be deprived of part of his costs on the ground

---

[29]   See, eg, *The Indian Endurance (No 1)* [1993] AC 410; *Fraser v HMLAD Ltd* [2006] EWCA Civ 738.
[30]   (1843) 3 Hare 100; *Johnson v Gore Wood & Co* [2002] 2 AC 1.
[31]   The word 'venue' is used here in the sense that one 'venue' is the use of machinery under the 2003 Act and the other is the use of a court to decide a claim to interference with light under the civil law.
[32]   See *Amalgamated Investment and Property Co Ltd v Texas Commerce International Bank Ltd* [1982] QB 84; *Johnson v Gore Wood & Co* [2002] 2 AC 1; *HIH Casualty and General Insurance Ltd v AXA Corporate Solutions Ltd* [2003] Lloyds Rep IR 1.

that the proceedings were unreasonable and disproportionate. Conversely, the local authority might well reject as frivolous a complaint which covered the same ground as an unsuccessful claim brought in a court, under s 68(2) of the 2003 Act.

LICENCES AND OTHER ARRANGEMENTS

2.24 An easement, creating an interest in land, may be distinguished from a personal licence not having this effect.[33] Unlike an easement, a licence cannot (generally) be taken advantage of by a successor in title of the licensee. Further, a licence (unlike an easement) is subject to revocation by the licensor.

2.25 A licence to open or maintain a window will not, therefore, ripen into an easement, will not benefit successors of the licensee, and is precarious. Indeed, the device of a written licence for such purposes is frequently used to prevent the acquisition of a light under s 3 of the Prescription Act 1832, as discussed in Chapter 7.

THE RIGHT TO LIGHT CONTRASTED WITH OTHER RIGHTS

Restrictive covenants

2.26 Restrictive covenants affecting freehold land are used to create a kind of private planning law, in a particular area. The efficacy of such covenants was considered by the leading case of *Tulk v Moxhay*,[34] which related to Leicester Square in London. It was held that a covenant taken on conveyance of land not to build on the land conveyed was enforceable against successors of the purchasers who had notice of the covenant, by those who retained the land for the benefit of which the covenant was taken.

2.27 The doctrine applies only to restrictive covenants, not positive obligations.[35] As in the case of easements, there must be a dominant tenement, though this need not be a separate plot of land. A different estate in the same land is sufficient.[36] The covenant must benefit the dominant tenement directly.[37] For the benefit of the covenant to 'run with' the dominant land (ie be enforceable by successors in title of the original covenantee who from time to time own the dominant land) it must be either annexed to it,[38] assigned or the covenant must have arisen as part of a building scheme.[39] By comparison with the right to light, the law relating to restrictive covenants is in some respects wider and in others narrower in the protection afforded.

2.28 First, whilst the law of easements is of universal application (except where excluded by agreement) restrictive covenants must be specifically imposed on land. There are no implied restrictive covenants.

---

[33] *IDC Group Ltd v Clark* [1992] 2 EGLR 184. Cf *Britel Developments (Thatcham) Ltd v Nightfreight (Great Britain) Ltd* [1998] 4 All ER 432.
[34] (1848) 2 Ph 774.
[35] *Rhone v Stephens* [1994] 2 AC 310.
[36] *Hall v Ewen* (1887) 37 ChD 74.
[37] *Rogers v Hosegood* [1900] 2 Ch 388.
[38] See Law of Property Act 1925, s 78. For the requirements for annexation of benefit of restrictive covenants see *Crest Nicholson Residential (South) Ltd v McAllister* [2004] 1 WLR 2409.
[39] *Elliston v Reacher* [1908] 2 Ch 374, 665, CA.

2.29   Secondly, restrictive covenants, like easements, require in effect a dominant and a servient tenement, though the terminology used is that of the 'benefited' and 'burdened' land. But, unlike easements, they also require the benefit of the covenant to be attached to the dominant tenement, whereas in the case of a right to light the easement attaches to the land automatically.

2.30   Thirdly, restrictive covenants if created after 31 December 1925 require protection by registration as land charges to be enforceable against successors of the covenantor.[40] This is not the case in relation to easements, apart from equitable easements.[41]

2.31   Fourthly, restrictive covenants, unlike easements, are capable of protecting views and general visual amenities. Indeed, this is one of their principal purposes.

2.32   Finally, however, restrictive covenants which are obsolete are potentially subject to modification by the Lands Tribunal under s 84 of the Law of Property Act 1925. A review of the principles of the legislation lies outside the scope of this book. Rights to light and other easements are not subject to this jurisdiction, which also applies to covenants imposed in certain long leases.[42]

LEASES

2.33   Covenants in leases may impose restrictions on lessee or lessor which may have the effect of preserving light to windows on the demised premises or premises of the lessor. One particular feature of the law relating to rights to light is that a lessee may, under s 3 of the Prescription Act 1832, acquire a right to light over his lessor's premises. Hence, leases frequently contain provisions negating the acquisition of such right.[43] By contrast, a right to light cannot be acquired under the doctrine of lost modern grant[44] against a freeholder where the property in question is the subject of a lease.

2.34   Subject to these points, a lessee acquires by virtue of s 62 of the Law of Property Act 1925 all quasi-easements actually enjoyed therewith, including all rights over the lessor's land which, immediately before the demise, were actually used and enjoyed whether as of right or by possession, with the demised premises. These will include a right to light, where the demised premises contain windows overlooking adjoining land of the lessor.[45]

2.35   Thus a lessee may effectively acquire a right to light as part of his lease. Such a right, however, expires with his lease, and arises (save where it is acquired by prescription) by virtue of the lease itself. Rights to light in general, however, exist in favour of and against freehold owners between whom there is no legal relationship.

---

[40]   Land Charges Act 1972, s 2(5); Land Registration Act 2002, ss 11, 29 and 32. In the case of covenants entered into prior to 1926, the equitable doctrine of notice continues to apply – Law of Property Act 1925, s 2(5).

[41]   See Chapter 1 at **1.13** and Chapter 14.

[42]   Law of Property Act 1925, s 84(12).

[43]   *Morgan v Fear* [1907] AC 425; *Haynes v King* [1893] 3 Ch 439; *Foster v Lyons & Co* [1927] 1 Ch 219; *Hapgood v JH Martin & Son Ltd* (1934) 152 LT 72; *Willoughby v Eckstein (No 2)* [1937] 1 Ch 167; and see Chapter 7 at **7.4–7.5**.

[44]   See Chapter 6 at **6.2**.

[45]   *Wheeldon v Burrows* (1879) 12 ChD 31; *Allen v Taylor* (1880) 16 ChD 355.

Chapter 3

EXTENT OF RIGHTS TO LIGHT

TEST OF SUFFICIENCY

Generally

3.1 As has already been noted,[1] no easement of light may be acquired by prescription or by grant in respect of land which has not been built on. However, the grant of a right of light in favour of a building not yet constructed is possible, subject to compliance with the rule against perpetuities.[2] In this regard a distinction may be drawn between the grant of a future right and the grant of a right of light in favour of a defined building which has not yet been constructed. The latter may not be subject to the rule.[3] Subject to this the right can only subsist in favour of defined apertures to buildings intended to admit light.

3.2 As explained in Chapter 2, a right of light is determined by reference to natural light from the sky falling upon window apertures in buildings. Once a right of light to a window in a building has been acquired (either by act of the parties or prescription) the *extent* of the dominant owner's right was summarised by Peter Smith J in *Midtown Ltd v City of London Real Property Co Ltd*[4] as follows:

> 'It is well established that the fact that light enjoyment by the relevant windows is diminished as a result of the proposed development, does not itself show the development constitutes a nuisance. The question to be posed is not what light is taken away, but what light is left, and whether the light is sufficient for normal purposes according to the ordinary notions of mankind having regard to the purposes for which the building was designed and the nature of that design: see *Colls v Home and Colonial Store Ltd* [1904] AC 179.'

In the recent case of *Regan v Paul Properties Ltd*[5] Mummery LJ said of the same case at [37]:

> 'The case is authority for the proposition that the test for infringement of the right to light is whether the obstruction complained of is a nuisance that is whether there is a substantial loss of light so as to render the occupation of the house less fit for occupation and uncomfortable according to the ordinary notions of mankind. It is not enough for the claimant simply to prove that the light is less than it was.'

Therefore for over 100 years the locus classicus has been the case of *Colls v Home and Colonial Stores* ('*Colls*'). The speech of Lord Lindley contains the following passage:[6]

---

[1] See Chapters 1 and 2
[2] See *Newham v Lawson* (1971) 22 P & CR 852; see generally *Dunn v Blackdown Properties* [1961] Ch 433; *Dano Ltd v Earl Cadogan* [2003] EWCA 782, [2003] HLR 66, [2004] 1 P&CR 13; and see **9.38**.
[3] Cf *Chaffe v Kingsley* [2000] 1 EGLR 104.
[4] [2005] 1 EGLR 65 at [55].
[5] [2006] EWCA Civ 1319.
[6] Per Lord Lindley in *Colls v Home & Colonial Stores Ltd* [1904] AC 179.

'. . . generally speaking an owner of ancient lights is entitled to sufficient light according to the ordinary notions of mankind for the comfortable use and enjoyment of his house as a dwellinghouse, if it is a dwellinghouse, or for the beneficial use and occupation of the house if it is a warehouse, a shop or other place of business. The expressions "the ordinary notions of mankind", "comfortable use and enjoyment", and "beneficial use and occupation" introduce elements of uncertainty; but similar uncertainty has always existed and exists still in all cases of nuisance, and in this country an obstruction of light has commonly been regarded as a nuisance, although the right to light has been regarded as a peculiar kind of easement.'

In *Allen v Greenwood*[7] Buckley LJ restated the rule in the following terms:

'The authority which must now be regarded as the leading case on this topic is undoubtedly the decision of the House of Lords in *Colls v Home and Colonial Stores Ltd* from which I think the following formulation of the principle can be distilled: the amount of light to which a dominant owner is entitled under a prescriptive claim is sufficient light, according to ordinary notions, for the comfortable or beneficial use of the building in question, again according to ordinary notions, for such purposes as would constitute normal uses of a building of its particular character. If the building be a dwellinghouse, the measure must be related to reasonable standards of comfort as a dwellinghouse. If it be a warehouse, a shop or a factory, the measure must be related to reasonable standards of comfort or beneficial use (for comfort may not be the most appropriate test in the case of such a building) as a warehouse, a shop or a factory as the case may be. These may very probably differ from the standards which would apply to a dwellinghouse. If the building be a greenhouse, the measure must in my opinion be related to its reasonably satisfactory use as a greenhouse.'

3.3   There were cases prior to *Colls*, which suggested the possibility of two other standards. The first of these looked at the amount of light necessary to the use made of the dominant building at the time the right to light was acquired. So in *Martin v Goble*[8] premises had acquired a prescriptive right to light at a time when they were used as a malt-house. Subsequently, the use of the premises was changed to that of a dwelling-house. The jury was directed that 'the house was entitled to the degree of light necessary for a malt-house, not a dwelling-house. Thus converting it from one to the other could not affect the rights of the owners of the adjoining ground'. The other standard was the actual amount of light received, rather than the amount necessary for ordinary purposes. Hence, on this basis, any effect on the light would be actionable, even if the room remained sufficiently well lit for ordinary purposes.[9] The rationale of the first standard was the unfairness of allowing the dominant owner to increase the burden on the servient owner by changing the use of the dominant building to one acquiring more light. The proponents of the second standard, however, stressed the unfairness of allowing the servient owner to interfere with the present or future rights which the dominant owner enjoyed from the quality of light he actually received. Many judicial disagreements resulted. The cases relating to these alterations must now be read as no longer representing the law insofar as they are inconsistent with *Colls*, for that authority clearly establishes that the correct approach is to apply a uniform standard to the amount of light to which the dominant building is entitled.

---

[7]   [1979] 1 All ER 819, CA.

[8]   *Martin v Goble* (1808) 1 Camp 320, 120 GR 971. See also *Lanfranchi v Mackensie* (1867) LR 4 Eq 427. *Martin v Goble* was dissented from in *Moore v Hall* (1878) 3 QBD 178, and considered overruled in *Dicker v Popham* (1890) 63 LT 379. In *Colls v Home and Colonial Stores Ltd* [1904] AC 179, Lord Davey (at 202) treated it as a case which involved alteration of the substance as opposed to the quality of the dominant tenement. The report of *Martin v Goble* does not suggest, however, that internal alterations had been carried out.

[9]   *Moore v Hall* (1878) 3 QBD 178 (*Martin v Goble* was dissented from).

3.4   The test, accordingly, as to whether an actionable nuisance by interference with light has been caused, is not by reference to the amount of light originally received through the aperture before the obstruction complained of, but whether the amount of light received after the obstruction is in place will enable the building (or that portion of it which receives light through the aperture) to continue to be enjoyed for ordinary purposes. The locality in which the dominant tenement is situated is probably of no effect in determining whether the standard is maintained:[10]

> 'The human eye requires as much light for comfortable reading or sewing in Darlington Street, Wolverhampton, as in Mayfair.'

The above test must be applied in a broad, common sense way. In *Colls* Lord Macnaghten stated that the court must distinguish between 'a partial inconvenience and a real injury to the plaintiff in the enjoyment of the premises', and the diminution of light must be 'such as really makes [the premises] to a sensible degree less fit for the purposes of business or occupation'[11] (citing Best CJ in *Back v Stacey*[12] and Tindall CJ in *Parker v Smith*[13]). The test is in principle the same whether the right to light has been acquired by prescription or by express grant[14] subject to any wording in the grant which evinces a clear intention to apply a different standard.

Relevance of actual and prospective layout and uses of affected areas

3.5   In establishing whether sufficient light continues to be received, it is necessary to have regard not only to the existing layout and purposes for which the building is used, but also foreseeable future changes in internal arrangements and uses.

3.6   This is illustrated by *Carr-Saunders v Dick McNeil Associates*.[15] In that case, the issue concerned the interference with light to the second floor of the plaintiff's building, which received light from four windows at the front and two at the rear. The front of the second floor had at one time been separately occupied by a lessee who used it as an office but the plaintiff, having obtained possession of the separately occupied part, used the whole floor initially as an open plan area for living accommodation. Subsequently, he converted the floor into six consulting rooms, with two rooms at the rear and four at the front, the rooms at the rear each incorporating one of the rear-facing windows. The defendant subsequently obstructed the light to the rear-facing windows, resulting in the consulting rooms in question suffering a significant loss of light. The defendant argued that the obstruction of light was not actionable since, had the plaintiff kept the whole of the second floor laid out in open plan, there would have been no significant effect by virtue of the interference with the light received to the rear windows on the light enjoyed by the second floor as a whole. The defendant argued that it was not open to a dominant owner by an act on his part to increase the burden on the servient tenement, and accordingly the internal partition works carried out by the plaintiff to form the separate consulting rooms should be disregarded in determining whether an actionable interference had occurred.

---

[10]   *Horton's Estate Ltd v James Beattie Ltd* [1927] 1 Ch 75 at 78. Approved in *Fishenden v Higgs and Hill Ltd* (1935) 153 LT 128.
[11]   At 186–188.
[12]   (1826) 2 C & P 465.
[13]   (1832) 5 C & P 438.
[14]   *Frogmore Developments Ltd v Shirayama Shokusan Co* [2000] 1 EGLR 97.
[15]   [1986] 2 All ER 888.

3.7   The court rejected this argument for three reasons: first, since the case was one of
a prescriptive right to light under s 3 of the Prescription Act 1832, the issue was not one
of whether there was an easement of access of light to a particular room in a building,
but to the building as a whole, so that the extent of the right was not necessarily to be
measured by the internal arrangements of the building. Secondly, the issue in a case of
nuisance was whether there was disturbance of the dominant owner in the comfortable
enjoyment, not of a particular room, but of his property. Thirdly, the dominant owner's
right to light was not measured by the particular use to which the dominant tenement
had been put in the past:[16]

> 'The extent of the dominant owner's right is neither increased nor diminished by the actual
> use to which the dominant owner has chosen to put his premises or any of the rooms in
> them: for he is entitled to such access of light as will leave his premises adequately lit for all
> ordinary purposes for which they may reasonably be expected to be used. The court must,
> therefore, take account not only of the present use, but also of other potential uses to which
> the dominant owner may reasonably be expected to put the premises in the future.'

3.8   The same principle had earlier been applied in *Colls*,[17] where Lord Davey said:[18]

> 'The easement is for access of light to the building, and if the building retains its substantial
> identity, or if the ancient lights retain their substantial identity, it does not seem to me to
> depend on the use which is made of the chambers in it, or to be varied by any alteration
> which may be made in the internal structure of it.'

He went on to say:[19]

> 'According to both principle and authority, I am of opinion that the owner of the dominant
> tenement is entitled to the uninterrupted access through his ancient windows of a quantity of
> light, the measure of which is what is required for the ordinary purposes of inhabitancy or
> business of the tenement according to the ordinary notions of mankind, and that the
> question for what purpose he has thought fit to use that light, or the mode in which he finds
> it convenient to arrange the internal structure of his tenement, does not affect the question.'

3.9   A corollary of this principle is that the court will consider not only present use of
a particular room, but also possible future uses. For example, if a room lighted by a
window enjoying a right to light is used as a scullery, an obstruction which reduces the
light received by the window below the acceptable standard is actionable despite the fact
that ordinary notions of mankind do not require sculleries to be well lit.[20]

3.10   As is clear from *Carr-Saunders v Dick McNeil Associates*,[21] internal partitioning
which results in the creation of small rooms in a previously open plan area which are
more significantly affected by an obstruction to light than the previous open plan area
would have been does not affect the plaintiff's right to complain. It is also clear that not
only actual sub-division but any future foreseeable sub-division must be taken into
account. Presumably, the converse also applies, so that if it is possible that a small room
might be thrown into a larger area, once again this would not affect the plaintiff's
position. Although normally the creation of an open plan area might be expected to
result in better light, this might not necessarily be the case, where the existing room is

---

[16]   Per Millett J at [1986] 2 All ER 888 at 894c–d.
[17]   [1904] AC 179.
[18]   Ibid, at 202–204.
[19]   *Colls v Home & Colonial Stores Ltd* [1904] AC 179 at 202–204.
[20]   *Price v Hilditch* [1930] 1 Ch 500 at 507–508 per Maugham J.
[21]   [1986] 2 All ER 888.

small and no part of it is far from the window in question. Throwing the existing room into a larger area can result in the area so formed being more sensitive to loss of light from the existing window, if no additional windows are available to light the enlarged area. This is because the light received by the parts of the newly formed space furthest from the existing window will be less well lit.

3.11 What future arrangements of the claimant's building's internal space are reasonably foreseeable is, presumably, a question of fact. Relevant matters, it is submitted, would include:

(1)   the structural possibilities of the building;

(2)   economic considerations, such as the cost of doing the work set against the likely benefit in terms of creation of lettable space;

(3)   whether before the work is done there is a need to obtain possession of the relevant area, and the prospects of this being achieved;

(4)   whether third party consents, such as from a landlord or holder of the benefit of a restrictive covenant, are required, and the prospects of such consents being obtained;

(5)   where applicable, the need for planning or listed building consent and the prospects of this being obtained.

Therefore regard may be had to any ordinary use to which the tenement is adapted during the prescription period, but the burden of the servient tenement is not to be increased by some subsequent alteration in its use or internal configuration. Regard cannot be had to the actual or potential use of the property for some special or extraordinary purpose (*Colls* per Lord Davey[22]). This is particularly so where the right has been acquired by prescription as opposed to an express grant; because rights acquired by prescription are to be measured by the actual enjoyment had during the prescriptive period

Relevance of impact of loss of light on particular locations within the affected area

3.12 A further matter of relevance in deciding whether sufficient light remains in any case is the location where loss has occurred. Loss in areas whose utility is marginal, or which are inherently unlikely to be used for purposes with high amenity value will be given less weight than loss of an area where there is a greater reasonable expectation of good natural light. So in *Smyth v Dublin Theatre Co Limited*[23] Meredith J said:

'. . . no inconvenience is felt by reason of the fact that portions of the room are in comparative darkness, provided the room as a whole is fairly well lit and a reasonable area near the window enjoys a sufficiency of direct light. If a plaintiff is unreasonable if he complains of defective lighting in corners of the room where adequate light is not to be expected and is generally comparatively useless . . . is he to be considered unreasonable if he

---

[22]   At 202–204.
[23]   [1936] IR 692 at 703, 705–706.

complains of defective light a few feet from the window, though such light is well above the expert's standard for a room as a whole, if near the window is a place where better light may be expected to be found?

...and interpreting the term "ordinary light" in a common sense manner I hold that a plaintiff is not claiming more than ordinary light simply because he claims a reasonable amount of direct light where he may expect to find it in a room laterally lighted ... If that much latitude is not given to the expression "ordinary light" the flexibility of the legal principle stressed in *Colls v Home & Colonial Stores* ([1904] AC 179, [1904–7] All ER Rep 5) is lost, and a rigid standard set up by experts is introduced.'

3.13 These remarks were cited with approval by Millett J in *Carr-Saunders v Dick McNeil Associates*.[24] In *Deakins v Hookings*,[25] Judge Cooke said:

'(i)   In a room that is already ill-lit every bit of light is precious.
(ii)   Save in an extreme case it would be difficult to say that once a living room (contrast a store) fell below 50/50 that the light left was adequate.
(iii) In considering whether a room where more than 50% remained well-lit regard should be had to the use to be made of the remainder and how bad, *vis-à-vis* that use, the remaining light was.
(iv) The test is not merely a statistical one; test (ii) provides a pretty irreducible minimum.'

Right to extraordinary light

3.14 The extent of light acquired may depend on the type of building. In *Allen v Greenwood*,[26] it was held that in the case of a right to light acquired by prescription, the extent of light acquired under s 3 of the Prescription Act 1832 was to be measured according to the nature of the building and the purposes for which it was normally used. In that case, the dominant building was a greenhouse, and it was held that the extent of light acquired by prescription was the right to that degree of light and the benefits of light including the rays of the sun required to grow plants in the greenhouse, and not just the amount of light required for illumination.

3.15 An alternative basis for the decision in *Allen v Greenwood* was that a right to an exceptional quantity of light could be acquired by prescription provided it had been enjoyed for the full prescriptive period to the knowledge of the servient owner. Thus, in some cases, at any rate where the light is acquired by prescription, there may be a right to an extraordinary quantity of light where there is the requisite degree of knowledge on the servient owner's part.

3.16 The principle that the amount of light to which the dominant owner is entitled may depend on the nature of the building and the purpose for which it is normally used has certain corollaries.

(1)   As was accepted in *Allen v Greenwood*, it does not necessarily follow that simply because a building is used as a greenhouse the dominant owner will have the right to such degree of light and warmth as is necessary for every conceivable use to which a greenhouse can be put. It seems that the extent of light to which the dominant owner is entitled would not be such as to enable him to use the

---

[24]   [1986] 2 All ER 888 at 893B.
[25]   [1994] 1 EGLR 190 at 193A–193B.
[26]   [1979] 1 All ER 819, CA.

greenhouse for 'exotic purposes'.[27] The growing of tomatoes and pot plants may be protected, but the growing of exotic orchids or plants whose natural habitat is tropical rain forest or western American desert may not.

(2)   It seems to be the case that where the building is a swimming pool, the dominant owner has no right to expect to receive the sun's rays on his bare skin. As Goff LJ said in *Allen v Greenwood*:[28]

> '. . . the defendants say that . . . the only complaint the plaintiffs can have is loss of heat or radiant properties, and they postulate the example of a swimming pool, part of which is fortuitously warmed by sunlight coming through a south window. They say, and I have no doubt rightly, that the owners could have no cause of action against one who, whilst leaving fully adequate light for the complete enjoyment of the swimming pool, so shaded the sun as to deprive it of this chance warmth.'[29]

3.17   It would seem to follow from the principles, first, that regard must be had to actual and potential foreseeable uses of the building in question, and, secondly, that the present use of the building is not to be regarded as fixing the extent of light required, that where the nature of a building is such as to require an extraordinary quantity of light, and the right to such light has been acquired, it is irrelevant that the present use of the building is not such as to require that quantity of light. For example, a greenhouse used for storage purposes, or simply derelict, will nonetheless be entitled to an extraordinary quantity of light within the above definition.

3.18   The dominant owner cannot, self-evidently, increase the burden on the servient owner by enlarging his windows (although the enlarged windows may ultimately acquire prescriptive rights to light). However, he is entitled to receive light to the full extent of the aperture, no account being taken of frames or glazing bars.[30] Equally, he cannot, by reducing the size of his windows, increase the burden on the servient owner. Thus if the dominant owner reduces the size of his window, and the servient owner erects a building which obstructs the light, the dominant owner has no claim if (taking into account the obstruction) sufficient light would have continued to be received through the window if its size had not been reduced.[31]

3.19   A further way in which a claimant may be able to establish a right to an extraordinary quantity of light is by virtue of an express or implied grant. In the case of an express grant, the extent of the rights granted will depend on the words used, construed in the factual matrix in which the transaction is set.[32] The words of a grant will be construed against the grantor in case of ambiguity.[33]

3.20   Where the premises in question are let, the lessor is under an implied obligation not to derogate from his grant.[34] This principle operates to prevent the lessor from acting in a way which interferes with the lessee's use of the premises for some particular

27   *Allen v Greenwood* [1979] 1 All ER 819 at 825F–825G.
28   [1979] 1 All ER 819 at 827D.
29   Presumably, the reference is to an indoor swimming pool whose position in this respect is analogous to that of a greenhouse. It is doubtful whether an *outside* pool could constitute a 'building' capable of acquiring rights to light – see Chapter 4 at **4.4** and **4.11**.
30   *Turner v Spooner* (1861) 1 Drew and Sm 467 62 ER 457.
31   *Ankerson v Connelly* [1906] 2 Ch 544; [1907] 1 Ch 678; see also Chapter 8 at **8.52**.
32   *Investors Compensation Scheme v West Bromwich Building Society* [1998] 1 All ER 98, HL.
33   See, eg, *Savill Brothers v Bethell* [1902] 2 Ch 523.
34   See, generally, *Hill and Redman's Law of Landlord and Tenant* (LNUK, 1988, looseleaf) vol 1, paras [6884]–[6900].

purpose for which they were let. Acts which may be prevented include those interfering with the light needed for the activity which at the time of the lease it was contemplated the lessee would carry on at the premises. So in *Herz v The Union Bank of London*,[35] the plaintiff was a diamond merchant, who held certain premises under a lease. His business depended on his being able to assess accurately the condition and value ('quality and water') of jewels; this activity required an extraordinary quantity of light. The defendants, owners of adjacent property, proposed to erect buildings which would interfere with the plaintiff's light, but not to an extent which could be actionable ordinarily. However, before the case, the defendants became the plaintiff's landlord by purchasing the premises he occupied, subject to his lease, which described him as a diamond merchant. The court granted the plaintiff an injunction, the Vice-Chancellor saying:

> 'But it is said that this is an ancient light in a dwelling-house: and an authority has been cited to shew that the Defendants are entitled to obscure or diminish the light to such an extent as would not interfere with the enjoyment of a mere dwelling-house. The case referred to certainly supports the proposition that, where the character of a building is altered to that which requires a greater quantity of light, the owner of adjoining land has a right to erect any obstruction which would not obstruct the light to an extent sufficient to injure it in its former state of enjoyment before the alteration. The principle of that decision is that no man is entitled by any act of his own suddenly to impose a new restriction on his neighbour; but the application of that principle was to a case where no right of personal enjoyment was interfered with, and where the Plaintiff did not even state who was in possession, but merely complained of an injury to his inheritance, and not to himself.

> The present case is of a different kind; the Defendants are the owners of the reversion, and the Plaintiff is described in the lease as a diamond merchant.

> There seems to be no sound principle on which, where the demise of the house is to a person known to sustain such a character as that any diminution of the light would disturb his enjoyment in that character, the reversioner can be allowed to withdraw or obstruct anything necessary to his enjoyment of the demised property in that character.'

3.21   Similarly, in *Frederick Betts Ltd v Pickfords Ltd*,[36] a lessor was held to have derogated from his grant when he converted what ought to have been an outside wall into a party wall under the London Building Act 1894 so that the lessee was obliged to block up his windows in the wall.

THE TEST OF WHETHER THERE HAS BEEN AN ACTIONABLE INTERFERENCE WITH LIGHT

Generally

3.22   Whether there has been an actionable interference is a question of fact. In the past some judges regretted the growing tendency to seek to answer the question by reference to measurements and scientific evidence. This tendency was lamented by Maugham J in *Price v Hilditch*:[37]

---

35   (1859) 2 Giff 686, 66 ER 287.
36   [1906] 2 Ch 87.
37   [1930] 1 Ch 500 at 504.

'I have had quite a considerable body of evidence on both sides, two experts for the plaintiff and two for the defendant, one or two lay witnesses for the plaintiff, and, I think, some six or seven witnesses of a lay character on behalf of the defendant. On one side it is alleged that the injury to the plaintiff's two rooms has been very serious, and on the other side it is denied that there has been any injury at all. I confess that for my part I would prefer, in cases of this kind where the injury is not, as it so often is, hypothetical, to deal with the matter very largely as depending upon the actual evidence of ordinary members of the public who have used the rooms before and after the alleged obstruction, and who could give positive evidence as to the injury, if any, which they have suffered.'

3.23   *Price v Hilditch* was an early case where expert evidence was called. In practice such evidence is now relied on in virtually every rights of light case, and it would be highly imprudent for a party not to have such material available except in a very clear case. However, it remains possible to rely on non-expert evidence and the evidence of lay witnesses as to the effect of the loss of light remains of importance for a number of reasons:

(1)   As will be seen below, the court's approach to the scientific tests generally adopted is that they do not lay down absolute rules as to what is or is not an actionable interference. There is what might be termed a band (in percentage terms) of loss of light which may or may not, depending on the circumstances, be actionable. In this borderline area the impact on witnesses, particularly the owner and occupier of the dominant tenement, may be important. As Judge Cooke said in *Deakins v Hookings*:[38]

> 'But it is not merely a question of statistics. The plaintiff's evidence makes it obvious to me that there is an appreciable drop in the comfortable occupation of the room going beyond the comparatively slight drop that the expert evidence alone would suggest. Whilst the expert evidence alone would be enough to say that there was an actionable interference but a slight one, the plaintiff's evidence goes to show that it is real and deleterious in terms of beneficial occupation and goes beyond the merely slight.'

(2)   It is of course possible that there may be divergence between the experts called for the respective parties: in such cases the importance of lay evidence is obvious.

(3)   When the court has to decide what relief ought to be granted the lay evidence may be of importance, both in deciding whether to grant an injunction or to leave the plaintiff to his remedy in damages, and, if the remedy is to be in damages, in assessing the level of such damages. On the first point, Lord Lindley said in *Colls v Home & Colonial Stores Limited*:[39]

> '. . . the good sense of judges and juries may be relied upon for adequately protecting rights to light on the one hand and freedom from unnecessary burdens on the other . . .'

Relevant matters will include the extent of the infringement, the effect on the plaintiff, and whether the effect of an injunction would be oppressive, which may involve comparison between the plaintiff's loss and the defendant's position if an

---

[38]   [1994] 1 EGLR 190.
[39]   [1904] AC 179 at 213.

injunction is granted.[40] It is clear that the convenience of the parties is a relevant matter. In *Price v Hilditch*,[41] for example, an injunction was refused because the inconvenience to the plaintiff of the interference with light to a room which was used as a scullery was minor.

3.24   As already noted, the test is whether the light left is sufficient for ordinary purposes. The geographical location of the premises, and the character of the neighbourhood in which they are situated are not relevant considerations.[42] In practice, the test which is used most commonly involves ascertaining whether at least half the room affected continues to receive an adequate quantity of light after the obstruction is in place. This is sometimes termed the '50/50' rule. However, as will be seen, it is somewhat misleading as it is not a rule of law and is not applied inflexibly. The 'amenity' impact of the loss of light is important. Further, the rising expectations and the emergence of various other tests, of sufficiency of daylight, including a British Standard,[43] suggest that broader criteria should now be applied.

3.25   The starting point is to evaluate the extent of the light lost. For these purposes, specialist surveyors have evolved the 'Waldram' method of measurement.[44] It is commonly accepted among rights of light surveyors that an adequate amount of daylight is available where 0.2% of the whole dome of the sky is visible at table-top height (a working plane of approximately 850 mm above floor level). The points to which such light penetrates are joined up to form a line called the Sky Factor Contour. The Sky Factor Contour is calculated (using a computer program) as it is before the alleged infringement and as it will be afterwards. The difference between the two contours can be measured so that the area (in square feet or square metres) of lost light can be calculated.

3.26   This method is based on the theory that a certain level of illumination is adequate for normal purposes. The unit of measurement is the 'lumen', itself based on measurement of the amount of light obtainable from the dome of the sky, excluding direct sunlight, during daytime. One lumen per square foot is equivalent to 0.2% sky factor. This is the accepted test for sufficiency of light.[45]

3.27   Accordingly, the Waldram method involves preparation of plans of each room or other area affected, showing the area that falls within the 0.2% sky factor contour lines before and after the obstruction is (or will be) in place. From calculations of the difference between the areas 'before' and 'after' it is possible to ascertain the extent of the area where after the obstruction is in place the light is no longer adequate. A full description of the Waldram method of measurement is given in Chapter 12

3.28   Surveyors also follow the practice of measuring lost light by reference to the Equivalent First Zone ('EFZ'). This works as follows. The affected room is divided into four equal zones: the zone nearest the window is called the front zone; the next zone back the first zone; the next zone back the second zone; and the last zone the makeweight area. The EFZ approach assumes that the most serious loss of light is in the front zone and that loss of light gets progressively less serious towards the back of the

40   See Chapter 11 at **11.72–11.129** for full consideration of the factors influencing the grant or refusal of an injunction.
41   [1930] 1 Ch 500.
42   *Horton's Estate Limited v James Beattie Limited* [1927] 1 Ch 75. See also **3.4**.
43   See Chapter 13 at **13.8**.
44   This topic is discussed in detail in Chapter 12.
45   See, generally, Chapter 12.

room. The area of lost light in the front zone is multiplied by 1.5; that in the first zone by 1; that in the second zone by 0.5; and that in the makeweight zone by 0.25. The resulting figures are then aggregated to arrive at the EFZ figure.

3.29 It will be appreciated at once that the EFZ figure will vary according to the depth of the affected room. A room which is particularly deep will have a higher EFZ of lost light than a shallower, more conventionally shaped room, but at the same time the effect of the lost light on the use of the room will be less because most of it never received light anyway. The adoption of the EFZ approach in such a case gives a misleading impression that the loss of light is much worse than it really is. In practice, the EFZ method is only used by rights of light surveyors to calculate compensation in cases where there had been an admitted actionable infringement. It is not used to decide whether an infringement has taken place.

3.30 The conventional way of approaching the question whether a diminished amount of light is sufficient is the so-called '50/50 rule'. This states that if the remaining area of light exceeds 50% of the area of the relevant room then no infringement has occurred. This test is not to be applied slavishly. The critical question is rather whether the reduction in light amounts to such a substantial interference with the use and enjoyment of his property by the dominant owner that it constitutes an actionable nuisance. That question is one of fact and judgment.

3.31 In *Carr-Saunders v Dick McNeil Associates*,[46] Millett J referred to the consensus of experts based on daylight contour plans by which a room might be regarded as adequately lit for all ordinary purposes if 50% or more of its area receives not less than 1 lumen per square foot at table level. The judge said:

'The 50/50 rule is not in my judgment to be applied without any regard to the shape and size of the room or the disposition of the light within the room to which it is applied. The justification of the 50/50 rule is that an owner is unreasonable if he complains that the corners or other parts of the room where good light is not expected are poorly lit, if the room as a whole remains well lit.'

3.32 In *Fishenden v Higgs and Hill*[47] the defendants were proposing to, and in the course of, erecting a building, opposite that occupied by the plaintiff under a lease, of substantially greater dimensions. Evidence was adduced from experts on both sides and agreed plans were put before Crossman J showing the relative size of the two buildings and the 0.2% contour lines in each affected room before and after the erection of the defendants' building.[48] Crossman J termed the contour line 'the grumble line'. The court considered and accepted the figures given in the plans for the percentage of each room which was well lit before the new building and the percentage which would be well lit after it was erected. The losses were substantial. Crossman J said:[49]

'I think the evidence goes to show that has been such an interference with the comfortable use and enjoyment of his house according to the ordinary requirements of mankind, on the evidence that I have; in fact, I think it is very nearly admitted to be so, because the view

---

[46]   [1986] 2 All ER 888.
[47]   (1935) 153 LT 128.
[48]   The plans were collected and incorporated in a book published by the plaintiff's expert, John Swarbrick FRIBA *Easements of Light* (BT Batsford Ltd, 1938).
[49]   At *153 LT 131.*

which Mr Pitts [the plaintiff's expert] has expressed, and I think is generally accepted, is that something like 50% of the ordinary shaped room ought to be adequately lighted within this so-called grumble line.'

3.33   Crossman J rejected an argument for the defendants that the grumble line was irrelevant because even after the loss of light the plaintiff would be no worse off than other persons in the locality. He granted the plaintiff an injunction. On appeal this was discharged, but the correctness of his approach to the question whether there had been an actionable injury was upheld. Maugham LJ (the judge in *Price v Hilditch*) expressed the view that the plans were *exceedingly useful*, whilst continuing to assert that *no hard and fast mathematical standards can be applied.*[50]

3.34   In *Cory v City of London Real Property Co*[51] the court again accepted expert evidence based on Waldram diagrams and granted an injunction. In *Ough v King*,[52] the Court of Appeal upheld the decision of the judge who had found there was an actionable interference even though more than half the room was well lit after the obstruction of light, the well lit area being reduced from 64.05% to 51.27%. It was held that the judge was entitled to have regard to the locality and the higher standards expected of comfort as years go by. Lord Denning MR said:[53]

'I would not myself be prepared to regard the figures 50/50 rule of Mr Waldram as a universal rule. In some cases a higher standard may be reasonably required.'

3.35   In *Deakins v Hookings*,[54] Judge Cooke likewise said that the 50/50 rule was not a rigid test, and that in some cases a higher standard might be appropriate having regard to changing expectations. He described the rule as 'a bare minimum' in the case of living rooms, and went on to say that regard should be had to the use to be made of that part of the room which was not well lit and how bad, vis-à-vis that use, the remaining light was.

3.36   In *Midtown Ltd v City of London Real Property Co Ltd*[55] Peter Smith J referred to and described the Waldram method of measurement and went on to say:[56]

'One test applied regularly as to whether a room is adequately lit is the so-called 50:50 rule. A room is considered to be adequately lit where 50% of the room is adequately lit for the purpose as set out above.'

3.37   In *Regan v Paul Properties DPF No 1 Ltd*[57] where the effect of the obstruction would have been to reduce the well lit area of the claimant's living room from 66% to 43.5%, an attack was made at first instance on the authority of the Waldram approach. Essentially this followed the line taken by the defendants in the *Fishenden* case. It was submitted that the claimant still enjoyed reasonable light for the locality, and that the 50/50 rule was not determinative. The court accepted that the rule was not a rigid one. Stephen Smith QC said:[58]

---

50   At p 143.
51   [1954] High Court of Justice, Chancery Division. Report published as a supplement to *The Right of Light* (Anstey and Chavasse) by Estates Gazette Ltd (1958).
52   [1967] 1 WLR 1547.
53   Ibid, at 1553B.
54   [1994] 1 EGLR 190.
55   [2005] 1 EGLR 65.
56   At [53].
57   [2006] EWHC 1941 (CH).
58   At [67].

'... it is a very useful guide which will apply to the majority of cases concerning infringements of rights to light, especially where the dominant tenement is a dwelling house and the room in question is a living-room, but it need not be followed in extraordinary circumstances.'

3.38 He rejected the defendants' argument as one which *would introduce a measure of uncertainty into an area where greater certainty would be advantageous.* He further rejected arguments based on the claimant's property remaining 'marketable', and on the living room remaining better lit than many others. The argument that no injury had been caused was not pursued on appeal.

3.39 Thus the present position remains that the basic rule is that laid down by *Colls*, and that in determining whether there is actionable infringement the court will generally apply the 50/50 rule. In the case of residential premises a somewhat higher degree of light may be expected

3.40 There was formerly thought to be a rule that if no obstruction projected above a line subtending an angle of 45° drawn from the base of the window in question no obstruction was established,[59] but this is not the case.[60] Equally, there may be no claim even if the obstruction extends considerably beyond the 45° line.[61]

3.41 The burden on a servient tenement cannot be increased by a voluntary action of the owner of the dominant tenement. Thus, in *Smith v Evangelisation Society*,[62] an action was started to restrain interference with light to a window in a room also lighted, at the beginning of the period of 20 years before the action was brought, by skylights. During that period, they had been blocked up. They were not ancient lights, but could only have been obstructed by the dominant owner himself. The court treated the skylights as reinstated, and declined to disregard the vertical light which the skylights would afford, even though it was established that for some purposes use of the vertical light would be unsatisfactory.

Stained or frosted glass

3.42 It is unclear whether a church or other building with stained or frosted glass windows, which however admit some light, is entitled to greater protection than a building with clear windows.[63] But it seems on principle that it ought to be, by analogy with the position of greenhouses.[64] There is some support for this view in *Attorney-General v Queen Anne Garden & Mansions Co*,[65] in which it was held that an unconsecrated memorial chapel could acquire, under s 3 of the Prescription Act 1832, a right to the light necessary not only for conducting services and confirmation classes but also for the designed illumination of the stained glass windows and mosaics. Whether this would also apply to an ordinary building constructed with tinted windows is an open question. On the one hand, the nature of the building is not such as to require a special quantity of light. On the other hand, the use of tinted windows may be important for comfort and privacy of the occupants or in terms the aesthetic

---

[59] *Hackett v Baiss* (1875) LR 20 Eq 494.
[60] *Ecclesiastical Commissioners v Kino* (1880) 14 Ch D 213; *Colls v Home & Colonial Stores Ltd* [1904] AC 179
at 210 per Lindley LJ; *Fishenden v Higgs and Hill Ltd* (1935) 153 LT 128 at 132.
[61] *Charles Semon & Co v Bradford Corporation* [1922] 2 Ch 737.
[62] [1933] Ch 515.
[63] *Newham v Lawson* (1971) 115 Sol Jo 446, 22 P&CR 852.
[64] See **3.14–3.17**.
[65] (1889) 60 LT 759.

appearance of the building. In practical terms, replacement of the existing glazing by clear glazing may be expensive or impractical for some reason. It is suggested that where a building is originally constructed with tinted glazing this may affect the quantity of light to which the owner is entitled, by prescription.

RELEVANCE OF NATURAL LIGHT FROM OTHER SOURCES

3.43   The general rule is that where a building has windows on more than one side, all of which are entitled to protection as ancient lights (ie they have prescriptive rights to light), the owners of the land on each side of the building can build only to such a height as, if a building of like height were erected on the other side, would not deprive the room of so much light as to cause a nuisance.[66]

3.44   The possibility of supplementing light by artificial light must, clearly, be disregarded in establishing whether a nuisance has been committed by an obstruction, a point confirmed by *Midtown Ltd v City of London Real Property Co Ltd*.[67] It may, however, be relevant on such matters as the extent of relief to be granted, and in particular whether an injunction rather than damages should be granted (see **3.52).**

3.45   Where an issue arises as to whether the dominant tenement has lost light to an actionable extent, account may be taken of light received through apertures which have not been the subject of an obstruction, including skylights.[68] However, where the other apertures enjoy no right to light, by prescription or grant, it appears that the light received through them ought to be ignored.[69]

3.46   The effect of obstructions to the dominant owner's light on the servient tenement must be considered globally, so that if the owner of the servient tenement raises one part of his building, but lowers another, the effect of the lowering must be balanced against the raising in deciding whether an actionable interference has occurred.[70]

3.47   In deciding whether an actionable interference has occurred, the court will not take account of the benefit received by the dominant tenement from light-reflecting surfaces. The principle is clear, where the light-reflecting surfaces (eg glazed tiles) are on the land of the servient owner, the rationale of the rule is that the dominant owner has no power to compel the servient owner to maintain the tiles in position or clean them. Such obligations, even if undertaken by the servient owner, would constitute positive covenants which would not be capable of running with the land.[71] It follows that efforts by those infringing rights to light to mitigate or avoid liability by offering to place reflective surfaces on the sides of their buildings nearest the plaintiff's premises will not succeed:[72]

> '. . . it is quite preposterous to say, "let us damage you, provided we apply such and such a remedy".'

[66]   *Sheffield Masonic Hall Co Limited v Sheffield Corporation* [1932] 2 Ch 17.

[67]   [2005] 1 EGLR 65.

[68]   *Smith v Evangelisation Society (Incorporated) Trust* [1933] Ch 515; *Fishenden v Higgs and Hill Ltd* (1935) 153 LT 128; *Midtown Ltd v City of London Real Property Co Ltd* [2005] 1 EGLR 65 at [53].

[69]   *Colls v Home & Colonial Stores Ltd* [1904] AC 179 at 211 per Lord Lindley; *Kine v Jolly* [1905] 1 Ch 480 at 493 per Vaughan-Williams LJ and at 497 per Romer LJ; [1907] AC 7 per Lord Atkinson.

[70]   *Davies v Marrable* [1913] 2 Ch 421.

[71]   *Rhone v Stephens* [1994] AC 310.

[72]   *Dent v Auction Mart Co* (1866) LR 2 Eq 238 at 251–252.

3.48   There seems little doubt that the same principle would apply even were the tortfeasor to offer to install a reflecting surface on the plaintiff's land, so that the plaintiff could himself gain access to it for repair and maintenance. The position would still remain that damage had been caused to the plaintiff's land by the obstruction to light, and there seems no reason why the plaintiff should be obliged to consent to have his premises altered so as to mitigate the liability of the defendant.

WHERE EXISTING WINDOWS DO NOT PROVIDE ADEQUATE LIGHT

3.49   It is also necessary to consider the position where the room was one where even before the obstruction less than 50% was adequately lit. In such circumstances, obviously the obstruction will not reduce the area of room well lit to below 50%. In this situation, the better view seems to be that this factor does not prevent the dominant owner complaining of an actionable injury. It is not for the servient owner to tell the dominant owner how he should construct his premises; further, if the dominant owner installs new larger windows in response to an obstruction, to maintain his light, the new apertures will not themselves (until the prescriptive period has elapsed) enjoy rights to light.[73] On the other hand, a dictum of Lord Robertson in *Colls v Home and Colonial Stores Ltd*[74] suggests that the dominant owner has to suffer the consequences of 'making one window where there should be five to give proper light, and living 20 years in this cave'. It is suggested that this reasoning would not now be followed (particularly given the modern need to obtain planning permission and listed building consent) at least in relation to parts of the dominant building which are of importance to its enjoyment. This view seems consistent with the decision in *Litchfield-Speer v Queen Anne's Gate Syndicate Ltd (No 2)*, discussed below.

3.50   Irish cases support the proposition that where premises are badly lit a small interference may be treated by the court as more serious than where they are well lit.[75] The same view was expressed by Judge Cooke in *Deakins v Hookings.*[76] Against this, in *Litchfield-Speer v Queen Anne's Gate Syndicate Limited (No 2)*,[77] an injunction was refused in respect of an interference with light in a kitchen which was already poorly lighted. It is submitted that where rooms or other areas are already ill lit, any reduction in the well lit area is proportionately more serious than in the case of a room where more than 50% is well lit prior to the obstruction, and that the Irish cases, although of only persuasive authority, should be followed. For the position where the dominant owner himself reduces the size of his windows see **3.18**. In *Fishenden v Higgs and Hill Ltd*[78] the respective rooms of the plaintiff were before the infringement well lit to the extent of 34.5%, 39.9%, 38.8%, 63% and 71.6%. The obstruction would reduce these figures to 10.9%, 14.9%, 19%, 25% and 40.15%. The Court of Appeal, setting aside the order of the court below for a mandatory injunction, made no reference to any distinction between those rooms currently over 50% well lit and those which were not. The basis of the decision was that the having regard to the conduct of the plaintiff and

---

[73]   See *Dent v Auction Mart Co* (1866) LR 2 Eq 238. See, generally, Hudson 'Light for Inadequate Windows' 48 Conv (NS) 408.

[74]   [1904] AC 179 at 181.

[75]   *O'Connor v Walsh* (1908) 42 ILTR 20; *McGrath v Munster & Leinster Bank* [1959] IR 313.

[76]   [1994] 1 EGLR 190. See **3.35**.

[77]   [1919] 1 Ch 407.

[78]   (1935) 153 LT 128.

the defendants, in particular the plaintiff's failure to make clear initially his full complaints about the design of the new building, it would be unfair to grant an injunction.

3.51   A particular problem arises where the relevant rooms in the dominant tenement are less than 50% well lit due to their configuration, for example, being long and narrow with a window at one end. In such cases all activities requiring light will need to take place in a limited area near the window whether the light is obstructed or not. The loss of light may make little practical difference to the utility of this area. There may be a sound argument for not treating such loss as unusually serious where this is the case.

RELEVANCE OF ARTIFICIAL LIGHT

3.52   Rights of light protect natural light. Although a reliable supply of cheap electricity is a feature of modern life in the developed world, in the only reported case on the point, *Midtown v City of London Real Property Co Ltd,*[79] the court has decisively rejected the suggestion that the availability, or indeed the necessity of habitually using artificial light for the activities in the dominant tenement should lead to a conclusion that no injury is caused. In the case before him, which concerned solicitors' offices, Peter Smith J said:[80]

'56 Despite the apparently depressing effect of the agreed statement, which shows a substantial diminution of the minimum amount of natural light to all of the offices on the Property, Mr Morgan QC, with characteristic boldness submits that given the locale, one should not address this impact solely by reference to natural light.

57 His argument is as follows. All of the rooms on the Property are habitually lit by artificial light whenever they are used. That has been the case as long as the present buildings have been in place and according to the evidence of Kendall Freeman, would be the position in the future if any refurbishment took place. This is reinforced, Mr Morgan QC submits, by the fact that the internal rooms, which receive no natural light whatsoever, are illuminated constantly by artificial light. This is despite the fact that those rooms are used by typing and ancillary staff, who would be working in circumstances where it is probably more important for them on a traditional analysis to have as much natural light as possible. Not unsurprisingly, the higher one's status is within the firm, the bigger a window that person receives. None of Kendall Freeman's witnesses showed that they needed natural light for the purposes of using the rooms. Further, none of them showed that in any realignment or redevelopment, that they would depart from that practice. Mr Morgan QC submits that this is in line with modern office practice where it is preferable to provide a constant level of light which is unchanging and this can only be achieved by permanent artificial light. That he submits, is why Kendall Freeman never use the offices with the lights off.

58 Mr Morgan QC produced a guide issued by the Chartered Institute of Building Service Engineers, "Lighting for Offices". He submits, that in accordance with that guide, these rooms in modern practice will always require artificial light, and that is demonstrated, by the present and prospective user. Given that reduction of natural light is irrelevant if the lighting is really provided by the artificial light. He pointed out that this is the practice in modern offices and he was reinforced in this submission, he contended; by the fact that there had never been any light dispute in the City (where an injunction has been sought), because everybody knew this was the practice.

---

79   [2005] 1 EGLR 65.
80   Ibid, at [61].

59 He also submitted that the time had come to recognise this "real" situation and dispense with rigid and unhelpful rules that had been devised in the past, such as the 50/50 rule.

60 He also submitted that one should not confuse the amount of light required for a task with the visual purposes of providing a view and increasing the general brightness of a room. Windows serve those purposes, but the only relevant purpose of the window is the third possible purpose (identified in the report, paragraph 3.1.2) namely, task illumination.

61 There are a number of potential difficulties about this submission. First, it would mean that there would never be a successful challenge to an infringement of light, because it could always be said, no matter how much actual light is taken away, it is always possible to fill the gap with artificial light. It is well demonstrated by the fact that the rooms in the Property, which have no natural light, are illuminated to the same standard by the constant electrical lighting as those, which have a natural light. No such argument so far as I am aware, has ever been put successfully or otherwise in any light case. Second, it undermines, in my view, the potential advantages that might appertain on a particular case, for natural light, which varies and might be better for specified tasks. The report itself (paragraph 3.1.2) identifies that the natural variation of daylight was valuable.

62 I was troubled about this submission because it was not supported by any kind of expert evidence. Further, it does not take into account potentially varied uses. If the Property has a right to light (as is the case), any other reasonable use to which it would be put, which might be diminished, should also be taken into account. In the instant case, in practical terms, no use is made of the natural light. It is not impossible however, for the Site to be redeveloped in a way, which incorporates more use of the natural light. If that takes place, that would have an impact on Midtown's use of, and enjoyment of its freehold title. Third, the lack of challenge in the City, might simply be, that most people adopt a pragmatic view, whereas the Claimants in this case are not willing to bargain away their rights, but wish to insist on them being enforced. It would not be appropriate to require their rights to be bargained away if they did not wish to do so. One always has to be alert to ensure that developments do not override rights simply by expropriation.

63 I have sympathy with the submissions. It may well be that in an appropriate case it is a right basis for challenging assumptions that have taken place as regards the preference of natural light to artificial light. However, on the evidence before me, I am not convinced that such a submission can be made out to challenge the case on the basis of no infringement. It does not follow however, that the submissions cannot be used for arguments based on remedy, i.e. refusing an injunction. I can see considerable force in that regard and I will revert to that further in this judgment.'

3.53   It is thought that these reasons are convincing. Further, despite Peter Smith J's expression of sympathy, it is thought the courts are unlikely to accept arguments to the effect that no injury has been caused since the claimant can use artificial light just as easily as natural light for two main reasons. First, it and parallel arguments have the potential to subvert the whole law of easements, not of rights of light alone. Why, for example, hold that a dominant owner has suffered injury to his right of way over a driveway if he has the option of a quick and relatively painless car journey which can bypass the obstructed route? Secondly, the interest protected is natural light, which cannot be assumed never to have special value in the future, depending on such matters as raised environmental standards and future uses of the dominant building or a replacement. For example, EEC Directive 89/954 of 1989 concerns minimum health and safety requirements for the workplace. Paragraph 8.1 of Annexes I and II require that *workplaces must as far as possible receive sufficient natural light*. This has been transposed into domestic law by statutory instrument.[81]

3.54   However, the availability and convenience of artificial light may be relevant to the grant of injunctive relief. This would particularly be the case where the room in question is small, and/or is only likely ever to serve an ancillary function such as toilet or store room. It would clearly be wrong (despite the actual outcome of *Midtown,* where an injunction was refused despite the extremely serious injury) to pay lip service to the rule that artificial light is irrelevant but decline to enforce the right specifically on the ground that it is available.

---

[81]   Workplace (Health, Safety and Welfare) Regulations 1992, SI 1992/3004 (as amended).

Chapter 4

BUILDINGS AND STRUCTURES CAPABLE OF ENJOYING RIGHTS TO LIGHT

GENERAL

4.1   As has already been stated in Chapter 1, no right to light can exist in favour of land which has no buildings on it. Further, a right can arise only in respect of light received through defined apertures in such buildings, intended for the purposes of admission of light. This is undoubtedly the position at common law. Section 3 of the Prescription Act 1832, which provides for the acquisition of a right to light based on 20 years' actual enjoyment,[1] provides that:

> 'When the access and use of light to and for *any dwellinghouse, workshop, or other building* shall have been actually enjoyed therewith for the full period of 20 years without interruption, the right thereto shall be deemed absolute and indefeasible . . .'

Thus the position under the 1832 Act is, broadly, the same as at common law, although the particular words of the statute fall to be considered in relation to any claim under its provisions.

4.2   There are therefore two questions: first, whether there is a building in existence which satisfies common law requirements or the statutory definition as the case may be, and, secondly, whether there are in existence in that building apertures sufficiently defined to give rise to a right to receive light through them. These questions may require to be considered in a number of contexts.

(1)   Where a question arises as to whether enjoyment of light has occurred for the necessary period to establish a prescriptive right, the date of the construction of the dominant building may be in issue.

(2)   The destruction or alteration of the dominant building may in some circumstances result in the right to light being lost. The effect of demolition and reconstruction is considered elsewhere in this book.[2] But in the case of a prescriptive right to light, it is clear that enjoyment for the necessary period is dependent on the continued existence of a building containing the apertures receiving light, or some other building which, by reason of the configuration of its apertures, can effectively be regarded as the successor thereto, and the maintenance of these apertures in a state such that light can penetrate into the interior of the building.[3] So windows permanently blocked on the inside will not qualify.

---

[1]   See Chapter 6 at **6.15–6.29**.

[2]   See Chapter 8 at **8.49–8.56**.

[3]   *Smith v Baxter* [1900] 2 Ch 138; *Tamares (Vincent Square) Ltd v Fairpoint Properties (Vincent Square) Ltd* [2006] EWHC 3589 (Ch), [2006] 41 EG 226, [2006] All ER (D) 10 (Sep), ChD (High Court of Justice, Chancery Division). See **4.15**.

(3)   Irrespective of issues of prescription, certain types of structure will not be
       regarded by the law as satisfying either the common law or statutory requirements
       for buildings or apertures capable of enjoying rights to light.

DECIDED CASES UNDER THE PRESCRIPTION ACT 1832, S 3

4.3   In a number of cases, the courts have considered the italicised wording of the
Act. The Act refers to 'other building'. These words have been held wide enough to
include ecclesiastical buildings,[4] a picture gallery,[5] a greenhouse[6] and a garage.[7]

4.4   In *Smith & Co (Orpington) v Morris*,[8] the county court judge gave consideration
to the question as to whether a window was situated in a 'building' within s 3 of the 1832
Act. He stated that the principal elements for consideration were as follows:

(1)   Did the structure give substantial shelter from the elements?

(2)   Was it one which ordinarily required light by means of windows or fixed
       apertures?

(3)   Did it have windows?

(4)   Was it so attached to the soil as to pass under a conveyance of the land without
       specific mention?

In *Smith*, although the garage was open sided, it was held that this fact was not
sufficient to deprive it of its character of a 'building'.

4.5   The position with regard to whether caravans and mobile homes are capable of
constituting buildings for the purposes of the Prescription Act 1832, s 3 has never
arisen. It is suggested that whether a caravan or mobile home is capable of constituting
a building for the purposes of the statute is a question of degree, depending on the
criteria identified in the case of *Smith & Co (Orpington) v Morris*, and in particular its
degree of annexation to the land.

4.6   In *R v Rent Officer of Northamptonshire Registration Area, ex parte Allen*[9] the
question arose as to whether a caravan was a 'house' for the purposes of the Rent
Act 1977. The caravan was fully mobile, but was connected to services, although all
services could be easily disconnected by hand. It was held that the caravan was not a
house, in view of its mobility and the possibility of disconnecting services.

---

4   *Ecclesiastical Commissioners v Kino* (1880) 14 ChD 213; *Attorney-General v Queen Anne Gardens and
     Mansions Co* (1889) 60 LT 759.
5   *Clifford v Holt* [1899] 1 Ch 698.
6   *Allen v Greenwood* [1980] Ch 119.
7   *Smith & Co (Orpington) v Morris* (1962) 112 LJ 702.
8   (1962) 112 LJ 702.
9   [1985] 2 EGLR 153.

4.7 On the other hand, in *Elitestone Ltd v Morris*,[10] it was held that a chalet or bungalow which rested on concrete foundation blocks in the ground constituted a house protected by the Rent Act 1977. Lord Lloyd stated of the bungalow:[11]

> 'It is not like a portacabin, or mobile home. The nature of the structure is such that it could not be taken down and re-erected elsewhere. It could only be removed by a process of demolition . . . if a structure can only be enjoyed in situ, and is such that it cannot be removed in whole or in sections to another site, there is at least a strong inference that the purpose of placing the structure on the original site was that it should form part of the realty at that site, and therefore cease to be a chattel.'

4.8 In the *Elitestone* case, the House of Lords reviewed earlier cases in which the distinction between chattels, and fixtures which form part of land was considered in the context of buildings. Relevant factors include the degree of annexation and the purpose of annexation, in the context of which the ease with which the structure may be moved is a relevant consideration. It is clear from the *Elitestone* case itself that the mere fact that the structure simply rests on the land without being actually attached to it will not prevent it becoming part of the land. It is probable that tents and other temporary structures are not included in the definition, though it has been held that a large marquee is capable of being a building in the context of the Town and Country Planning Act 1990.[12] However, it is unlikely that any temporary structure will be in position continually for the prescriptive period.

4.9 It is suggested that these cases provide helpful guidance as to the circumstances in which a mobile home or freestanding building not attached to land may constitute a building for the purposes of the Prescription Act 1832, s 3. It seems clear that, in general terms, a caravan, if capable of being moved, will not constitute a building, even if it is connected to services. In the case of large mobile homes which cannot readily be moved, and freestanding buildings which are, however, not permanently attached to the land, the question is one of degree, but it is submitted that there may well be circumstances in which they are capable of constituting 'buildings', provided that they have the appearance of buildings and contain apertures through which light is received. A further issue is whether the condition of the building is relevant to whether it qualifies under s 3. If it is grossly dilapidated and incapable of occupation can it be said to be a dwellinghouse, workshop, or other building at all? In *Boss Holdings Ltd v Grosvenor West End Properties Ltd*[13] it was held that for the purposes of the Leasehold Reform Act 1967, s 2 premises were not a house where they were gravely dilapidated. The decision turns to an extent on the relevant statutory definition, which required the premises to be designed or adapted for living in. It is suggested nevertheless that it is arguable that premises which are incapable of occupation may not qualify under the 1832 Act. In support of this point, it can be said the 1832 Act is intended to preserve the amenity of light[14] not sterilise land by useless easements.

---

[10] [1997] 2 All ER 513, HL.

[11] [1997] 2 All ER 516B.

[12] *Skerritts of Nottingham Ltd v Secretary of State for the Environment Transport and the Regions (No 2)* [2000] 2 PLR 102.

[13] [2006] EWCA 594.

[14] 'Enjoyed' does not imply pleasure, merely convenience in this context: *Cooper v Straker* (1888) 40 ChD 21; *Smith v Baxter* [1900] 2 Ch 138; *Tamares (Vincent Square) Ltd v Fairpoint Properties (Vincent Square) Ltd* [2006] EWHC 3589 (Ch), [2006] 41 EG 226, [2006] All ER (D) 10 (Sep), ChD (High Court of Justice, Chancery Division).

4.10   In the somewhat unusual case of *Duke of Norfolk v Arbuthnot*,[15] an issue arose as to whether part of a church constituted a 'building'. The church in question was constructed in the form of a Latin cross with a central tower. The plaintiff claimed ownership of that portion of the church east of the tower, that would normally be occupied by the chancel, and erected a wall across the west end of it so as to separate it structurally from the rest of the church. The defendant pulled down part of this wall, alleging that the portion claimed by the plaintiff was the chancel of the parish church, and that even if it were not, the parishioners were entitled either by prescription at common law or by virtue of a lost grant, or under the Prescription Act 1832, s 3 to light from the part claimed by the plaintiff. The plaintiff established that he owned the eastern part of the building, and that it was not the chancel of the parish church. The defendant's claim to have the wall separating the east end of the church from the remainder removed, which was in the form of an iron grille, also failed. The defendant relied on common law prescription, the Prescription Act 1832, s 3 and a lost grant, but all three bases of claim were rejected. In relation to the Prescription Act 1832, Bramwell LJ doubted whether the church could be considered a building within s 3 of the 1832 Act, although he gave no reason for his (tentative) view on the point, which was not necessary for the decision nor referred to by the other members of the court. It is submitted that the dictum cannot be accorded significant weight, given these points, the wording of the 1832 Act, and the other decided cases and what constitutes a 'building'. In *Ecclesiastical Commissioners v Kino*,[16] it was assumed that a church was a building capable of acquiring a right to light.

4.11   In *Harris v De Pinna*,[17] the issue arose as to whether a structure used for the storage of timber was a 'building' for the purposes of the 1832 Act. The structure consisted of several floors or stages, and was substantially constructed with upright timber standards fixed in stone bases built on solid piers. The standards were tied together with longitudinal baulks or cross-beams which supported floors or stages of solid planks, and were also connected by diagonal braces. The ends of the floors were open and unglazed, and served to admit light and air for drying timber. Light and air were received for the structure over the defendant's yard. The defendant commenced building over the yard, and the plaintiff, the owner of the structure, brought an action to restrain interference with light and air. It was held that the claim in relation to light failed. Two points were taken: the first was that the structure was not a 'building' within s 3 of the 1832 Act. At first instance, Chitty J accepted this argument, holding that although the structure was a structure, it was not a building within s 3.[18] The Court of Appeal did not find it necessary to decide the point, dismissing the claim on the ground that the structure contained no defined apertures through which light was received, Cotton LJ saying:[19]

> 'All that you protect is the access of light through the windows which have been substantially in the same place where they are at the time when the action is brought, for 20 years; and in my opinion it will not do in order to establish a right, to show that though at some time light did not come in through a particular access, at other times it did, and that sometimes it came in through one and sometimes through another opening, which was there in the structure of the building, which would admit light. Here we have evidence that the timber was stored and placed in these structures in different ways from time to time. What is the consequence? It may be, and the evidence of the plaintiffs has not negatived it, that at one time the timber

---

[15]   (1880) 5 CPD 390.
[16]   (1880) 14 ChD 213.
[17]   (1886) 33 ChD 238.
[18]   Ibid, at 249.
[19]   Ibid, at 257.

would be so piled up that no light would come in from the aperture which there might be at, say, the eastern end of the building, and that when the timber was piled differently it came in through the eastern, and could not come in through the western aperture. Very true, during all that time the erection of the building may have enjoyed light, but it has not enjoyed, in my opinion, such access as will give a right to it to the occupier. In order to do that it must be shown that there has been a definite access, I do not say through a window, but through some part of the building and that there has been enjoyed in the building for the statutory period, the light which has come in through that definite mode or means of access.'

4.12 Decisions in the context of other legislation as to what constitutes a 'building' are of little assistance and, in *Harris v De Pinna*, Chitty J at first instance declined to treat as persuasive cases on the meaning of 'building' in the Metropolitan Building Act 1855.[20] It is submitted that the word 'building' in s 3 is to be construed ejusdem generis with the earlier expressions, so that in general a building must have walls and a roof enclosing an interior space. Thus structures such as spectator stands[21] and walls[22] would not constitute a building, although they are undoubtedly structures.

THE TYPE OF APERTURE PROTECTED

Aperture must be defined

4.13 As is clear from the passage in *Harris v De Pinna* cited above, a right of light can be established only in relation to a defined aperture whose purpose is to admit light. An aperture used for an unglazed door will not qualify[23] on the ground that admission of light through such an aperture is fluctuating and uncertain. Peterson J said:[24]

'If a door is at one time fully open and at another time only partially open, what is the aperture through which the light has been enjoyed, and what is the amount of light which has been enjoyed during the period of prescription.'

He also held that, in the particular context of s 3 of the Prescription Act 1832, it applied only to windows or apertures in the nature of windows and not to apertures with doors in them, which were primarily constructed for the purpose of being closed and thus excluding light. The position, therefore, seems to be that both at common law and under s 3, a prescriptive right to light cannot be acquired in respect of apertures with unglazed doors in them. This would not, however, apply to glazed doors which admit light even when closed.

4.14 Modern commercial buildings frequently employ glazed curtain walling supported by steel and concrete frames, as opposed to load-bearing masonry external walls. In such construction, it cannot be said that there are in reality 'apertures' at all. A court would, given the prevalence of the method of construction, be unlikely to find that such buildings are incapable of acquiring rights to light. It is submitted that the 'aperture' can properly be regarded as that part of the whole area between floor and ceiling slabs intended to admit light.

---

[20] For use of the word 'building' in other statutory contexts, see, eg, Town and Country Planning Act 1990, s 336; Party Wall etc Act 1996, s 6.
[21] Cf *City of Westminster v London County Council* [1902] 1 KB 326.
[22] Cf *Mills and Rockleys Ltd v Leicester City Council* [1946] KB 315.
[23] *Levet v Gas Light and Coke Co* [1919] 1 Ch 24.
[24] [1919] 1 Ch 27.

Partially obscured windows

4.15   Clearly, the fact that the window in question has curtains or blinds which are drawn at different times or seasons of the year does not prevent such a window being treated as enjoying a right to light. The same also applies where the window has external shutters capable of being opened and closed.[25] Permanent obstruction of the window by the dominant owner, for example, by boarding up, may, depending on the circumstances, result in the aperture not acquiring a right to light, or in any acquired right to light being treated as abandoned.[26] In *Smith v Baxter*,[27] it was held that a permanent boarding up of two windows prevented them acquiring a prescriptive right to light, but the position was different with regard to another window which had been covered with shelving. In *Tamares (Vincent Square) Ltd v Fairpoint Properties (Vincent Square) Ltd,*[28] it was held that two windows which though they retained their glazing had been permanently blocked on the inside with panelling during the prescriptive period had not acquired prescriptive rights to light.

4.16   The right to light arises in relation to any part of the structure which contains a defined aperture for the admission of light, even though the aperture forms part of the structure of the building which also serves as a wall or roof, for example, the glazed wall of a greenhouse or the glazed roof of a conservatory.[29] The dominant owner's right extends to the full size of the aperture, no account being taken of window frames or glazing bars.[30]

Apertures between different parts of the same building

4.17   In *Duke of Norfolk v Arbuthnot*,[31] the facts of which have already been outlined, Bramwell LJ expressed doubt as to whether a prescriptive right to light could arise in respect of light passing through part of a building owned by the plaintiff and thence via an arch to part owned by the defendant, on the ground that the arch existed for the common benefit of two buildings. Reasons for this doubt were not articulated, but it is a possible view that the right to light arises only in respect of apertures in the external envelope of a structure, so that no prescriptive right to light can arise in relation to the further diffusion of light once it has passed through the external envelope. Thus those whose premises derive light via a glazed atrium, for example, would not be protected.

4.18   It is suggested that this view is not correct. There is no logical reason why there should be no right to light which passes through part of a building before arriving at the plaintiff's premises. This view is supported by *Tisdall v McArthur & Co (Steel & Metal) Ltd*[32] in which it was held that the existence of a transparent glass roof over a yard which provided light to the plaintiff's windows did not prevent the acquisition of a prescriptive right to light.[33]

---

[25]   *Cooper v Straker* (1888) 40 ChD 21.
[26]   See, generally, Chapter 8 at **8.9–8.19**.
[27]   [1900] 2 Ch 138.
[28]   [2006] 41 EG 226 (High Court of Justice, Chancery Division).
[29]   *Easton v Isted* [1903] 1 Ch 405.
[30]   *Turner v Spooner* (1861) 1 Drew and Sm 467, 62 ER 457.
[31]   (1880) 5 CPD 390.
[32]   [1951] IR 228.
[33]   See also *Barnes v Loach* (1879) 4 QBD 494.

Incomplete/unoccupied premises

4.19 It appears that once a building is sufficiently structurally completed to be recognisably such, the fact that it remains unfinished will not prevent a right to light arising by prescription. In *Courtauld v Legh*,[34] a house was structurally completed, the roof finished, the floors laid, and the windows put in, but not internally completed nor fit for habitation. It was held that a right to light in respect of the windows had been acquired. In *Collis v Laugher*,[35] it was held that for the purposes of the date of commencement of the 20-year period necessary to establish a prescriptive right to light under s 3 of the Prescription Act 1832, enjoyment commenced when the exterior walls of the building with the spaces for the windows were completed, and the building was roofed in, even though the windows themselves had not been installed. This case must of course be distinguished from the situation where the external walls are not constructed to a sufficient stage to have inserted in them the defined apertures for windows. Thus the construction of a steel and concrete frame for a building, without walling, would probably not give rise to an entitlement to a prescriptive right to light. Where a building enjoying rights to light is demolished, the rights it enjoys do not necessarily end for all time; if there is an intention on the part of an owner to rebuild they may be regarded as simply in abeyance.[36]

---

[34] (1869) LR Exch 126.
[35] [1894] 3 Ch 659.
[36] See Chapter 8 at **8.49–8.50**.

Chapter 5

ACQUISITION OF RIGHTS OF LIGHT I –
BY ACTS OF THE PARTIES

SUMMARY

5.1   In this chapter the way in which rights of light may be acquired by the acts of the parties is considered. This chapter will therefore look at express grants and implied grants and those cases where a right of light may arise by operation of law or under a statute.

EXPRESS GRANT

5.2   It is comparatively rare for an easement of light to be created by express words of grant as between freeholders. More frequently one finds deeds entered into between owners of adjoining buildings, or provisions in conveyances or transfers of parts of land formerly in one ownership which contain covenants restricting buildings and other erections that can be constructed so as to protect existing rights to light.[1] There is no reason in principle, however, why an express grant cannot be effected. In order for a legal easement of light to be granted, a deed is required.[2] An equitable easement may be created otherwise than by deed.[3] An uncompleted agreement to grant a legal easement is a classic example of an equitable easement. There is a difference between the way in which legal easements and equitable easements are protected in order to bind successors of the original parties.

Unregistered land

5.3   In the case of unregistered land, a legal agreement will be valid as a legal interest in land under s 1 of the Law of Property Act 1925 and no registration under the Land Charges Act 1972 is required. In the case of unregistered land, an equitable easement created since 1925 is void against a purchaser for money or money's worth of a legal estate in the land subject to it, unless registered prior to completion of the purchase.[4] The fact that the purchaser has notice of it will not prevent the easement being void against him.[5]

---

[1]   See, eg, *Potts v Smith* (1868) LR 6 Eq 311.
[2]   Law of Property Act 1925, s 52.
[3]   Law of Property Act 1925, s 53.
[4]   Land Charges Act 1972, s 4(6).
[5]   Law of Property Act 1925, s 199(1)(i).

Registered land

5.4   On first registration of the title to land the following rules, in summary, apply.

(1)   A legal easement will be an overriding interest under Sch 1, para 3 to the Land
Registration Act 2002 ('LRA 2002'). However, in practice, the title deduced will
refer to such a legal easement and the easement will be noted on the title under the
Land Registration Rules 2003[6] ('LRR 2003'), r 35 and 38.

(2)   An equitable easement does not qualify as an interest which overrides under the
law in force after 13 October 2003. So any newly created equitable easement must
have been registered under the Land Charges Act 1972, or it will not be entered on
the register. Equitable easements created before 13 October 2003 which had the
status of overriding interests under s 70(1)(a) of the Land Registration Act 1925
will continue to do so by virtue of the provisions of Sch 12, para 10 to LRA 2002.

(3)   Easements created by estoppel are not seemingly subject to any particular means
of protection under LRA 2002. In practice they may be the subject of a notice on
the register if referred to in panel 13 of the FR1 form.

In practice rights of light are only likely to fall within (1) above on first registration. On
dispositions of registered titles, only those entries on the register of legal or equitable
easements will bind the disponee. Equitable easements will not bind a disponee if not so
noted. However, legal easements (even if not noted on the register) may bind the
disponee if they satisfy the factual conditions in Sch 3, para 3 to LRA 2002 and thereby
take effect as interests which override. An express grant or reservation of an easement
(ie a right of light) must be completed by notice on the register under s 27 of LRA 2002
until which point it takes effect in equity only.[7]

5.5   For an easement to be validly granted, the grantor must in general have sufficient
interest in the servient land to create a valid easement over it. Easements granted over
land belonging to third parties may, however, take effect by way of acquiescence, or
estoppel in some circumstances.[8] For example, where the third party allows access over
his land in return for a right in return such as the maintenance of encroaching
foundations. Likewise, if there is an express grant of an easement over land to which the
grantor has no title, but he then acquires title, he and his successors will be bound by
estoppel.[9] Where the grantor has only a limited interest in the land over which he
purports to grant the easement, the extent of the easement will be determined by his
interest at the time of the grant, without taking into account subsequent events. So in
Booth v Alcock,[10] the grantor of an easement of light had at the time of the grant only
a lease over the servient tenement. He subsequently acquired the fee simple, but it was
held that the grant was restricted in duration to the length of the lease which the grantor
had at the date of the grant.

5.6   Where the rights of the grantor to dispose of his land are subject to statutory
constraints, he cannot lawfully grant an easement in excess of his powers. This point

---

6   SI 2003/1417.
7   This is so only if the title to the servient tenement is registered. LRA 2002, ss 27 and 132. Further details on
         the registration of rights of light expressly granted are set out in Chapter 14. See also *Ruoff & Roper*:
         Registered Conveyancing (Sweet & Maxwell, looseleaf) ch 36.
8   See, eg, *ER Ives Investments Ltd v High* [1967] 1 All ER 504, CA.
9   *Rowbotham v Wilson* (1857) 8 E&B 123; 8 HLC 348.
10   (1873) 8 Ch App 663.

used to be taken on dispositions by trustees, or life tenants under the Settled Land Act 1925.[11] The importance of these restrictions, insofar as they apply to former trustees for sale, has been greatly reduced by the Trusts of Land and Appointment of Trustees Act 1996. Trustees of land now have all the powers of an absolute owner unless expressly restricted.[12] It remains the position that when authority is required the grant of an easement which is not authorised will be of no effect.[13]

5.7   In the same way as a competent grantor is required, no easement can be granted in excess of the interest of the grantee in the dominant tenement. This is consistent with the general principle that easements are appurtenant to land, so that they can only subsist for as long as the interest in land to which they relate subsists. Where the grant is to someone with a limited interest, who subsequently becomes the owner of the dominant tenement, the easement may enure for the benefit of the freehold if the terms of the grant contemplated that this should be the case.[14] For perpetuity considerations, see **9.38** below.

5.8   An easement of light may also be reserved by the vendor of land.[15] The reservation must normally be in clear terms.[16] Apart from this, an easement may be held to have been reserved by implication but such a reservation will be found to exist only where the facts are not reasonably consistent with any explanation other than such an easement was intended to be reserved.[17]

5.9   An express easement of light may be granted by a lease. The effect of such a grant was considered in *Frogmore Developments Ltd v Shirayama Shokusan Co*[18] in the context of its (alleged) inconsistency with intended development of nearby land, which adjoined the former GLC County Hall in London. It was held that the grant of 'the right to free and unobstructed passage of light and air to the premises at all times' entitled the lessee to receive light at a level which did not fall below that required for the ordinary purposes for which the premises could be used. This authority demonstrates how important it is to advise clients where reservations are on the title (whether reserved in transfers of the freehold, or on grants of leases) that such reservations (eg of light) may impose a severe constraint on the client's development or building plans.

GRANT BY IMPLICATION

5.10   An easement may be inferred where a conveyance or other document does not grant it expressly, but uses terms consistent with the existence of the easement. In *Roberts v Karr*,[19] the description of land in a release as abutting on a road was held to

---

[11]   See, eg, Settled Land Act 1925, s 49(1), which authorises the grant and reservation of easements, and s 41 of the same Act in regard to the grant of leases.

[12]   Trusts of Land and Appointment of Trustees Act 1996, s 6(1).

[13]   See, eg, *Oakley v Boston* [1976] QB 270 (consent required to grant of an easement under Ecclesiastical Leases Acts 1842 and 1858 but not obtained). See also *Re St Clement, Leigh-on-Sea* [1988] 1 WLR 720. See **6.33**, for the issues arising where property is governed by ecclesiastical law.

[14]   *Rymer v McIlroy* [1897] 1 Ch 528.

[15]   See Law of Property Act 1925, s 65 and the *Shirayama* case at footnote 22.

[16]   *Wheeldon v Burrows* (1879) 12 ChD 31 at 49 per Thesiger LJ.

[17]   *Re Webb's Lease* [1951] Ch 808 at 829 per Jenkins LJ; *Peckham v Ellison* (1998) 77 P&CR D27, CA (right of way).

[18]   (1997) ChD (unreported).

[19]   [1809] 1 Taunt 495.

preclude the grantor from asserting that the grantee was not entitled to access over a verge which separated part of the land granted from that road.

5.11 An easement may be held to have been granted by implication, based on the intended use of the property the subject of a lease for sale.[20] In *Browne v Flower*,[21] Parker J considered the position of an implicit grant of an easement of light, saying:

> 'Once again, though possibly there may not be known to the law any easement of light for special purposes, still the lease of a building to be used for a special purpose requiring an extraordinary amount of light might well be held to preclude the grantor from diminishing the light passing to the grantee's windows, even in cases where the diminution would not be such as to create a nuisance within the meaning of recent decisions . . .'

There seems no reason in principle why these words should be limited to the situation where the lessee or other grantee is claiming an extraordinary quantity of light. If the purpose for which premises are leased or granted contemplate the receipt of light in any quantity through existing or, indeed, proposed apertures a right to receive such light might arise by implication. This may well be of importance in the case of specialised premises, such as drawing offices, and will become more generally important if statutory requirements regarding health and safety at work lead to the imposition of a standard entitling employees to work in environments with direct sky illuminations. Current regulations require lighting at work places to be 'so far as is reasonably practicable, . . . by natural light'.[22] This does not impose on the employer a duty to ensure that natural light is available, save except so far as it is 'reasonably practicable'. It would presumably not be the case that it would be reasonably practicable to provide natural light where the terms on which the employer occupied the relevant premises did not confer on him a right to prevent the windows being obscured so as to limit or exclude natural light. It is, however, possible to envisage circumstances where it might be argued that since the contemplated purpose for which premises were being leased or purchased involved at least some obligation on the part of the purchaser to provide natural light to the work places of those whom he proposed to employ there, there was by implication a grant of an easement of light.[23] It is an open question at present as to how far (i) the statutory obligations on lighting in places of work can be said to affect the question whether an interference with light should be considered actionable and (ii) to what extent the presence of such lighting should determine the grant or refusal of an injunction and any damages in lieu; see Chapters 3 and 11 for further discussion of these two issues.

GRANT UNDER THE RULE IN *WHEELDON V BURROWS*

5.12 This case[24] finds its foundations in the principle of implied grant. It is, in effect, an early formulation of s 62 of the Law of Property Act 1925 but the rights that pass are

---

20   *Lyttleton Times Co Limited v Warners Limited* [1907] AC 476; *Yankwood Limited v Havering London Borough Council* [1998] EGCS 75.

21   [1911] 1 Ch 219 at 226.

22   Construction (Health Safety and Welfare) Regulations 1996, SI 1996/1592, reg 25. See also the Management of Health and Safety at Work Regulations 1999, SI 1999/3242, especially Sch 1. See *Midtown v CLRP Co* [2005] EWHC 33 Ch at [58] per Peter Smith J, noting the CIBES Lighting Code for Offices (access via www.cibse.org).

23   For a case where the grant in a lease of a right to light was held not to be limited by implication from surrounding circumstances, see *Frogmore Developments Ltd v Shirayama Shokusan Co Ltd* (1997) ChD (unreported). See **5.9**.

24   (1879) 12 ChD 31.

limited by comparison to that section, an exception being the agreement for a lease which does not count as a conveyance for the purposes of s 62.[25] The principle itself is neatly set out by Thesiger LJ:

> '... that, on the grant by the owner of a tenement of part of that tenement as it is then used and enjoyed, there will pass to the grantee all those continuous and apparent easements (by which, of course, I mean quasi-easements), or in other words all those easements which are necessary to the reasonable enjoyment of the property granted, and which have been and are at the time of the grant used by the owners of the entirety for the benefit of the part granted.'

5.13   The rule, therefore, usually operates on the sub-division of a parcel of land. For example, if a parcel of land under common ownership is divided into part A, which is retained and part B, which is disposed of, the rule confers by implication on the transferee of part B the benefits of any rights to light over part A that the former owner of both parts exercised over the land prior to its sub-division. The rule also applies where the common owner subdivides and sells the subdivided property simultaneously, retaining no land himself.

5.14   *Wheeldon v Burrows* was itself a case that concerned the right of access to light over the servient tenement. Access to light is regarded as both continuous and apparent and necessary for the reasonable enjoyment of the land and does not therefore suffer from the problems of easements (such as rights of way) for which proof of use or necessity is required.[26] Thus, in *Swansborough v Coventry*,[27] Trindall CJ said:

> 'It is well established by the decided cases, that where the same person possesses a house, having the actual use and enjoyment of certain rights, and also possesses the adjoining land, and sells the house to another person, although the lights be new, he cannot, nor can anyone who claims under him, build upon the adjoining land so as to obstruct or interrupt the enjoyment of those lights.'

Sale of part of land, where vendor retains the remainder

5.15   Where buildings on the land being disposed of have yet to be built but the vendor is aware, either at the time of the disposition or during any prior agreement for the disposition, that the land is being acquired for building purposes, the principle applies equally and the right attaches to the buildings when built.[28]

5.16   The transfer of rights by implication may itself be negatived or modified by circumstances, but the onus of establishing this is on the grantor. Therefore, where the grantor makes it clear in express terms that he intends to build on part A (the retained land), the grantee cannot complain if his access to light is restricted by such construction.[29] If, however, the grantee is aware of only a general intention to build, such as by describing the retained land as 'building land', then this is insufficient to negative the implication.[30]

---

[25]   See *Borman v Griffith* [1930] 1 Ch 493.
[26]   For example, *Borman v Griffith* – the case itself provides a useful review of the rule in *Wheeldon v Burrows* at 499.
[27]   (1832) 9 Bing 305 at 309.
[28]   *Frederick Betts Ltd v Pickfords Ltd* [1906] 2 Ch 87.
[29]   *Birmingham, Dudley & District Banking Company v Ross* (1888) 38 ChD 295.
[30]   *Broomfield v Williams* (1897) 1 ChD at 602; *Frogmore Development Ltd v Shirayama Shokusan Co Ltd* (1997) ChD (unreported).

5.17   Where a grantor who sells part of his land does not expressly reserve in that grant an easement of light in favour of the part he has retained, he will normally not be held to have reserved such a right by implication.[31] Such reservation should, therefore, be expressly stated in the grant. The general rule is that grants are construed against the grantor, and this principle applies to exclude, in general, the implication of reservations in favour of the grantor, as explained at **5.21**. The correct approach is for the court to interpret the terms of the grant by considering the instrument and the surrounding circumstances in conjunction.[32]

5.18   However, where a vendor disposes of two plots of land simultaneously, which are adjacent to each other, both conveyances are treated as grants under the rule in *Wheeldon v Burrows* and therefore each part acquires by implication the same easements over any other as it would if that other part had been retained by the vendor.[33] This rule applies equally to testamentary dispositions and voluntary conveyances inter vivos.[34]

Lease of part of land, where the landlord retains the remainder

5.19   As with an outright sale of land, the formal grant of a lease over part B of land of the lessor, will allow the lessee to acquire by implication, for the term of the lease, any right to the access of light over the retained land (part A), which it can be shown was actually enjoyed by the part let at the date of the lease.

5.20   During the term of that lease, any later lease or grant of the retained land must take effect subject to the right to the access of light to the let land.[35] If, however, there was never any formal grant of the original lease over the let land (eg there was an agreement only to create a lease), the rights of the original informal lessee may still be protected by registration or actual occupation of the part let.

5.21   Where a lessor, in demising part of his land over which light is received to his retained land, fails to reserve in favour of the part retained an easement of light over the part demised, the retained land will normally enjoy no right to light during the term of the lease.[36] For an easement of light to arise under the principle, it is not necessary for the common owner to be actually in possession of both parts of his land before he simultaneously disposes of both parts.[37]

5.22   The application of the principle was described by Mellish LJ in *Leech v Schweder*[38] as follows:

> 'It is perfectly established that if a man owns a house, and owns property of any other kind adjoining that house, and then either conveys the house in fee simple or demises it for a term

---

[31]   *Wheeldon v Burrows* (1879) 12 ChD 31 at 49. See also **5.8**. For the effect of a reservation, see the Law of Property Act 1925, s 65.

[32]   *St Edmundsbury and Ipswich Diocesan Board of Finance v Clark (No 2)* [1975] 1 All ER 772, CA; *Frogmore Developments Ltd v Shirayama Shokusan Co Ltd* (1997) ChD (unreported). For the extent of 'surrounding circumstances' see, generally, *Investors Compensation Scheme Ltd v West Bromwich Building Society* [1998] 1 All ER 98, HL.

[33]   *Russell v Watts* (1884) 25 ChD 559 – see especially Fry LJ at 584.

[34]   *Phillips v Low* [1892] 1 Ch 47.

[35]   *Thomas v Owen* (1888) 20 QBD 225.

[36]   *Re Webbs Lease* [1951] Ch 808; *Frogmore Developments Ltd v Shirayama Shokusan Co Ltd* (1997) ChD (unreported). See also *Peckham v Ellison* (1998) 77 P&CR D27, CA.

[37]   *Barnes v Loach* (1879) 4 QBD 494.

[38]   (1874) 9 Ch App 463 at 472.

of years to another person, a right to light unobstructed by anything to be erected on any land which at the time belonged to the grantor passes to the grantee.'

The implication may be negatived by surrounding circumstances, as where it is well known to the purchaser or lessee that the grantor or lessor intends to develop his retained land in a way which may interfere with the light to the buildings (actual or proposed) on the land conveyed or let.[39] The onus of negativing the implication of an easement lies on the grantor.[40] Care should be taken when granting leases in particular to ensure that any reservation of the right to build on adjoining land (whether by the lessor or third parties) is wide enough and does not infringe the principle of non-derogation from grant; see **5.32**.[41]

LAW OF PROPERTY ACT 1925, S 62

5.23 This is now the main way in which the right to easements which are not mentioned in the conveyance are impliedly granted and overlays the rule in *Wheeldon v Burrows*. The section applies to conveyances made after 31 December 1881 which was when s 6 of the Conveyancing Act 1881, which preceded s 62 of the Law of Property Act 1925, came into effect.

5.24 Section 62 of the Law of Property Act 1925 provides that:

'(1) A conveyance of land shall be deemed to include and shall by virtue of this Act operate to convey, with the land, all buildings, erections, fixtures, commons, hedges, ditches, fences, ways, waters, watercourses, liberties, privileges, easements, rights, and advantages whatsoever, appertaining or reputed to appertain to the land, or any part thereof, or, at the time of conveyance, demised, occupied, or enjoyed with, or reputed or known as part or parcel of or appurtenant to the land or any part thereof.

(2) A conveyance of land, having houses or other buildings thereon, shall be deemed to include and shall by virtue of this Act operate to convey, with the land, houses, or other buildings, or outhouses, erections, fixtures, cellars, areas, courts, courtyards, cisterns, sewers, gutters, drains, ways, passages, lights, watercourses, liberties, privileges, easements, rights and advantages whatsoever, appertaining or reputed to appertain to the land, houses, or other buildings conveyed, or any of them, or any parts thereof, or, at the time of conveyance, demised, occupied, or enjoyed with, or reputed or known as part or parcel of or appurtenant to, the land, houses, or other buildings conveyed, or any of them, or any part thereof.'

5.25 By conveyance, is meant virtually any instrument which transfers or creates a *legal* estate in freehold or leasehold land.[42] The term does not include, therefore, agreements which create equitable interest only.[43] Where they apply, the general words of s 62 can only be excluded by express terms.[44]

---

[39] *Birmingham, Dudley and District Banking Co v Ross* (1888) 38 ChD 295; *Godwin v Schweppes Ltd* [1902] 1 Ch 926.

[40] *Broomfield v Williams* [1897] 1 Ch 602; *Pollard v Gare* [1901] 1 Ch 834; *Swansborough v Coventry* (1832) 9 Bing 305; *Myers v Catterson* (1889) 43 ChD 470.

[41] See *Paragon Finance v CLRP Co* [2002] 1 EGLR 97.

[42] Law of Property Act 1925, s 205(1)(iii).

[43] *Borman v Griffith* [1930] 1 Ch 493. Which is of itself sufficient to create an express equitable easement – see **5.2**.

[44] Law of Property Act 1925, s 62(4); *William Hill (Southern) Ltd v Cabras Ltd* (1987) 54 P&CR 42 at 46. For recent authority on the scope of s 62 see *Harbour Estates v HSBC Bank* [2005] Ch 194.

5.26   Section 62 has the effect of passing to the transferee of land the benefit of existing easements, profits, privileges and rights which appertain to the land conveyed, or are indeed reputed to appertain to it, or which at the date of the conveyance are enjoyed with that land. This will include rights of light in the course of being acquired, even though precarious.[45] It is not thought that the *benefit* of a written consent within s 3 of the Prescription Act 1832 (as to which see **6.24**) will pass under s 62.[46] As appears in Chapter 6, such a consent (if effective) prevents the assertion of a prescriptive claim to light by the dominant owner ('A'). The benefit of such a consent will pass to any successor of A ('B') because B acquires the dominant land with the benefit of the consent and no prescriptive claim can arise while that consent is in force and unrevoked. Section 62 simply has no part to play here. The same observation is made as to the effect of s 63 of the Law of Property Act 1925 considered at **5.30**.

5.27   As an owner of land cannot have an easement over his own land, there is clear authority that s 62 operates only where there has been diversity of ownership, or occupation of the dominant or servient tenement prior to the conveyance. This is because where no such divergence exists there can be no easement to pass under s 62.[47]

5.28   However, strictly, the views of Lords Edmund-Davies and Wilberforce are obiter dicta albeit of high authority.[48] In the case of quasi-easements of light, as opposed to other easements, it appears in any event that where there is unity of occupation, s 62 is still capable of applying. This was decided in *Broomfield v Williams*.[49]

5.29   As with the rule in *Wheeldon v Burrows*, the presence of light over land is not difficult to show. Therefore, a right to the access of that light will be transferred under s 62 even where there has been a unity of ownership provided the right has been exercised by and for the benefit of the land conveyed and not just for the common benefit of the two properties. Where the land is not in common ownership no such problem arises. It should be noted that the court retains an equitable jurisdiction to rectify any conveyance which mistakenly transfers to a grantee more rights than were intended in a relevant contract for sale.

LAW OF PROPERTY ACT 1925, S 63

5.30   Section 63 of the Law of Property Act 1925 provides that:

> '(1)   Every conveyance is effectual to pass all the estate, right, title, interest, claim, and demand which the conveying parties respectively have, in, to, or on the property conveyed, or expressed or intended so to be, or which they respectively have power to convey in, to, or on the same.

---

[45]   *Midtown v CLRP Co* [2005] EWHC 33 Ch at para 23 per Peter Smith J.

[46]   This point arises where there is a consent provision in a lease (falling within *Haynes v King* [1893] 3 Ch 439) where the successor in title to the landlord acquires the freehold. Section 62 does not operate to pass the benefit of the consent proviso in the lease to the new owner of the freehold.

[47]   *Sovmots Investments Ltd v Secretary of State for the Environment* [1979] AC 144 at 176C per Lord Edmund-Davies. Lord Wilberforce expressed the same view. But see a contrary view expressed by the Court of Appeal in *P&S Platt v Crouch* [2003] EWCA Civ 1110. It is arguable, as is stated at **5.28**, that in rights of light claims diversity of occupation is not required; see *Broomfield v Williams* [1897] 1 Ch 602.

[48]   For comment, see C Harpum (1977) 41 *Conveyancer* 415; (1979) 43 *Conveyancer* 113; (1978) 42 *Conveyancer* 449.

[49]   [1897] 1 Ch 602.

(2)   This section applies only if and as far as a contrary intention is not expressed in the conveyance, and has effect subject to the terms of the conveyance and to the provisions therein contained.

(3)   This section applies to conveyances made after the thirty-first day of December, eighteen hundred and eighty-one.'

5.31   There have been attempts in two recent authorities to use s 63 to pass the benefit of a break clause in a lease and the benefit of a restrictive covenant over freehold land. In each case the argument failed. Section 63 is really designed to deal with a situation where the grantor has a lesser estate than he purports to grant. It is suggested that in the light of these two authorities s 63 does not operate to pass any right of light which would otherwise pass under s 62.[50]

UNDER THE OBLIGATION NOT TO DEROGATE FROM GRANT

5.32   This principle is a general rule applying to all conveyances and is not restricted to cases involving easements. This is because it is based upon the presumed intention of the parties to the relevant grant. Therefore, in that a grantor should not do anything to render the disposal nugatory, the principle has been described as one 'of common honesty'.[51] The rights acquired pursuant to an application of the principle binds successors in title of the grantor and are available to successors in title of the grantee.

5.33   The principle finds clear judicial expression in the judgment of Parker J in *Browne v Flower*, where His Lordship said:[52]

'But the implications usually explained by the maxim that no-one can derogate from his own grant do not stop short with easements under certain circumstances there will be implied on the part of the grantor or lessor obligations which a strict user of the land retained by him further than can be explained by the implication of any easement known to the law. Thus, if the grant or demise be made for a particular purpose, the grantor or lessor comes under an obligation not to use the land retained by him in such a way as to render the land granted or demised unfit or materially less fit for the particular purpose for which the grant or demise was made.'

5.34   Therefore, the immunities acquired by virtue of the principle depend upon the common intention, to be gathered either from the express words of the grant or the circumstances in which it was made. No complaint can be made if an act by the grantor does not make the land granted unfit for a particular purpose or only achievable at a greater expense or with less convenience.[53]

5.35   The principle has been applied so as to bind those deriving title from the grantor, irrespective of whether they have notice of the grantor's obligation.[54] In *Johnston and Sons Ltd v Holland*,[55] in which earlier cases were reviewed, the principle was held to

---

[50]   See *Harbour Estates v HSBC Bank plc* [2005] Ch 194 and *Sugarman v Porter* [2006] EWHC 331 Ch at [31]–[44].

[51]   *Harmer v Jumbil (Nigeria) Tin Areas Ltd* [1921] 1 Ch 200 at 235 and see *Johnston and Sons Ltd v Holland* [1988] 1 EGLR 264.

[52]   [1911] 1 Ch 219 at 225.

[53]   *O'Cedar Ltd v Slough Trading Company Ltd* [1927] 2 KB 123 at 127.

[54]   *Cable v Bryant* [1908] 1 Ch 259.

[55]   [1988] 1 EGLR 264, CA.

apply to acts done by the grantor on land which he did not own at the date of the grant. This may be of considerable importance in rights of light situations, and may effectively preclude a vendor of land on which a building exists, or on which the erection of such a building is contemplated, from using land which he later acquires so as to interfere with the light received over it to the purchasers of the building, whether existing at the date of the sale or contemplated at that time. It is immaterial whether the purchaser's building would otherwise enjoy a prescriptive right to light. Reference should also be made to *Paragon Finance v CLRP Co*[56] referred to at **5.19**.

UNDER STATUTORY PROVISIONS

5.36   Easements may be granted expressly by statute, or may arise by the exercise or performance of powers or obligations contained in those statutes. One example of this is where a public body which compulsorily purchased land under a statutory power may need additional rights over adjoining land in order to carry out the purposes for which the land is being purchased. However, it should be noted that there is no implied right to create new easements which did not exist prior to the compulsory purchase[57] except insofar as they may exist as quasi-easements under either the rule in *Wheeldon v Burrows*, or s 62 of the Law of Property Act 1925.[58] This lack of creative power is confirmed by silence in the Acquisition of Land Act 1981, which is the primary Act by which the government, local authorities and other bodies obtain land by compulsory purchase. Therefore, it is now the norm for specific Acts to contain express provision for the creation of new rights within their powers for compulsory purchase.

5.37   Where land is compulsorily purchased which has existing easements, these are transferred in the normal way under s 62 and the usual implications for successors in title apply. There are not many circumstances under which it would be envisaged that a right to light would specifically be required in an Act of Parliament, except, for example, insofar as DEFRA requires land for experimental farms.

5.38   Another form of statutory provision which creates an easement of sorts, is that which permits the laying and repairing of pipes, wires and cables. These are not clear easements because the statutory undertaker does not acquire the land and as such there is no dominant tenement. This was considered in *Newcastle-under-Lyme Corporation v Wolstanton Ltd*[59] where Morton LJ, agreeing with and quoting Evershed J at the first instance, stated:

> 'They have by force of the statute the exclusive right to occupy for the purposes of their statutory undertaking the space in the soil taken by the pipes . . . but that exclusive right of occupation which continues so long as the Corporation carry on their undertaking, does not depend upon or involve the vesting in the plaintiff corporation of any legal or equitable estate in the land.'

5.39   The conclusion reached by JF Garner[60] is that these 'rights given by statute are *sui generis*, and fit in with no known other jurisprudence concept and amount to an exclusive right to occupy the space or can be occupied by the actual pipes themselves'.

---

56   [2002] 1 EGLR 97.
57   *Sovmots Investments v Secretary of State for the Environment* [1979] AC 144.
58   See **5.12–5.29**.
59   [1947] Ch 427 at 456.
60   20 *Conveyancer* 208 at 213.

Acts which enable these activities include: the Electricity Act 1989,[61] the Telecommunications Act 1984[62] and the Water Industry Act 1991,[63] but once again in terms of rights to light these type of provisions are of little or no significance.

5.40   Chapter 8 considers the way in which rights of light may be extinguished under statutory provisions.

---

[61]   Schedule 4.
[62]   Schedule 2.
[63]   Section 159.

Chapter 6

ACQUISITION OF RIGHTS TO LIGHT II – BY PRESCRIPTION

SUMMARY

6.1   An easement of light may be acquired by prescription in one of the following ways:

(1)   by proving continuous enjoyment since time immemorial, which in practice means showing enjoyment back many hundreds of years and potentially since 1189. This is known as 'common law prescription'. Only freehold owners can claim the right by this means;

(2)   by proving at least 20 years' continuous enjoyment back from the time when proceedings are issued. Such enjoyment must comply with the requirements of the Prescription Act 1832, and a claim is a prescriptive one based on that Act. Unique to rights to light, and only under this Act, a tenant may claim rights to light, both for and against a freehold owner and even against his own landlord;

(3)   by claiming that light has been enjoyed for any period of at least 20 years and that enjoyment has been a fictitious grant of such a right by a person capable of making such a grant. Only freehold owners can claim the right by this means. This is known as a claim based on 'lost modern grant'. It saves having to prove enjoyment since 1189 and avoids having to prove enjoyment for at least 20 years back from the issue of proceedings as required by the Prescription Act 1832.

Any claim to rights to light can be based on any of these prescriptive heads of claim, and in some cases all three heads can be relied upon if the facts so warrant. It is rare, however, for a claim to be based (let alone succeed) upon common law prescription.

COMMON LAW PRESCRIPTION

6.2   The acquisition of an easement of light by prescription at common law requires proof of enjoyment from time immemorial, which in practical terms means from the beginning of legal memory being 1189, that being the first year of the reign of Richard I. The date was fixed by the Statute of Westminster in 1275 and remains fixed.[1]

6.3   As can be imagined, particularly with regard to the easement of light which depends on apertures in buildings for its enjoyment, proof of enjoyment back so many centuries has increasingly become impossible. To overcome this, the courts have adopted

---

[1]   See, generally, Nash '1189 and the limit of legal memory' (1989) 139 NLJ 1763.

a presumption that a right to light proved to have been long enjoyed, and without any evidence that enjoyment began at a date after 1189, was a right which had existed for a period commencing with the beginning of legal memory. Thus in *Aynsley v Glover*,[2] evidence of an 80-year-old witness was accepted as establishing the presumption of enjoyment since 1189, in circumstances where the date of building of the dwellings receiving light could not be proved.

6.4   It is equally possible to rebut the presumption by showing that the building can be proved to have been built at a date since 1189.[3] In the light of access to historical records such as Ordnance Survey maps and photographs, the National Monument Record maintained by English Heritage, local registers and Tithe and Enclosure maps it is often easier to rebut the presumption than establish it. In places such as the City of London, it is only in the case of certain churches which escaped the Great Fire and a few other ancient buildings (such as exist in Cloth Fair near Smithfield) where even the remotest possibility of establishing a common law prescriptive claim exists. The same may be true in places such as Bristol and York where 'ancient' buildings still exist.[4]

6.5   It is also possible to rebut the presumption of long enjoyment by showing that at some time since 1189 the dominant and servient titles were in common ownership. The same result may occur where it can be shown that both tenements were in common possession (as opposed to common ownership – e g by a tenant) but that conclusion is not altogether clear.[5]

6.6   Enjoyment of light, if claimed by prescription at common law, must be by a freehold owner against a freehold owner. This is because the right, if acquired, depends on the presumption of a grant by the absolute owner of the freehold. Although there is an exception to this rule when claims under the Prescription Act 1832 ('the 1832 Act') are made (where a tenant may acquire an easement of light – see **6.17** and **6.30** for the detail of this), in claims made at common law, the grant must be for and against the fee simple.[6] The same point (ie the need to show a 'presumed grant') can also arise where there is a limit on the capacity of the servient owner to grant an easement and where it would be ultra vires (beyond the power) for the grant to have been made. Thus, in the case of the Church Commissioners where no consent can be shown to the grant, no grant can be presumed.[7] The same limitations may apply to fiduciaries, commoners[8] and the National Trust (where inalienable land is concerned). One other exception arises, rarely, where the claimant is a tenant with the right to enlarge his lease into a fee simple under s 153 of the Law of Property Act 1925.[9] In practice, it is important to check the capacity of the presumed grantor at any stage of the period for which enjoyment is claimed. There are also some areas of property law where esoteric points have to be watched. One of them is where the title was formerly copyhold; this will emerge from the

---

2   (1875) 10 Ch App 283.
3   See, eg, *Wheaton v Maple & Co* [1893] 3 Ch 48 – property built in 1852; *Bowring Services v Scottish Widows Fund and Life Assurance Society* [1995] 1 EGLR 158 – property shown to have been built after the Second World War where aerial photographs showed the bomb site after destruction of the predecessor building during the Blitz in 1940.
4   Historical research resources available on the Internet and in public libraries and from local historical societies may assist in dating apertures. Where buildings are listed the particulars of listing will also assist. Buildings which qualify for the enjoyment of light since 1189 are extremely rare and in practical terms claims so based are hardly ever made, if at all.
5   See Chapter 8 at **8.6–8.8**.
6   *Wheaton v Maple & Co* [1893] 3 Ch 48.
7   *Oakley v Boston* [1976] QB 270. See **6.33** for rights of light claims over ecclesiastical property.
8   *Paine v St Neots Gas & Coke Co* [1938] 4 All ER 592; [1939] 3 All ER 812, CA.
9   *Bosomworth v Faber* [1992] NPC 155, CA.

register. Whilst rare, they may still require consideration and the general principles are mentioned here. In cases where a period of enjoyment of light prior to 1 January 1926 (on which date all copyholds were converted to freeholds) is material and the title of the dominant land was copyhold prior to that date for any period of the period of enjoyment relied upon a number of different and difficult problems arise. Because it is rare to rely on such historic enjoyment, a summary of principles to be applied should suffice here.

(1)   A copyholder may acquire a right to light against land owned by a third party, in the name of the Lord of the copyholders' manor.

(2)   A copyholder may not acquire a right to light against his Lord unless the custom of the manor permits it. In many cases, the application of the principle that a use has a lawful basis (*omnia praesemuntur*[10]) will allow the presumption that the custom was to allow the use.

(3)   If enfranchisement of the copyhold was under the Copyhold Act 1894 or earlier Acts, the right to light will survive. It may not survive if enfranchisement was not statutory, and no rights to light were reserved to the copyholder.[11]

6.7   The enjoyment of the light claimed as an easement by prescription at common law must have been enjoyed 'as of right' and this means openly, without consent and without the use of force. (This rule is often described by textbooks using the Latin words 'nec vi [ie not by force] nec clam [ie not secretly] nec precario [ie not by consent]'.) In the case of an easement of light it is hard to see how enjoyment can otherwise be than by the open use of a window, or other aperture, and in modern times force seems an inappropriate and unlikely vehicle for securing the enjoyment of light. However, in the context of neighbour disputes, it is not unknown for alleged obstructions to light to be torn down during the dead of night, if not during broad daylight. It has been held by the Court of Appeal (in a case concerning a right of way), that user enjoyed after its exercise becomes contentious (and which can be continued to be enjoyed only by the physical removal of obstructions), ceases to be as of right.[12] Thus, in the case of an easement of light, enjoyment after the matter becomes contentious (eg by forcible removal of an obstruction, or the cutting down of a tree, or hedge or even, possibly, the sending of a letter challenging the user) will not be 'as of right' at common law. (Note, however, the different position which applies to the easement of light claimed under the 1832 Act at **6.21**, where enjoyment does not have to be as of right.) As to enjoyment by consent, evidence of permission other than in written form in light cases is rare, and mere acquiescence in the enjoyment (by not objecting to the aperture receiving light) will not prevent acquisition by prescription at common law, for such acquiescence is an essential ingredient in the establishment of the right by this means.[13] Enjoyment must not be inconsistent with a statute or custom. Thus enjoyment of light through an aperture in a building constructed in breach of planning control may not be capable of supporting a prescriptive claim at common law. As to custom, where the Custom of

---

[10]   The law presuming the lawfulness of the act or thing done unless the contrary is shown.
[11]   See *Derry v Sanders* [1919] 1 KB 223.
[12]   *Newnham v Willison* (1987) 51 P&CR 8; *Smith v Brudenell-Bruce* (2002) 2 P&CR 51.
[13]   *Mills v Silver* [1991] Ch 271.

London applies, that too prevents a claim to the easement of light by prescription at common law.[14] It is thought that there is no longer a special custom in existence in York which affects light.[15]

6.8   It is possible to acquire the right to an easement of light by prescription at common law even though the enjoyment may have been by the dominant owner in a mistaken belief as to his rights against the servient owner.[16] The explanation is that the claimant may believe that he has the right to the easement of light (e g from a grant) but this belief (in error) does not prevent the enjoyment from being acquiesced in by the servient owner who does not share the same belief.[17] It is only in the rare instance where both dominant and servient owners share the same (erroneous) belief as to the origin or existence of the right that it can be said that there is no assertion of any right which is being acquiesced in. Only then may such a shared belief prevent a claim in prescription at common law from succeeding.[18]

6.9   There is sometimes difficulty in establishing the knowledge of the servient owner of the enjoyment of the easement of light. For the purposes of claims under common law prescription, it must be shown that the freeholder has known of and acquiesced in the enjoyment.[19] The presence of a tenant on the servient land may in law affect the freeholder's knowledge. At common law (and note for the reasons set out at **6.16** the different situation which governs claims under the 1832 Act), the actual or presumed knowledge of the freehold reversioner will determine how far he is bound by the presence of the apertures on the dominant land which are to acquire the right to the easement of light. It would seem that if the windows in the dominant land were there before the grant of the tenancy, the reversioner of the tenancy of the servient land will be bound.[20] The position where the windows were first opened during the currency of the tenancy of the servient land is less clear. The answer may depend on whether the windows had at the time the tenancy commenced the appearance of ancient lights.[21] In broad terms, it may be said that the longer the building is on the dominant land with its apertures in place, the more likely it is that the court will find in favour of a prescriptive claim succeeding and uphold the presumption that the freehold reversioner of the servient land knew of it.[22] The extent of the servient owner's knowledge derived via an agent (e g a managing surveyor) must depend on the individual acts and circumstances.[23]

LOST MODERN GRANT

6.10   The doctrine of lost modern grant has its origin in the increasing difficulty which the courts encountered when it was necessary in the seventeenth and eighteenth centuries to establish the presumption of enjoyment of an easement back to 1189. Thus, by analogy with the period of 20 years fixed by the Statute of Limitations 1623, it became possible to assert that enjoyment of an easement for 20 years, without any other

---

14   See **6.13**.
15   See **6.13**.
16   *Bridle v Ruby* [1989] 1 QB 169.
17   See *Mills v Silver* [1991] Ch 271.
18   See *Bridle v Ruby* above and also *Chamber Colliery v Hopwood* (1886) 32 ChD 549, where both servient and dominant owners believed that the enjoyment of the easement was for the term of the lease.
19   See **6.13**.
20   *Cross v Lewis* (1824) 2 B&C 686, 107 ER 538.
21   Ibid, per Abbot CJ.
22   *Pugh v Savage* [1970] 2 QB 373.
23   *Diment v Foot* [1974] 1 WLR 1427.

lawful explanation, could be presumed to have had its origin in a grant. The grant was, of course, fictional. The word 'modern' no doubt refers to the fact that the presumed grant post-dates 1189.[24] It is considered that the Crown is bound by claims to light based on lost modern grant.[25]

6.11 It is possible to establish acquisition of an easement of light by the application of the doctrine if it can be shown that there has been enjoyment both by and against the freehold owners of the dominant and servient tenements for a period of at least 20 years.[26] Although it has been argued that an easement of light cannot be acquired by the application of this doctrine (as considered by the Eire Supreme Court in *Tisdall v McArthur & Co*,[27] by reference to the obiter remarks of Farwell LJ in *Hyman v Van Den Bergh*),[28] there seems no logical reason why such an easement should not be capable of acquisition under this head, and recent authority in 1996 states that this view is correct.[29] The period of 20 years is not a fixed one (cf the 1832 Act), and it can be claimed for any period of time during which the right was capable of being enjoyed. This is in contrast with claims under the 1832 Act where the relevant 20-year period must run continuously back from the date of the commencement of the action determined by the actual or notional issue of a Claim Form under the Civil Procedure Rules 1998 (CPR).[30]

6.12 If there is no evidence to show that the grant could not have been made (e g by incapacity of one of the parties, the absence of a requisite consent, or the fact of common ownership), the court will adopt the legal fiction that a grant was made.[31] It is only if there is evidence that it is impossible for a grant to have been made that the court will refuse to apply the fiction. Mere circumstantial evidence showing that a grant was unlikely will not displace the fiction. (See **6.6**).[32]

6.13 Cases where it has been impossible to assert the fiction have arisen in the following circumstances.

(1) Where the presumed grantor cannot grant the right, for example, a right of light over consecrated ground which cannot be granted by faculty.[33]

(2) Where there is evidence that the consent of a third party is required for a grant, which has never been obtained, such as the consent of the Church Commissioners.[34]

(3) Where the enjoyment of the right can be attributed to permission, or tolerance, such permission not being a grant in itself.[35] However, the enjoyment of the easement under a mistaken belief that the right has been conferred, or by the tacit

---

24   *Dalton v Angus* (1881) 6 App Cas 740 is the leading authority on the origin of the doctrine of lost modern grant.
25   See **6.29**.
26   *Simmons v Dobson* [1991] 1 WLR 720.
27   [1951] IR 228.
28   [1908] 1 Ch 167 at 176–178.
29   See *Marlborough (West End) Ltd v Wilks Head and Eve* (1996) ChD (unreported) per Lightman J.
30   SI 1998/3132. See **6.16**.
31   *Tehidy Minerals v Norman* [1971] 2 QB 528.
32   Ibid, at 532, 552.
33   *Re St Martin's Le Grand York* [1990] Fam 63. See **6.33**.
34   *Oakley v Boston* [1976] QB 270. For the rules affecting property governed by ecclesiastical law see **6.33**.
35   *Bridle v Ruby* [1989] 1 QB 169.

acquiescence of the owner of the servient land, will not preclude establishment of the right by application of the doctrine.[36]

(4)   Where the Custom of London applies. This Custom applies so as to give the right to freehold (not leasehold) building owners within the area of the City of London to build on their 'ancient foundations' to any height without regard to the effect on neighbouring properties of the loss of light. Originally, the Custom extended only to houses, but in *Perry v Eames*,[37] the Custom was held to apply to non-residential premises, namely the Old Bankruptcy Court in Basinghall Street. Ancient foundations have not been satisfactorily defined in any modern authority, but it is suggested that the Custom applies to a freehold owner rebuilding within the 'footprint' of foundations formerly occupied by a building which has been demolished. Thus demolition of an existing building and replacement within that 'footprint', albeit with modern piled foundations, should be within the Custom. What is within the area of the City of London is capable of alteration by legislation, both primary and subordinate, and in any case on the fringe of the City it is necessary to check the extent and location of the City of London Corporation's boundary with that of an adjoining London Borough. The City Solicitor can supply the information, both current and historic, which may be required. It is not clear what happens to the right to claim the benefit of the Custom if a building within the City boundary ceases to be so as a result of boundary changes. It is thought that if redevelopment takes place at a date when all or part of the foundations of the building to be rebuilt are no longer in the City, the Custom may no longer apply as the building is not 'in the said City' according to the terms of the Custom. (The terms of the Custom as certified by the Recorder of the City of London in *Plummer v Bentham*,[38] are set out in Appendix 3.) The Custom was applied in *Bowring Services v Scottish Widows Fund and Life Assurance Society*[39] demonstrating that in cases where no prescriptive right can arise under the Prescription Act 1832[40] the existence of the Custom can be fatal to a claim based on lost modern grant, as well it might also be to a claim based on common law prescription. The existence of the Custom of London is important in the City as it can offer a defence to any claim for infringement where prescription at common law or under the 1832 Act has been lost for some reason. There are no customs surviving elsewhere in England and Wales which apply in rights of light claims. It is thought that the Custom of York has been abandoned and no longer survives, although no recent case has tested this proposition. By contrast with the position in London, the Custom in York only gave the right to build to any height on land which had *not* been built up, and that may account for the demise of the Custom of York within what is now a fully developed city centre.

(5)   Where the user lacks the qualities required for a prescriptive claim at common law (ie not 'as of right' being enjoyed either with force, or secrecy, or by consent).[41]

6.14   Even though the doctrine relies on a fiction, a claimant or counter-claiming defendant seeking to assert a lost modern grant in his statement of case must set out the dates at, or before or between which he alleges that grant was made.[42]

---

[36]   Ibid; *Mills v Silver* [1991] Ch 271 and see **6.8**.
[37]   [1891] 1 Ch 658.
[38]   (1757) 1 Burr 248, 97 ER 297.
[39]   [1995] 1 EGLR 158.
[40]   See **6.13**.
[41]   See **6.7**.
[42]   *Tremayne v English Clays Lovering Pochin & Co* [1972] 1 WLR 657.

PRESCRIPTION ACT 1832, S 3

6.15 The text of the material provisions of this Act (referred to in this part of the chapter as 'the 1832 Act') is set out in Appendix 1.

6.16 In summary form, and by way of introduction to the complex questions which arise under the 1832 Act, an easement of light can be acquired under s 3 of the 1832 Act provided:

(1) the light has been enjoyed for the benefit of *a building*;

(2) the light has been *enjoyed continuously for a period of at least 20 years* reckoned *back from the date on which the action challenging or asserting the right was commenced* (which is the date of the commencement of the action itself and not the date of a counter-claim asserting or challenging the right);

(3) the light has been enjoyed *without consent* of the servient owner or anyone on his behalf;

(4) the light has been enjoyed *without interruption*;

(5) the right is *not asserted against the Crown*.

6.17 The right may be claimed under the 1832 Act by a tenant of the dominant land, both against the freeholder of the servient land and against any tenants of his. The principle will apply even where the freehold owner of the servient land is the same as the owner of the dominant land.[43] In practice, the precise extent of the rights to light (if any) acquired by a tenant under the 1832 Act will depend on the terms of any lease or underlease.[44] This is an important difference from other easements where enjoyment has to be both by and against the fee. It does not matter that the freehold owner of the servient land may be unable to make a grant, for example, because of a statutory restriction on his rights. The Act operates without any presumption of a grant. It is quite permissible to claim a right to light not only under the Act, but under the fiction of a lost modern grant – which in the latter case does require a presumption of a grant and thereby capacity to grant it.[45] The following important points of principle under s 3 should be noted.

The enjoyment of light must be for the benefit of a building

6.18 Whilst it is not strictly necessary to have 'apertures', in practical terms, the building cannot benefit from the enjoyment of light other than through openings through which light can pass.[46] It is not necessary to prove actual occupation of the building for actual enjoyment under s 3 to commence.

6.19 This is an important point when dealing with evidence as to the time during which there has been enjoyment under s 3. The date at which a building was completed to the extent of being able to enjoy light, which in most cases will be the time at which the structure can be said to have contained the apertures, will be the critical date for the

---

[43] *Morgan v Fear* [1906] 2 Ch 406, affirmed by the House of Lords at [1907] AC 425.
[44] See Chapter 7.
[45] See **6.4** and *Tapling v Jones* (1865) 11 HLC 290.
[46] See, generally, Chapter 4.

start of the right rather than a later date when occupation commenced.[47] Thus evidence from the planning and building control departments of the relevant local authority and from those involved in the construction process such as architect, clerk of works or building contractor, may be important in dating the time from which the building was capable of enjoying the access of light.

6.20   'Building' has been defined by the court so as to include not just houses and offices but also:

–   a greenhouse;[48]

–   a church and a chapel;[49]

–   a church in the City of London.[50]

But a structure for storing and seasoning timber and exhibiting it for sale was not a building within s 3 of the 1832 Act.[51] A modern example of a similar structure which would not be a building would be a car port.[52]

There must be continuous actual enjoyment of the right for at least 20 years back from the date on which the action asserting or challenging that right was commenced[53]

6.21   Unlike other easements claimed by prescription, s 3 of the 1832 Act does not require enjoyment of light to be 'as of right'. But there must be factual evidence of enjoyment.[54] Section 4 of the 1832 Act (see Appendix 1) has the effect that the claimant must show this continuous period of enjoyment calculated back from the commencement of the action, which in practical terms will be the date on which the claim form is issued by the court under either Part 7 or Part 8 of the CPR.[55] It is an open question whether a reference to the Adjudicator to HM Land Registry under LRA 2002 and the Land Registration Rules 2003 is a 'suit or action' within s 4 of the Prescription Act 1832. If it is not, the 20-year period remains undefined at the date of the reference to the Adjudicator. There is no binding authority on the point at present.[56] It is suggested that an application under r 74 of the 2003 Rules in Form AP1 to register a right of light claimed by prescription is not a 'suit or action'. It is suggested further that a reference to the Adjudicator may be within the definition of the words 'suit or action', either as a matter of construction, or as a matter of policy, in order to avoid the need to bring a separate claim in the High Court or county court. But at present the matter remains undecided. It is believed that the Adjudicators take the view that such a

---

[47]   *Courtauld v Legh* (1869) LR 4 Ex 126; *Collis v Laugher* [1894] 3 Ch 659. See also Chapter 4 at **4.19**.
[48]   *Allen v Greenwood* [1980] Ch 119.
[49]   *Ecclesiastical Commissioners v Kino* (1880) 14 Ch 213.
[50]   *A-G v Queen Anne Gardens & Mansion Co* (1889) 60 LT 759 the Guards' Chapel in Westminster.
[51]   *Harris v De Pinna* (1886) 33 ChD 238.
[52]   See also Chapter 4 at **4.11** and **4.13**.
[53]   In practice, enjoyment for a period of more than 19 years may suffice – see below, and also Chapter 7 and Chapter 8 at **8.20**.
[54]   *Hyman v van den Bergh* [1908] 1 Ch 167 at 172; *Marlborough (West End) Ltd v Wilks Head and Eve* (1996) ChD (unreported).
[55]   *Colls v Home & Colonial Stores* [1904] AC 179.
[56]   There is no definition of 'suit or action' in the 1832 Act. Compare s 15(1) and 38(1) of the Limitation Act 1980 and see the discussion of what is an 'action' in *JA Pye (Oxford) Ltd v Graham* [2000] Ch 676, at 699–703, per Neuberger J. (This question did not arise in that claim on appeal to the Court of Appeal and the House of Lords; see [2003] 1 AC 419, at 439C).

reference is to be treated as a 'suit or action'. Much may also turn on the date to be given to the start of the period for the purposes of s 3. The date of the creation of the apertures may lead to a dispute as to whether the relevant period of 20 years (or 19 years and one day) has passed since the date on which the 'claim' is brought. Should the date for the purposes of s 4 of the 1832 Act be the date of the application in form AP1? This is thought to be unlikely. There are two other dates: first, the date of referral from the Chief Land Registrar to the Adjudicator (under r 5 of the Land Registration (Referral to the Adjudicator to HM Land Registry) Rules 2003[57] (a possibility); and, secondly, the date of the entry of the reference by the Adjudicator under r 5 of the Adjudicator to Her Majesty's Land Registry (Practice and Procedure) Rules 2003[58] (another possibility). The difference between these two latter dates is usually very short (5–7 days, for example). Either of them may be the correct date for the period under s 4 assuming that the reference is a 'suit or action'. The dates themselves may be critical for the purposes in assessing whether the period of enjoyment under the 1832 Act is sufficient. The position is uncertain at the time of writing (April 2007) and there may be other relevant dates which a party may want to rely upon depending on the date from which enjoyment of the light is being asserted.

6.22 In cases where the servient land is owned by infants, or tenants for life, or other persons with a disability (e g patients or persons under a disability) enjoyment of light against such persons for the period of their disability is still effective under s 3, as the right is said to be absolute and indefeasible if enjoyed for the 20-year period. Therefore, any periods of disability are not excluded by virtue of s 7 of the 1832 Act, which has no application to s 3. It is also important to note that the alternative 40-year period set out in s 2 of the 1832 Act does not apply to rights of light.[59]

6.23 For the right to have been 'actually enjoyed' there must be evidence that light was received by the building and so received as an easement. Thus blocking up of windows for long periods will prevent enjoyment[60] but not temporary obstructions, or nightly drawing of blinds, or closing of shutters for periods when a business is shut, for example, during a weekend or Bank Holiday.[61] The fact of non-enjoyment is an important one and a trap into which security-minded property owners can fall. A common modern instance is the internal boarding up of windows for security reasons (e g in 'self store' buildings) and this fact will mean that the 'actual enjoyment' ccases and cannot be claimed at a later date when the right is in issue. The same trap is created by the use of screens or show cards across the upper storey windows in high street stores. It is also important to distinguish such non-enjoyment from the other ways in which an easement of light may be lost under the 1832 Act. These are:

–   abandonment (see Chapter 8 at **8.9**); and

–   submission to an interruption within s 3 of the 1832 Act (see **6.26**).

It is suggested that it may be possible to avoid the trap of non-enjoyment by informing owners of land over whose land the light is derived that notwithstanding the boarding up, the light is still to be treated as actually enjoyed. But this seems artificial in concept

---

[57]   SI 2003/2114.
[58]   SI 2003/2171.
[59]   *Perry v Eames* [1891] 1 Ch 658.
[60]   *Smith v Baxter* [1900] 2 Ch 138, applied in *Tamares (Vincent Square) Ltd v Fairpoint Properties (Vincent Square) Ltd* (2006) 41 EG 226. See also Chapter 8 at **8.9–8.19**.
[61]   See Chapter 7 and Chapter 8 at **8.20–8.48** for prevention of acquisition by light obstruction notices and other means by which the enjoyment of the right may be interrupted.

and may not work to preserve the right under the 1832 Act. (Note that under **6.21** the period of actual enjoyment must run continuously back from the actual or notional issue of a claim form. So unless the period of non-enjoyment is short, the claim based on the 1832 Act will fail.) There is no set period of time by which non-enjoyment will lead to a loss of rights. Whether opaque advertising screens placed on the front of buildings while redevelopment of the interior is being carried out amounts to the loss of actual enjoyment is a moot point. There must be a risk of the loss of actual enjoyment if the light received is substantially diminished for a fair period of time. It must also be shown that enjoyment was between two different occupiers of the dominant and servient land. This is important where buildings are occupied by the same tenants of the same landlord, for in such a case the same tenants cannot acquire light against each other. (See below for the various situations which can arise under this head where landlord and tenant are concerned.)

The enjoyment must have been without consent or agreement in writing

6.24   Such consent or agreement must be in writing and may be signed either by the owner of the servient land, or by the dominant owner, or by a tenant of either, or someone else in occupation. It does not have to be signed by both parties. This means that a person with a lesser interest than the freehold can bind the freeholder – even without the knowledge or consent of the latter, and that is why well-drawn leases will contain provisions preventing tenants from agreeing to light being enjoyed by consent.[62] The consent must be between the servient owner and the dominant owner (either freeholders or leaseholders).[63]

6.25   What amounts to a written consent may sometimes be difficult to discern in certain deeds and documents. It is clear that a mere exception of the right to light will not amount to a consent under s 3. What is necessary is a provision which positively authorises the owner of the adjoining (servient) land to build as he pleases.[64] This is why in conveyances or transfers and in leases there is invariably an exception of light to the grantor coupled with a declaration that the grantor may build on his adjoining land to any height, etc whether or not that interferes with the light enjoyed by the land conveyed, transferred or let.[65] A stone inscription reserving the right of the servient owner to build to a defined distance will not be an agreement in writing for the purposes of s 3.[66] The famous sign 'Ancient Lights' is not evidence of consent, but rather an assertion that lights are being enjoyed.

There must not have been an interruption of the enjoyment

6.26   Section 3 of the 1832 Act states that the actual enjoyment of the light must have been for the full period of 20 years without interruption. Section 4 of the 1832 Act[67] states that, to be an interruption for the purposes of the Act, it must have been submitted to or acquiesced in for one year after the dominant owner has had notice of the interruption and of the person making the interruption or causing it to be made. What, therefore, is an 'interruption'? It is any obstruction of the enjoyment of the light caused by the servient owner (or by a third party) and the erection of buildings is an

---

62   *Hyman v Van Den Bergh* [1908] 1 Ch 167; *Marlborough (West End) Ltd v Wilks Head and Eve* (1996) ChD (unreported) per Lightman J, and see Chapter 7 at **7.4–7.6**.
63   *Hyman v Van Den Bergh* [1908] 1 Ch 167.
64   *Haynes v King* [1893] 3 Ch 439.
65   See *Foster v Lyons* [1927] 1 Ch 219; *Willoughby v Eckstein* [1937] Ch 167.
66   *Ruscoe v Grounsell* (1903) 89 LT 426.
67   Set out at Appendix 2.

obvious example of this.[68] But a fluctuating obstruction such as packing cases or freight containers may not be an interruption.[69] A light obstruction notice registered under the Rights of Light Act 1959[70] will from the date of registration, whether as a contemporary or as a final notice, amount to an interruption if no action is taken by the dominant owner to challenge it by action within one year of such registration.[71]

6.27 It is necessary for the person creating the interruption to make it clear to the dominant owner who has created or authorised it. The mere fact that a building or structure is put up may not be enough.[72] Quite apart from placing the name of the servient owner on the offending structure, the service of a letter referring to the nature of the interruption and stating who has authorised it would be enough to satisfy s 4. A light obstruction notice under the Rights of Light Act 1959 when registered will contain a reference in the register to the person causing the Notice to be registered, and by s 3(6) of the 1959 Act, such registration is treated as an interruption under s 4 of the 1832 Act.[73] To disprove submission to or acquiescence in the interruption requires action to be taken which shows that the dominant owner has been unwilling to accept the interruption, and this opposition must be made clear to the servient owner by words, or actions. A solicitor's letter served on the servient owner or the commencement and service of an action are the types of act which will displace any submission to or acquiescence in an interruption. In the case of the light obstruction notice under the Rights of Light Act 1959, opposition by an action claiming a right to light with a claim to set the notice aside would be enough. Uncommunicated objections or grumbles are not enough.[74] But it is very important to do any of these things within one year, and in most cases an immediate solicitor's letter (even as a protective measure prior to negotiations) is essential.

6.28 It is a by-product of s 4 that if there has been enjoyment for *over* 19 years followed by an obstruction which has not been acquiesced in for one year, and where an action is brought after 20 years have run (but within one year of the obstruction), the easement of light may be claimed under the 1832 Act – even though there has not been enjoyment for a full period of 20 years. This is sometimes known as the 'nineteen years and a day' rule. It is important to note that the enjoyment claimed must be for over 19 years (hence the 'day'), for if the action is commenced in a case where enjoyment prior to obstruction has been for only 19 years the action will fail as 20 years' user cannot be established.

Examples

(1) A's building was constructed and the apertures were in place by 1 January 1987. B obstructs A's light (by a light obstruction notice ('LON')) registered on 1 October 2006. If A brings a claim on 1 June 2007 he can establish 20 years' user and has not submitted to the interruption for one year.

---

[68] *Plasterers' Co v Parish Clerks' Co* (1851) 6 Ex 630.
[69] *Presland v Bingham* (1889) 41 ChD 268.
[70] See Appendix 2 for light obstruction notices. See also Chapter 7 at **7.11–7.14** and Chapter 8 at **8.31–8.34**. The term 'light obstruction notice' is not used in the Rights of Light Act 1959 but is a convenient shorthand for a notice registered under the provision of s 2.
[71] Rights of Light Act 1959, s 3, set out at Appendix 1; *Bowring Services v Scottish Widows Fund and Life Assurance Society* [1995] 1 EGLR 158.
[72] *Seddon v Bank of Bolton* (1882) 19 ChD 462.
[73] See, generally, Chapter 7 at **7.14** and Chapter 8 at **8.37**.
[74] *Dance v Triplow* [1992] 1 EGLR 190, CA; *Bowring Services v Scottish Widows Fund and Life Assurance Society* [1995] 1 EGLR 158.

(2)   A's building was constructed and the apertures were in place by 1 January 1988. B obstructs A's light (as before by a LON) registered on 1 October 2006. If A brings his action before 2 January 2007 he is too soon for he cannot establish 20 years' enjoyment.

To preserve the 19 years and a day rule where an interruption is caused by a light obstruction notice being registered, s 3(4) of the 1959 Act gives the dominant owner 'credit' for one year back from the date of the commencement of the enjoyment of light. Thus, in the second example, even if credit of one year is given back to 1 January 1986, any action brought before 2 January 2006 is too soon.

The right to acquire an easement of light under s 3 does not run against the Crown

6.29   This has the effect of rendering many servient owners subject to the fact that they cannot acquire rights to light against buildings which are in Crown ownership. This requires care to be taken in examining titles which are or which have been in Crown ownership. 'The Crown' will include not only Her Majesty in right of Her Crown (eg St James' Palace) and Her Royal Duchy of Lancaster (eg land to the south of the Strand), but will also include the Royal Duchy of Cornwall (eg the Kennington Estate in South London), the Crown Estate (eg Regent's Park in London) and government departments. The Crown may also feature as a freehold land owner following the dissolution of companies and the vesting in the Crown (or the appropriate Royal Duchy) as bona vacantia, or (following disclaimer by the Treasury Solicitor) in escheat. Before 1969 the Post Office was an office of the Crown and therefore an easement of light could not be acquired as against Post Office buildings. Other de-nationalised bodies may fall into the same category. In recent times, with sales of surplus NHS and MOD land in city centres, the exemption of the Crown is of some importance.[75] Custom (eg the Custom of London) cannot be used to prevent a right to light being acquired under s 3 of the 1832 Act.[76] Under the Human Rights Act 1998 it is a moot point whether this immunity survives and this point is discussed at Chapter 15. In practice it is understood that those advising the Crown (in the sense used above) are reluctant as a matter of policy to claim the benefit of the immunity, although no formal position has been adopted to this effect. As is stated at **6.10** above, the Crown is bound by claims to light based on lost modern grant.

6.30   The effect of the Human Rights Act 1998 on the Crown's 'immunity' is considered in Chapter 15.

LANDLORD AND TENANT

6.31   Because the easement of light can be acquired by and against persons with a lesser interest than a freehold, complex situations can arise where properties are the subject of claims to light which are tenanted. In general terms an easement of light must be annexed to an estate and enjoyment by a tenant is in law the enjoyment of the landlord. The enjoyment of the right by a succession of tenants is sufficient. The vital

---

[75]   See *Perry v Eames* [1891] 1 Ch 658 and *Wheaton v Maple & Co* [1893] 3 Ch 48.
[76]   See **6.13**. See also *Salters Co v Jay* [1842] 3 QB 109, 114 FR 448; *Truscott v Merchant Taylors Co* (1856) 11 Exch 855, 156 ER 1074; *Perry v Eames* [1891] 1 Ch 658 – all cases decided on the interrelation between s 3 of the 1832 Act and the Custom of London.

question will be whether the term of the lease, its terms and other events (such as surrenders) will have any affect on a claim by the tenant, or his landlord to a right of light.[77]

Examples

(1)   Block A is adjacent to Block B and the common owner of the freehold is landlord C. C grants a lease of Block A to D. C does not reserve any rights to light to himself, nor does he reserve the right to build on Block B to any height. D can acquire an easement of light for the benefit of Block A against his own landlord C and can prevent his landlord from rebuilding Block B in such a way that interferes with the light to Block A.

(2)   The same facts arise as in (1) save that Block B is owned by E. Once again, C can prevent E from rebuilding in a way which interferes with the easement acquired under s 3.

(3)   If the facts are the same as under (1) or (2) but there are a succession of tenants during the 20-year period of Block A, each on the same terms, the result will be the same.[78] But if during that period a new lease is granted reserving rights to light to the landlord and the right to rebuild Block B, the tenant of Block A will not have acquired a right to light, as during the 20-year period he has enjoyed light by consent.[79]

(4)   If a tenant of A surrenders the lease during the period, and the facts are as in (1) or (2) above, the successor tenant will have the right under s 3.[80]

(5)   If the tenant of Block B acquires the reversion during the 20-year period and the tenant of Block A is holding on the terms set out in (1) above, the latter will have acquired the right under s 3.[81]

(6)   If there is a surrender of the lease of Block A so that the freeholder of that Block obtains possession, he cannot acquire a right to light against Block B if he is still the owner of the freehold of it. He cannot acquire an easement against himself. But if by the time the surrender and retaking of possession occurs he is no longer the owner of Block B, he can continue to assert his rights against it.[82]

(7)   Where the tenant under a lease enjoys light by consent within s 3 of the 1832 Act, he cannot claim any right of light under that Act against his lessor.[83]

6.32   It should be plain from the examples above that, in cases where the easement of light is in issue between buildings that are or have been let during the relevant 20-year

---

[77]   See *Midtown v CLRP Co* [2005] EWHC 33 Ch at [8]–[24] per Peter Smith J.
[78]   *Fear v Morgan* [1906] 2 Ch 415.
[79]   See *Haynes v King* [1893] 3 Ch 439.
[80]   *Fear v Morgan* [1906] 2 Ch 415.
[81]   *Richardson v Graham* [1908] 1 KB 39.
[82]   *Fear v Morgan* [1906] 2 Ch 415; *Richardson v Graham* [1908] 1 KB 39.
[83]   As is stated above, the tenant's enjoyment is the relevant enjoyment. Such enjoyment may be by consent because of the terms of the lease which allows the landlord to redevelop his adjoining land; see **6.25**. See *Marlborough (West End) Ltd v Wilks Head and Eve* (1996) ChD (unreported). The effect of such a situation can be disastrous for the landlord and this is why the 'best' form of lease allows the tenant to enjoy light prescriptively, but reserves them to the landlord.

period, great care must be taken to understand the history of the freehold title and the leasehold title and to see the leases that may have been granted by the dominant owner. Chapter 7 considers this further in the context of preventing rights to light from being acquired.

ECCLESIASTICAL PROPERTY

6.33 Special (and complex) rules apply to the ownership of land and the grant or acquisition of interests in lands which is subject to ecclesiastical law. (Such property – referred to here as 'ecclesiastical property' – will usually be either consecrated land, or vested in the Church Commissioners, or the Bishop, or the incumbent for other purposes.) Such ecclesiastical property will usually be subject to special rules concerning ownership, disposition and the grant of rights for its benefit and over it.[84] Property vested in the Church Commissioners as part of their investment funds, or land vested in the Governors of Queen Anne's Bounty, is not subject to these special rules. Because of the special rules which apply to ecclesiastical property, certain principles apply in respect of the easement of light which may be claimed against it. Specialist advice must be taken in cases where these issues arise.

6.34 In summary, the principles which apply where a right of light is claimed against ecclesiastical property are as follows.

(1) An easement of light cannot be granted by a deed of grant, but rather by either a licence or a faculty. The same applies to an implied grant under s 62 of the Law of Property Act 1925; see **5.23**. Therefore there can be no claim to light over consecrated land (eg a churchyard) under s 62.[85]

(2) An easement of light can only be acquired over ecclesiastical land by prescription under the doctrine of lost modern grant where it is possible to presume a lost faculty granting that right. This is because either the incumbent (freehold owner) has only a limited power to create easements, or because the consent of a third party is required, such as the Church Commissioners.[86]

(3) As to acquisition of a right of light under the 1832 Act, there is doubt about whether this can be done against consecrated land. It is suggested that as the acquisition of the right does not depend on a presumed grant there is no reason why such a right of light should not be acquired. Moreover, a right of light is not usually inconsistent with the original purpose for which the consecrated land is to be used (eg as a churchyard).[87]

It is, however, possible for a consecrated building to acquire a right of light by normal means, ie by lost modern grant or under the 1832 Act.[88]

---

[84] For the law on such property in detail see Hill *Ecclesiastical Law*; Newsom *The Faculty Jurisdiction of the Church of England*; and *Halsbury's Laws of England*, (2003 reissue, 4th edn) vol 8(1).

[85] *Re St Martin Le Grand, York* [1990] Fam 63 at 76–77 per Coningsby QC Ch. But compare *Re St Clement's* [1988] 1 WLR 720 at 728 per Cameron QC Ch. The difference may lie in the distinction between consecrated ground and that vested in the Church for other purposes and whether in the former case prescription can be asserted on any footing.

[86] See s 9 of the Church Property (Miscellaneous Provisions) Measure 1960 (as amended) and s 60 of the Pastoral Measure 1983 for restrictions.

[87] See *Re St Martins* (above) at 71.

[88] *Ecclesiastical Commissioners v Kino* (1880) 14 Ch 213.

Chapter 7

ACQUISITION OF RIGHTS TO LIGHT III – PREVENTION OF ACQUISITION

SUMMARY

7.1 There are three ways in which an easement of light may be prevented from being acquired:

(1) by agreement between the dominant and servient owners (and in the case of tenanted properties by agreement between landlord and tenant);

(2) by physical interruption; and

(3) by use of the Rights of Light Act 1959.

BY AGREEMENT

7.2 It is open to the dominant and servient owners to agree that neither of them will acquire any light for, or against, the buildings on their respective titles. When there are sales off of parts of the property formerly in common ownership, it is commonplace to see the usual declaration that the purchaser will not be entitled to acquire any right to light against the land retained by the vendor or any successor as owner of that land. This will negate any implied grant under s 62 of the Law of Property Act 1925[1] or ss 19(3) and 22(3) of the Land Registration Act 1925, or in the case of dispositions made after 13 October 2003, under s 27(7) of the Land Registration Act 2002.[2]

7.3 It is equally commonplace to see rights to light being reserved to a vendor, but as explained in Chapter 6 at **6.25**, that will not prevent a right to light being acquired under s 3 of the Prescription Act 1832[3] (or possibly by lost modern grant) by the purchaser or his successor unless it is also stated that any enjoyment is precarious; an example being the clause giving the adjoining owner (the former vendor) the right to build how he pleases.[4]

7.4 In the context of landlord and tenant, the only sure way of preventing acquisition by tenants, if there are no other difficulties such as those arising from the

---

[1] See Appendix 1.
[2] For conveyancing and land registration issues see Chapter 14. If s 62 is *not* excluded application may be made to note the easement on both the dominant and servient titles under the Land Registration Rules 2003, SI 2003/1417, r 74. For further detail on this topic see *Ruoff & Roper: Registered Conveyancing* (Sweet & Maxwell, looseleaf) 36.023 and C Harpum *Registered Land* (2002) 8.12.
[3] See Appendix 1.
[4] *Haynes v King* [1893] 3 Ch 439; *Marlborough (West End) Ltd v Wilks Head & Eve* (1996) ChD (unreported) per Lightman J.

principle of non-derogation from grant, is to include provisions in a lease as set out at
7.5. The same provisions should also be in any underlease or lesser interest, although it
is thought that an absence of such terms would not allow the underlessee (or person
claiming a derivative interest) to claim a right to light as the rights of such a person
could not be greater than the headlessee. But the point is not entirely free from doubt in
the light of the potentially wide scope of the principle derived from *Fear v Morgan*[5] that
a tenant can acquire a right to light under the 1832 Act in his own right and against the
tenant of the common landlord.[6] It follows that there can be no acquisition of rights to
light against the tenant of the common landlord if the claimant cannot establish that
right against the landlord himself. An example of this arose in *Wheaton v Maple & Co*,[7]
where the landlord was the Crown and, accordingly, no claim could be made against a
tenant of the Crown. Likewise, where the common landlord has reserved rights to light
to himself and has reserved the right to build to any extent on any of his adjoining land,
one tenant of the landlord cannot assert a right to light against a neighbouring tenant of
the same landlord.[8]

7.5   The provisions suggested are as follows:

(1)   a term reserving all rights to light enjoyed by the demised property to the landlord.
        This stops any tenant claiming light independently of his landlord, and also
        enables the landlord to settle claims for interference without being obliged to
        account for any part thereof to the tenant in satisfaction of its interest. This ought
        to stop underlessees from claiming any right to light;

(2)   a covenant preventing the tenant from asserting any claim to light against any
        neighbouring building of the landlord;

(3)   a declaration that, in respect of any neighbouring building of the landlord, he has
        the right to rebuild without limit;

(4)   a covenant by the tenant not to stop up, etc any windows on the demised property.
        This has more to do with preventing abandonment than acquisition, but is
        mentioned here for completeness;

(5)   a covenant by the tenant to report any actual or threatened obstructions or light
        obstruction notices,[9] any planning applications and any adjoining owner notices.
        As under (4), this may have more to do with preventing the loss of rights.
        However, it is to be noted that, in the context of the light obstruction notice
        ('LON'), as service of the proposed notice will invariably be on the tenants of the
        servient building and as the owner of that building will want to prevent
        acquisition of a right to light over it by the dominant building,[10] this reporting
        obligation is important.

---

5   [1906] 2 Ch 415.
6   *Wheaton v Maple & Co* [1893] 3 Ch 48; *Willoughby v Eckstein* [1937] 1 Ch 167; *Blake and Lyons Ltd v Lewis
      Berger & Sons Ltd* [1951] 2 TLR 605.
7   [1893] 3 Ch 48.
8   See *Blake and Lyons Ltd v Lewis Berger & Sons Ltd* [1951] 2 TLR 605 and *Paragon Finance v CLRP Co*
      [2002] 1 EGLR 97.
9   The term 'light obstruction notice' is not used in the Rights of Light Act 1959, but is convenient shorthand
      for a notice registered under the provisions of s 2.
10   See **7.10**. See also s 7 of the Rights of Light Act 1959 which defines 'owner' as including a lessee for a term
      of years certain with not less than 7 years unexpired when the application to register the light obstruction
      notice is being made. A covenant against any such lessee applying to register a notice under the 1959 Act
      may be prudent and may be expressed independently or as part of the covenant referred to in (4) above.

7.6   Another form of agreement which will prevent a right to light from being acquired is to give permission to the dominant owner to build (up to a given height or according to defined plans) or to impose, by way of a restrictive covenant, a limit on building.[11] In addition, it is agreed between the parties that any light enjoyed by the dominant owner pursuant to the permission granted is by consent. In London, it is common to find deeds regulating light in this way where both dominant and servient owners agree in such terms and, accordingly, neither have enforceable rights to light against each other, and can only enforce the terms of any restrictive covenant as to height, etc.[12]

BY PHYSICAL INTERRUPTION

7.7   Prior to the implementation of a nationwide planning control regime from 1 July 1948, it was conventional to erect an obstruction (a 'spite screen') to prevent the acquisition of light under the 1832 Act. If that screen complied with s 4 of that Act and remained unchallenged for one year, a right to light could not be asserted under the 1832 Act in view of the 'interruption' caused by it. The Town and Country Planning Act 1947 which came into force on this date effectively put an end to the erection of spite screens, as planning consent was unlikely to be granted for a structure which was not only unsightly but which was also intrusive on the amenities of the neighbouring land.[13] Although the Town and Country Planning Act 1947 has been superseded, subsequent legislation has maintained and indeed extended the principle that 'development' (including building and engineering operations) requires planning permission.

7.8   Thus for over the past 50 years the primary manner of preventing light from being acquired has not been by means of the use of physical obstructions – whether classed as spite screens or otherwise. Clearly, anything by way of a structure will usually need express planning consent under the Planning Acts.[14] The general development orders under successive town planning legislation permit certain works without the need to apply for planning permission. However, those orders have never allowed obstruction of the necessary size to be effective for this purpose.[15]

7.9   It is, however, important to note that the fact that a building has been erected and has been consented to may prevent the assertion of a right to light under the 1832 Act, if there has been submission to or acquiescence in it for one year.[16] In modern developments, it is not inconceivable that a building goes up apace while the parties' advisers discuss the pros and cons of its effect on the light to the dominant building. If one year has gone by, and the new building has been up for that time, an interruption has occurred and all rights under the 1832 Act are lost. It may be possible to fall back on lost modern grant, but not in the City of London.[17]

---

[11]   See *City of London Corporation & Anor v Intercede 1765 Ltd & Anor* [2005] EWHC 1691 Ch for the interpretation of such types of agreement, with the significant emphasis on the terms of the plans and elevations showing height limits and their extent.
[12]   See Chapter 9 for further analysis of such deeds.
[13]   For planning law generally, see Chapter 13.
[14]   See Chapter 13 at **13.4** for the meaning of this expression.
[15]   See (currently) the Town and Country Planning (General Permitted Development) Order 1995, SI 1995/418 (as amended). The main provisions relating to building operations are in Sch 2, Part 2.
[16]   See Chapter 6 at **6.26** and *Dance v Triplow* [1992] 1 EGLR 190.
[17]   See Chapter 6 at **6.13**.

BY THE USE OF THE RIGHTS OF LIGHT ACT 1959

7.10   The Rights of Light Act 1959 (called in this part of this chapter 'the 1959 Act') came into force on 16 October 1959. Its provisions now set out the accepted manner in which rights to light can be prevented from being acquired.[18] The 1959 Act operates essentially by allowing the creation of a *notional* obstruction of light received by a building over the land of another. The terminology and procedures under the 1959 Act are set out in detail in Chapter 8 at **8.33**. In this chapter, we consider the practical aspects of operating the 1959 Act.

7.11   A light obstruction notice may be used in two situations in order to prevent a right of light from being obtained. First, where it is believed that the building on the dominant land is about to acquire the benefit of 20 years' user, the emergency procedure referred to below should be used. Even if the notice is challenged within one year of registration, if the evidence is such that the apertures in the building have not been in situ for 20 years (allowing if necessary for the 'nineteen years and a day' rule referred to in Chapter 6 at **6.28** and preserved by s 3(4) of the 1959 Act), the servient owner will have been successful in claiming that the building on the dominant land has not acquired a right to light. This may be of vital importance if the servient owner is planning his own development which would otherwise infringe the light to the building on the dominant land.

7.12   The second instance where the registration of the notice may be used to good effect in preventing the acquisition of a right to light is as follows. The owner of the servient land has plans to develop at some time in the future and is reasonably confident that out of the dominant owners whose light may be affected by the development, some may not have acquired 20 years' user in respect of their buildings, and others may well not object to any notice within one year of registration. In the latter case, they will be deemed to have consented to an interruption[19] and unless they can rely on lost modern grant, they will be unable to assert any right to light. Clearly, there is a degree to which a gamble is being taken, but even if challenges are made to the notices within time, the servient owner can 'flush out' any problems in advance of the plans for development being finalised. This course may also avoid last-minute injunctions being threatened.

7.13   The effect of a light obstruction notice, once registered, is that it is intended to be equivalent to the obstruction of light to the dominant building across the servient land which would be caused:[20]

> ' . . . by the erection, in such position on the servient land as may be specified in the application, of an opaque structure of such dimensions (including, if the application so states, unlimited height) as may be so specified.'

As such, it amounts to an obstruction to the access of light to the dominant building and an interruption from the date of registration.[21] Such a notice will have that effect until it is cancelled. It will also have that effect until it has been registered for one year. In the case of a notice registered under a temporary certificate (see below), the notice will have effect only until the date fixed for its expiry (which cannot be longer than 6 months from registration), unless before that date application has been lodged with the

---

[18]   See Appendix 1 for the text of the 1959 Act.
[19]   See Chapter 6 at **6.27–6.28**, Chapter 8 at **8.37**, and s 3(6) of the 1959 Act.
[20]   Section 2(2)(b) of the 1959 Act.
[21]   Section 3(1) of the 1959 Act.

local authority for registration of a notice based on a definitive certificate. The significance of the reference to one year is due to the need to tie in with s 4 of the Prescription Act 1832 and the concept of an 'interruption'.[22]

7.14   By s 3(6) of the 1959 Act, the notice, once registered, takes effect as if all persons interested in the dominant building have notice of it and on whose behalf it is registered. Unless and until any action is brought (within time), the persons interested in the dominant building are deemed to acquiesce in the obstruction caused by the notice, according to its terms. Once an action is brought, there is no longer any submission to or acquiescence in the notional obstruction. In order to maintain the 'nineteen years and a day' rule, s 3(4) gives the dominant owner the benefit of that rule by treating the commencement of enjoyment as having commenced one year earlier, if that would allow the dominant owner to challenge the notice under s 3(3). If the action fails, the court can direct that the dominant owner is deemed to have submitted to or acquiesced in the notice as if the action had not been brought (s 3(6) proviso).[23]

7.15   The first stage in any application to register a notice under the 1959 Act is, therefore, to define the location and height of the notional obstruction on a plan. In practice, the height is left as an unlimited one. Of some difficulty is the need to take account of projections (this may require two notional obstructions placed against the faces of the servient buildings), and to take account of apertures on the dominant building where there is no doubt that a right to light exists. This calls for care in defining both the height and the width of the notional obstruction.

7.16   The second stage is to make an application in Form 1.[24] With this application should be lodged two copies of the proposed application in Form A to the Local Land Charges Rules 1977.[25] It is to this form that the plan of the suggested notional obstruction will be annexed. The Registrar will direct what notices should be given to those affected and who appear to have an interest in the dominant building. In practice, the applicant will supply the Registrar with a list of all such persons. It is only in cases where there is doubt or difficulty that advertisements need to be directed, and if this is thought to be a possibility, a draft advertisement and suggested place for its publication should also be supplied to the Registrar on this application. In most cases, Special Delivery with tracked delivery is recommended. It is sometimes necessary to serve a large number of occupational tenants in an office block or a block of flats, but all have interests which may be affected and they must be served.[26]

7.17   The third stage is to give notice to all persons who appear likely to be affected by the registration of the notice, by serving a copy of the application on those directed to be served, and in such manner as the Registrar shall have directed at stage two.[27]

7.18   The fourth stage is to notify the Registrar that the directions as to service or notification have been complied with. This usually requires dispatch of the recorded delivery and advice of receipt records with copies of all letters served and any newspaper

---

[22]   See Chapter 6 at **6.27–6.28**.

[23]   See Chapter 6 at **6.28** for examples of the effect of s 3(4).

[24]   Prescribed by r 21 of the Lands Tribunal Rules 1996, SI 1996/1022, set out in Appendix 2. Form 1 is an application for the issue of a certificate that adequate publicity has been given to those affected by the proposed application to register the light obstruction notice.

[25]   SI 1977/985. See Appendix 2.

[26]   Lands Tribunal Rules 1996, r 22. See Appendix 2.

[27]   Ibid, r 22(3). See Appendix 2.

or other advertisements placed. If satisfied, the Registrar will issue a definitive certificate that adequate notice has been given to those likely to be affected by the registration of the notice.[28]

7.19   The fifth stage is to apply for registration at the Local Land Charges Registry of the application (Form A) with the Registrar's definitive certificate of notice in Form 3 granted at stage four.[29] The registered notice will remain on the register for 21 years from the date of registration.[30]

7.20   In cases where there is exceptional urgency (e g the dominant owner is likely to be close to acquiring 20 years' enjoyment allowing for the credit of one year under s 3(4)) the emergency procedure may be invoked. This requires the making of an application to the Registrar of the Lands Tribunal for the issue of a certificate that, in the opinion of the Lands Tribunal, the case is one of exceptional urgency and that, accordingly, a light obstruction notice should be registered forthwith as a temporary notice, for such period as may be specified in the certificate. The period cannot exceed 6 months.[31] This is, in effect, an additional element to stage two under **7.16**. The applicant needs not only to have identified who is to be served and in what manner, but also why the matter is one of exceptional urgency. Form 1 is used for this purpose using the additional paragraph as regards exceptional urgency. It is prudent to have cogent evidence which can be placed before the Registrar in order to make out the case of exceptional urgency. The commonest reason is the fear (no doubt backed up by evidence of construction, etc) that the dominant owner's building is about to acquire user of light for the 20-year period, and allowing for the 'credit' of one year under s 3(4). If the emergency certificate is granted in Form 2, that will allow registration of the notice in the Local Land Charges Register, for the period given in the certificate. It cannot last for more than 6 months.[32] The servient owner must then apply for a definitive certificate.

7.21   It is important to note the following practical features of this procedure.

(1)   A temporary light obstruction notice will take effect as a notional obstruction and is something which will be an interruption from the date of registration.[33] It is, therefore, vital to challenge such a registration within one year from that date, for otherwise rights under the 1832 Act will be lost, and although reliance may be placed on the lost modern grant, that will be to no avail in the City of London where the Custom of London applies.[34] In practical terms, the challenge which should be made is to issue a claim form asserting the right to light for the benefit of the dominant building and asserting the fact that the light obstruction notice is an actionable interference to those rights. The same effect can be achieved by a counter-claim within one year in existing proceedings; see the definition of 'action' in s 7(1) of the 1959 Act. Note that no challenge can be made once the light obstruction notice has ceased to have effect.[35] This is important where temporary certificates are registered.

---

28   Ibid, r 24 and Form 3. See Appendix 2.
29   Local Land Charges Rules 1977, SI 1977/985, r 10, see Appendix 2.
30   Ibid, r 10(6)(b). See Appendix 2.
31   Section 2(3)(b) of the 1959 Act and Lands Tribunal Rules 1996, r 23. See Appendices 1 and 2.
32   Lands Tribunal Rules 1996, r 23(2).
33   *Bowring Services v Scottish Widows Fund and Life Assurance Society* [1995] 1 EGLR 158.
34   See Chapter 6 at **6.9**.
35   Section 3(3) proviso of the 1959 Act.

(2)   Where a temporary light obstruction notice is registered, it is vital to complete the registration of the permanent light obstruction notice based on the definitive certificate before the expiry of the period specified for the temporary registration. If this is not done, there will be a break in the period of the year which is so vital if an interruption is to be claimed.

(3)   A challenge to the issue of a certificate by the Registrar of the Lands Tribunal may be made by way of judicial review.[36] A declaration to set aside such a certificate sought by a claim form in an ordinary civil action and not in an application for judicial review is an abuse of the process and will be struck out.[37] In this context, it is important to note the need to ensure that the evidence placed before the Registrar should be as comprehensive as possible in order to avoid a later challenge that the evidence (eg of exceptional urgency) was so slender, or non-existent with the result that the emergency certificate should be set aside.

(4)   The issue of a certificate under the 1959 Act by the Registrar of the Lands Tribunal is not a decision which can be the subject of an appeal by way of case stated under s 3(4) of the Lands Tribunal Act 1949 to the High Court.[38]

7.22   The 1959 Act applies to Crown land.[39] This includes land in which the Royal Duchies have an interest, as well as land owned by the Crown Estate and by government departments. Thus, it is possible for such bodies to use the 1959 Act to prevent the acquisition of light by adjoining owners, whereas the position remains that a right to light cannot be acquired against Crown land under s 3 of the Prescription Act 1832. Section 4 of the 1959 Act expressly preserves that position.

7.23   Finally, it may be relevant to consider how far the 1959 Act affects right to light claims made under the fiction of lost modern grant.[40] Although the words 'or otherwise' occur after the words 'by virtue of the Prescription Act 1832' in s 3(1) of the 1959 Act, when determining the entitlement of the dominant owner to a right to light, there is a school of thought which believes that the 1959 Act does not affect directly the fiction of lost modern grant. The concept of the light obstruction notice and its duration for one year is designed to challenge a right to light claimed under the 1832 Act. The framework of the 1959 Act does not fit into the fiction of a lost modern grant as a claim on this footing can be based on enjoyment for any period of 20 years and that does not have to be a period running back from the actual or notional date on which a claim form is issued. There is no concept of an interruption in lost modern grant claims. The point has not, however, been decided. However, it might be open to a servient owner to rely on the registration of the light obstruction notice to show the impossibility of a grant during the time for which such registration had been effective. Thus the notice displaces the fictional grant during the period of its registration. The dominant owner must then rely on a period of enjoyment earlier than the date of registration of the notice, if he can. The same point might also be open to the servient owner to take when asserting

---

36   See CPR Part 54 and rules thereunder. See the notes to Part 54 in the current Practice books for the distinction between claims which are appropriate for judicial review and those which are properly regarded as ordinary civil claims to be brought under CPR Part 7 or 8. The precise scope of the boundary between what may be regarded as a public law claim and a private law claim, as set out in *O'Reilly v Mackman* [1983] 2 AC 237 and in *Roy v Kensington and Chelsea and Westminster FPC* [1992] 1 AC 624, is unclear. See, for a recent example of this distinction, *Rusby v Harr* [2006] EWCA Civ 865, (2006) Lawtel, 7 June, CA.

37   *Bowring Services v Scottish Widows Fund and Life Assurance Society* [1995] 1 EGLR 158.

38   Ibid. For case stated procedure see CPR Part 52 PD.

39   See s 4.

40   See Chapter 6 at **6.10–6.14**.

abandonment, and this is a point likely to be taken where the dominant owner must assert enjoyment for a period some years back because of the existence of the notice. The law requires clarification here for as long as a lost modern grant claim can be asserted.

Chapter 8

EXTINGUISHMENT OF RIGHTS OF LIGHT

SUMMARY

8.1　A right to light may be extinguished in the following ways:

(1)　by agreement between those interested in the dominant and servient tenements;

(2)　by unity of ownership of the dominant and servient land;

(3)　by permanent abandonment;

(4)　by interruption;

(5)　by demolition or alteration of the dominant building, in some situations;

(6)　under certain statutory provisions relating to compulsory purchase and appropriation of land for planning purposes.

Reference is made in this chapter to certain other matters, which although not strictly a matter of extinguishment, lead to the loss of rights of light. A right of light may be lost (or not acquired) by non-enjoyment of the light, or by submission to or acquiescence in an interruption for the purposes of the Prescription Act 1832 ('the 1832 Act').[1]

EXTINGUISHMENT BY AGREEMENT

8.2　An easement of light may be released by agreement between the owner of the dominant and servient tenements. Since an easement is an interest in land the release must be in writing,[2] and to effect a release of the legal estate ought to be by deed.[3] Care needs to be taken to ensure that all those entitled to and subject to the easement are parties to the deed, otherwise there is a risk that the objective may not be achieved. This could give rise to particular difficulties where not only the freeholder of the dominant building but also tenants are entitled to rights of light acquired under the 1832 Act by

---

[1]　See Chapter 6 for details of how a prescriptive right of light may not be acquired. These other matters are referred to in this Chapter in order to remind readers of the distinction between extinguishments in 'pure' terms and instances where the right may not be acquired. Note the fact that once the enjoyment of the right of light becomes contentious and when it may be obstructed the prescriptive right under the 1832 Act may be lost: *Newnham v Willison* (1987) 56 P&CR 8; *Smith v Brudenell-Bruce* (2002) 2 P&CR 51; see Chapter 6 at **6.7**.

[2]　Law of Property Act 1925, s 53.

[3]　Ibid, s 52.

20 years' user.[4] In these situations, there may be real uncertainty about the identity of the dominant owners, although clearly only those with legal interests in their land, and whose premises receive light through defined apertures over the servient land, will qualify. In the case of a building of multiple occupation, the task of tracing not only the occupying tenants, but also the owners of mesne interests in those parts of the building enjoying the rights to light may be laborious and fail to be exhaustive. This can cause problems where it is desired to redevelop the servient building in a way which may interfere with the dominant building's light.

8.3   In these cases, where it is desired to achieve agreement to extinguish rights to light, various expedients can be used. One is to obtain warranties and indemnities from those who appear to be the sole or main dominant owners, to the general effect that they:

(1)   warrant that there are no other dominant interests;

(2)   give indemnities against losses arising from any claims by either identified holders of interests in the dominant tenement or by potential claimants generally.

This approach has the merit of simplifying negotiations in a redevelopment situation, and also (subject to the solvency of the covenantors) has the effect of capping the developer's liability. It also discourages attempts by the covenantors to encourage claims by others, either in return for a share of any compensation achieved or as a lever to extract further concessions from the developer. On the other hand, it presupposes a willingness on the part of those giving the warranties and/or indemnities to expose themselves to possibly onerous liabilities, and is unlikely to be attractive except where substantial consideration passes in return.

8.4   Another approach is to rely on the Rights of Light Act 1959 (see below), combined with a deed of release executed by the known dominant owners. If a light obstruction notice[5] is registered under this Act and not challenged within a period of one year, the right to light is extinguished. Therefore, if the known dominant owners have bound themselves by agreement not to take steps to assert their rights, hence raise no challenge to the notice, once the notice has been in effect for one year (assuming no other claimants have commenced proceedings in the meantime), the possibility of such further claims is excluded. This procedure has the advantage of certainty, but involves a long timescale. Neither procedure, of course, itself guarantees that no adverse claims will be made. However, provided agreement has been reached with those having the major interests in the dominant tenement before the redevelopment starts, other claimants may, in practice, be reluctant to assert rights to the point of seeking interim injunctive relief to prevent building work proceeding, given the risk that they run on their undertakings in damages.[6] Equally, the failure to seek an interim injunction is likely to place substantial difficulties in the way of obtaining a mandatory order for removal of that part of the redevelopment which they allege infringes their rights at trial.[7] Hence there may be a need for a developer to factor in an element of calculated risk both as to whether all potential claims to rights to light have been identified and

---

[4]   See Chapter 6 at **6.17**, **6.24** and **6.30**.
[5]   The term light obstruction notice is not used in the Rights of Light Act 1959, but is a convenient shorthand for a notice registered under the provisions of s 2.
[6]   See Chapter 11 at **11.88**.
[7]   See Chapter 11 at **11.97–11.108**.

their agreement obtained, and whether any who did not fall within these categories in practice pose a threat to the development proceeding.

8.5   Deeds may make provision for determination of easements on notice. The precise terms of the provision for determination must be strictly complied with.[8] An easement may be extinguished by implied agreement, where the dominant owner authorises the servient owner to erect a building which must inevitably interfere with the easement of light. In these circumstances, the dominant owner is estopped from reasserting his right subsequently, on the ground that it would be inequitable for him to do so.[9] In general, for the estoppel to be established, it must be shown that the dominant owner was aware of the existence of his right, or at least had a suspicion as to the true position.[10]

EXTINGUISHMENT BY UNITY OF OWNERSHIP

8.6   A man cannot have an easement over his own property.[11] Therefore, provided the freehold of both dominant and servient tenements is vested in the same person any easement of the one over the other is extinguished.

8.7   It appears to be the case that extinguishment operates only where the *freehold* of both tenements is vested in the same person. Accordingly, it does not operate where, for example, the same person owns the freehold of one tenement but simply a leasehold interest in the other. In such cases, it seems that whilst in practice a person in occupation of both properties in such circumstances cannot exercise the easement, it does not disappear but is simply suspended.[12] In *Simper v Foley*,[13] Page Wood V-C said:

> 'I apprehend it is clear that the effect of an union of the ownership of dominant and servient tenements for different estates is not to extinguish an easement of this description, but merely to suspend it so long as the union of ownership continues; and that upon a severance of the ownership the easement revives.'

8.8   In the case of easements of light, it is also to be remembered that under s 3 of the 1832 Act a right to light may be acquired in respect of and against land where the same person is the freeholder of both the dominant and servient tenements, but where the dominant (as well as possibly also the servient) tenements are in occupation of lessees.[14] It seems to follow that unity of ownership of dominant and servient tenements will not extinguish easements enjoyed by a lessee. Thus in *Richardson v Graham*,[15] the owner of a dominant tenement which had acquired a right to light by 20 years' user leased it to the plaintiffs, and then sold it (subject to the lease) to the defendant. It was held that the right to light continued during the term of the plaintiff's lease. The original owner of the dominant tenement could not have interfered with the easement without derogating

8   *Wallshire Limited v Advertising Sites Limited* [1988] 2 EGLR 167, CA.
9   Cf *Taylors Fashions Limited v Liverpool Victoria Trustees Co Limited* [1981] 1 All ER 897; *Re Basham Deceased* [1987] 1 All ER 405. See also *Gillett v Holt* [1998] 3 All ER 917 and *Snell's Equity* (31st edn) Ch 10, for the law of estoppel in detail.
10   *Armstrong v Sheppard & Short Limited* [1959] 2 All ER 651; *Taylor Fashions Limited v Liverpool Victoria Trustees Co Limited* [1981] 1 All ER 897 at 912B.
11   *Kilgour v Gaddes* [1904] 1 KB 457.
12   *Thomas v Thomas* (1835) 2 CM&R 34.
13   (1862) 2 J&H 555 at 563.
14   *Frewen v Philipps 11 CBNS 449*; *Robson v Edwards* [1893] 2 Ch 146; *Morgan v Fear* [1907] AC 425. See Chapter 6 at **6.17**, **6.24** and **6.30**.
15   [1908] 1 KB 39.

from his grant to the plaintiffs, and the defendant could be in no better position. The right to light enured in favour of the plaintiffs against the defendant.

PERMANENT ABANDONMENT

8.9   A right to light is a continuous easement, in the sense that enjoyment of it requires no human intervention.[16] A right to light is enjoyed by virtue of the configuration of the dominant tenement, not because any particular individual is using it at any particular moment. Under this heading it is important to distinguish abandonment of an easement of light from its non-acquisition (in prescription claims) by non-enjoyment during the relevant 20-year period or, in cases under the 1832 Act, from cases where the claim can be defeated by showing that actual enjoyment for the 20 years running back from the date of the issue of the claim form has not been present, or where there has been an interruption within s 4 of that Act.[17]

8.10   However, the law recognises that a right to light may become abandoned. The general criteria required for abandonment of an easement were described by Lord Justice Buckley in *Tehidy Minerals Ltd v Norman*[18] as follows:

> 'Abandonment of an easement or of a profit àprendre can only we think be treated as having taken place where the person entitled to it has demonstrated a fixed intention never at any time thereafter to assert the right himself or to attempt to transmit it to anyone else.'

See also *Wilson's Brewery Ltd v West Yorkshire Metropolitan Borough Council.*[19]

8.11   It is clear, therefore, that an intention to abandon a right to light will only be established by clear evidence that the dominant owner has an intention no longer to rely on the right. Although (in theory) simple statements, documentary or, indeed, even oral evidence ought to suffice, provided repeated sufficiently often and emphatically. In practice, the issue is almost invariably one whose answer depends on the inferences to be drawn from external acts and circumstances surrounding the dominant and servient tenements. In some cases, the issue seems to have been approached simply as one involving an inquiry whether the acts of the dominant owner with respect to the apertures show an intention to no longer use them for the enjoyment of light. If the dominant owner blocks up his windows in a permanent way, and makes no use of them for a prolonged period, abandonment has been held possible.

8.12   On the other hand, in other cases, the courts have held that this is insufficient, and that the right to light will be held to have been abandoned only if, additionally, the owner of the servient land has acted in reliance on the actions of the dominant owner, so that he would be prejudiced if the right to light were held enforceable. The preponderance of authority is probably (just) in favour of the latter view.[20] On this view the doctrine of abandonment is similar to the doctrine of proprietary estoppel.[21] The

---

[16]   See Chapter 1.
[17]   See **8.20** and Chapter 6 at **6.7** and **6.21**. For the effect of non-continuous enjoyment see *Tamares (Vincent Square) Ltd v Fairpoint Properties (Vincent Square) Ltd* [2006] 41 EG 226.
[18]   [1971] 2 QB 528 at 553D.
[19]   (1977) 34 P&CR 224. For recent authority on abandonment of easements generally see *City of London Corpn & Anor v Intercede 1765 Ltd & Anor* [2005] EWHC 1691 Ch.
[20]   See Christine J Davis 'Abandonment of an Easement: Is it a question of intention only?' [1995] Conv 291.
[21]   For proprietary estoppel generally, *Snell's Equity* (31st edn) ch 10, 10-15–10-28.

alternative view, however, has some support, including at least one recent authority,[22] and does have the merit of rendering unnecessary any inquiry as to whether the servient owner has suffered detriment. The authorities are reviewed below.

8.13   It is submitted that, on the authorities, abandonment can occur in either way, although this has been expressly recognised in only one case.[23] Whichever approach the courts have adopted, it appears always to have been assumed that there could be no abandonment unless the dominant owner knew of his right.[24] This seems correct in principle. Just as acquisition of an easement of light by prescription is based on conduct and knowledge, abandonment should also be so based; unless the existence of what is being abandoned is known of by the possessor, he can hardly be said to have impliedly agreed to relinquish it.

8.14   In *Moore v Rawson*,[25] the plaintiff, who had in the wall of his building windows which were ancient lights, pulled down the wall and replaced it with a blank wall having no apertures 17 years before the action. The defendant subsequently, 3 years before the action, erected a building near to the plaintiff's new wall. About 3 years later, the plaintiff opened windows in the same position as the ancient lights in his new wall, and sued the defendant for obstruction. It was held that the action must fail, since the plaintiff had by his actions abandoned the right to light formerly enjoyed by the ancient lights. The decision was based on the ground that since the defendant had acted to his detriment by constructing his building without reference to the supposed right of the plaintiff, it would be unjust to grant an injunction. Abbott CJ also stated that by erecting a blank wall the plaintiff might have induced someone to buy the servient land.

8.15   *Moore v Rawson* was approved and followed in *Cook v Mayor of Bath*,[26] a case on obstruction of a right of way. In *Winter v Brockwell*,[27] a case pre-dating *Moore v Rawson*, the court applied the same principle. A parol (oral) licence was given by the dominant owner of a right to light and air received over a yard, to the servient owner to erect a skylight over the yard; the effect of this structure was to obstruct the light and air (the main problem apparently relating to smells). It was held that the dominant owner could not revoke the permission, once acted on, at all events without tendering to the servient owner a sum representing the expenses incurred in erecting the structure. This case might suggest that the dominant owner can re-assert his rights provided it is equitable for him to do so. Such a right is recognised in other contexts, probably in the doctrine of promissory estoppel.[28] However, the case should probably not be read as extending thus far. The structure could easily be removed without major damage to the fabric of the buildings surrounding the yard, and there were clearly issues of risk to health involved. The erection of substantial and permanent buildings by the servient owner was not, therefore, in question.

8.16   In *Stokoe v Singers*,[29] where the allegation of abandonment of the right to light failed, the dominant owner had blocked up his windows for 20 years; the apertures

---

22   *Marine and General Mutual Life Assurance Society v St James Real Estate Co Ltd* [1991] 2 EGLR 178 and see **8.17**.

23   *Stokoe v Singers* (1857) 8 EL&BL 31 at 120–121; see also **8.16**.

24   Cf *Obadia v Morris* (1974) 232 EG 333.

25   [1824] 3 B&C 332; 107 ER 756.

26   (1868) LR 6 Eq 177.

27   (1807) 8 East 308, 103 ER 359.

28   See, generally, *Snell's Equity*. Sometimes called '*High Trees*' estoppel (see *Central London Property Trust Ltd v High Trees House Ltd* [1947] KB 130).

29   (1857) 8 EL&BL 31, 120 ER 12.

remained visible (the blocking up having been by means of rubble built up within them) as did the iron bars on the outside of the windows. A purchaser of the servient land then proposed to build so as to obstruct the windows, and the plaintiff, the successor to the dominant owner, then re-opened the windows. The judge's direction to the jury, approved on appeal, was to the following effect.

(1)   The right to light to the plaintiff's windows continued until lost.

(2)   There should be a verdict for the plaintiff unless:
       (a)   his predecessor had by blocking up the windows manifested an intention of permanently abandoning them; or
       (b)   they thought that the windows had been kept so closed as to lead the defendant to alter his position in the reasonable belief that the lights had been permanently abandoned.

This case recognises the two alternative methods of abandonment, one of which involves only the simple manifestation of an intention to abandon, without any alteration in the servient owner's position. This seems to have been the basis of the decision in *Lawrence v Obee*,[30] where a blank wall had replaced a window formerly in it for over 20 years. Although this was also a case in which the defendant had subsequently erected a building (an allegedly malodorous privy), it was not suggested (at least expressly) that this amounted to alteration of the servient owner's position. On the other hand, the decision may be explicable on this ground.

8.17   More recently, in *Marine and General Mutual Life Assurance Society v St James Real Estate Co Ltd*,[31] abandonment by simple evidence of intention has received backing in principle although the claim failed on the facts (since although the windows had been blocked up the apertures were retained, without the sills or reveals being broken). It was said that:

> 'It is clear that the windows were closed up in such a way that they could be reopened without keying into the brickwork of the walls. The procedure followed seems to have been, in summary, that a sleeve was put round the edges of the window, leaving the cill in place, and brickwork was laid within the sleeve. Thus, as appears from the photographs that were before me, the position of the apertures is clearly visible. Nevertheless I agree with the submission of the Defendant's Counsel that the closing up is solid, substantial and uses materials similar to the walls. I have no reason to doubt that, as Counsel submitted, the "infill" panels are perfectly capable of lasting the life of the building.'

8.18   Nevertheless, the court held, applying *Tehidy Minerals Ltd v Norman*,[32] that the right to light had not been abandoned. The wall with windows had not been pulled down and replaced by a blank wall. Window apertures had been filled in with brick, but the sills remained and the position of the apertures was clearly visible.

8.19   By contrast, in *Smith v Baxter*,[33] the boarding up of windows for a prolonged period was held to amount to abandonment.[34] This suggests that the issue as to what degree of prominence in the obstruction of the window is required to evidence abandonment is ultimately one of fact. In the context of abandonment it is necessary,

---

[30]   (1814) 3 Camp 514, 170 ER 1465.
[31]   [1991] 2 EGLR 178.
[32]   [1971] 2 QB 528. See also **8.10**.
[33]   [1900] 2 Ch 138.
[34]   See also Chapter 4 at **4.15**.

finally, to mention one issue which arises when buildings are being demolished or altered. Will the right of lights which may have been enjoyed by the old building be lost when the demolition, or alteration takes place? This question is answered at **8.49**.

INTERRUPTION

Actual interruption

8.20   Under the Prescription Act 1832, s 3,[35] 20 years' actual enjoyment of light gives rise to a right to light under that Act. However, by s 4 of the same Act:

'Each of the respective periods herein-before mentioned shall be deemed and taken to be the period next before some suit or action wherein the claim or matter to which such period may relate shall have been or shall be brought into question; and . . . no act or other matter shall be deemed to be an interruption, within the meaning of this statute, unless the same shall have been or shall be submitted to or acquiesced in for one year after the party interrupted shall have had or shall have notice thereof, and of the person making or authorising the same to be made.'

8.21   The combined effect of ss 3 and 4 of the 1832 Act is that where light has been actually enjoyed for a period of more than 19 years prior to interruption, the right is capable of becoming 'absolute and indefeasible' under s 3, since no interruption for a period of at least one year, prior to the expiry of the 20-year period, is possible. However, until the period of 20 years has run, the dominant owner has no right capable of being relied on or giving rise to legal rights.[36] Thus, in *Lord Battersea v Commissioners of Sewers for the City of London*,[37] the plaintiffs sought an injunction to restrain the defendants from building so as to interfere with access of light to their premises. The buildings on the defendant's site had been demolished between May and October 1875. In 1895, the plaintiffs commenced proceedings against the defendants to restrain the construction of a new development on the defendants' land, asserting that their windows had since 1875 acquired a right to light under s 3 of the 1832 Act. In July 1895, the plaintiffs sought an interlocutory injunction to restrain the defendants from building so as to interfere with the access of light. They claimed that since more than 19 years had passed since the old buildings on every part of the defendants' site had been pulled down, the defendants could do nothing to defeat the plaintiffs' right to light, even though the plaintiffs had not, at the time the motion for an interlocutory injunction came on for hearing, enjoyed the light for the full period of 20 years (because some of the buildings on the defendants' site had been demolished only in October 1875, hence the 20-year period would be completed only in October 1895).

8.22   The court held that the plaintiffs had not established their right to the light received by their premises over the defendants' land in its state following the demolition of the buildings in 1875. North J said:

'That section [ie s 4] to my mind, strongly bears out, on this point, what Section 3 says, because the period of years – the 20 years – is to be "next before the suit or action wherein the claim is made". What I am asked to do now is to say that it is quite sufficient that the 20 years shall be calculated, not 20 complete years before action, but 20 years, 19 years, and

---

[35]   See Chapter 6.
[36]   *Bridewell Hospital (Governors) v Ward, Lock, Bowden & Co* (1893) 62 LJ Ch 270; *Lord Battersea v Commissioners of Sewers for the City of London* [1895] 2 Ch 708.
[37]   [1895] 2 Ch 708.

rather more of which is before action, the rest of the 20 years being made up during the continuance of the action. It seems to me that such a contention is directly contrary to the meaning of these two Sections. I think, therefore, that the action can only be brought after the period of 20 years has elapsed.'

8.23   However, the court's conclusion did not preclude the plaintiffs from relying on a right to receive light to their premises to the extent enjoyed over the defendants' land *prior* to the demolition of the defendants' buildings in 1875. Therefore, an interlocutory injunction was granted restraining the defendants from building higher than the buildings existing in July 1875 so as to obscure the plaintiffs' windows. Thus whilst the combined effect of ss 3 and 4 of the 1832 Act is that after enjoyment has existed for more than 19 years it is capable of ripening into an absolute and indefeasible right, the right arises only once the 20-year period has elapsed.

8.24   An interruption for the purposes of the 1832 Act requires either physical obstruction of the light or a notional obstruction under the Rights of Light Act 1959 (considered below). The physical obstruction may be due to the act of the servient owner or a stranger.[38] However, the mere commencement of legal proceedings by the servient owner does not amount to an interruption.[39] It is also established that the dominant owner's obstruction of his own light does not amount to an interruption within the meaning of the Act.[40] But such activity may be evidence of abandonment. It may also be evidence of non-enjoyment during the 20-year period relied on: see **8.9**.

8.25   There is no clear authority which establishes whether the interruption means *any* act which amounts to diminution of the light, even to a small (and possibly non-actionable) extent, or whether, in order to qualify as an interruption, the obstruction must be such as to be actionable. It is suggested that the latter must be the case, since the 1832 Act is concerned with rights to light, and if in a particular case an obstruction is not so substantial as to give rise to a claim, there seems no basis on which the provisions of the Act should be brought into play.

8.26   In order to defeat the acquisition of a right to light under s 3, the interruption must be acquiesced in for one year. The notion of acquiescence implies knowledge that the obstruction exists. Submission or acquiescence is a 'state of mind', as Birkett LJ said in *Davies v Du Paver*.[41] The person in question, before he can be said to acquiesce, must have some notice of the existence of the obstruction. The mere presence of the obstruction is not enough for these purposes.[42] In *Seddon v Bank of Bolton*,[43] Fry J suggested in the course of argument that written notice was required,[44] but the actual point did not arise for decision since the court held that the plaintiff had failed to discharge the burden of proof in establishing her right to light. But at p 469 of the report, Fry J did express the view, obiter, that the defendants had not shown the kind of notice which would have made the obstruction an interruption under s 4. Quite what notice is sufficient, other than expressly in writing, is open to debate. It is submitted that notice in writing is not necessary; it is, in practice, improbable that such notice would be given, and the terms of the 1832 Act do not expressly require it.

---

[38]   *Plasterer's Company v Parish Clerks Company* (1851) 6 Exch 630; *Davies v Williams* (1851) 16 QBD 546.
[39]   *Reilly v Orange* [1955] 2 QB 112.
[40]   *Smith v Baxter* [1900] 2 Ch 138.
[41]   [1953] 1 QB 184 at 203.
[42]   *Glover v Coleman* (1874) LR 10 CP 108; *Seddon v Bank of Bolton* (1882) 19 ChD 462. See Chapter 6 at **6.27**.
[43]   (1882) 19 ChD 462.
[44]   (1882) 19 ChD 462 at 464.

8.27 Assuming the dominant owner becomes aware of the obstruction, whether he acquiesced in its continuation for the one-year period is an issue of fact.[45] Evidence to negative acquiescence may take many forms. Clearly, the most decisive evidence of non-acquiescence is the commencement of legal proceedings to vindicate the right interrupted, although this is not an essential requirement.[46] Other types of evidence of non-acquiescence include:

(1)   protests made in anticipation of the interruption;[47]

(2)   refusal to act on a permission given by the servient owner (it being implicit in such permission that the existence of the right is denied);[48]

(3)   other manifestations of dissent or dissatisfaction.

8.28 Section 4 of the 1832 Act refers to submission or acquiescence. The fact that something is submitted to (even reluctantly) does not prevent it amounting to submission or acquiescence within s 4. In *Glover v Coleman*,[49] Brett J said:

> 'Acquiescence . . . would mean not active agreement, but what might be called a tacit, a silent agreement, – a submission to a thing by one who is satisfied to submit. The question for the jury, therefore, upon a suggested acquiescence, would be, whether the plaintiff, although he has not specifically agreed that the thing should be done, has submitted to it, and has been satisfied to submit. Now, "opposition", on the other hand, I should say, would mean dissent or dissatisfaction manifested by some act of opposition. "Submitted to" in this part of the Section, seems to me to be something intermediate between a submission by one satisfied to submit and a dissatisfaction manifested by some act of opposition.'

In the same case, Grove J drew a distinction[50] between *'mere grumbling, or complaining to a member of his family, or expressing dissatisfaction to a third party'*, which would not amount to an act of opposition, and *'protests . . . made to the party causing the interruption'*, which would be capable of amounting to non-acquiescence.

8.29 In *Dance v Triplow*,[51] it was held that the following acts did not prevent the plaintiff from having acquiesced in an interruption of his right to light for more than one year:

(1)   complaining to the local planning authority about a proposed revision of the planning consent obtained by the defendants;

(2)   consulting solicitors concerning the defendant's use of a weed killer which had drifted across the boundary.

---

[45]   *Bennison v Cartwright* (1864) 5 B&S 1.
[46]   *Glover v Coleman* (1874) LR 10 CP 108.
[47]   *Davies v Du Paver* [1953] 1 QB 184.
[48]   *Ward v Kirkland* [1967] 1 Ch 194 at 231G–232F.
[49]   (1874) LR 10 CP 108 at 119.
[50]   (1874) LR 10 CP 108 at 121.
[51]   (1992) 1 EGLR 190; (1991) 64 P&CR 1.

8.30   The same case also establishes that the burden of proving non-acquiescence lies on the dominant owner once the interruption has lasted for more than one year. This is consistent with the general rule that it is for the person asserting the right to light to establish their case.[52]

Notional interruption

8.31   The Rights of Light Act 1959 ('the 1959 Act') introduces a statutory method of interruption without the need for the erection of a physical obstruction. The mechanism provided by the Act is a light obstruction notice, a notional physical obstruction notionally erected on the land of the giver of the notice. Registration of the light obstruction notice as a local land charge is deemed to constitute notice to those affected. The light obstruction notice remains effective for one year, this period mirroring the length of time during which an obstruction must continue under s 4 of the 1832 Act. If those affected by the notice fail to take and protect their rights within the one-year period, their rights to light will be extinguished to the same extent as if an actual physical obstruction had been erected for that period in the position specified in the light obstruction notice.

8.32   The 1959 Act was passed to remedy two problems which had arisen as a result of the Second World War. The first was that during the War many buildings had been destroyed, and by the time the Act was passed had not been rebuilt. This led to the possibility of rights to light being acquired by neighbouring buildings over the sites on which these buildings had formerly stood. Secondly, the enactment of the Town and Country Planning Act 1947 required planning permission for the erection of physical obstructions which were formerly used to prevent the acquisition of rights to light under the Prescription Act 1832. In practice, the need for planning permission resulted in the practice of erecting such obstructions falling off. The combined effect of these matters was perceived to give rise to a risk that many areas of land might be sterilised for development in future. A committee under Mr Justice (later Lord Justice) Harman (this is commonly known as 'the Harman Committee') was appointed to consider the problem, and reported in May 1958.[53] The Harman Committee Report sets out the problem, and provides a useful guide to the interpretation of the 1832 Act, which resulted from the Report.[54]

8.33   Sections 2 and 3 of the 1832 Act lay down the basic framework. The basic concept is the creation by s 2 of a notional obstruction brought into being by a notice under the section. Although the Act does not define such a notice except in terms of its being a notice under s 2, such notices are generally referred to as 'light obstruction notices', and this terminology will be used here. Section 2(1) provides that for the purposes of preventing the access and use of light from being taken to be enjoyed without interruption, any person who is an owner of land ('the servient land') over which light passes to a dwellinghouse, workshop or other building ('the dominant building') may apply to the local authority in whose area the dominant building is situated for the registration of a light obstruction notice. By s 7(1), the term 'owner' bears a special meaning. It applies to:

(1)   the freeholder;

---

52   Cf *Seddon v Bank of Bolton* (1882) 19 ChD 462.
53   Report of the Committee on the Law Relating to Rights of Light (Cmnd 473).
54   See Appendix 3 for relevant extracts.

(2)   a tenant under a fixed-term lease having not less than 7 years unexpired;

(3)   a mortgagee in possession where the interest mortgaged is either the freehold or a lease with not less than 7 years unexpired.

8.34   The key provision of the Act is s 3(1), which provides that once a light obstruction notice is registered under the Act the access of light to the dominant building across the servient land shall be treated as obstructed to the same extent, and with the like consequences, as if an opaque structure, of the dimensions specified in the application:

(1)   had on the date of registration of the notice been erected in the position on the servient land specified in the application, and had been so erected by the person who made the application; and

(2)   had remained in that position during the period for which the notice has effect and had been removed at the end of that period.

8.35   A light obstruction notice is therefore notionally a physical obstruction of light to the dominant building received over the servient land. The obstruction ceases to have effect after one year;[55] this ties in with s 4 of the 1832 Act, set out at **8.20**. There is no need for the notional obstruction to remain in position for more than one year to be effective as an interruption under the 1832 Act, and equally a period of less than one year would not be sufficient. As has been pointed out above, since no interruption of less than one year can be effective under the 1832 Act to prevent the 20-year period being established, enjoyment for more than 19 years is capable of ripening into a prescriptive right.[56] The 1959 Act applies the same regime to notional obstructions created by light obstruction notices, by s 3(4). The actual wording of the subsection is to the effect that where at any time during the period for which a light obstruction notice is in force:

'. . . the circumstances are such that if the access of light to the dominant building had been enjoyed continuously from a date one year earlier than the date on which the enjoyment thereof in fact began, a person would have had a right of action in any court . . . in respect of the registration of the notice, that person shall have the like right of action . . .'

8.36   By s 7(1), 'action' includes a counter-claim.[57] Where the notional obstruction creates an actionable interference to the dominant building, the owner has the same right of action in respect of the registration of the notice as he would have had in respect of a physical obstruction of the same dimensions as those described in the notice. The remedies available are declaratory relief, and an order directing cancellation or variation of the notice, as the court may determine.[58] Cancellation of the light obstruction notice would generally be predicated on the basis of the court deciding that the entire obstruction was unlawful, a variation on a decision that only part of the obstruction created an actionable interference.[59] For obvious reasons, injunctive relief is not available. The 1959 Act makes no provision for an award of damages suffered by

---

[55]   See s 3(2)(b).
[56]   See **8.21**.
[57]   Now a Part 20 claim under the Civil Procedure Rules 1998, SI 1998/3132 ('CPR').
[58]   See s 3(5).
[59]   See *Hawker v Tomalin* [1969] 20 P&CR 550.

reason of the notional obstruction. This is no doubt consistent with the absence of any *actual* obstruction, since there has been no interference with the light in fact received by the dominant building.

8.37 As has been seen in relation to s 4 of the 1832 Act, the issue of acquiescence is relevant in deciding whether there has been an interruption of the light for a sufficiently long period to defeat the acquisition of a prescriptive right.[60] The 1959 Act introduces for the purposes of s 4 of the 1832 Act a special regime in relation to light obstruction notices. The two key features of the regime are:

(1)   registration of the light obstruction notice is deemed to be notice of the obstruction to all those interested in the dominant building;

(2)   until the light obstruction notice is challenged in legal proceedings, all persons interested in the dominant building are deemed to acquiesce in the obstruction, but from the date of legal proceedings no person is deemed to acquiesce in the obstruction.[61]

Thus where the 1959 Act applies, it is unnecessary to inquire into either the state of mind of the person alleged to have acquiesced or as to whether the acts in relation to the obstruction amounted to acquiescence: it is simply necessary to see whether legal proceedings to challenge the notice were commenced within one year of its registration, even if not by the particular claimant. There is a proviso that if the court dismisses a particular claimant's claim, it may direct that the regime shall continue to apply as if the action had not been brought. The purpose of this is to prevent the light obstruction notice from being deprived of effect by virtue of an unsuccessful claim. The court's power is discretionary.

8.38 The 1959 Act lays down a number of detailed requirements as to:

(1)   the giving of notice to those likely to be affected by a light obstruction notice before such a notice is registered;

(2)   the form of the notice;

(3)   registration of the notice.

The aim of these provisions is twofold: first, they are designed to ensure that those interested in the servient land become aware of the proposed registration of the light obstruction notice, and do not lose their rights by failing to challenge within the one-year period from registration the notice, in circumstances where they had no notice of the proposal to register it. Secondly, there is the need to protect purchasers of the dominant building: since there will be no physical evidence of a light obstruction notice visible on inspection of the dominant building, a purchaser might be led to conclude that windows looking over the servient land had acquired prescriptive rights to light. It is, therefore, necessary to ensure that light obstruction notices are registered in some publicly available register for inspection by prospective purchasers. The 1959 Act achieves this by providing that light obstruction notices are to be registered as local land charges under the Local Land Charges Act 1975.

---

[60]   See **8.27–8.30**.

[61]   See s 4(6).

8.39   Before an application can be made to a local authority for registration of a light obstruction notice, appropriate publicity must be given to the proposed application. The 1959 Act deals with this in s 2(3), by providing that an application is to be accompanied by a certificate issued by the Lands Tribunal.[62] The certificate may be in one of two alternative forms:

(1)   a certificate under s 2(3)(a) certifying that adequate notice of the proposed application has been given to all persons who in the circumstances existing at the time when the certificate is issued appear to the Lands Tribunal to be persons likely to be affected by the registration of a notice in pursuance of the application;

(2)   a certificate under s 2(3)(b) certifying that in the opinion of the Lands Tribunal the case is one of exceptional urgency, and that accordingly a notice should be registered forthwith as a temporary notice for such period as may be specified in the certificate.

Certificates issued under s 2(3)(a) are known as definitive certificates, and those issued under s 2(3)(b) as temporary certificates. The purpose of a temporary certificate is to enable a light obstruction notice to be erected where otherwise the period of 19 years uninterrupted enjoyment of light would be completed before the procedure for obtaining a definitive certificate, and registration, could be effected. In order to prevent the emergency certificate procedure being used to bypass the definitive certificate procedure, provision is made for emergency certificates to have only a limited life, following which a definitive certificate must be obtained.

8.40   The procedure for obtaining certificates is laid down in Part VI of the Lands Tribunal Rules 1996.[63] Rule 21 provides that an application for a certificate of the Lands Tribunal under s 2 of the 1959 Act is to be in Form 1 in Sch 1 to the Rules.[64] It must be accompanied by two copies of the application which the applicant proposes to make to the local authority in whose area the dominant building is situated. By r 22, on receipt of an application the Registrar of the Lands Tribunal is to determine what notices are to be given whether by advertisement or otherwise to persons who appear to have an interest in the dominant building, the subject of the proposed application. The Registrar must require the applicant to provide any documents or information which it is in his power to provide. By r 22(3), the notices that the Registrar determines shall be given under r 22 must be given by the applicant, who is to notify the Registrar in writing once this has been done, setting out full particulars of the steps he has taken.

8.41   In the case of an application for a definitive certificate, the Registrar will require the following information:

(1)   the identities of all those interested in the dominant building who could qualify as 'owners' within the 1959 Act, s 7;

(2)   the business addresses and registered offices of the person so identified;

(3)   the full address and location of the dominant building.

---

[62]   Established under the Lands Tribunal Act 1949.
[63]   SI 1996/1022.
[64]   See Appendix 2.

The proposed applicant will be required to write letters to all those so identified, giving them notice of the proposed application to the local authority, and enclosing a copy of that proposed application and any plan which is to accompany it.

8.42 The identity of the potential 'owners' may be capable of ascertainment from a property search at the Land Registry: however, such a search may not reveal the names of all potential owners. This is less of a problem than it was because, since 13 October 2003, (in general terms) only leases for a term of less than 7 years are not registrable under the provisions of ss 4 and 27(2)(b) of the Land Registration Act 2002.[65] Before that date leases had to be for a term of 21 years to be registrable under the old Land Registration Act 1925. Therefore the risk that potential 'owners' may not be traced by a Land Registry search is now less. There is therefore usually a requirement imposed that a copy of the proposed application to the local authority be sent to the dominant building addressed simply to the 'occupier'. Following notification to the Lands Tribunal that the relevant notices have been served, the Registrar will issue the definitive certificate in Form 3 in Sch 1 to the Lands Tribunal Rules.[66]

8.43 Where the application includes an application for a temporary certificate authorising the registration forthwith of the proposed notice, the applicant will need to include in his application details of the reasons which make the case one of exceptional urgency. It is desirable to accompany the application in these circumstances by an affidavit verifying the facts.[67] Strictly, such evidence is not necessary in the first instance (though the Registrar may require it). Whether there is an accompanying affidavit or not, the application should contain a full explanation of the reasons for the application being made as one of urgency. An example of the type of situations where this would be the case would be if the dominant building had been completed 18 years or thereabouts prior to the application, so that there was a real risk of the 19-year period elapsing shortly.

8.44 A temporary certificate cannot last longer than 6 months.[68] Form 1 in Sch 1 to the Lands Tribunal Rules envisages a composite application both for a temporary and definitive certificate. The Registrar may, therefore, grant a temporary certificate in respect of a proposed application, and give directions at the same time as to the notices to be given to those affected, preparatory to the grant of a definitive certificate. The applicant can then, having given the appropriate notification to those likely to be affected by the light obstruction notice, apply to the Registrar for the definitive certificate, and obtain it within the 6-month period.

8.45 It is not possible to challenge the Registrar's decision to issue a temporary certificate except by way of judicial review proceedings under CPR Part 54.[69] Once the relevant certificate has been obtained, the applicant applies to the relevant local authority (in whose area the dominant building is situated) for registration of the notice in respect of which the certificate has been given as a local land charge under the Local Land Charges Act 1975. The procedure is governed by the Local Land Charges Rules 1977.[70] By r 10(1), an application is to be in Form A and be accompanied by the

---

[65] See ss 4 and 27(2)(b) and *Ruoff & Roper: Registered Conveyancing* (Sweet & Maxwell, looseleaf) 7.005–7.006 for the detailed provisions.
[66] See Appendix 2.
[67] Affidavit evidence may be adduced before the Lands Tribunal under Lands Tribunal Rules 1996, rr 33 and 38.
[68] Lands Tribunal Rules 1996, r 23(2).
[69] *Bowring Services Ltd v Scottish Widows Fund and Life Assurance Society* [1995] 1 EGLR 158.
[70] SI 1977/985. See Appendix 2.

certificate of the Lands Tribunal. On receipt of the application and certificate, the registering authority (ie in the local authority for the purposes of the Local Land Charges Act 1975 in whose area the dominant building is situated) must register the notice in accordance with r 6. Rule 6(1) provides for registration by reference to the land in the area of the registering authority, and r 6(2) provides for the registration by entering in the part of the register appropriate for that charge the particulars specified in Sch 2 to the Local Land Charges Rules 1977 in relation to that Part. The relevant part of the register for light obstruction notices is Part 11.[71] Part 11 requires information with regard to the notice to be entered under the following heads:

(1)   Description of charge.

(2)   Description of dominant building.

(3)   Name and address of applicant and short description of his interest in the servient land.

(4)   Position and dimension of structure to which registration equivalent.

(5)   Date of temporary Lands Tribunal certificate (if any) and of its expiration.

(6)   Date of definitive Lands Tribunal certificate.

(7)   List of documents filed.

(8)   Date of registration.

8.46   Form A in Sch 1 to the Local Land Charges Rules 1977 envisages that the application will be accompanied by a plan showing the location of the servient land and the position of the notional obstruction on it. The form of application envisages that the notional obstruction will be of unlimited height. Normally, the notional obstruction will be shown on the plan attached to the application, but the form of application also allows for the possibility of notional obstructions on all the boundaries of the servient land. One advantage of the notional obstruction introduced by the 1959 Act is that it is possible to 'position' it so as to obstruct windows in any position irrespective of the practical problems of erecting an actual obstruction of the requisite dimensions and in the desired position. This can be important where the dominant building has acquired an extra storey. The notice can be positioned to obstruct the new windows without interfering with the windows lower down, which may already enjoy indefeasible rights.[72]

8.47   It must be remembered that the Lands Tribunal will not issue a definitive or temporary certificate without having before it the draft application to the local authority. It is not, therefore, possible to register a light obstruction notice in a form different from that in respect of which the Lands Tribunal has issued its certificate.

8.48   Where a temporary certificate accompanies the application to the registering authority, the registering authority is to cancel the registration of the notice if no definitive certificate has been filed, on the expiration of the period of operation of the

---

[71]   See Local Land Charges Rules 1977, r 3. See Appendix 2.
[72]   Contrast the practical problem faced by a servient owner erecting an actual obstruction to upper windows and lower windows enjoying established light – see *Tapling v Jones* (1865) 11 HLC 290.

temporary certificate.[73] Where a notice is registered following the issue of a temporary certificate, and the applicant subsequently obtains a definitive certificate before the temporary certificate expires, the period of 12 months within which the light obstruction notice must be challenged under s 3(2) of the 1959 Act runs from the date of registration of the notice pursuant to the temporary certificate. In *Bowring Services Limited v Scottish Widows Fund and Life Assurance Society*,[74] the plaintiff failed in its effort to challenge a light obstruction notice in circumstances where on 12 August 1991 the light obstruction notice was registered pursuant to a temporary certificate, which was expressed to expire within 4 months unless a definitive certificate was lodged. The definitive certificate was issued on 8 October 1991. The plaintiff commenced proceedings to challenge the light obstruction notice in October 1992, more than 12 months after the initial registration of the light obstruction notice, but within 12 months of the issue of the definitive certificate. It was held that the plaintiff's challenge had been made too late to prevent the notice being effective as an interruption of the plaintiff's enjoyment of light. The court also dismissed the plaintiff's argument to the effect that the Registrar's decision to issue the temporary certificate was invalid, holding that the only way of challenging this would be by way of judicial review proceedings.

DEMOLITION OR ALTERATION OF THE DOMINANT BUILDING

8.49   Since a right to light inherently depends on the existence of defined apertures in a building, the disappearance of the building, or the relevant part containing the apertures, may affect whether the right to light continues to exist. This question raises similar issues as to whether there has been abandonment by blocking up windows,[75] but goes further, requiring consideration of the effect for this purpose of either the complete demolition of the dominant building, or the demolition and/or remodelling of the wall in which the windows enjoying rights to light are situated.

8.50   Dealing first with demolition, it is clear in principle that the demolition of the dominant building may result in the disappearance of rights to light enjoyed with it but, equally, that this is not always necessarily the case. In *Ecclesiastical Commissioners v Kino*,[76] a church containing windows enjoying rights to light was demolished, although wooden structures were erected to show the position of the former windows. The owner of neighbouring land asserted that the effect of this demolition was to bring to an end the rights to light enjoyed by the windows. This argument was rejected. It was held that the fact that there were no existing windows did not prevent the plaintiffs obtaining an injunction, on the basis that they intended to rebuild making use of the pre-existing right to light for the new building. The effect of the demolition was simply to suspend enjoyment of their rights.[77] It is suggested that the best way of ensuring that any argument of the type asserted by the neighbouring owner in *Kino* is defeated is for the owner of the property being developed to write formal letters to adjoining owners over

---

73   Local Land Charges Rules 1977, r 10(6).
74   [1995] 1 EGLR 158.
75   See **8.17–8.18**.
76   (1880) 14 ChD 213. The church concerned was St Dionis Backchurch, situated on the western corner of Fenchurch St and Lime St just after the junction of Fenchurch St with Gracechurch St. The windows in question ran along the south side of the former nave of the church just below the roof and were above the site of the 'low buildings' owned by the claimant lying between the south side of the church and Fenchurch St. In the 1990s the same site (which was then being redeveloped) led to other disputes over rights of light with adjoining owners.
77   See also *Staight v Burn* (1869) 5 Ch App 163.

whose land the development site derives light stating that notwithstanding the demolition of the building, rights of light for the benefit of the new building will be maintained and are not to be treated as abandoned. In the absence of any such letter much may depend on the time during which the site is vacant. The significance of not losing such rights as may have been enjoyed by the old building is of course dependant on the new building having coincident rights. As to this see the paragraphs immediately below.

8.51   Where the dominant building undergoes alterations, so that the windows enjoying rights to light are replaced by new windows, whether the right to light is lost depends on a number of matters. The general principle is that alterations to windows will not destroy the right to light enjoyed by them, provided there is coincidence between at least part of the old and the new apertures.[78] The right to light, however, will not extend to those portions of new apertures opened in the dominant building which do not coincide with the apertures which previously enjoyed a right to light, nor, obviously, to wholly new apertures (unless and until they acquire prescriptive rights to light of their own). Where the new operations coincide partially with the old ones, the claimant is entitled to have his prescriptive rights protected. It is thought that in such cases damages may be awarded for the whole loss to the building,[79] on the basis that the obstruction of the new lights inevitably involves obstruction of the old.

8.52   Thus where a window enjoying rights to light is increased in size, the right to light applies to only that portion of the larger aperture which is coincident with the pre-existing window, but equally the right to that portion is not lost by the enlargement. Where the effect of the alteration is to *reduce* the size of the existing window, the position is that the right to light remains, but the dominant owner cannot complain about any subsequent building work of the servient owner which obstructs the light received from the newly reduced window, if the light would have remained adequate notwithstanding the obstruction if the window had remained at its original size.[80] In *Ankerson v Connelly*,[81] the defendant redeveloped his land, and reduced the size of windows enjoying rights to light, resulting in the light received being reduced by at least three-quarters. The plaintiffs, owners of the servient tenement, then erected hoardings sufficient to obstruct the defendant's windows in their altered condition. There was evidence that, but for the reduction in size, the obstruction would not have caused actionable interference to the windows. It was held that the defendant had no right to complain.

8.53   In *WH Bailey & Son Limited v Holborn & Frascati Limited*,[82] the same principle was applied where the obstruction to the window arose not directly from the dominant owner's acts, but by acts of another servient owner, to which the plaintiff had assented. Sargant J said:[83]

> 'I think myself that the true view of the law is suggested by a passage in the 8th edition of Gale on Easements where at p. 547 the learned author says: "It would seem clear that after an alteration in an ancient window whereby its size was decreased, the dominant proprietor would not be entitled to prevent the erection of buildings which, though obstructing the altered window, would not, before the alteration, have caused an illegal obstruction within

---

[78]   *Tapling v Jones* (1865) 11 HLC 290.
[79]   On the principles discussed in Chapter 11 at **11.50**.
[80]   *Ankerson v Connelly* [1906] 2 Ch 554; [1907] 1 Ch 678.
[81]   [1906] 2 Ch 544; affirmed [1907] 1 Ch 678.
[82]   [1914] 1 Ch 598.
[83]   Ibid, at 602–603.

the rule laid down in *Colls'* case. This principle was applied in *Ankerson v Connelly*". Converting that passage from a negative proposition into a positive proposition and applying it not to an alteration of a window but to an alteration of the light coming over adjoining property brought about with the assent or permission of the owner of the dominant tenement, it seems to me that it is true to say that an obstruction of light coming over adjoining property acquiesced in or consented to by the owner of the dominant tenement does not entirely negative his right to an easement of light over other adjoining property, though it does not give him any further right over that second adjoining property, so as to prevent the erection of a building which he could not have prevented had he not assented to the prior obstruction of light over the first adjoining property.'

8.54 Where the effect of the alterations to the dominant building is to destroy the identity between the old and the new apertures, the right to light may be lost. De minimis coincidence will not be enough to preserve the right.[84] It is, therefore, of practical importance for a dominant owner who proposes to carry out work to a building enjoying rights to light both to keep an accurate survey record of the position of any such windows which are to be demolished, and to ensure that the new apertures are in the same position as the old. In *News of the World Limited v Allen Fairhead & Sons Limited*,[85] a claim to rights to light in respect of a redeveloped building replacing an original building enjoying such rights failed for lack of proof of the position of the original windows. This was so even though the court accepted that there was some coincidence between certain of the old and new apertures, albeit the extent was unclear. In practice experienced rights of light surveyors should have no real difficulty in determining the extent of the 'old' and 'new' light, and the measurement of losses, although much may depend on the extent of the coincidence.

8.55 Where the plane of the window, or the position of the wall in which it is situated, is altered, whether the right to light is preserved cannot be answered simply by reference to coincidence between the old and the new aperture. The courts' approach has been to uphold the continuation of rights to light provided the light continues to be received by the dominant building in the same general position as when the pre-existing window was in existence. In *National Provincial Plate Glass Insurance Co v Prudential Assurance Co*[86] Fry J said:

'. . . I find nothing whatever in the statute [ie the Rights of Light Act 1832] which refers expressly to a window or aperture. I find in the statute a reference to the access of light, and in my view the access of light might be described as being the freedom with which light may pass through a certain space over the servient tenement . . .'

The principle has been applied to:

(1)   replacement of a dormer window with a skylight;[87]

(2)   setting back a wall, replacing in it windows in the same position and of the same sizes as in the original wall;[88]

---

[84]   *Ankerson v Connelly* [1906] 2 Ch 554; [1907] 1 Ch 678.
[85]   [1931] 2 Ch 402.
[86]   (1877) 6 ChD 757 at 764.
[87]   *National Provincial Plate Glass Insurance Co v Prudential Assurance Co* (1877) 6 ChD 757.
[88]   *Barnes v Loach* (1879) 4 QBD 494.

(3)   setting back a wall, and insertion in it of a window at a different angle to the original.[89]

8.56   How far can the old and new windows be 'out' before there is a lack of coincidence?

•   In practice the question of whether there is coincidence between old and new apertures will depend on the evidence to show such coincidence – if any.

•   In the horizontal plane, specially drawn elevations will reveal the coincidence by the effect of the superimposition of the elevations to the old and new buildings.

•   In the vertical plane, ground plans will show how far the walls with the apertures in them have moved in or out from their original position.

•   It will be a matter of degree as to how far such new apertures will be coincident. In some cases there may be a high degree of coincidence. In others only a few windows out of many will be coincident. As the general principal is that the dominant owner cannot increase the burden on the servient owner, moving the new walls out by more than about 3 feet (or one metre) in the vertical plane will lead to a loss of coincidence.[90]

•   In any event accurate drawings of the old and new buildings will be essential if coincidence in either plane is to be established.

EXTINGUISHMENT UNDER STATUTORY PROVISIONS

The power to override an easement of light

8.57   Part IX of the Town and Country Planning Act 1990 (in this section referred to as 'the 1990 Act') provides for certain local authorities to acquire land compulsorily for development and planning purposes.[91] By s 237 of the 1990 Act:

'(1)   Subject to subsection (3), the erection, construction or carrying out or maintenance of any building or work on land which has been acquired or appropriated by a local authority for planning purposes (whether done by the local authority or by a person deriving title under them) is authorised by virtue of this section if it is done in accordance with planning permission, notwithstanding that it involves—
  (a)   interference with an interest or right to which this section applies, or
  (b)   a breach of a restriction as to the user of land arising by virtue of a contract.
(2)   Subject to subsection (3), the interests and rights to which this section applies are any easement, liberty, privilege, right or advantage annexed to land and adversely affecting other land, including any natural right to support.
(3)   . . .
(4)   In respect of any inference or breach in pursuance of subsection (1), compensation—

---

[89]   *Bullers v Dickinson* (1885) 29 ChD 155.

[90]   The late John Anstey expressed the view that you were safe in moving your windows out by a foot (300mm), probably all right in moving them out by 2 ft in (800mm) getting a bit dubious if they moved out 3'5" (1020mm) and almost certainly out of Court if they moved out by 5 ft 8 in (2900mm). (Metric conversions approximate.) There is no specific judicial authority for this view, but in practice these are the margins within which the standards will work.

[91]   See 1990 Act, s 226. For the meaning of 'required' see *Chesterfield Properties v Secretary of State for the Environment* [1997] NPC 122; (1997) *The Times,* August 1; LTL 24 July 1997.

(a) shall be payable under section 63 or 68 of the Lands Clauses Consolidation Act 1845 or under section 7 or 10 of the Compulsory Purchase Act 1965, and

(b) shall be assessed in the same manner and subject to the same rules as in the case of other compensation under those sections in respect of injurious affection where—

    (i) the compensation is to be estimated in connection with a purchase under those Acts, or

    (ii) the injury arises from the execution of works on land acquired under those Acts.

(5) Where a person deriving title under the local authority by whom the land in question was acquired or appropriated—

    (a) is liable to pay compensation by virtue of subsection (4), and

    (b) fails to discharge that liability,

the liability shall be enforceable against the local authority.

(6) Nothing in subsection (5) shall be construed as affecting any agreement between the local authority and any other person for indemnifying the local authority against any liability under that subsection.

(7) Nothing in this section shall be construed as authorising any act or omission on the part of any person which is actionable at the suit of any person on any grounds other than such an interference or breach as is mentioned in subsection (1).'

The effect of this provision is that private rights (including easements of light) are overridden, where they affect the use of land held for planning purposes where development is carried out in accordance with planning permission. This applies not only to development by the local planning authority itself but also to any person deriving title from it.[92] It is possible for authorities who wish to take advantage of these provisions to enter into agreements with developers whereby the freehold interest is transferred to the authority for the purpose of allowing it to exercise its powers under s 237 (or similar powers) and for agreements to provide that the developer will carry out the development under a lease (thereby deriving title under the authority) with provisions allowing the freehold title to revest in the developer at the completion of the development. The developer will indemnify the authority against the liability to pay the compensation under s 237(4). The major concern of the parties to such arrangements is that they are not subject to challenge by way of judicial review. The acquiring or appropriating authority must satisfy itself that the exercise of the statutory power to override the easement is necessary and that it is a proper exercise of the power.[93]

8.58 In *R v City of London Council, ex parte Master Governors and Commonalty of the Mystery of the Barbers of London*,[94] it was held that where a local authority has acquired and held land for planning purposes, s 237(1) of the 1990 Act enabled land initially acquired or appropriated for planning purposes, and developed, to be redeveloped notwithstanding that the effect of the development was to interfere with rights to light. It was also held that the section applied notwithstanding that the local

---

[92] See 1990 Act, s 236(8). See also Sch 6 to the Regional Development Agencies Act 1998, and Sch 20 to the Local Government Planning and Land Act 1980 which contain similar (but not identical) provisions.

[93] See *R v Leeds City Council ex parte Leeds Co-operative Society* (1996) 73 P&CR 70. See *Ford Camber Ltd v Deanminster Ltd & anor* [2006] EWHC 1961 (Ch) (subject to appeal in early 2007) and *Standard Commercial Property Securities Ltd v Glasgow City Council* [2006] UKHL 50; [2006] 47 EG (CS) 181 for recent cases where 'schemes' were upheld. But note the limits of such 'schemes' and the ever prevalent risk of judicial review under CPR Part 54.

[94] [1996] 2 EGLR 128. See also *Midtown v CLRP Co* [2005] EWHC 33 Ch for an application of this section, the court holding that there must be a factual link between the development which is the subject of the claim and the original acquisition or appropriation. In *Midtown* that link was missing: the court's decision on that aspect of the case and the construction of s 237 meant that the submissions of counsel on the alleged non-conformity with human rights did not have to be determined. See Chapter 15 for Human Rights Act 1998 matters.

authority had itself covenanted with the dominant owner not to obstruct its light and air.[95] That was a case where the developer (as lessee of the City of London Corporation) derived title from the Corporation and the developer was accordingly able to take the benefit of the section. Compensation for the exercise of the power to override is based on the 'injurious affection' measure; see **8.61–8.62**.

Compulsory purchase

8.59   Where land acquired compulsorily is subject to a right of light, the acquiring authority is neither obliged nor empowered to acquire those rights compulsorily. The dominant owner in respect of such an easement is not entitled to a notice to treat, but only to compensation for the injury. Where land acquired has the benefit of an easement, that easement will pass to the acquiring authority.[96]

8.60   Various statutes empower public and private bodies to acquire land compulsorily. Such acquisition is generally subject to the Land Compensation Act 1961, the Compulsory Purchase Act 1965 and the Acquisition of Land Act 1981. Where land compulsorily acquired has the right of an easement, that easement will pass to the acquiring authority.[97] Generally, when powers are given by statute to acquire land compulsorily, the whole of the landowner's interest must be purchased, unless the relevant provision authorises acquisition of a lesser right, such as an easement.[98] So in *Sovmots Investments Ltd v Secretary of State for the Environment*,[99] it was held that a local authority's power to purchase compulsorily land for housing did not extend to the compulsory creation of easements for services, and of access and support, incidental to the compulsory purchase of a number of maisonettes in an open complex which was not itself intended to be acquired. Lord Wilberforce said:

> 'A power to acquire a right over land cannot authorise compulsion of an owner of land not being acquired to grant new rights over that land.'

Where land is acquired compulsorily, its value will be assessed taking into account the benefit of any easement of light it enjoys, as part of its open market value.[100]

---

[95]   But see *Thames Water Utilities Ltd v Oxford City Council* (1999) 77 P&CR D16, holding that s 237 did not authorise breaches of covenant by subsequent *use* of buildings erected in reliance of power under the section. This was because the judge found that as the compensation could only be for the effect of the *execution of the works*, and not for the effect of the subsequent *use of the property*, s 237 could not be deployed so as to override a user covenant. Whether the decision in this authority is right is open to doubt. It is inconsistent with earlier observations by Chadwick J in *Brown v Heathlands Mental Health NHS Trust* [1996] 1 All ER 133. Fortunately in rights of light cases it will be the execution of the work (i e the building being erected) which interferes with the right of light. So compensation under s 237(4) will be payable for that and the section can be used to override the easement of light. In other cases where, eg, a user covenant stands in the way of the development, the decision in *Thames Water* stands in the way and it will be for a future case taken to the Court of Appeal to make the law here more rational. It is thought that the decision of the judge in *Thames Water* is wrong and that it is ripe for the challenge.

[96]   See *Halsbury's Laws of England* (2003 reissue, 4th edn) vol 8(1), [30]–[31].

[97]   [1977] 2 All ER 385, HL.

[98]   Ibid, at 393g.

[99]   Land Compensation Act 1961, s 5(2).

[100]   Consider also in this context the effect of the exercise of powers under Part XI and in particular s 352 of the Housing Act 1985 (fire precautions in houses in multiple occupation) and the effect of an order – which may interfere with an easement. It appears that the exercise of such powers does not extinguish the easement: see *Jones v Cleanthi* [2006] EWCA Civ 1712, right of way and access to bin store blocked off. This point may arise, eg, where an order under Part XI requires an aperture to be closed up. It seems from that authority that any right of light enjoyed by the apertures will not be extinguished once and for all.

The effect of the exercise of the statutory powers to override or acquire

8.61   Where the effect of compulsory acquisition is to interfere with a right to light enjoyed over the land compulsorily acquired, the general principle is that if the interference would have been actionable, but for being authorised by statute, the dominant owner has no right to action.[101] Instead, he may make a claim for compensation for injurious affection of his land, depending on the statutory provisions under which the compulsory acquisition has been authorised. Such a claim may be made under s 68 of the Lands Clauses Consolidation Act 1845, or s 10(1) of the Compulsory Purchase Act 1965. The measure of compensation is, in principle, the same as for damages in tort. The damage must not be too remote.[102] Betterment (ie the general increase in the value of the property affected by reason of the execution of the works) is not taken into account, so it should not be deducted from any loss in value overall.[103] When the obstruction of light interferes not only with windows in the claimant's building enjoying rights to light, but also with windows not enjoying such rights, compensation may be claimed for the effect on the building as a whole, not limited to damage arising from obstruction of the windows enjoying rights to light. This was decided in *Re London Tilbury and Southend Railway Company and Gowers Walk School Trustees*.[104] The basis for the decision was that the obstruction to the windows in the building which did not enjoy rights to light inevitably obstructed the light received by the windows that did.

Lord Esher MR said:[105]

> 'If . . . a person puts up buildings, the inevitable consequence of their erection being to obstruct ancient and modern lights, should not be taken to have foreseen that in obstructing the one he would obstruct the others. If that were proved in a common law action the plaintiff would be entitled to damages for the whole of the consequences of the wrongful act of obstructing ancient lights, which would include damage to the new as much as to the old lights. If so, it seems to me obvious that compensation must be given under the statute to the same extent.'

Lindley LJ stated:[106]

> ' . . . they [the railway company] have infringed the rights of the trustees by darkening certain ancient windows, and as a consequence of that they have diminished the value by an amount found by the arbitrator to be 1450*l*. That is the necessary consequence of their wrongful act. On what principle are the railway company not to pay for that diminution in value? The railway company say they might have blocked up all the modern windows; but to this the trustees may reply, that more than this has been done, that their rights have been infringed, and that, though no action will lie because the infringement is authorized by an Act of Parliament, their case falls within the 16th section of the Railways Clauses Act, and that the consequence is that full compensation must be made, which full compensation is the difference between the value of the land as it was and as it is at present.'

Lopes LJ put the matter succinctly:[107]

---

101   See *Brown v Heathlands Mental Health NHS Trust* [1996] 1 All ER 133.
102   *Rickett v Metropolitan Railway* (1867) LR 2 HL at 175.
103   *Eagle v Charing Cross Railway* (1867) LR 2 CP 638; *Halsbury's Laws of England*, [358]–[360].
104   (1889) 24 QBD 326, decided under s 16 of the Railways Clauses Consolidation Act 1845. Cf the same principle applied in the award of damages at common law. See Chapter 11 at **11.50–11.51**.
105   Ibid, at 329–330.
106   Ibid, at 332.
107   Ibid, at 332–333. See also Chapter 11 at **11.50**.

'... having regard to the position of the windows of the school buildings, it is physically impossible to obstruct the light to the new, without at the same time obstructing the light to the ancient windows.'

8.62   However, it is clear that no claim will be for injury which could not have been caused at common law,[108] although it seems that establishing a diminution in the value of the claimant's land may not be an essential prerequisite to a claim.[109] No claim lies for temporary interference caused by the execution of works, as opposed to the permanent obstruction resulting from the construction (once complete) on the land acquired.[110] The measure of compensation relates to injury to the land of the claimant, not to a loss personal to the landowner or relating to some particular use of his land.[111] There is no claim for a 'ransom' which the landowner might have sought to extract to grant a release of his rights.[112] This is in contrast to his private law position, where damages may be assessed on this basis, if an injunction is refused. Compensation is normally assessed by the Lands Tribunal,[113] acting either under the relevant statutory provision or s 1 of the Land Compensation Act 1961.

---

[108]   *Wildtree Hotels Ltd v Harrow London Borough Council* [2001] 2 AC 1.
[109]   *Eagle v Charing Cross Railway* (1867) LR 2 CP 638.
[110]   *Wildtree Hotels Ltd v Harrow London Borough Council* [2001] 2 AC 1.
[111]   *Argyle Motors (Birkenhead) Ltd v Birkenhead Corporation* [1974] 1 All ER 201, HL.
[112]   *Wrotham Park Settled Estates v Hertsmere Borough Council* [1993] 2 EGLR 15, CA.
[113]   See Chapter 11 at **11.119–11.127**.

Chapter 9

DEEDS REGULATING RIGHTS TO LIGHT

GENERALLY

9.1   Agreements between owners of nearby buildings with respect to rights of light and air are not uncommon where the buildings are located in established city centres. They are useful to facilitate development in various situations. First, they may contain an express grant of a right of light (this topic is dealt with in Chapter 5). Secondly, they may provide total or partial release of existing prescriptive rights of light, so enabling a nearby servient landowner to construct a new building which would otherwise infringe the rights of light in question. Thirdly, they may take the form of a mutual agreement between landowners that each of them will in future be entitled to raise his own building within certain limits without objection by the other. Fourthly, they may provide that no prescriptive easement of light will in future be acquired in favour of the windows in a proposed or indeed already constructed new development which has not yet acquired such rights. This particular aspect of the topic is discussed more fully in Chapter 7. These four basic ingredients may be combined in the same document. Such agreements are normally by deed, given that they involve dispositions of land, but there are no prescribed or generally adopted forms and, in practice, their phraseology and content differ quite widely.[1] This and the absence of significant numbers of reported decisions of the courts on disputed issues arising from such deeds inevitably complicates discussion of the subject. What follows therefore is more in the nature of general guidance which is not necessarily definitive.

9.2   The following will be considered in more detail:

- terms providing for payment of compensation;

- terms allowing infringement of existing lights;

- terms authorising the construction of new buildings, and whether in any particular case they are restrictive or permissive;

- terms excluding the future acquisition of rights of light;

- the legal effectiveness of rights of light deeds;

- the effect of the Contracts (Rights of Third Parties) Act 1999; and

- some points for draftsmen will also be briefly noted.

---

[1]   For forms of grants of easements of light generally, see *Encyclopaedia of Forms and Precedents* (Butterworths, 2005 reissue) vol 13(1), paras 1670–1681.

TERMS PROVIDING FOR PAYMENT OF COMPENSATION

9.3   Where the parties have agreed that a sum is to be paid for permission to erect a new building, the deed will provide for this. The deed should specify whether the payment is inclusive or exclusive of VAT. A time for payment should be specified if the sum to be paid is intended to be compensation for the effect of a new building on the light received through the windows of the building of the payee. The permission given by the payee for the new building should be expressed to be conditional upon such payment being actually made.

9.4   In some cases, the deed will simply contain a recital that the sum has been paid. The function of recitals is to narrate the history leading up to the making of the agreement in question or to express in general terms the intention with which the agreement was made.[2] Recitals are an aid to construction, but they cannot control, cut down or qualify operative parts of the contract which are clear.[3] The effect of a recital that a certain sum has been paid is not, in equity, conclusive against an original party, but may be relied on by a subsequent purchaser provided he has no notice of non-payment.[4]

TERMS ALLOWING INFRINGEMENT OF EXISTING LIGHTS

9.5   It is usual, where the deed is intended to give permission for a development which would infringe the dominant owner's right to light, for the deed to recite the fact that the dominant owner has certain rights which will be affected by the new development of the servient owner. It is highly desirable for the deed to incorporate drawings showing the location of the windows in question in plan and elevation. Failure to do so can lead to uncertainty, increasing over time as buildings are altered and plans mislaid, as to which windows in the dominant building were acknowledged to have rights of light and in respect of which the permission relates. The purposes of such provisions are, first, to make it clear that the subject matter of the deed is relaxation of existing rights to light enjoyed by the dominant owner and, secondly, to preclude the servient owner from seeking to evade the provisions of the deed by arguing that the dominant owner's building did not in fact enjoy rights of light at all. In this regard it is important to note the distinction between provisions which allow existing rights of light to be overridden, and those which may have the effect of preventing rights of light coming into existence in the future by virtue of prescription.[5] A provision which allows the construction of a new building notwithstanding its effect on existing rights to light will not operate as a general release of current rights of light except insofar as the new building affects them (as to which see **9.14**), nor will it preclude the dominant owner from acquiring rights of light from new windows in his building in future, unless this is specifically provided for. The draftsman therefore needs to consider whether the agreement should address and provide for these matters. This may be particularly important if the dominant owner wishes in the future to redevelop his own building and wishes to be free of the risk of the owners of the new building asserting rights of light against him. Often the deed permitting a new building owner may contain express provisions allowing the dominant

---

[2]   See K Lewison *The Interpretation of Contracts* (Thomson Sweet & Maxwell, 3rd edn, 2004) ('Lewison') para 10.09.

[3]   Lewison, paras 10.10, 10.11.

[4]   Lewison , para 10.18, and see Law of Property Act 1925, s 68.

[5]   *Marlborough (West End) Ltd v Wilks Head and Eve* [1996] NLD 138. Referred to in *Midtown Ltd v City of London Real Property Co Ltd* [2005] 1 EGLR 65.

owner to redevelop his building in future, subject to agreed restrictions on the dimensions of any new building. Since the form of the new building will not have been fixed, these limits are defined schematically by light angles (see **9.15–9.16**).

9.6   Deeds may, for example, contain a provision which entitles the covenantee (dominant owner) to alter his building, notwithstanding that the light to the permitted building is affected. Frequently, this is backed up by a provision that the light to the relevant windows of the permitted building is to be regarded as enjoyed by the consent of the owner of the dominant building. Another common provision is one to the effect that the agreement is to enure for the benefit and burden of both parties, and to apply to successors in title, and to be an agreement within s 3 of the Prescription Act 1832, so that there is to be no prescriptive acquisition of a right to light in respect of the permitted building. It is possible for such terms to bind the freeholder of the dominant land even though he is not a party and the tenant of that land has entered into such an agreement.[6]

TERMS AUTHORISING THE CONSTRUCTION OF NEW BUILDINGS

9.7   Terms under which one owner authorises the other owner to construct a new building, notwithstanding the possible effect of this on the light received by the building of the owner giving authorisation, lie at the heart of most rights of light deeds. Frequently they give rise to problems of interpretation, due to failure of those who drafted them to identify the extent and effect of the permission granted. For the purpose of the discussion it is assumed the authority has been given by a dominant owner to a servient owner, but this is not necessarily the only situation which arises in practice. For example, the dominant owner may himself wish to incorporate in the deed permission to extend or replace his own existing building some time in the future, and to guard against the chance that this may raise issues as to its effect on the light to the servient owner's new building.

9.8   The first issue which can arise is whether the authorised building is restricted to the actual building which is proposed at the time of the deed (presuming it was duly constructed), or whether the permission is wide enough to encompass some or all of:

(1)   the right to replace the authorised building in the event of its accidental destruction;

(2)   the right to demolish the authorised building and rebuild it;

(3)   as in (2) above, but allowing the servient owner to replace the authorised building with one of different external design provided the external dimensions of the authorised building are not exceeded;

(4)   as in (2) above but allowing the owner to replace the authorised building with one which may or may not be of greater or lesser external dimensions than the authorised building but which replacement does not have any greater affect on the light being received over the land of the owner granting authorisation than the authorised building.

---

6   See Chapter 6 at **6.24**.

A further issue which arises is the territorial extent of the effect of the deed. Do any limits on the dimensions and design of the authorised building apply to the whole of it, including parts remote from the dominant owner's windows, or only to those parts which are relevant to the dominant owner's light?

9.9   Many deeds are framed by reference to a particular proposed building to be erected by the servient owner, and provide that the servient owner is at liberty to erect a building as shown on certain drawings, which are defined as 'the works'. This provision is often reinforced by a provision to the effect that the consent is limited to the execution of the works as defined 'but not further or otherwise' or by a provision that the works cannot be varied without the consent of the dominant owner.

9.10   By reference to the questions identified in the preceding paragraph, it is thought that, based on general reasoning and the authorities discussed below, as far as (1) and (2) are concerned, in general the permission granted by such a deed allows rebuilding to the same design both in the event of accidental destruction and following demolition. The intent of the deed is to confer a permanent permission without limit of time. As to (3), the same reasoning would seem to apply. The words 'not further or otherwise' are apt (at least in the absence of counter-indications) only to apply to external dimensions and not to detailed design matters, which cannot have been contemplated as being relevant to the effect of the authorised building on the light of the dominant owner.

9.11   Question (4) is less straightforward. Computer-aided design enables the effect on light of buildings of different massing to be calculated accurately, and may produce a structure which offers more internal space than a building within the envelope of the authorised building without affecting the light of the dominant owner more, but which in some parts exceeds the dimensions of the authorised building (but may be smaller than those dimensions in other parts). It could be argued that since the purpose of the deed is to protect light and air, provided the proposed building has no greater effect than one built within the dimensions of the authorised building, the deed allows it. On the other hand, there are objections to this argument. First, the impact of the new design may have been carefully tailored to the current window configuration of the dominant owner's building and produce less satisfactory results by comparison with the authorised building if this were to change. Secondly, the intention of the deed may generally be discerned as limiting the effect on light by restricting the size of any new building. The mechanism adopted may be criticised as crude, but construing the deed as if it intended to adopt a mechanism using a light standard base reference point could be said to go beyond legitimate processes of construction. To some extent the issue depends on the particular wording used, and how far the dimensions of the authorised building are given prominence in the deed by citing them or incorporating scale drawings. In general, however, it is thought that wording of this kind does indeed restrict the external dimensions of any new building within those of the authorised building.

9.12   In this connection a distinction is sometimes drawn between *permissive* and *restrictive* deeds. A *restrictive* deed is one which, on its true construction, limits the permission to one particular building in terms of profile and dimensions. A *permissive* deed is said to be is one which grants permission for any building provided that the effect of it on the light of the authorising owner is no greater than the particular building in contemplation. This approach to construction is useful but tends to mask the range of possible issues noted above.

9.13   Where the words of the deed are not clear, it is necessary to approach questions of construction by considering all the terms of the deed, and the matrix of fact including anything which would have affected the way in which the language of the document would have been understood by a reasonable man.[7] However, evidence of the subjective intention of the parties is not admissible.[8] Thus in *Rabin v Gerson Berger Association Limited*,[9] it was held that evidence of the advice of counsel was not admissible to interpret a deed prepared on the basis of that advice. Likewise, oral evidence is generally inadmissible to add, vary or contradict the deed.[10]

9.14   Authorities on rights of light deeds support the general approach indicated above. In *Cemp Properties (UK) Limited v Dentsply Research and Development Corporation (No 2)*,[11] a deed executed in 1934 allowed the servient owner to erect a new building. The deed provided that he should:

> '... have full liberty and power to erect the new building in accordance with the plan annexed hereto but not otherwise.'

The plan showed a three-storey building which permitted light to the bottom sill of a window (described as window B in the deed) at an angle of 54.5° from the horizontal. The permission given by the deed was determinable on notice. Morritt J said:[12]

> 'The other point at issue is whether the 1934 deed would permit the erection of a new building so as to infringe the rights to light of the five apertures to the same, but to no greater extent than the 1934 deed allowed. The third recital states that the building owner:
>
> > "... is desirous of erecting ... new buildings of greater height which threaten to interfere with the ancient lights ... and to diminish the access of light and air ... and the plan annexed hereto indicates the manner in which such ancient lights will be effected."
>
> The plan referred to merely shows the flank wall of the proposed new building consisting of a ground and three upper floors topped by a parapet. Various light angles are shown, the material one being a line which shows that the top of the parapet permits the access of light to window B at an angle of 55.5. There is no other indication of the nature or design of the new building.
>
> Clause 1 provided that:
>
> > "... the building owner and the persons rightfully claiming under it shall have full liberty and power to erect the said new buildings in accordance with the said plan annexed hereto but not otherwise."
>
> Clause 2 enabled the owners of 1–5 Poland Street at any time thereafter to raise the height or alter the elevation of 1–5 Poland Street or to pull down and erect any new buildings according to such plans and elevations and in such manner as they should consider proper.

---

7   *Investors Compensation Scheme Ltd v West Bromwich Building Society* [1998] 1 All ER 98, HL; see also *Prenn v Simmonds* [1971] 3 All ER 237; *Reardon Smith Line Limited v Hansen-Tangen* [1976] 3 All ER 570, HL.

8   *Stroude v Beazer Homes Ltd* [2005] EWCA 265.

9   [1986] 1 All ER 374. See *Investors Compensation Scheme Ltd v West Bromwich Building Society* [1998] 1 All ER 98 at 114J per Lord Hoffmann.

10   *Jacobs v Batavia and General Plantations Limited* [1924] 1 Ch 287; *Rabin v Gerson Berger Association Limited* [1986] 1 All ER 374; Lewison op cit, para 2.07.

11   [1989] 2 EGLR 196.

12   Ibid, at 202C–202E.

...

In my judgment the 1934 deed authorised any building provided that it did not infringe the rights to light to the five apertures to any greater extent than the plan indicated. The permission granted was not expressed to be temporary. The purpose of the deed and the plan showed that the parties were concerned only with position and height of the flank wall of the proposed new building. The parties were not concerned at all with which particular bricks formed the wall and the parapet. In my judgment, therefore, on a proper construction of the 1934 deed, the owners of the site were entitled to put up a new building with a flank wall facing 1–5 Poland Street in the same position and to the same height as shown on the plan.'

9.15 In the *Cemp* case, the two important features of the deed were that the outline of the new building was shown purely schematically, and there was a light angle shown running from a particular window sill. The use of a light angle or angles tends to show that there is less concern with the particular permitted building, and that the true intent is simply to prevent construction beyond the line formed by the angle.

9.16 The effect of the incorporation of plans and sections of the parts of the authorised building nearest to the building of the dominant owner, and the territorial extent of the effect of the deed, were considered in *Mayor and Commonalty and Citizens of the City of London and another v Intercede (1765) Ltd and another*.[13] A mutual right of light deed between two owners with buildings on opposite sides of the street allowed the owner of one of the buildings to erect a new building to a height not exceeding the height indicated by the red colour on a drawing. The drawing showed only the facades of the buildings. In the case of the relevant building the drawing also showed two heights, 80 ft to the pediment and 108 ft 3 in to the top of the facade. It also showed a line with an angle of 75° running from the outside edge of the pediment to the top of the facade. The owner of the relevant building wished to develop it with a building higher than 108 ft 3 in. The other owner contended that the deed prohibited any development of the relevant building exceeding 108 ft 3 in in height over the whole site of it. The court held that the height restriction only applied at the facade, and that it was permissible to exceed the height restriction provided the higher part was sufficiently far from the street facade not to intersect the line.

9.17 Whether a deed authorising construction of a new building has any effect on the dominant owner's rights to light beyond waiving his right to complain that the erection of the authorised building and, depending on the answer to the issues identified above, any successor building is a nuisance depends on the words used. It is unlikely that the dominant owner would be taken to have waived his right to sue for nuisance arising from excessive noise and vibration arising from the construction works, and probably he could not be restrained from challenging the planning permission for the new building in the absence of any express term to that effect, since the waiver only extends to his common law rights.

9.18 In the absence of any provision to the contrary, the authorisation will not by implication grant any immediate right of light to the authorised building. The authorised building will, however, in due course, acquire rights of light by prescription over the dominant owner's building. This situation arose in *Marlborough (West End) Ltd v Wilks Head and Eve*[14] where the issue was whether the effect of a deed was to preclude the possibility of a prescriptive right to light arising in future. Deeds sometimes

---

13   [2005] EWHC 1691 (Ch).
14   20 December 1996, High Court of Justice, Chancery Division; [1996] NLD 138.

make provision to exclude this by wording designed to amount to an agreement in writing under s 3 of the Prescription Act 1832, either generally or by authorising the dominant owner to alter his own building in future, for example, by raising it up to a certain height. Whether such provisions are effective depends on their precise wording: see **6.25**. A mere reservation will not amount to such an agreement. There must be a positive authorisation to build notwithstanding any effect on light.

TERMS EXCLUDING THE FUTURE ACQUISITION OF RIGHTS OF LIGHT

9.19　As already noted, one aim of rights of light deeds may be to preclude the possibility of prescriptive rights of light arising in future under s 3 of the Prescription Act 1832 in favour of windows in a new building. The deed may thus provide it is to enure for the benefit and burden of both parties, and to apply to successors in title, and to be an agreement within s 3 of the Prescription Act 1832, so that there is to be no prescriptive acquisition of a right to light in respect of the permitted building. Section 3 of the Prescription Act 1832 makes specific provision for this in its wording:

> '. . . unless it shall appear that the same was enjoyed by some consent or agreement expressly made or given for that purpose by deed or writing . . .'

9.20　It is possible for such terms to bind the freeholder of the dominant land even though he is not a party and the tenant of that land has entered into such an agreement.[15] No registration of such an agreement seems to be required under the Land Registration Act 2002. There are ways, however, in which such agreements are affected by registration. First, on first registration the applicant is under a duty to make full disclosure to the Land Registry of relevant documents under r 24 of the Land Registration Rules 2003.[16] Under r 36 agreements preventing the acquisition of rights of light can be entered in the property register of the affected land. Secondly, on subsequent dispositions such agreements may be noted on the register under r 76. See, generally, Chapter 14.

LEGAL EFFECTIVENESS OF RIGHTS OF LIGHT DEEDS

9.21　Although the fact that rights to light deeds are frequently employed suggests that legal effectiveness is unquestioned, their legal enforceability can raise difficult questions.

Between original parties

9.22　No difficulty arises in principle where questions of enforcement arise between original parties to the deed. Ordinary contractual principles apply, so that both benefit and burden of the deed are fully enforceable, subject to the normal rule that injunctive relief, as opposed to claims for damages, is not granted as of right.[17]

---

[15]　See Chapter 6 at **6.24**.
[16]　SI 2003/1417.
[17]　See generally Chapter 11.

Position of successors in title

9.23   Rights to light deeds may have a somewhat hybrid quality, imposing various types of obligations, such as obligations not to build (or only to build to a certain extent), obligations to pay money, obligations to build and retain reflective wall coverings, and acknowledgements that light is enjoyed by licence only. As far as the position of successors in title is concerned, each of these categories can raise different questions.

9.24   Insofar as the deed in question restricts building, it can be regarded as imposing a restrictive covenant. Where the deed is permissive, it may be doubtful whether it can be regarded as imposing a restrictive covenant, but it is thought that since in substance the effect of a permissive deed is still to restrict the dimensions of a new building this point gives rise to no difficulty.[18] Assuming this is the case, the benefit of the restrictive covenant is taken by the owners of the land intended to be benefited, provided the benefit of the covenant is annexed to the land. Where the deed predates 1 January 1926 the rules relating to annexation of restrictive covenants require that the dominant and servient lands are clearly defined and that express words of annexation of the benefit of the covenant be used.[19] In the case of covenants entered into after 1925, s 78(1) of the Law of Property Act 1925 facilitates the annexation of the benefit of a covenant to land of the covenantee, provided the land intended to be benefited is clearly identified.[20] It is essential that the covenantee retains land capable of being benefited, and that it must be capable of being ascertained with reasonable certainty.[21]

9.25   As regards the burden of restrictive covenants, in the case of covenants entered into after 1925, they are not enforceable against purchasers for valuable consideration unless registered under the Land Registration Act 2002[22] or the Land Charges Act 1972.[23] It would therefore be prudent in the case of rights to light deeds to ensure that they are duly noted on the register of the covenantor's title.

9.26   In the case of other covenants, it is necessary to distinguish between transmissibility of benefit and burden. Dealing first with benefit, a successor in title may enforce a covenant provided:

- it touches and concerns land;[24]

- it relates to clearly identifiable land;

- it has been entered into with someone having an interest in the land intended to be benefited;[25]

- the person seeking to enforce the covenant must have an interest in the land;[26]

---

[18]   See A Francis *Restrictive Covenants and Freehold Land* (Jordans, 2nd edn, 2005) ('Francis') Ch 3, 3.1.

[19]   *J Sainsbury v plc v Enfield Borough Council* [1989] 1 EGLR 173.

[20]   *Federated Homes v Mill Lodge Properties* [1980] 1 All ER 371; *Crest Nicholson Residential (south) Ltd v McAllister* [2004] 1 WLR 2409, CA.

[21]   *Formby v Barker* [1903] 2 Ch 539; *Renals v Cowlishaw* (1879) 11 ChD 866; *Crest Nicholson Residential (South) Ltd v McAllister* [2004] 1 WLR 2409, CA; and see generally Francis, Ch 8.

[22]   Land Registration Act 2002, ss 11, 32.

[23]   Land Registration Act 1925, ss 20, 50; Land Charges Act 1972, s 2(5).

[24]   *P & A Swift Investments v Combined English Stores Group plc* [1989] AC 632; *Cardwell v Walker* [2004] 2 P & CR 9.

[25]   See Law of Property Act 1925, s 78(1).

[26]   Ibid; *Smith v River Douglas Catchment Board* [1949] 2 All ER 179, CA.

• the agreement must show an intention that the benefit of the covenant be transmissible.

9.27   In practice, it is likely that these requirements will be satisfied in many cases. The question of the transmission of the burden of covenants is, however, more problematic, since in the case of both positive covenants and negative covenants which are not restrictive covenants, the general rule is that successors in title are not bound. This rule was reaffirmed in *Rhone v Stephens*.[27] It is subject to various statutory exceptions,[28] but these are unlikely to have much practical impact.

9.28   The rule that the burden of positive covenants is not enforceable against successors in title explains why, where the dominant tenement benefits from natural light reflected from light-coloured glazed bricks on the servient owner's wall, this light is not taken into account when assessing whether some interference has or will occur. The reasoning is that there is no power to compel the servient owner to maintain the reflective surface in position or to clean it.[29] In practice, rights to light deeds do sometimes make provision to the effect that the new building shall contain glazed surfaces and that these shall be maintained. Such terms bind the original parties only.

9.29   Positive covenants may be enforced indirectly against successors under the principle relating to benefit and burden laid down in such cases as *Halsall v Brizell*,[30] under which, where a right over property is enjoyed on the condition of performance of a positive obligation, enjoyment of the right may be restrained if the positive obligation is not performed. Thus, in *Halsall v Brizell*, a deed relating to the development of land contained provisions granting rights of way to owners of individual plots, and further provisions imposing on them an obligation to contribute to common upkeep costs. It was held that a successor to an original covenantor who owned the plot was liable to contribute to the upkeep costs, Upjohn J saying:[31]

> 'If the defendants did not desire to take the benefit of this deed, for the reasons that I have given they could not be under any liability to pay the obligations thereunder. They do desire, however, to take the benefit of this deed. They have no right to use the sewers which are vested in the plaintiffs, and I cannot see that they have any right, apart from the deed, to use the roads of the park which lead to their particular house . . . the defendants cannot rely on any way of necessity nor on any right by prescription, for the simple reason that, when the house was originally sold in 1851 to their predecessor in title, he took the house on the terms of the deed of 1851 which contractually bound him to contribute a proper proportion of the expenses of maintaining the roads and sewers, and so forth, as a condition of being entitled to make use of those roads and sewers. Therefore it seems to me that the defendants cannot, if they desire to use their house as they do, take advantage of the trusts concerning the user of the roads contained in the deed and the other benefits created by it without undertaking the obligations thereunder. On that principle it seems to me that they are bound by this deed, if they desire to take its benefits.'

---

27   [1994] 2 AC 310.
28   For example, Local Government (Miscellaneous Provisions) Act 1982, s 33; Town and Country Planning Act 1990, s 106.
29   *Dent v Auction Mart Co* (1866) LR 2 Eq 238 at 251–252. See Chapter **3.47**.
30   [1957] Ch 169.
31   Ibid.

9.30   It is clear that the principle does not extend so as to oblige the successor to a covenantor to perform positive obligations if he wishes to take any benefit under a deed, but is restricted to those obligations intimately connected with his enjoyment of property rights.[32]

THE EFFECT OF THE CONTRACTS (RIGHTS OF THIRD PARTIES) ACT 1999

9.31   The Contracts (Rights of Third Parties) Act 1999 reformed the rule of privity, which, in general terms, prevents a person who is not a party to a contract enforcing that contract, or taking a benefit under it.[33] The Act allows a person who is not a party to a contract to enforce a term of it if either the contract expressly provides that he may, or if the term sought to be enforced purports to confer a benefit on him. The latter alternative right to enforce is excluded if it appears that the parties did not intend the term to be enforceable by the third party.[34]

9.32   The third party who claims the right to enforce the term must be expressly identified in the contract, either by name, or as a member of a class, or as assuming a particular description. But he need not be in existence when the contract is entered into.[35]

9.33   The remedies available to a third party are those remedies which would have been available to him had he been a party to the contract, but any enforcement is subject to and must be in accordance with any terms of the contract.[36]

9.34   Section 2 of the 1999 Act contains restrictions upon the manner and extent to which the principal parties can rescind, vary or extinguish rights under the contract so as to affect the third party's rights. The remaining sections of the Act[37] concern procedural matters in enforcement proceedings by the third party, and specific exception of contracts from the Act.

9.35   The impact of the 1999 Act upon the agreements relating to rights to light would appear to be as follows:

(1)   The Act affects only the rights of a third party to enforce a term of the contract where it expressly says he may, or where the term is for his benefit. The third party cannot be liable for the burden of agreements unless he is an actual party to the agreement.

(2)   Agreement to grant rights to light may, conceivably, confer a benefit on others, such as adjoining landowners. Unless the contracting parties define who is the third party with the (potential) right to enforce the term, the Act will have no

---

[32]   *Rhone v Stephens* [1994] 2 AC 310 per Lord Templeman; distinguishing *Tito v Waddell (No 2)* [1977] 3 All ER 129. See also *Thamesmead Town Ltd v Allotey* [1998] 3 EGLR 97, CA.

[33]   The Act came into force on 11 November 1999, but does not apply to contracts entered into between that date and 11 May 2000, unless the contract specifically provides that the Act is to apply to it. In respect of contracts made after 11 May 2000, the application of the Act is as described above.

[34]   Section 1(1) and (2).

[35]   Section 1(3). See *Avraamides v Colwill* [2007] BLR 76.

[36]   Section 1(4) and (5).

[37]   Sections 3–8.

bearing on the matter whether there is an express provision as to third party enforcement, or whether there is a purported conferment of benefit.[38] Thus, it is only where the contract to grant the right has, as its aim, the inclusion of others as beneficiaries of the grant, that the Act will have any relevance.

For instance, if there is a contract for the sale of land between A and B, and A is retaining adjoining land, and A, as a term of the contract, agrees to execute a grant of light over his retained land in B's favour, only C, another adjoining landowner, could not enforce that term.[39] But if such a contract incorporated a further term that C could ask for a grant of light in his favour from A, or if C was defined in the contract as a person in existence and having the potential right to enforce the term, the Act would give C the right to do so.

(3)   The same principles set out at (2) above will apply to other contracts concerning rights to light, such as agreements to vary such rights, or to extinguish or release them. In the case of such variation and release, one foreseeable difficulty created by the Act is the right of third parties, such as tenants in one of the buildings affected, to claim the benefit of a contract to vary or release rights. For example, it may be that a variation or release has been agreed between the parties in terms by which it is intended that such tenants are *not* to have rights to light which they may enjoy varied or released. Conversely, the parties may want to bind everyone to a variation or release, in which case the agreement should be carefully drawn so as to achieve this. In the former case, the parties to the agreement should exclude the right of third parties to enforce any terms under the Act by expressly stating that: (i) the parties do not intend that any terms of the agreement are to be enforceable by any person not a party; and (ii) (for the avoidance of doubt) rights conferred by the Act are excluded from persons who might otherwise be within its scope. In the latter case, where the aim of a variation or release is to encompass all those with potential rights to light, there should be no need to consider any exclusion or modification of rights under the Act in view of the fact that all persons who are intended to be caught by the variation or release are either parties, or will be made expressly subject to the burden of the agreement by those having a higher title.[40]

9.36   In general terms, the 1999 Act requires the parties, and those drafting agreements for them, to consider whether any terms are going to have an effect on the rights of third parties, and whether such third parties ought to have the right to enforce any terms of the agreement between the principal parties. It is suggested that, in the context of rights to light, the answer to the last question will be no, and, therefore, the sensible course is to exclude the Act expressly.

DRAFTING ISSUES

9.37   Deeds should always contain plans and sections of the existing and proposed buildings sufficient to establish the precise parameters of the permissions or limitations confirmed or imposed in the text. These should be cross-referred to the relevant paragraphs of the operative part of the deed. In some cases, it may be useful to supplement these with isometric preparations of the affected area, to show the relationship of the relevant buildings.

---

[38]   Section 1(1) and (3).
[39]   Even s 56 of the Law of Property Act 1925 could not come to his aid: *Beswick v Beswick* [1968] AC 58.
[40]   See Chapter 8 at **8.3**.

PERPETUITIES

9.38 A grant of an easement arising at a future date can offend the rule against remoteness of vesting which is one branch of the rule against perpetuities. If a grant infringes the rule, the grant may be void. The law of perpetuity and, in particular, the rule against remoteness of vesting, is complex and the reader is referred to textbooks on Property Law such as *Megarry & Wade: The Law of Real Property* in its current edition.[41] However, the immediate grant of such an easement, such as an easement of light, will not offend the rule provided it takes effect immediately, or within a defined period; such as the period allowed, under the Perpetuities and Accumulations Act 1964, s 1, of 80 years. It seems clear that a 'consent' under s 3 of the Prescription Act 1832 is not the grant of a legal interest, so the perpetuity rules and in particular, the rule against remoteness of vesting, have no application to such consents. The fact that a prescriptive easement of light may ripen at a future date into a legal easement does not, it is suggested, bring the rule against remoteness of vesting into play. Finally, the fact that a right of light may be broken at a future date does not bring about the vesting of any interest at that date, so once again the Perpetuity Rule has no application.[42]

CHECKLIST

9.39 The following points may provide a useful checklist for rights of light deeds:

- whether the deed is permissive or restrictive in terms;[43]

- the extent to which the design of the permitted building may be changed;

- where the size or height of new building is restricted, whether the restrictions apply to the whole site of the permitted building , or only to some parts, for example, those directly affecting the dominant owner's light;

- whether the permitted building may be demolished and replaced with some other building within certain defined parameters, for example, of height and within defined light angles;

- whether the permitted building can be rebuilt in the case of accidental loss;

- provisions preventing windows in the permitted building acquiring future rights of light over the dominant owner's building;

- provisions allowing the dominant owner to redevelop his own building at some time in the future notwithstanding any effect on the permitted building.

9.40 Certain general points, common to all deeds, must be taken into account:

(1) In order to be legally effective, it is desirable that all those interested in each property be parties to the deed, including mortgagees. Otherwise, there is a risk

---

[41] See *Dunn v Blackdown Properties* [1961] Ch 433 and C Harpum *Megarry & Wade: The Law of Real Property* (Sweet & Maxwell, 6th edn, 1999) at 7-023, 7-130 and 7-135.

[42] See *Dano v Earl Cadogan* [2003] 2 P&CR 10 for the application of this principle to Restrictive Covenants.

[43] See **9.12**.

that the deed may prove impossible to enforce against a recalcitrant owner of some interest in one of the areas of land concerned. There may also, of course, be difficulties for a party who seeks to rely on the deed if he or his predecessor was not a party.

(2) Where the deed on its true construction is intended to be made with a party, and that party is named in the deed, that party is entitled to enforce covenants of the covenantor even though he has not himself executed the deed. The rationale of this rule is that since there is no obligation placed on the covenantee, it is not essential that he should have executed the deed before he can enforce it.

(3) Even where obligations are imposed on the covenantee, he may be able to enforce the deed notwithstanding that he has not executed it.[44] Where the covenantor has not executed the deed, he will not be bound at law but he may be bound in equity if he takes the benefit of property under the same deed.[45] Section 1 of the Law of Property (Miscellaneous Provisions) Act 1989 has relaxed the requirements for the execution of a deed, by removing certain formal requirements. However, by s 1(2), an instrument is not to be a deed unless it makes clear on its face that it is intended to be a deed by the person making it or the parties to it whether by describing itself as a deed or expressing itself to be executed or signed as a deed or otherwise. The deed must also be validly executed. Section 1(3) of the same Act prescribes the method of execution of a deed by an individual.

(4) Section 56(1) of the Law of Property Act 1925 extends those persons who may take the benefit of a covenant, by enabling any party who can show that, as a matter of construction, the benefit of a covenant is intended to be vested in him to take the benefit of it even though he is not named as a party to the deed.[46]

(5) It is normal for rights to light deeds to recite the interest of each of the parties to the deed in the property concerned, as freeholder, mortgagee, and lessee or otherwise. In practice, depending on the subject matter of the deed, it may not be necessary for those holding only short-term leases to be parties, and this may not be practical in the case of a building of multiple occupation. It is, of course, always necessary to bear in mind that if such parties enjoy rights to light which are to be infringed by a development of a neighbouring building, their rights will not be affected by agreement between the freeholders of their building and the owner of the site on which the new building is to be erected. It is necessary, therefore, to make separate provision for compensation for their loss, assuming the right to claim such compensation is not excluded by the terms of their leases (in practice, relatively unlikely except where the new building is owned by their lessor).

(6) Where the deed provides for an easement to arise in the future, the rule against perpetuities applies. Therefore, the deed must be framed to ensure that the easement cannot arise further in the future within 21 years after the expiration of lives in being or a specified number of years not exceeding 80.[47] When land is not

---

[44]   *Morgan v Pike* (1854) 14 CB 473; *Northampton Gas Light Co v Parnel* (1855) 15 CB 630.

[45]   *Formby v Barker* [1903] 2 Ch 539.

[46]   *Re Ecclesiastical Commissioners for England's Conveyance* [1936] Ch 430; *Beswick v Beswick* [1968] AC 58. See also **9.33** in respect of rights under the Contracts (Rights of Third Parties) Act 1999.

[47]   Perpetuities and Accumulations Act 1964, s 1(1).

described at the date of the grant as part of the dominant tenement, a provision for it to be designated as such in the future will be used for perpetuity.[48]

(7)   Registration of provisions which create restrictive covenants in the charges register of the burdened property will be required.

---

48   *London and Blenheim Estates Ltd v Ladbroke Retail Parks Ltd* [1993] 4 All ER 157, CA.

Chapter 10

PROCEEDINGS FOR INFRINGEMENT OF RIGHTS TO LIGHT I – CAUSES OF ACTION, PARTIES, LIMITATION AND VENUE

CAUSES OF ACTION

10.1 Actionable interference with a right to light constitutes the tort of private nuisance. The term 'nuisance' is properly applied only to such unreasonable use of land as interferes with the enjoyment by the plaintiff of rights in land.[1] Nuisances may be of various kinds and may involve (a) encroachment on the claimant's land, (b) physical damage to his land or buildings, works or vegetation thereon, or (c) undue interference with the comfort and enjoyment of his land. In the case of nuisances of the first two kinds, the character of the neighbourhood is not relevant in deciding whether a nuisance has occurred.[2] It appears to be the case that injury to a right of light falls within the second category.[3] It is certain that in the case of an injury to an easement of light the character of the neighbourhood is not relevant. 'The human eye requires as much light for comfortable reading or sewing in Darlington Street, Wolverhampton, as in Mayfair.'[4] There is a peculiarity in claims for nuisance for infringement of easements (including rights of light) that the action can succeed only if an easement is established to exist. Generally, ordinary claims for nuisance depend simply on whether the matters complained of are an actionable wrong under the general law.[5]

10.2 It is established that no claim lies for invasion of privacy by overlooking or obstruction of a view or prospect.[6] Where the right to light is protected by a contract, an action lies against the contract breaker under the terms of the agreement. The same applies where breach of a right to light deed is in question.

10.3 Restrictive covenants may have the effect of preventing the erection of buildings which interfere with light, and they may also be employed to protect privacy and views by prohibiting the erection of buildings on the land burdened by the covenant.

---

[1] Newark 'The Boundaries of Nuisance' (1949) 65 LQR 480, cited by Lord Goff of Chieveley in *Hunter and Others v Canary Wharf Ltd* [1997] AC 655, HL at 687G, and referred to in *Hussain v Lancaster City Council* (1998) 77 P&CR 89, CA at 108–109 per Hirst LJ.

[2] *St Helens Smelting Co v Tipping* (1865) 11 HLC 642 at 650 per Lord Westbury; *Halsey v Esso Petroleum Co Ltd* [1961] 1 WLR 683.

[3] In *St Helens Smelting Co v Tipping* Lord Westbury considered that material injury to property included 'sensible injury to the value of property'. This suggests that where the effect of the activities on the enjoyment of the property is significant the character of the neighbourhood may not be relevant even if there is no physical injury to property.

[4] *Hortons' Estate Ltd v James Beattie Ltd* [1927] 1 Ch 75 at 78.

[5] For the requirements of the tort of nuisance generally, see *Halsbury's Laws of England* (4th edn, reissue 1997) vol 34, paras 9–14 and 16–30.

[6] See, generally, Chapter 2 at **2.6**.

Restrictive covenants may, in appropriate cases, be in force against the owner for the time being of the servient land by the owner for the time being of the dominant land, even where there is no privity of contract or estate between them.[7]

PARTIES

Claimants

10.4   It is established that in order to maintain an action in private nuisance, the claimant must be the owner or occupier of the land affected.[8] Therefore, a person on premises as a mere licensee has no right of action.[9] Thus, in principle, a right of action is available to freeholders, tenants in occupation, and others with a legal right to occupy the premises affected but not to licensees.[10] In the case of tenants, the protection extends only to those in whom the tenancy is vested at the date of the wrong, hence a tenant who has assigned his interest cannot make a claim, even if he subsequently resumes possession following the absconding of the assignee. Presumably, the same rule would apply where, following the insolvency of the assignee and the disclaimer by its liquidator of the term of the lease under the Insolvency Act 1986, a vesting order is made in favour of the original tenant or an intermediate assignee under ss 181 and 182 of that Act.

10.5   Those who have legal interests in the premises, whether as freehold or leasehold, may maintain an action in nuisance provided the injury to light affects the permanent value of their interest. Thus, in *Shelfer v City of London Electric Lighting Co*,[11] it was held that a reversioner had a right of action where his property was injured by vibration from the operation of a generating station. In *Jesser v Gifford*[12] it was held that a reversioner could sue in respect of damage caused by obstruction to ancient lights.[13] In *Midtown Ltd v City of London Real Property Co Ltd*[14] the court was prepared to allow a claim for damages of a landlord of commercial premises (let to tenants) which had purchased the freehold as a speculative investment. It is not clear whether a reversioner can bring an action to prevent a right of light being acquired over his land. This situation could arise where new windows are constructed by an adjoining owner which receive light over the land of the neighbour. Unless some action is taken to obstruct the new windows, they will acquire rights to light after 20 years enjoyment under s 3 of the Prescription Act 1832. In practice, the reversioner's remedy would be to register a light obstruction notice under s 2 of the Rights of Light Act 1959.[15]

---

7   For the law of restrictive covenants, see A Francis *Restrictive Covenants and Freehold Land: A Practitioners' Guide* (Jordans, 2nd edn, 2005).

8   *Hunter and Others v Canary Wharf Ltd* [1997] AC 655, HL.

9   *Hunter and Others v Canary Wharf Ltd* [1997] AC 655, HL at 692 per Lord Goff of Chieveley overruling *Khorasandjian v Bush* [1993] 3 All ER 669, CA. For the position of premises occupied collectively by companies in the same group as licensees, see *Butcher Robinson & Staples Ltd v London Regional Transport* [1999] 36 EG 165. See also Murdoch 'Who can sue in Nuisance?' *Estates Gazette* (1999) No 28, 17 July, p 120 and **11.30**.

10 For the distinction between a lease and a licence, see *Street v Mountford* [1985] AC 809, and generally *Hill & Redman's Law of Landlord and Tenant* vol 1, paras 549–900. In general, a person in exclusive possession of premises paying rent will be considered a tenant.

11 (1895) 1 Ch 287, CA.

12 (1767) 4 Burr 2141.

13 See also *Wilson v Townend* (1860) 1 Drew & Sm 324; *Shadwell v Hutchinson* (1829) 3 C&P 615.

14 [2005] 1 EGLR 65.

15 See generally Chapter 7. Reversioners (including long leaseholders with intermediate interests) would be 'owners' within s 7 of the 1959 Act.

Defendants

10.6   The liability of the actual tortfeasor is undoubted: it is not necessary to establish that he owns the servient tenement. Thus, in the case of a building infringing a right to light, the contractor erecting the building may be liable for creating the nuisance.[16] Liability of the tortfeasor continues in respect of consequential damage, even after he has parted with possession of the building and is unable to remedy the situation.[17] It is not necessary for the tortfeasor to have any interest in the land in question. Liability may also arise not only in respect of acts actually done, but also in respect of acts authorised, where the person in question has power to prevent the acts being done. So in *Ridewood v Jalnarne*[18] an owner of a dominant tenement over which a right of way ran was held liable for the wrongful acts of visitors who parked on the roadway. It was present when the illegal parking occurred, had the ability to prevent it by terminating the licence of those parking illegally to use the right of way, and permitted the illegal activities to continue. In *Chartered Trust Plc v Davies*,[19] a case involving a claim for derogation from grant under a lease, a landlord of a shopping mall was held liable to one of his tenants for the effect on the tenant's business for authorising the erection of a pawnbrokers' sign outside an adjacent unit, and failing to prevent queuing by prospective customers of the pawnbroker in the common parts of the mall.[20] In *Lippiatt v South Gloucestershire County Council*[21] a landowner was held liable for repeated acts of nuisance committed on neighbouring land by travellers whom it knew to be based on its land.

10.7   An occupier of land is liable for a nuisance even though he has not created it, if he continues it while in occupation.[22] An occupier is also liable for nuisance created after he becomes the occupier if he has actual or constructive notice of its existence, or if he continues a nuisance with actual or constructive notice of its existence, and does not take reasonable steps to bring it to an end.[23] Making use of a building which constitutes a nuisance amounts to adoption.[24]

10.8   Where a person purchases a building which is let to tenants, he is liable for nuisance created by the original reversioner, even though he has no right to abate the nuisance under the terms of the lease.[25]

10.9   Therefore, in general, the persons who are likely to be responsible in law for nuisances caused by the erection of obstructions to light will include the following:

(1)   the building contractor erecting the building;

(2)   the landowner on whose land the building is being erected, if the building is being erected with his authority;

---

[16]   *Thompson v Gibson* (1841) 7 M&W 456.
[17]   *Rosewell v Prior* (1701) 12 Mod 635 at 639.
[18]   (1989) 61 P&CR 143.
[19]   [1997] 2 EGLR 83, CA.
[20]   Cf the earlier case of *Hilton v James Smith & Sons (Norwood) Ltd* [1979] 2 EGLR 44.
[21]   (1999) *The Times*, April 9, CA.
[22]   *Rosewell v Prior* (1701) 12 Mod 635; *Thompson v Gibson* (1841) 7 M&W 456.
[23]   *Goldman v Hargrave* [1966] 2 All ER 989, PC; *Leakey v National Trust for Places of Historic Interest or Natural Beauty* [1980] 1 All ER 17, CA; *Sedleigh-Denfield v O'Callaghan* [1940] 3 All ER 349, HL.
[24]   *Sedleigh-Denfield v O'Callaghan* [1940] 3 All ER 349 at 358 per Viscount Maugham.
[25]   *Sampson v Hodson-Pressenger* [1981] 3 All ER 710.

(3)   the tenant or other occupier directly authorising the erection of the building in question.

10.10 Where the servient tenement changes hands, the new owner will be liable for continuing the nuisance. Where the servient property is the subject of a lease, the general rule is that the landlord is not liable for nuisaces committed by his tenant unless he has authorised the tenant to commit the nuisance. But where the landlord has powers of management of his property sufficient to pursue the cessation of the nuisance, he may remain liable if he fails to exercise them.[26] The court will not grant an injunction against a landlord who is not able under the terms of the lease to take any steps to restrain future continuation of the nuisance.[27]

10.11 In many cases, leases contain tenant's covenants prohibiting any acts by the tenant on the demised premises which constitute a nuisance. It is thought that the existence of such a covenant, coupled with failure by the landlord to take steps to enforce such a covenant in the event of the tenant obstructing a neighbour's light, might be sufficient, on the principles discussed above, to make the landlord liable to the dominant owner whose light has been interfered with. It is clear that the grant by the landlord of a lease to a developer requiring or authorising the erection of a building which will interfere with a right to light would also be sufficient to result in him incurring liability.[28] In *Tetley v Chitty*[29] it was held that the landlord of a go-kart track was liable for nuisance caused to those living in the vicinity, since the noise created by his tenant was an ordinary necessary consequence of the operation of the go-karts, and there had been implied consent to the creation of the nuisance. On the other hand, it is clear that a landlord is not liable for nuisances committed by his tenant elsewhere than at the demised premises.[30]

10.12 Where the landlord re-lets premises after a nuisance upon them has been created, if he knew or ought to have known of the nuisance before re-letting, he is liable for the nuisance which occurs.

10.13 One point to be considered, in selecting the appropriate defendant, is the extent of the remedy being sought. In *Barnes v Allen*[31] the court refused to grant a mandatory injunction to require a building to be demolished for infringement of light, where the action was brought against the lessee alone, without joining the freeholder. This decision is clearly correct. It cannot be right to order the destruction of property in which a person has an interest without them having an opportunity to go before the court, save in exceptional circumstances.

10.14 It may be necessary to join the freeholder in cases where there is doubt whether a claim against a lessee alone will succeed. For example, a claim based on the Prescription Act 1832 might not succeed against the lessee alone (because of an interruption) and a claim based on lost modern grant would require joinder of the freeholder.

26   *Smith v Scott* [1973] 1 Ch 314; *Elizabeth v Rochester on Medway City Council 26 April 1983, CA*; *Hussain v Lancaster City Council* (1998) 77 P&CR 89, CA; *Chartered Trust Plc v Davies* [1997] 2 EGLR 83.
27   *Celsteel Ltd v Alton House Holdings Ltd* [1986] 1 All ER 608, CA.
28   Cf *Burt v Victoria Graving Dock Co* (1882) 47 LT 378; *Winter v Baker* (1887) 3 TLR 569; *Jenkins v Jackson* (1888) 40 ChD 71; *Tetley and others v Chitty and others* [1986] 1 All ER 663.
29   [1986] 1 All ER 663.
30   *Hussain v Lancaster City Council* (1998) 77 P&CR 89, CA.
31   (1927) 164 LT Jo 83.

LIMITATION

10.15 An interference with a right to light constitutes the tort of nuisance. Under the Limitation Act 1980, s 2, claims must be brought within 6 years of the date the cause of action accrues. The interference with a right to light constitutes a continuing nuisance, with a right of action accruing afresh every day.[32] However, damages can be recovered for only that part of the loss which arose during the relevant period before the commencement of proceedings or, arguably, the assessment of damages.[33] It is considered that the Latent Damage Act 1986 does not apply to such claims, as the action is not one where it is necessary to show any want of care on the part of the defendant.[34]

10.16 In some cases, the dominant owner may have a concurrent claim for breach of contract, if the right to light arises pursuant to an agreement – either an express grant, or a covenant (eg in a lease) not to obstruct light to certain windows. The limitation period for claims based on simple contracts is 6 years from the date of the breach. Whether the defendant will be deemed to be in continuing breach of contract during every day that this state of affairs continues will depend on the wording of the contract. In some cases, the breach may be a single breach committed on a certain date. This could arise, for example, if there was an agreement to construct a particular new building in a certain way so as not to obstruct the dominant owner's right to light. Once the new building has been constructed otherwise than as agreed, the cause of action is complete. In most cases, however, where there is a simple covenant not to obstruct windows, it is thought that the breach continues as long as the state of affairs exists.[35] Where the obligation is contained in a deed, under s 8 of the Limitation Act 1980, the period of limitation is 12 years.

10.17 By the proviso to s 36(1) of the Limitation Act 1980, it is provided that the time-limits, inter alia, relating to ss 2, 5 and 8 of that Act shall not apply to any claim for, inter alia, an injunction or other equitable relief, except insofar as such time-limit may be applied by the court by analogy in like manner as the corresponding time-limit under any enactment repealed by the Limitation Act 1939 was applied before 1 July 1940. By s 36(1) of the Limitation Act 1980 various time-limits under the Act do not apply to claims for specific performance, injunctions or other equitable relief 'except in so far as any such time limit may be applied by the court by analogy in like manner as the corresponding time limit under any enactment repealed by the Limitation Act 1939 was applied before 1 July 1940'. Section 36(2) provides that nothing in that Act affects any equitable jurisdiction to refuse relief on the ground of acquiescence or otherwise.

10.18 Limitation periods are imposed by statute, rather than common law. The first statute, the Limitation Act 1623, did not apply at all to equitable claims. However, by the time the Limitation Act 1939 came in to force in 1940 the courts had evolved a doctrine under which statutory limitation periods would in effect be applied by analogy to equitable claims by denying relief where a legal claim for the same subject matter would be time barred.[36] It is considered that this rule would be applied to claims for interference with rights of light, though it is unlikely to arise in practice given that the

---

32 See Chapter 11 at **11.38**.
33 *Hardy v Ryle* (1829) 9 B&C 603.
34 Cf *Iron Trades Mutual Insurance v JK Buckenham* [1990] 1 All ER 808 at 821.
35 Cf *Midland Bank Trust Company v Hett, Stubbs & Kemp* [1979] Ch 384.
36 *Compania de Seguros Imperio v Heath (REBX) Ltd* [2001] 1 WLR 112; *P & O Nedlloyd BV v Arab Metals Co* [2005] EWHC (Comm) 1276.

interference with a right to light is a continuing wrong. It is more likely that a claimant who fails to act to prevent the erection of a building which interferes with his light will establish his legal claim but be refused relief by way of the equitable remedy of injunction. A further problem where the claimant delays in seeking equitable relief lies in the equitable doctrine of laches.[37] This requires the court to have regard to the length of the delay and the nature of acts done during the period which affect either party and may make it unjust to allow the claim to proceed.[38] It is unclear whether the doctrine of laches can apply so as to debar the claimant from equitable relief even if he starts his action within the relevant limitation periods laid down by the Limitation Act 1980. It is thought that, in general, it ought not to apply, given that Parliament has laid down a period during which the right of action should be available.[39] In practice, given that interference with rights to light is a continuing cause of action, the issue is unlikely to arise directly, although it may be of relevance in considering whether to grant a mandatory injunction at trial to obtain the removal of the offending structure.[40]

VENUE

10.19 Actions for infringement of rights to light may be brought in the High Court and the county court, and are governed by the Civil Procedure Rules 1998 ('CPR') as supplemented by Practice Directions ('PD') issued under the authority of the Civil Procedure Act 1997, s 5. The reader is referred to specialist works on Civil Procedure and Practice, including the one-volume *Civil Court Service*, published by Jordans, which is issued twice a year. Guidance as to the appropriate venue is provided by the High Court and County Courts Jurisdiction Order 1991 ('HCCCJO').[41] Claims where the statement of value (see **10.20**) does not state that the claimant expects to recover more than £15,000 should not be started in the High Court.[42] Where the monetary claim is likely to exceed £50,000 or the property in issue is valuable the normal venue for rights of light claims will be the Chancery Division of the High Court. Procedure in the Chancery Division is regulated by the CPR and the *Chancery Guide*.[43] In other cases the best venue will be the county court, particularly where proximity to the court is necessary for the convenience of witnesses. Transfer between High Court and county court is regulated by Part 30 of the CPR and statutory provisions of the County Courts Act 1984, ss 40–42.

10.20 Under the CPR claims may be started using Part 7 or 8. In general Part 7 is to be used when there are likely to be disputed issues of fact, and Part 8 is appropriate where the issues which arise are primarily ones of law, such as the interpretation of documents. Claims of nuisance involving rights to light will normally therefore be initiated under Part 7. The Particulars of Claim must comply with CPR Part 16, and in particular r 16.4, and should contain the following information:

(1)   The claim should identify the dominant land owned or occupied by the claimant and the servient land owned or occupied by the defendant. Frequently a plan is

---

[37]   See *Lindsay Petroleum Company v Hurd* (1874) LR 5 PC 221; *Nelson v Rye* [1996] 2 All ER 186.

[38]   See *Garcia v De Aldama* [2002] EWHC 2087 (Ch).

[39]   Cf *Re Pauling's Settlement Trusts* [1962] 1 WLR 86.

[40]   See Chapter 11.

[41]   SI 1991/24, as amended.

[42]   See HCCCJO, art 4A.

[43]   See *Civil Court Service* (Jordans) Section 5.

attached for this purpose and this is encouraged by CPR PD16 para 7.1. The registered title numbers should be given if possible.

(2)   A statement of the claimant's interest in the dominant land (whether as owner, tenant or otherwise).

(3)   A statement that there is a building on the claimant's land through the windows in which light is received over the defendant's land. It is useful to attach plans and elevation drawings with the apertures numbered where these are numerous or not readily distinguishable from other apertures in respect of which no claim is made.

(4)   The enjoyment of such light must be asserted to be enjoyed as of right, so as to give rise to an easement. For example, it may be pleaded that by reason of actual enjoyment for 20 years or upwards, or by virtue of an express grant of which details are given in the Particulars.

(5)   The illegal acts of the defendant should be identified, for example, the construction of a building on the servient land which interferes with the claimant's right to light or will do so when erected.

(6)   The injury (actual or threatened) to the claimant's rights should be set out.

(7)   Claims for damages, prohibitory or mandatory injunctive relief, and declarations as appropriate. Any special damage should be set out in detail.

(8)   The claim must contain a statement of value where the claim includes a claim for damages.[44] Claims for interest must comply with CPR, r 16.4(2).

(9)   Where an injunction or declaration is sought, the claim must comply with CPR PD16 para 7.1.

10.21 The claimant may attach to or serve with his statement of case a copy of any document which he considers necessary to his claim, including an expert's report.[45] This may be useful where such a report has been finalised before proceedings are commenced.

10.22 Frequently, where building work is about to start, or is in progress, which threatens to interfere with the claimant's light, an application for an interim injunction will be required. CPR, r 25.2 allows an interim injunction to be granted before proceedings are started in urgent cases.[46]

---

[44]   CPR, r 16.3(2).
[45]   CPR PD16 para 13.3(3).
[46]   See also Chapter 11 at **11.69**. The considerations relating to interim injunctions are also discussed in Chapter 11.

Chapter 11

PROCEEDINGS FOR INFRINGEMENT OF RIGHTS TO LIGHT II – REMEDIES

GENERAL OVERVIEW OF REMEDIES AVAILABLE

11.1 The law provides various remedies in respect of infringements of rights to light. These may be considered under the following headings:

(1) Abatement.

(2) Damages at common law.

(3) Injunctions, which may be divided into:
    (a) interim injunctions including *quia timet* interim injunctions; and
    (b) final injunctions.

(4) Damages in addition to or substitution for an injunction, to which special principles apply.

(5) Declaratory relief.

11.2 The decision of which remedy to claim, and in what terms, is a matter of considerable practical importance for those aggrieved by a threatened or actual infringement of a right to light. This is particularly the case where the claimant seeks an injunction. One particularly frequent dilemma which a claimant may face is whether to apply to the court for an interim injunction in advance of trial to restrain the defendant from commencing and/or further continuing with building works which the claimant alleges will (when the resulting building is complete) obstruct his light. It is a virtually invariable requirement of the grant of such an injunction that the claimant must give an undertaking to compensate the defendant for any loss the defendant suffers if it transpires that the injunction ought not to have been grant ('undertaking in damages'). This can expose a claimant to the possibility of incurring onerous liabilities, where the allegedly infringing building is a sizeable commercial development, where the delay between the grant of an interim injunction and the trial of the case may be months, if not longer. On the other hand, the courts are generally reluctant to grant the claimant a mandatory injunction to order the removal of that part of the defendant's works which infringe the claimant's right to light where the claimant has not at least sought an interim injunction, whether or not he has been granted one. The claimant may therefore find himself in the unenviable position of having to decide whether to seek an interim injunction to protect his light in the knowledge that if at trial the court concludes that the injunction should not have been granted his undertaking in damages may be enforced, but if on the other hand he does not seek such an injunction, and the offending building is completed by the date of trial, his chances of obtaining mandatory relief to have it removed are greatly diminished. These matters are fully explored below.

11.3 The assessment of damages also gives rise to areas of difficulty. The principles governing common law damages are entirely separate from those governing equitable damages. Equitable damages, granted most frequently in lieu of a final injunction, are intended to reflect the loss due to the permanent infringement of the claimant's right, as well as past loss.[1]

11.4 In addition to legal remedies, the law in theory recognises certain limited forms of self-help by way of abatement of a nuisance.[2] In early medieval times, from which the common law originates, self-help was not regarded with disfavour, and indeed even private war was recognised as a legitimate pastime for the barons until prohibited by Henry I. The modern climate, however, is decidedly against self-help, and it is suggested that an aggrieved party should resort to it only in unusual circumstances. It remains, nevertheless, of more than academic relevance.

Procedural matters

11.5 Of the remedies enumerated above, the first, abatement, does not require recourse to court proceedings. The remainder can be sought only in such proceedings. It is therefore necessary to refer briefly to the procedure for claims in relation to rights to light in the civil courts. This will also, it is hoped, enable readers who do not have a legal background to follow case reports more easily.

11.6 The civil courts at first instance in England and Wales are the High Court of Justice and the county courts. The High Court is part of the Supreme Court, which also includes the Court of Appeal but not the House of Lords, the ultimate Court of Appeal.[3] The county courts are also established by statute, and are located throughout the country on a regional basis.[4] From both High Court and county courts, appeals lie (with permission of the court of first instance or the Court of Appeal) to the appropriate higher court. This will be either the next highest tier of court (eg to the High Court where the original decision is that of a county court) or to the Court of Appeal, depending on the nature and subject matter of the original decision. Very broadly, appeals against final judgments lie to the Court of Appeal from both High Court and the county courts. This is provided by the Access to Justice Act 1999 (Destination of Appeals) Order 2000.[5] Appeals are regulated by Part 52 of the Civil Procedure Rules[6] (see below), which derive their force from the Civil Procedure Act 1997. Appeals lie with permission from the Court of Appeal to the House of Lords[7] as the ultimate Court of Appeal for the whole of the UK. The procedure for such appeals is laid down by practice directions of the House of Lords. In limited instances direct appeals from decisions of the High Court to the House of Lords are possible. For such an appeal to be made there must be a point of general public importance in issue, certified by the judge. A certificate can be issued in two situations. The first is where the issue relates to statutory interpretation, and the second to the situation where binding authority at Court of Appeal or House of Lords level binds the High Court in reaching

---

[1]   See **11.122**.
[2]   See **11.9**.
[3]   Established originally in 1873; see now the Supreme Court Act 1981 and the Civil Procedure Act 1997.
[4]   See County Courts Act 1984. Their location is wholly unrelated to counties, a local government unit which itself no longer exists in many areas of the country. For the organisation of the Supreme Court and the county courts generally see *Halsbury's Laws of England* (4th edn, reissue 1997) vol 10, paras 501 et seq.
[5]   SI 2000/1071.
[6]   SI 1998/3132.
[7]   See Administration of Justice (Appeals) Act 1934, s 1.

its decision. Permission is required from the House of Lords.[8] Certain matters may be referred to the European Court of Human Rights, either during domestic proceedings or by way of further appeal. Rights of light have not so far achieved this distinction, though the law relating to easements certainly can involve human rights issues. These are discussed in Chapter 15.

11.7 English law has never been codified, and is still based generally on the common (unwritten) law, supplemented by the rules of equity developed by the Court of Chancery. There were historically important differences in the law applied and the remedies available in the common law courts and the Court of Chancery, the most important of which for the law of easements were that the common law courts could not grant injunctions or award specific performance and the Court of Chancery could not award damages. However, in 1854 the common law courts were for the first time given limited jurisdiction to award injunctions auxiliary to verdicts for the plaintiff, and the Court of Chancery was in 1858 empowered to award damages in addition to or in substitution for an injunction or specific performance, by the Chancery Amendment Act of that year, known as Lord Cairns' Act. The jurisdiction is now contained in s 50 of the Supreme Court Act 1981 in the case of the High Court and Court of Appeal and s 38 of the County Courts Act 1984 in the case of county courts. The enactment of the Judicature Acts of 1873–1875 merged the common law courts and the Court of Chancery into the High Court, part of the Supreme Court, and provided that common law and equitable remedies were available in all divisions of the High Court. Where there was a conflict the rules of equity were to prevail.[9] The High Court was and remains divided into divisions which tend to deal principally with different kinds of work.[10] Property matters including easements are normally dealt with in the Chancery or Queen's Bench Divisions. A claimant can start proceedings in any division subject to the power of the court to transfer the case to another division or the county court.[11] County courts are not part of the Supreme Court and are governed by separate statutory provisions, currently contained principally in the County Courts Act 1984. They have most of the powers of the High Court, subject to certain limitations.[12] Following the coming into force of the Civil Procedure Rules 1998[13] ('CPR') on 26 April 1999, which regulate procedure in the county courts, High Court and Court of Appeal, a complete recasting of civil procedure has occurred in relation both to the High Court and the county courts, and the Court of Appeal. Prior to that time, civil procedure was governed in the High Court and the Court of Appeal by the Rules of the Supreme Court in various versions, the last of which came in to force in 1965.[14] These rules were divided into Orders and further subdivided into Rules. In the county court, the County Court Rules, the latest version of which was the County Court Rules 1981,[15] applied. The House of Lords was and continues to be governed by its own standing orders. Readers unfamiliar with the courts may find it helpful to bear these changes in mind when considering the terminology used in cases. Two particular points of nomenclature should be noted. First, under the CPR the person initiating a claim is known as the 'claimant', and the person defending the claim as the 'defendant'. In previous terminology, the person initiating a claim for nuisance was known as the 'plaintiff', and

---

8   See Administration of Justice Act 1969, Part II and para 1.12 of the Practice Directions Applicable to Civil Appeals issued by the Judicial Office of the House of Lords.
9   See Supreme Court Act 1981, s 49.
10   See Supreme Court Act 1981, ss 5, 61.
11   See Supreme Court Act 1981, s 65; County Courts Act 1984, s 40.
12   County Courts Act 1984, s 38; County Courts Remedies Regulations 1991, SI 1991/1222.
13   SI 1998/3132.
14   SI 1965/177.
15   SI 1981/1687.

this term occurs universally in the cases decided before the CPR came into force. It also continues to be used in the rest of the common law world, including, for example, the United States, Canada, Australia and New Zealand. Therefore, in the text the editors use the term 'claimant', in accordance with modern usage, save when referring to or discussing the (fairly numerous) cases where the report uses the older term either because the case predates the CPR or because it comes from a non-English jurisdiction. Secondly, the CPR refer to injunctions obtained prior to trial as *interim* relief, the former description being *interlocutory* relief.

11.8   As already noted the law relating to rights of light is part of the common law which has not been codified. The main statutory provisions are those of the Prescription Act 1832 and the Rights of Light Act 1959, both considered elsewhere in this work. Apart from these the law is to be found in judicial decisions. It is the obligation of every judge to follow previous decisions which are binding on him. This involves the court in identifying the scope and effect of relevant previous decisions. It may consider that the earlier decision is not binding because the relevant passage(s) in the judgment or judgments relied on were not part of the actual decision in the case, but were remarks in passing (obiter dicta). Or it may consider that the earlier decision was flawed because it overlooked some relevant law (per incuriam). It may consider that the earlier decision was based on its own facts and does not establish any principle of relevance. Finally, it may exceptionally conclude that though an earlier decision should be authoritative the judgments are so conflicting or unclear the case cannot be relied on. Subject to these points, a lower court is bound by decisions of the Court of Appeal and the House of Lords. Earlier decisions of courts of coordinate jurisdiction are persuasive, particularly if the earlier decision has stood for a long time or was reached following full argument on the relevant issue, but not as such binding. The same applies to decisions of foreign courts at any level and of the Privy Council. For these purposes the organs of the European Convention on Human Rights are not foreign courts. The European Court of Human Rights is not bound by its previous judgments, and may depart from them for cogent reasons, for example, changes in social conditions. However, it usually follows them in practice. The Court of Appeal is generally bound by its previous decisions. The House of Lords is not bound by its previous decisions but will not normally depart from them save for good reason.[16]

ABATEMENT

General

11.9   Abatement is a remedy achieved by the act of the aggrieved party, by physical removal of the structure which interferes with the light to which that party is entitled. The remedy is hedged around with a number of restrictions discussed below and is best avoided if at all possible, given the increasing disfavour shown by the courts to self-help remedies. Nevertheless, it remains available, and is described below. In *Burton v Winters*[17] Lloyd LJ said:[18]

---

[16]   See generally *Halsbury's Laws of England* (4th edn, reissue 1997) vol 37, paras 1237 et seq.
[17]   [1993] 3 All ER 847, CA.
[18]   Ibid, at 851; see also *Cooperative Wholesale Society Limited v British Railways Board* (1995) NPC 200, (1995) *The Times*, December 20.

'Ever since the assize of nuisance became available, the courts have confined the remedy by way of self-redress to simple cases such as an overhanging branch, or an encroaching root, which would not justify the expense of legal proceedings, and urgent cases which require an immediate remedy.'

In the light of these criteria, it is thought that the practical ambit of abatement in rights to light disputes is limited; few cases involving rights to light are as simple or urgent as those given by Lloyd LJ.

Abatement and the criminal law

11.10 Attempts at abatement may in some circumstances involve potential consequences under the criminal law if what is done exceeds the boundaries of the right to abate. In general, damage to the property of another is a criminal offence. Under s 1(1) of the Criminal Damage Act 1971:

'A person who without lawful excuse destroys or damages any property belonging to another intending to destroy or damage any such property or being reckless as to whether any such property would be destroyed or damaged shall be guilty of an offence.'

It has been held that 'damage' includes permanent or temporary impairment of value or usefulness, as well as physical harm.[19] Thus the simple removal from the ground and laying down on the ground of a fence alleged to have stopped light, for example, would fall within the statute.

11.11 Section 5(2)–(4) of the Criminal Damage Act 1971 provides as follows:

'(2) A person charged with an offence to which this section applies shall, whether or not he would be treated for the purposes of this Act as having a lawful excuse apart from this subsection, be treated for those purposes as having a lawful excuse—

   (a) ...
   (b) if he destroyed or damaged or threatened to destroy or damage the property in question ... in order to protect property belonging to himself or another or a right or interest in property which was or which he believed to be vested in himself or another, and at the time of the act or acts alleged to constitute the offence he believed—
      (i) that the property, right or interest was in immediate need of protection; and
      (ii) that the means of protection adopted or proposed to be adopted were or would be reasonable having regard to all the circumstances.

(3) For the purposes of this section it is immaterial whether a belief is justified or not if it is honestly held.

(4) For the purposes of subsection (2) above a right or interest in property includes any right or privilege in or over land, whether created by grant, licence or otherwise.'

It is thought that a person who destroyed a building or fence which he believes obstructs his light could, depending on the facts, avail himself of a defence under s 5(2) of the Act. For the purposes of s 5(2), 'property' bears the extended definition in s 5(4), which seems clearly wide enough to include an easement of light. This is to be contrasted with the interpretation of 'property' in s 10(1) of the Act, in which property is defined as:

'Property of a tangible nature, whether real or personal ...'

---

[19] *Morphitis v Salmon* [1990] Crim LR 48, DC.

The defendant would, however, have to show that at the time of the acts in question[20] he had an honest belief, first, that his easement of light '*was in immediate need of protection*', and secondly, that the means of protection adopted 'were ... reasonable having regard to all the circumstances'. However, he does not have to show that the belief he actually entertained was justified, provided it was honestly held (see s 5(3)).

11.12 It ought, therefore, in principle, to be possible for a defendant to secure his acquittal provided he can establish the necessary honest belief. However, he may well face certain difficulties. First, his alleged honest belief that his easement 'was in immediate need of protection' might well be challenged. It could be said with some force that, given the availability of civil legal remedies for interference with light, and given that the interference with light does not cause any direct or permanent damage to the dominant owner's property, there would be no honest basis for such a person to believe that his easement was in immediate need of protection. Further, the word 'immediate' involves the application of an objective test. There must be evidence on which it could be said that the defendant believed that immediate action had to be taken to do something that would otherwise be a crime in order to prevent the immediate risk of something worse happening.[21]

11.13 It is further a question of whether acts of this kind could be said to be 'in order to protect property'. Once again, the test is objective. It could be said against a defendant in these circumstances that the removal of the building or screen in question was not carried out for this purpose, given the availability of remedies by Act of law. The law also recognises a common law defence of acts carried out to protect property[22] but it seems established that for these purposes property means tangible property and does not include incorporeal hereditaments.

11.14 Finally, reference should be made to s 9 of the Theft Act 1968, under which the offence of burglary is committed by someone who enters a building as a trespasser with the intention, inter alia, 'of doing unlawful damage to the building or anything therein'.[23] The criteria of unlawful damage are the same as in the Criminal Damage Act 1971. The offence applies only where there is entry to a 'building', which it seems may also include an unfinished building.[24] Therefore, although abatement is not directly prohibited by criminal law, there is a far from negligible risk that a person purporting to exercise a power of abatement might face a criminal charge.

Limits of the remedy

11.15 Returning to the limitations on the right of abatement in civil law, the right to carry out works of abatement may be exercised both on the dominant owner's land and on the land of the servient owner (in practice, of course, the latter situation is more likely).[25] The right to abate, however, arises only when an interference with the easement has occurred, and not on account of a threatened interference alone. Thus, in *Morrice v Baker*,[26] Haughton J said:

---

[20]   See *Cresswell v DPP* [2006] EWHC 3379 (Admin).
[21]   *Johnson v DPP* [1994] Crim LR 673, DC.
[22]   *Cresswell v DPP* [2006] EWHC 3379 (Admin) at [28].
[23]   Theft Act 1968, s 9(1) and (2).
[24]   Cf *R v Manning* (1871) LR I CCR 338.
[25]   *R v Rosewell* (1699) 2 Salk 459; *Thompson v Eastwood* (1852) 8 Exch 69.
[26]   *3 Bulst 196 81 ER 165.*

'... you have come too soon, to cast this down before it was made, for if he have an intent to build a wall, and lays the foundations, you ought not to disturb him for this his inception, you cannot pull this down.'

11.16 The acts of abatement must go no further than strictly necessary to abate the nuisance. Thus, in *Greenslade v Haliday*,[27] the plaintiff, who had a right to irrigate a meadow by placing a dam of loose stones across a small stream and occasionally a board or fender, fastened the board by means of two stakes which had never been done by his predecessors. The defendant, who had rights on the same stream, removed the stakes and the board also. It was held that the defendant was entitled to remove the stakes, which gave the board a character of permanency, but was not entitled to remove the board. Tindal CJ said:[28]

'... the defendant has done more than she ought to have done. The board in dispute was fastened by stakes, which was not usual; but the defendant, instead of removing the stakes alone, removed the board also. If a party who had a right to a stone weir were to erect buttresses, one who should oppose the erection of the buttresses could not justify demolishing the weir as well as the buttresses.'

Similarly, in *Lagan Navigation Co v Lambeg Bleaching, Dyeing and Finishing Co*,[29] the cutting away of banks to allow the escape of flood water was held unjustifiable because the defendant failed to prove it had not caused unnecessary damage. In *Cooperative Wholesale Society v British Railways Board*,[30] where abatement of a nuisance caused by a decrepit wall was in issue, it was held that the right extended only to demolishing the wall, not rebuilding it. And, in the case of light, where only part of a building erected by the servient owner obstructs the dominant owner's light, the dominant owner is entitled only to pull down so much of the new building as actually obstructs the light.[31] If there is a choice between possible methods of abatement, that which causes the least damage must be selected.[32] However, if either alternative would interfere with third party rights, or those of the public, it cannot be adopted, and it then becomes necessary to adopt that which is more onerous to the wrongdoer.[33] Unnecessary damage during the course of abatement will be an actionable trespass.[34] However, where reasonable abatement inevitably involves further adverse consequences to the offending obstruction, it is submitted that the person carrying out the abatement works is not on that account liable: for example, if demolition of the offending part of the building inevitably involves the removal or collapse of other parts.[35]

11.17 In general, a person wishing to carry out abatement works on the land of another must give that other notice, except in the case of emergency or where there is a danger to persons or property and no reasonable opportunity to give notice.[36] It follows that in the not uncommon case of obstruction to light caused by trees, the dominant owner is within his rights to abate the interference with light by cutting down so much of

---

[27]   (1830) 6 Bing 379, 130 ER 1326.
[28]   Ibid.
[29]   [1927] AC 226.
[30]   (1995) NPC 200, (1995) *The Times*, December 20.
[31]   *Penruddock's case* (1597) 5 Co Rep 100(b); *James v Haywood* (1630) 1 William Jones 221; *Cooper v Marshall* (1757) 1 Burr 259.
[32]   *Roberts v Rose* (1865) LR 1 Ex 82.
[33]   Ibid, per Blackburn J at 89.
[34]   *Lagan Navigation Co v Lambeg Bleaching, Dyeing and Finishing Co* [1927] AC 226.
[35]   Cf *Kawkwell v Russell* (1856) 2 LJ Ex 34.
[36]   *Jones v Williams* (1843) 11 M&W 176; *Lemmon v Webb* [1894] 3 Ch 1 at 13 per Lindley LJ.

the servient owner's trees as overhang his land.[37] However, in *Lemmon v Webb*[38] two members of the Court of Appeal stressed that it would be desirable to give notice in all cases.[39] Kay LJ said:

> 'No-one but an ill-disposed person would do such an act without previous notice. There was no emergency in this case. The defendant has acted in an unneighbourly manner, and I cannot help thinking he intended to cause annoyance.'

The Court of Appeal deprived the defendant of the costs of the action. It would seem, therefore, it would be prudent in all cases for notice to be given. Further, in the House of Lords, where the judgment of the Court of Appeal was affirmed, Lord Macnaughten suggested[40] that the rule would not necessarily apply:

> 'to the case of trees so young that the owner might remove them intact if he chose to lift them, or to the case of shrubs capable of being transplanted ...'

11.18 It is not entirely clear whether the right to carry out abatement works to trees exclusively on one's own side of the boundary without notice to the neighbour whose trees they are is limited to removing those lengths of the tree's boughs which project over the boundary, or whether in addition the dominant owner may reach across the boundary, by means of a lopper or hedge cutter, for example, to cut further portions of the tree lying on the servient owner's side of the boundary. In *Lemmon v Webb* it is clear that the Court of Appeal and the House of Lords proceeded on the basis that only those portions on the dominant owner's side of the boundary could be cut, but in the earlier case of *Pickering v Rudd*[41] the defendant had removed a Virginia Creeper growing in the plaintiff's garden, but which had spread over the side of the defendant's house, by means of ropes and scaffolding suspended over the plaintiff's garden without touching the surface of the plaintiff's premises. Lord Ellenborough directed the jury that the question was whether in removing the mischief the defendant had done any damage to the tree which might have been avoided, upon which there was a verdict for the defendant. This case might support the proposition that, provided there is no actual touching of the ground on the other side of the boundary, leaning over the boundary at a higher level to cut trees which constitute a nuisance is permissible. In the more recent case of *Dayani v London Borough of Bromley*[42] it was held that the right to abate nuisance caused by a fallen tree must be exercised reasonably and with due regard to the need to avoid unnecessary damage to the property of the landowner on whose land the tree stood.

11.19 It is, however, submitted that *Pickering v Rudd* should be approached with caution, and that the better view is that expressed in *Lemmon v Webb*. Further, in *Anchor Brewhouse Developments Ltd v Berkeley House (Docklands Developments) Ltd*,[43] it was held that trespass to land caused by the oversailing of a crane jib entitled the landowner to injunctive relief, a decision incompatible with the reasoning of Lord Ellenborough in *Pickering v Rudd* that no trespass was committed if a bullet was

---

[37]   *Lemmon v Webb* [1894] 3 Ch 1; [1895] AC 1.
[38]   [1894] 3 Ch 1, CA.
[39]   See Lopes LJ at [1894] 3 Ch 18, and Kay LJ at [1894] 3 Ch 24.
[40]   [1895] AC 1 at 7.
[41]   (1815) 4 Camp 219.
[42]   [2001] BLR 503.
[43]   [1987] 2 EGLR 173.

fired across a field but did not fall to the ground in the field. It appears established from the *Anchor Brewhouse* decision, and earlier authorities referred to therein,[44] that trespass to airspace is always actionable.

11.20 In the result, it is submitted that it is not permissible to overhang the boundary in order to remove those portions of a tree which give rise to a nuisance. Therefore, in the not uncommon case of nuisance caused by fast-growing conifers, where the majority of the foliage obstructing the light forms a comparatively high but narrow column on the servient owner's land, topping of such trees would be permissible only with due notice to the servient owner, save where an emergency arises.

11.21 Finally, the abatement must not give rise to a breach of the peace. This is in line with the general reluctance of the court to sanction self-help. Thus, in *Hale De Portibus Maris*,[45] it is said:[46]

> 'Any man may justify the removal of a common nuisance either at land or by water, because every man is concerned in it ... but because this many times occasions tumults and disorders, the best way to reform public nuisances is by the ordinary courts of justice.'

Relationship of abatement with legal proceedings for the same wrong

11.22 Abatement by act of a party will prevent a subsequent claim in legal proceedings for the same remedy.[47] But there seems no reason why a claim should not be maintained for damage sustained prior to the abatement,[48] because since interference with light is a continuing nuisance, damage is suffered every day whilst the nuisance continues prior to the abatement. The contrary dictum of Lord Atkinson in *Lagan Navigation Co v Lambeg Bleaching, Dyeing and Finishing Co*[49] to the effect that exercise of the right of abatement destroys any right of action in respect of a nuisance is probably to be regarded as confined to claims for abatement or future loss alone.[50]

11.23 It was formerly an open question as to whether the right to pursue the remedy of abatement survived legal proceedings in which a mandatory injunction to remove the nuisance was refused. Clearly, it would not be exercisable if the court dismissed the claim on the basis that no easement was found to exist, but in other cases, if the court either at the interim stage or the final stage of the action refused a mandatory injunction, the position was less clear: in *Lane v Capsey*[51]Chitty J in the context of the failure of a claim for a mandatory injunction at trial, left the point open. In *Burton v Winters*[52] it was held by the Court of Appeal that a right of abatement did not survive the conclusion of legal proceedings in which a mandatory injunction was refused. Conversely, there is no obligation to exercise a right of abatement as a precondition of

---

[44]   In particular, *Kelsen v Imperial Tobacco Company Great Britain and Ireland Ltd* [1957] 2 QB 334; *Woollerton and Wilson Ltd v Richard Costain Ltd* [1970] 1 WLR 411.
[45]   *1 Harg Tracts* 87.
[46]   Cited with approval by Kay LJ in *Lemmon v Webb* [1894] 3 Ch 1 at 19.
[47]   *Baten's case* (1610) 9 Co Rep 53b at 55a; *Burton v Winters* [1993] 3 All ER 847 at 851d.
[48]   *Kendrick v Bartland* (1679) 2 Mod Rep 253.
[49]   [1927] AC 226 at 244.
[50]   Cf *Clerk & Lindsell on Torts* (17th edn, 1995) para 29–24.
[51]   [1891] 3 Ch 411.
[52]   [1993] 3 All ER 847, CA.

exercising a right to claim damages or an injunction.[53] In *Leakey v National Trust of Places of Historic Interest or Natural Beauty*[54] Megaw LJ said:[55]

> 'But in any event, if there were such a right of abatement, it would ... be because my neighbour owed me a duty. There is, I think, ample authority that, if I have a right of abatement, I also have a remedy in damages if the nuisance remains unabated and causes me damage or personal injury.'

DAMAGES AT COMMON LAW

General principles

11.24 In this section we consider damages awarded at common law for nuisance. The subject of damages awarded in addition to or in lieu of an injunction (equitable damages) is dealt with separately at **11.122** et seq.

11.25 Damages at common law are normally awarded to compensate the claimant for wrong done. In certain limited circumstances, the court may award aggravated or exemplary damages.[56] The principle governing an award of compensatory damages is that the measure of such damages is:[57]

> 'That sum of money which will put the party who has been injured, or who has suffered, in the same position as he would have been in if he had not sustained the wrong for which he is now getting his compensation or reparation.'

11.26 A general principle is that damages for nuisance are not recoverable if they are too remote. For damages to be recovered from the wrongdoer, it is necessary to establish:

(1)   that the wrongdoer has caused the damage concerned;

(2)   that damage of the type which has occurred was a reasonably foreseeable consequence of the wrongdoer's acts or omissions.[58]

So, in *The Wagon Mound (No 1)*,[59] it was held that there was no liability for an oil spill in a harbour which resulted in a fire due to ignition of some oil which in turn had been lit by a fire which had started in cotton waste floating on the surface of the water. The ignition of the cotton waste had occurred due to sparks from the plaintiff's welding operations. It was held that damage of this kind was not reasonably foreseeable. In *RJ Tilbury & Sons (Devon) Ltd v Alegrete Shipping Co Inc & anor*[60] a claim for economic

---

[53]   *Lemmon v Webb* [1894] 3 Ch 1 at 24 per Kay LJ; *Smith v Giddy* [1904] 2 KB 448; *Edwards (Job) Ltd v Birmingham Navigations* [1924] 1 KB 341 at 356 per Scrutton LJ; *Bradburn v Lindsay* [1983] 2 All ER 408.
[54]   [1980] 1 All ER 17.
[55]   Ibid, at 34.
[56]   But it is now unlikely that exemplary damages are available for nuisance: *Kuddus v Chief Constable of Leicestershire* [2002] 2 AC 122.
[57]   Per Lord Blackburn in *Livingstone v Rawyards Coal Co* (1885) 5 App Cas 25 at 39.
[58]   *Overseas Tankship (UK) Ltd v Morts Dock and Engineering Co Ltd The Wagon Mound (No 1)* [1961] 1 AC 388.
[59]   Ibid.
[60]   [2003] EWCA Civ 65.

loss from the inability of a supplier of whelks to fulfil contracts to supply markets in Korea, due to oil pollution of the fishing grounds, was held to be too remote to constitute damage by contamination.

11.27 Where, however, the type of damage is foreseeable, but its extent is not, all damages are recoverable even if the extent of the injuries suffered by the claimant is greater than could have been foreseen.[61] But the limit to this principle is illustrated by *Balfour Beatty Construction (Scotland) Ltd v Scottish Power Plc*.[62] In that case, the pursuer received a supply of electricity from the defender under contract, at a construction site where it was constructing an aqueduct. The power supply failed whilst the pursuer was in the process of conducting a continuous pour of concrete, for which electricity was essential. As a result of the failure of the supply the entire day's work was rendered abortive. It was held that the pursuer was not entitled to recover, since damage arising from failing to achieve a continuous pour was not of a foreseeable kind.

11.28 Where, however, damage of a particular kind is foreseeable, the defendant is liable for all loss of that kind, and recovery is not reduced by the fact that the claimant is, for example, abnormally sensitive. This is sometimes referred to as 'the egg shell skull' rule.[63] The wrongdoer 'must take the victim as he finds him'.[64] Thus, if the claimant is unusually susceptible, either physically or mentally,[65] the risk of this increasing the claimant's loss is on the defendant. However, the defendant is not obliged to take the claimant as 'a quarrelsome litigious perfectionist'.[66]

Loss due to claimant's impecuniosity

11.29 As a general rule, a defendant is not responsible for increased loss which flows solely from the claimant's impecuniosity.[67] However, this principle does not apply in relation to failure to mitigate loss, or where the impecuniosity is not the sole cause of the loss in question.[68]

Recovery on behalf of third parties

11.30 The general principles governing title to sue are dealt with in Chapter 10. This section covers the scope of an individual claimant's claim. It is a well-established general rule that a claimant can recover in tort only in respect of his own loss, and not in respect of loss suffered by others.[69] This may have important ramifications in the case of claims for damage caused by loss of light. A distinction must be drawn between claims relating to injury to the value of the property affected and loss of amenity claims. In the former case, the nature of the claim (or claims) is for injury to a property interest. A party with an interest in the building (whether in possession or reversion), which he can show has been damaged by the injury to the light to the building, is entitled to maintain a claim in respect of damage to his interest. Thus there may be claims by occupying tenants, mesne

---

61   *Hughes v Lord Advocate* [1963] AC 837; *Parsons v Uttley Ingham & Co Ltd* [1978] QB 791.
62   (1994) 71 BLR 20, HL.
63   See *Dulieu v White* [1901] 2 KB 669.
64   Per Lord Wright in *Bourhill v Young* [1943] AC 92 at 109.
65   See *Kremin v Duke Street Investments Ltd* (1992) CILL 806.
66   Ibid, at 809.
67   *Liesbosch, Dredger (Owners) v SS Edison (Owners)* [1933] AC 499.
68   *Dodd Properties (Kent) Ltd v Canterbury City Council* (1980) 1 WLR 433; *Mattocks v Mann* (1992) *The Times*, June 19.
69   There are some circumstances where, in contrast, a party may recover substantial damages even though he has suffered little or no loss, if this was envisaged when the contract was made (*Linden Gardens Trust Ltd v Lenesta Sludge Disposals Ltd* [1993] 3 WLR 408, HL).

landlords and the freeholder. On the other hand, it is not possible, generally, for any of such parties to claim for loss which in truth falls on others. Thus if, for example, company A owns the building, but its subsidiary, company B, occupies the building as tenant of company A, both company A and company B have separate claims, but it is not possible for company B to claim for the whole loss.[70] Where the occupying entity or entities are simply licensees, they cannot maintain a claim even for their own loss.[71]

11.31 Equally, from a defendant's point of view, care needs to be taken when considering issues of payment of compensation for loss of light, and compromises of actions in which some (but not all) of those interested in the affected building pursue claims. A practical view may need to be taken as to whether, on the one hand, to take the risk of further claims or, on the other hand, to insist on some type of indemnity from those who are claimants against the possibility of future claims.[72]

11.32 On the other hand, where the claim is for inconvenience and loss of amenity, only those who actually suffer such loss may claim it.[73]

11.33 In the case of 'one man' companies, the court may, in appropriate circumstances, be prepared to allow the proprietor of the company to recover loss which, nominally, has been sustained by the company, on the ground that in reality that loss has been sustained by the proprietor. Thus, in *Esso Petroleum v Mardon*,[74] plaintiffs who were individuals were held entitled to recover damages from the defendant for breach of contract and misrepresentation which led them to enter a lease of a filling station, although the lease had actually been taken in the name of a company which they owned. In *DHN Food Distributors Ltd v Tower Hamlets Borough Council*[75] a claim by a holding company for disturbance following compulsory purchase was allowed even though the premises in question were occupied by a subsidiary. The court held that it was possible to look at the realities of the situation and pierce the corporate veil. Conversely, in *Kremin v Duke Street Investments Ltd*,[76] an individual plaintiff was held entitled to recover loss sustained by private companies he controlled, arising from claims for, inter alia, nuisance caused to the plaintiff.

Claims by reversioners

11.34 There may be many interests in the dominant land. In the case of a freehold owner in possession, no difficulty arises. He is not only directly affected by the infringement of light but is the owner of the whole interest in the dominant land, and, therefore, competent to claim in respect of all damage. Where the interest in the dominant land is split between a tenant or tenants and reversioners, the general rule is

---

[70] *Richard Roberts v Douglas Smith Stimson* (1988) 46 BLR 50; possibly the principle does not apply where the holding company has no claim of its own – *George Fisscher (Great Britain) Ltd v Multi Construction Ltd* (1992) CILL 795.

[71] *Hunter v Canary Wharf Ltd* [1997] AC 655; *Butcher Robinson & Staples Limited v London Regional Transport* [1999] 3 EGLR 63. See also Chapter 10 at **10.4**.

[72] See **8.3**, and generally Chapter 9.

[73] Although in *Credit Suisse v Beegas Nominees Ltd* [1994] 1 EGLR 76 the (corporate) plaintiff tenant of a building recovered general damages for breach of a repairing covenant in a lease for inconvenience experienced by staff and customers, no consideration seems to have been given to the question of whether the tenant was entitled to claim on behalf of such third parties and it is suggested the decision is suspect. In *Yankwood v London Borough of Havering* [1998] EGCS 575, it was suggested that the award was on the basis of being intended to compensate the plaintiff for loss of business.

[74] [1975] QB 819.

[75] [1976] 3 All ER 462, CA.

[76] (1992) CILL 806.

that each party holding an interest in the land is entitled to maintain an action in respect of his own loss. In the case of those whose interests are not in possession (mesne tenants and freeholders), it is now well established that they are entitled to bring claims for the injury to their interest, provided the interference with the land is of a sufficiently permanent nature to affect the value of that interest.[77] The requirement that the injury must be of permanent character would, presumably, exclude transient obstructions which have no effect on the value of the interest of the claimant. In the case of the erection of a permanent obstruction, no difficulty is likely to arise but the position may be less clear-cut where the obstruction is, though temporary, potentially more than transient, for example, due to scaffolding which will be struck when the relevant building work is complete. But it is thought that an obstruction can still be regarded as permanent even if it is not constructed of orthodox building materials, and may be readily removed, if the evidence shows that it is intended that it shall remain permanently in position.[78]

11.35 It is clear that the calculation of the damage suffered by a reversioner for injury to light is potentially complex. Relevant factors will include the length of the occupational lease, the length of the interest held by the reversioner (if he is not the freeholder) and the effect on the income received by the reversioner as a result of the interference. If the injury to the claimant is small, applying normal valuation principles, it is generally less likely that the claimant would be granted an injunction, as opposed to being left to his remedy in damages.[79] In practice, the court is generally likely to be more receptive to claims for injunctions brought by occupiers rather than to claims from reversioners, at least where the amount of damage to the reversion is small.

Retention of rights to light by reversioner by agreement

11.36 Under s 3 of the Prescription Act 1832, a leaseholder can acquire a prescriptive right to light against both his landlord and other tenants of his landlord.[80] To counter this, leases may contain a clause along the lines that the lessee:

> '... shall not be or become entitled to any right of access to light or air to the demised premises which would in any way restrict or interfere with the user of the remainder of the building or any adjoining or neighbouring or nearby property for building or any other purpose.'

11.37 The effect of such provisions in relation to prescriptive claims is considered in Chapter 7.[81] But they may also, if suitably worded, operate both to preclude light claims by the lessee against both the landlord and third parties and to reserve to the landlord the right to claim the damages for full value of the infringement as if he were in possession, on the argument that the lessee will have reduced his bid for the premises owing to the absence of protection against interference with light. The validity of the argument of course depends on the facts of each case. It may be very difficult, in practice, to show any loss where the premises have been disposed of on a long lease prior to the infringement occurring.

---

[77]   *Jesser v Gifford* (1767) 4 Burr 2141; *Shadwell v Hutchinson* (1829) 3 C&P 615 (claim by trustee); *Battishill v Reed* (1856) 18 CB 696; *Metropolitan Association v Petch* (1858) 5 CBNS 504; *Midtown Ltd v City of London Real Property Co Ltd* [2005] 1 EGLR 65.

[78]   *Metropolitan Association v Petch* (1858) 5 CBNS 504; *Baxter v Taylor* (1832) B&Ad 72; c f *Mumford v Oxford Worcester and Wolverhampton Railway Company* (1856) 1 H&N 34.

[79]   *Shelfer v City of London Electric Lighting Co* [1895] 1 Ch 287 and see **11.94**.

[80]   *Morgan v Fear* [1907] AC 425.

[81]   See Chapter 7 at **7.6** in particular.

Situation where the wrongful state of affairs continues after an initial award of damages

11.38 Interference with light is a continuing nuisance, in other words one whose effect is regarded by the law as carrying on from day to day as long as the interference remains in place. Three corollaries follow from this.

(1)   The claimant is entitled to recover damages in respect of the whole period of his ownership during which the interference with light continues.

(2)   Successive owners can sue in respect of the damage occurring during their ownership since the cause of action is a continuing one.[82]

(3)   If the damages are to be assessed as at the date of trial, but the claimant is entitled to bring successive actions in the future, as long as the injury continues.

11.39 The principles governing successive awards of damages now have limited practical importance given that all courts now have power to grant injunctive relief, or damages in lieu. But prior to the middle of the nineteenth century, the common law courts could award only damages (but not injunctions) and, conversely, courts of equity could not award damages.[83] Successive claims for damages for infringement of light were, therefore, common.[84]

11.40 Thus, in *Shadwell v Hutchinson*,[85] the plaintiff brought an action for obstruction of lights to a building. The principal argument of the defendant was that he was entitled to rely on the Custom of London, under which buildings on ancient foundations could be raised to any height.[86] The court having ruled against the defendant both on this point and on the argument that the plaintiff as a trustee could not maintain the action, the jury awarded one shilling damages. In subsequent proceedings between the same parties,[87] the plaintiff made a claim for damages for the obstruction caused by the infringing building from 28 November 1828 to the time of the second action. It was admitted that the obstruction of light was in just the same state as at the time of the former action. The plaintiff was awarded damages of £100.

11.41 From the plaintiff's point of view, the need to bring successive actions was obviously unsatisfactory. Historically, its consequences were mitigated by the practice which grew up in the common law courts of awarding what were in effect penal damages in the second action if the obstruction to light was not removed. Thus in *Shadwell v Hutchinson*, the damages in the second case of £100 were clearly assessed by the jury at a figure designed to deter the defendant from maintaining the obstruction. In *Battishill v Reed*,[88] a case of wrongful encroachment rather than interference with rights to light, the defendant paid 30 shillings into court, which he claimed was sufficient to compensate the plaintiff for the actual damage. The jury were directed to consider

---

[82]   *Whitehouse v Fellowes* (1861) 10 CBNS 765; *Delaware Mansions Ltd v Westminster City Council* [2000] BLR 1, CA.

[83]   See **11.122**.

[84]   The common law courts were first empowered to grant injunctions in relation to nuisance by the Common Law Procedure Act 1854, ss 79–81. The Chancery Court was empowered to award damages in lieu of an injunction by the Chancery Amendment Act 1858 ('Lord Cairns' Act').

[85]   (1829) 3 C&P 615.

[86]   For the Custom of London, see **6.13**.

[87]   (1830) 4 C&P 335.

[88]   (1856) 18 CB 696.

whether the amount paid into court was sufficient to cover the actual damage, and decided that it was. On appeal, it was held that the jury were right, Jarvis CJ saying:

> 'I think the Jury did right to give, as they generally do, nominal damages only in the first action; and if the defendant persists in continuing the nuisance, then they may give such damages as may compel him to abate it, but not, as was insisted here, the difference between the original value of the premises and their present diminished value.'

11.42 All the judges in *Battishill v Reed* recognised that it would not be permissible for the plaintiff to call evidence of the diminution in the value of his building caused by the obstruction, on the ground that this would be inconsistent with the principle on which damages were awarded. It would not be open to a plaintiff to make a claim based on permanent injury to the capital value of his building, and at the same time be able to pursue successive claims for injury accruing from day to day.

11.43 A partial alleviation of the inconvenience of having to take successive proceedings is provided by the principle that damages are to be assessed down to the date of the assessment.[89] Thus in the case of a continuing cause of action, damages can be assessed not simply from the date of commencement of the cause of action to the date proceedings were issued, but to the date of trial or assessment of damages, if later.

11.44 Although the rule that interference with light is a continuing cause of action remains of importance for the purposes of the Limitation Act 1980,[90] the procedural issues it formerly gave rise to have been eliminated by the changes in the organisation of the courts and the availability of injunctive relief in both the High Court and the county court as already described. It is now possible for a claimant to seek an injunction to prevent future interference with his right to light, or damages in substitution for such an injunction, along with damages for past interference if relevant. The power to award damages in substitution for an injunction is extremely important[91] since it opens the door to the court to withhold an injunction in favour of compensating the claimant by way of damages not only for loss suffered up to trial but for the permanent prospective loss of his right to light. This power gives rise to two difficult issues. The first is when should the court refuse an injunction to prevent future interference with a right to light and, secondly where it does so how should the damages be calculated?

11.45 It is not clear whether it still remains open to a claimant to follow the former practice and pursue successive actions for damages only. It is suggested that this is technically possible, but unwise, for the following reasons:

(1)   Given the availability of injunctive relief in every court, and the power to award damages in lieu of an injunction, the claimant would be obliged in his first action to specify whether he is claiming damages at common law or in lieu of an injunction.[92] If no damages in lieu of an injunction are sought in the first action, the claimant would probably be held to have disentitled himself from injunctive relief or damages in lieu in future.

---

[89]   This was formerly embodied in RSC Ord 37, r 6, but is not reproduced in the CPR. However, it is thought that the principle continues to apply. See *Hole v Chard Union* [1894] 1 Ch 294, CA for an example of the former principle.

[90]   See Chapter 10 at **10.15**.

[91]   The actual provisions of the Act of 1858 were repealed but have been held to have been preserved by subsequent legislation, see *Leeds Industrial Co-operative Society v Slack* [1924] AC 851. See now Supreme Court Act 1981, s 50; County Courts Act 1984, s 38(1).

[92]   *Jaggard v Sawyer* [1995] 2 All ER 189, CA per Millett LJ.

(2)   The court would probably not be prepared to award in effect penal damages in the second action, since the purpose of such damages was to dissuade the defendant from continuing with the wrong, whereas the court would have had power in all cases to grant the claimant an injunction, which was not the position prior to the nineteenth-century reforms discussed above. Therefore, the court would not now award such damages, confining the claimant to actual loss established.

(3)   Having regard to point (1), arguably the second claim could be struck out under CPR, r 3.4 on the basis that the second claim infringes the principle laid down in *Henderson v Henderson*[93] that:

> '... the court requires the parties ... to bring forward their whole case, and will not (except under special circumstances) permit the same parties to open the same subject of litigation in respect of a matter which might have been brought forward as part of the subject matter in contest ... The plea of res judicata applies except in special cases, not only to points upon which the court was actually required by the parties to form an opinion and pronounce a judgment, but to every point which properly belonged to the subject of litigation, and which the parties, exercising reasonable diligence, might have brought forward at the time.'

Measure of damages at common law

11.46 The basic measure of damages for injury to land caused by nuisance is diminution in the value of the land.[94] This will, therefore, be the appropriate measure where the injury is permanent, and is not subsequently abated by the removal of the offending obstruction, either voluntarily or by reason of a court injunction. The claim is not restricted to that suffered by the particular part of the building which enjoys ancient lights, but extends to diminution in the value of the whole of the building, including those parts whose windows do not enjoy ancient light.[95] Such damages are sometimes termed 'parasitic', in that the claimant is entitled to recover not only the loss caused by the obstruction of apertures enjoying the easement but also loss caused by the darkening of those which do not. The principle seems clearly established where the same obstruction affects not only ancient lights but also windows which enjoy no rights to light in the same building. In such cases, the claimant is entitled to sue for loss to the building as a whole.[96] It seems that the principle also extends to entitle the claimant to claim not only for injury to the building with ancient lights, but also the depreciation to other buildings or land which will be affected by the obstruction. So in *Griffith v Richard Clay & Sons Limited*[97] the plaintiff owned two houses fronting a street, the front

---

[93]   *Henderson v Henderson* (1843) 3 Hare 100 at 114–115 per Wigram V-C. See also *Talbot v Berkshire County Council* [1994] QB 290. The principle applies only where the subject matter of the second action could have been determined in the first and involves a cause of action asserted by one party against the other: *Barrow v Bankside Agency Ltd* [1996] 1 WLR 257; *Special Effects Ltd v L'Oreal SA* [2007] EWCA Civ 1. In *Bradford and Bingley Building Society v Seddon* [1999] 4 All ER 216, it was held that mere relitigation in circumstances falling short of cause of action or issue estoppel did not necessarily give rise to abuse of process, and that the maintenance of a second claim which could have been part of an earlier one, or which conflicted with an earlier one, should not in itself be regarded as an abuse of process. In such cases, the claimant was not required to establish special circumstances to justify his litigation. See also *Johnson v Gore Wood & Co (No 1)* [2002] 2 AC 1, where it was held that the mere fact that a claim or defence could have been raised in the earlier proceedings did not make it an abuse of process. The court should adopt a broad merits-based approach.

[94]   *Hunter and Others v Canary Wharf Ltd* [1997] AC 655, HL.

[95]   *Re London Tilbury and Southend Railway Company and Gower's Walk School Trustees* (1889) 24 QBD 326; *Scott v Goulding Properties Limited* [1973] IR 200.

[96]   Ibid.

[97]   [1912] 2 Ch 291.

windows of which were ancient lights. He also owned a piece of land to the rear of the houses, and adjacent thereto. The defendants wrongly obstructed the plaintiff's ancient lights. The plaintiff's houses were dilapidated, and he intended to demolish them and redevelop the whole site (including the land at the rear) as a warehouse or factory. It was held that he was entitled to recover not only for diminution in the value of the houses but also for the effect of the wrongful obstruction on the value of the land at the rear. Cozens Hardy MR stressed that the plaintiff's site taken as a whole was small (48 x 43 feet) and obviously must be used as one building site. He stated:[98]

'... the plaintiff is entitled to recover for all the damage caused which was the direct consequence of the wrongful act and so probable a consequence that, if the defendant had considered the matter, he must have foreseen that the whole damage would result from that act ...'

11.47 In *Wills v May*[99] the plaintiff was held entitled to recover for loss due to diminution in value not only of the house whose ancient lights were obstructed but also the neighbouring house which he proposed to redevelop along with it, notwithstanding that the neighbouring house's site might not be immediately ripe for development. Thus 'parasitic' damages may be recovered in two situations:

(1)   where the obstruction of ancient lights also obstructs windows which have no right to light damage for all the loss to the building is recoverable;

(2)   where the obstruction of ancient light affects the value of neighbouring property owned by the claimant which it is foreseeable will be developed by the claimant together with the property whose ancient lights are obstructed.[100]

11.48 Where a nuisance causes physical damage to property, the remedial cost may in appropriate circumstances be recoverable, but it is difficult to conceive of such a claim being made for loss of light, except (conceivably) if the effect of obstructing the ancient light to a greenhouse were to cause damage to an exotic plant.[101]

11.49 Where the effect of the loss of light results in the premises losing amenity value damages may be recovered. Such damages may include damages for injury to health, and inconvenience. There is a lack of authority on how such damages should be calculated in practice, although, in *Bone v Seale*,[102] it was said that the court should follow the principles applicable to damages for loss of amenity in personal injury cases.[103] It is also appropriate to have regard to claims by tenants against landlords for breach of covenant, insofar as they shed light on the approach of the court to claims based on loss of amenity suffered by occupiers of premises due to unlawful activities. Such cases, however, should be approached with caution given the wide difference between the effect of loss of light and such matters as dust, noise from building works and other physical disturbances.[104]

---

[98]   Ibid, at 298.

[99]   [1923] 1 Ch 317.

[100]   See also *Horton v Colwyn Bay and Colwyn Urban District Council* [1908] 1 KB 327, and Hudson 'Parasitic Damages for Loss of Light' 39 Conv, p 116.

[101]   For the possibility of a greenhouse acquiring a right to an exceptional quantity of light, see Chapter 3 at **3.14**.

[102]   [1975] 1 All ER 787, CA.

[103]   See also *Halsey v Esso Petroleum Co* [1961] 1 WLR 683; *Bunclark v Hertfordshire CC* [1977] 2 EGLR 114.

[104]   For some examples of damages awards covering these factors, see Franklin 'More Heartache: A Review of the Award of General Damages in Building Cases' 8 Const LJ 318.

11.50 Probably, a claimant who suffers loss of light may maintain a claim for damages for injury to health caused by the loss of light, if it is the foreseeable consequence of the defendant's wrongful act. Certainly, damages for inconvenience are recoverable.[105]

11.51 Damages for economic loss are undoubtedly recoverable in claims for nuisance, subject to issues of remoteness and foreseeability. Thus, in *Dodd Properties (Kent) Limited v Canterbury City Council*,[106] damages for nuisance were awarded representing dislocation of the plaintiff's business during the period when building works were carried out. In *Andreae v Selfridge & Co*[107] damages for loss of business due to noise and vibration caused by building works were awarded. In *Collingwood v H & C Stores*[108] damages were awarded for obstruction to the plaintiff's premises by the erection of a hoarding, assessed by reference to loss of trade. In *Yankwood Limited v Havering London Borough Council*[109] again damages were awarded by reference to interference with business. Another possible claim could be the extra expense of installing and running additional lighting systems, or having the existing lighting on for longer each day (though in practice claims of the latter kind are hard to prove). Provided it is reasonably foreseeable, loss sustained by inability to let the premises is recoverable: this is certainly the position in claims for breach of covenant for quiet enjoyment,[110] on the basis that such damages fall within the first limb of the rule in *Hadley v Baxendale*,[111] as arising in the usual course of things. Given that the test of reasonable foreseeability in contract is more restrictive than in tort,[112] there seems no reason why such damages should not be recoverable in tort.

11.52 In cases involving trespass, the courts have made awards of damages assessed by reference to a reasonable sum for the use made by the defendant of the claimant's land. Thus, in *Whitwham v Westminster Brymbo Coal Company*,[113] the defendants tipped spoil on the plaintiffs' land. Damages were assessed not by reference to the diminution in the value of the land, but by reference to a reasonable licence fee which the plaintiffs could have sought in return for granting the defendants the facility. Lindley LJ said:[114]

> 'The Plaintiffs have been injured in two respects. Firstly, they have had the value of their land diminished; secondly, they have lost the use of their land, and the Defendants have had the use of it for their own benefit. It is unjust to leave out of sight the use which the Defendants have made of this land for their own purposes, and that lies at the bottom of what are called the wayleave cases.'

The same principle has been applied in subsequent cases.[115]

11.53 In *Stoke-on-Trent City Council v W & J Wass Limited*[116] Nicholls LJ said:[117]

---

[105]   *Moore v Buchanan* (1966) 197 EG 565 (a right of way case).
[106]   [1980] 1 All ER 928, CA.
[107]   [1938] Ch 1.
[108]   [1936] 3 All ER 200.
[109]   [1998] EGCS 75.
[110]   *Mira v Aylmer Square Investments Limited* [1990] 1 EGLR 45.
[111]   (1854) 9 Exch 341.
[112]   *Czarnikow v Koufos* [1969] 1 AC 350, and see *McGregor on Damages* (Sweet & Maxwell, 17th edn, 2003) 6-144–6-177.
[113]   [1896] 2 Ch 538, CA.
[114]   [1896] 2 Ch 538 at 542.
[115]   See, eg, *Penarth Engineering Company v Pounds* [1963] 1 Lloyd's Rep 359; *Inverugie Investments v Hackett* [1995] 1 WLR 713, PC.
[116]   [1988] 3 All ER 394.
[117]   Ibid, at 402.

'It is an established principle concerning the assessment of damages that a person who has wrongfully used another's property without causing the latter any pecuniary loss may still be liable to that other for more than nominal damages. In general, he is liable to pay, as damages, a reasonable sum for the wrongful use he has made of the other's property. The law has reached this conclusion by giving to the concept of loss or damage in such a case a wider meaning than merely financial loss calculated by comparing the property owner's financial position after the wrongdoing with what it would have been had the wrongdoing never occurred. Furthermore, in such a case it is no answer for the wrongdoer to show that the property owner would probably not have used the property himself had the wrongdoer not done so.'

11.54 In *Lawson v Hartley-Brown*[118] this principle was applied to a case of trespass by building works, by a landlord constructing additional floors on top of a building demised (together with its air space) to the tenant. Damages were assessed by reference to a reasonable figure that would have been agreed, taking into account the advantage to the defendant, and the disturbance and potential loss of profit to the plaintiffs, at 1.5 times the annual rent payable by the plaintiffs to the defendant.

11.55 This measure of damages is likely to have relatively limited application in the field of rights to light. If the obstruction is permanent in nature, the claimant is likely to seek injunctive relief: if it is refused, damages in lieu of an injunction will be assessed on the basis of the principles discussed below.[119] If the claimant, at the time he commences proceedings, is not entitled to injunctive relief his damages for permanent obstruction will normally be assessed by reference to the diminution in value of his land. However, the 'wayleave measure' may, it is thought, be an appropriate basis of claim for a temporary obstruction to light: the claimant and the defendant would notionally have bargained to allow the defendant to infringe the claimant's right, and reached a figure taking into account the benefit and cost to both sides. The same general approach would probably be adopted by the court in assessing the measure of damages for trespass by oversailing by a crane on a construction site, which is subsequently removed, and other similar transient acts of trespass.

Interest

11.56 By s 35A of the Supreme Court Act 1981 and s 69 of the County Courts Act 1984, courts have power to award interest on damages. The claim for interest must be pleaded in the claim.[120] In general, where the damages represent compensation for financial loss, the claimant will be granted interest at a reasonable commercial rate over the period from the date the loss was sustained, until judgment.[121] The appropriate rate is one which properly compensates the claimant, not one taking into account the profit the defendant wrongfully made out of withholding the money. In commercial cases, interest is intended to reflect the rate at which the claimant would have had to borrow money to supply the place of that which was held. The special position of the individual claimant should be disregarded.[122] Where the claimant is at all material times in credit at the bank, the interest should be assessed by reference to the amount of interest lost by the claimant, rather than a borrowing rate.[123]

---

[118]   (1995) 71 P&CR 242.

[119]   See **11.122–11.134**.

[120]   CPR, r 16.4.

[121]   See *Kuwait Airways Corp v Kuwait Insurance Co SAK (No 2)* [2000] Lloyd's Rep IR 678.

[122]   *Tate & Lyle Distribution v GLC* [1982] 1 WLR 149; *Shearson Lehman Hutton Inc v Maclaine Watson & Co Ltd (No 2)* [1990] 2 All ER 723.

[123]   *Amstrad Plc v Seagate Technology Inc & Another* (1997) 86 BLR 34.

11.57 Where the claimant is awarded a sum assessed by reference to wrongful use of land, interest is not awarded, on the ground that it would produce a double recovery situation.[124]

Taxation

11.58 In *British Transport Commission v Gourley*[125] it was held that in awarding damages account must be taken of the tax which would have been payable on the sums which have been lost as a result of the tort. For the rule to apply, it is necessary that:

(1)   the sums for the loss of which the damages awarded constitute compensation would have been subject to tax;

(2)   the damages awarded to the claimant would not themselves be subject to tax.

11.59 Where the claim is for diminution in value to land, the first factor will not arise. If the claimant deals in land, so that the land is trading stock, the rule in *BTC v Gourley* will not apply, because the claimant will be liable to tax on the asset. Interest is normally taxable at the hands of the recipient, hence again the rule in *BTC v Gourley* will not apply. Where appropriate, the court can investigate the claimant's tax position in detail. The court should not necessarily ignore the effect of taxation where the damages are taxable, if this would be to produce over-compensation to the claimant.[126]

11.60 Care should be taken when releasing existing rights to light to ensure that, so far as possible, the party releasing those rights does not unwillingly incur either a capital gains tax,[127] or income tax charge. The release of the right may be a disposal of an asset within ss 21 and 22 of the Taxation of Chargeable Gains Act 1992, noting in particular s 22(1)(c). In addition, it may be open to Her Majesty's Revenue & Customs in certain cases to treat sums paid for releases as gains within the technical and complex provisions of Part 13, Chapter 3, ss 752–772 of the Income Tax Act 2007, in force 6 April 2007, thus causing an income tax charge under s 758 of the same Act. Under s 770, it is possible to seek advance clearance if it is thought that this section may apply. In any event, tax advice taken before any deal is done is a wise precaution. Finally, if a release is expressed to be for consideration in money or money's worth, stamp duty, now Stamp Duty Land Tax (SDLT), will be payable on the document recording the release, ad valorem, at the rate in force when the agreement is made, unless certified to be for value under the current threshold for ad valorem duty. Specialist tax advice should be taken, in particular on SDLT, on releases of rights of light which are potentially chargeable to SDLT as land transactions under Finance Act 2003, s 49. In addition, for VAT purposes complex questions may arise whether the grant of a right of light is a supply within the charge to VAT or is exempt under Group 1 of Sch 9 to the Value Added Tax Act 1994.[128]

---

[124]   *Whitwam v Westminster Brymbo Company* [1896] 1 Ch 894. See *McGregor on Damages*, 15-043.
[125]   [1956] AC 185. See generally *McGregor on Damages*, Ch 14, especially 14-037–14-040.
[126]   *Amstrad Plc v Seagate Technology Inc & Another* (1997) 86 BLR 34.
[127]   See Taxation of Capital Gains Act 1992.
[128]   For further reference see VAT Notice 742 and for specific discussion of this issue, see *Estates Gazette* (2007) Vol 3, 3 February, 304.

INJUNCTIONS

General principles

11.61 Under s 37(1) of the Supreme Court Act 1981:[129]

'The High Court may by order (whether interlocutory or final) grant an injunction … in all cases where it appears to the court to be just and convenient to do so.'

11.62 An injunction is a command by the court directed to a particular person to do or abstain from doing a certain act or acts. In a sense, all court orders granting a remedy require certain things to be done, but many types of court order are not injunctions, for example, a judgment for a sum of money, or an order that one party pay the other's costs. Relief by way of injunction was originally granted by the Court of Chancery alone. The Court of Chancery administered a system of rules known as 'Equity'; hence injunctions are a species of *equitable relief*. The distinction between those courts which can and cannot grant equitable relief by way of injunction has practically ceased to exist, as already noted. However, the principles of law as evolved in Equity continue to apply.[130] The most important of these is that an injunction will only be granted to protect some legal or equitable right. So there is no power to grant an injunction, for example, to prevent someone erecting a wall to block a view. In *Day v Brownrigg*[131] Jessel MR said:

'You must have in our law injury as well as damage … If a man erects a wall on his own property and thereby destroys the view from the house of the Plaintiff he may damage him to an enormous extent. He may destroy three-fourths of the value of the house, but still, if he has the right to erect the wall, the mere fact of thereby causing damage to the Plaintiff does not give the Plaintiff a right of action.'

11.63 It is not sufficient for the claimant to argue that he has an expectation or hope of acquiring such a right in the future. In the case of a claim based on a right to light, it would not be possible for a claimant to seek an injunction on the ground that he has a prescriptive right to light, if the necessary period has not elapsed, nor would he be entitled to object to the registration of a notice under the Rights of Light Act 1959 on the ground that its effect will be to prevent him acquiring such a right.[132] There is, however, no doubt that the court can award an injunction to restrain a nuisance including an interference with a right to light, and that such a claim can also be brought by a reversioner where the premises are occupied by a tenant, provided the nuisance will cause permanent damage to the reversioner's interest. An injunction is always a discretionary remedy and cannot be claimed as of right. This does not mean that the court should act capriciously. As a general rule a party who establishes his legal right is entitled to an injunction[133] to restrain or remedy an infringement of it. And injunctions may be granted to protect a claimant against a threatened injury which has not yet occurred in certain circumstances, by *quia timet* relief, considered below.

11.64 However, there are a number of general exceptions. First, the court will be less ready to grant a mandatory than a prohibitory injunction, and may vary the terms of an

---

[129] The position in the county court is the same, subject to certain statutory restrictions that are not material for claims in relation to rights to light – see County Courts Act 1984, s 38(1).

[130] *Day v Brownrigg* (1878) 10 Ch D 294.

[131] (1878) 10 Ch D 294 at 307.

[132] See Chapters 7 and 8.

[133] *Imperial Gas Light Co v Broadbent* (1859) 7 HLC 600; *Fullwood v Fullwood* (1879) 9 Ch D 176.

injunction to avoid oppression. So in *Jordan v Norfolk County Council*[134] the plaintiff established that a sewage pipe had been laid through his land without permission. The court awarded damages and an injunction under which the defendant had to remove the pipe and restore the land to its former condition. The injunction specified that trees must be replanted 'as far as reasonably practicable' according to a scheme prepared by a landscape architect to be appointed. However, the scheme produced involved costs about ten times the value of the land. The court, faced with this cost, which had not been foreseen originally, varied the order. Under the order, as varied, a scheme to restore the land was to be prepared by an architect on the basis of a cost proportionate to the value of the land concerned. The original order had not contemplated expense of the level involved in the original scheme. On the other hand, it is no objection to an injunction generally that compliance will be inconvenient or expensive.[135] In the case of erection of buildings which infringe the claimant's right to light a mandatory injunction may be ordered to compel demolition, though the grant of such a remedy is not automatic.[136] Secondly, an injunction may also be refused if it would be ineffective, for example, where the relevant act has already occurred. Thirdly, an injunction will be refused if it would involve an indirect attempt specifically to enforce the type of obligation the court will not generally enforce in this way.[137] Fourthly, the claimant may forfeit his right to an injunction by inequitable conduct, for example, by misleading the court or if he is not really interested in an injunction as opposed to financial compensation.[138] Finally, a claim to an injunction may be refused if the claimant has been guilty of acquiescence or laches. Acquiescence involves implied waiver of the right, for which purpose something more than mere inaction is required. The test is whether it would be unconscionable to allow the claimant to enforce his rights, whether those rights are legal or equitable.[139] Laches involves similar considerations, but can arise through mere lapse of time, where this has caused prejudice to the other party.

11.65 An injunction may also be refused where damages would be an adequate remedy, for example, where the illegal act has already taken place and there is no risk of it being repeated.[140] In the case of future injury the same applies, but it is well established that an injunction will in many instances be granted to restrain a future nuisance. The circumstances where the court will grant an injunction to restrain future interference with rights of light are considered below.[141] The fact that the claimant has suffered very small or nominal damage will not disentitle him from being awarded an injunction, and indeed may itself be a good reason for granting such an injunction, particularly in the case of injury to land. Any other rule could lead to property rights being expropriated with impunity. Thus injunctions have readily been granted to restrain trespass even where the claimant has not suffered significant injury from the acts complained of, for example, where the jib of a tower crane oversails the claimant's land.[142] On the other hand, a court is not bound to grant an injunction in such circumstances, and may award damages in substitution for an injunction under the power originally contained in

---

[134] [1994] 1 WLR 1353.

[135] *Pride of Derby and Derbyshire Angling Association v British Celanese Ltd* [1953] Ch 149.

[136] See **11.105–11.107**.

[137] *Co-operative Insurance v Argyll Stores* [1988] AC 1; *Internet Trading Clubs Ltd v Freeserve (Investments) Ltd* [2001] EBLR 102.

[138] *Istil Group Inc v Zahoor* [2003] 2 All ER 252 at [111]; *Blue Town Investments v Higgs and Hill plc* [1990] 1 WLR 696.

[139] *Gafford v Graham* [1999] 3 EGLR 75, CA; *Shaw v Applegate* [1977] 1 WLR 970, CA.

[140] *Desk Advertising Co Ltd v ST Dupont* (1973) 117 SJ 483.

[141] See **11.91–11.121**.

[142] *John Trenberth Ltd v National Westminster Bank Ltd* (1979) 39 P&CR 104; *Anchor Brewhouse Ltd v Berkeley House (Docklands Developments) Ltd* [1987] 2 EGLR 173.

Lord Cairns' Act.[143] No injunction (final or interim) can be granted in general against the Crown,[144] save in prerogative proceedings (including judicial review).[145] This applies to emanations of the Crown, importantly (for present purposes) the Crown Estates Commissioners.[146] Crown immunity does not extend to bodies created by statute (e g local authorities). However, it is established that where the legislative has entrusted a statutory body with functions to be discharged in the public interest, and has given that body power to acquire and hold land for the purpose of discharging that function, private easements affecting the land will not be enforced by injunction or damages. The aggrieved party's remedy lies exclusively in a claim under compulsory purchase legislation.[147] For compulsory purchase and extinguishment under statutory powers, see **8.56–8.61**.

Classification of injunctions

11.66 Injunctions may be classified in various ways.

(1) *Prohibitory/mandatory*. A prohibitory injunction prevents certain acts being done, whereas a mandatory injunction requires the defendant to take positive steps. In the context of rights to light, a typical prohibitory injunction would be one preventing the defendant from building so as to obstruct the claimant's light. A mandatory injunction would be one requiring the defendant to remove so much of a building as obstructs the claimant's light.

(2) *Final/interim*. A final injunction is one which the court grants at the trial of the action, and which will (almost invariably) be phrased so as to have permanent effect. An interim injunction is one granted prior to the trial of the action, to protect the claimant's rights prior to trial. It is not uncommon, for example, for a claimant in a rights to light case to seek an interim injunction to prevent the defendant from starting or continuing building which may infringe the claimant's rights to light until the case can be tried.

Quia timet injunctions/injunctions where actual injury to the claimant's rights has already occurred

11.67 In general an injunction is granted to restrain or require the remedy of a breach of the claimant's rights which has already occurred. By contrast, a *quia timet* injunction is granted to prevent a wrong before it occurs, where there is a very strong probability that substantial harm would be caused to the claimant which would not be adequately remedied by a damages claim. 'But no one can obtain a quia timet order by merely saying "Timeo"; he must aver and prove that what is going on is calculated to infringe his rights.'[148] The onus is on the claimant to satisfy the court that damage will necessarily be occasioned to him in the future.[149] The claimant in order to obtain a *quia timet* injunction must show a very strong probability on the facts that grave damage will accrue to him in the future.[150]

---

[143] See *Jaggard v Sawyer* [1995] 2 All ER 189, CA and **11.122–11.134**.
[144] See *Halsbury's Laws*, vol 24, para 824.
[145] See Supreme Court Act 1981, s 31 and *M v Home Office* [1993] 3 All ER 537, HL.
[146] For the position of the Crown Estate see *Halsbury's Laws*, vol 12(1), paras 278ff.
[147] *Brown v Heathlands Mental Health NHS Trust* [1996] 1 All ER 133.
[148] See *A-G for the Dominion of Canada v Ritchie Contracting and Supply Co Ltd* [1919] AC 999 at 1005.
[149] *White v Mellin* [1895] AC 154.
[150] *Redland Bricks Ltd v Morris* [1970] AC 652; *Drury v Secretary of State* [2004] 2 All ER 1056, CA.

Without notice/with notice injunctions

11.68 An injunction without notice is one granted on an application by one party without the other party being given notice, whereas a with notice injunction is one which is granted after hearing both parties. Without notice applications for injunctions are exceptional, and normally arise in two situations. First, where the case is one of exceptional urgency, so that the claimant needs instant intervention from the court without time being allowed for the normal notice to be given to the defendant enabling the defendant to participate. Secondly, certain types of application for interim injunctions would have their purpose defeated were the defendant initially to be notified of them, for example, applications for injunctions to restrain the defendant from disposing of or dealing with his assets prior to trial (so-called 'freezing' orders).[151]

INTERIM AND QUIA TIMET INJUNCTIONS

Introduction

11.69 In this section are considered the principles governing the grant of interim injunctions including *quia timet* injunctions. In practice, a claimant faced with an actual or apprehended injury to his rights of light as a result of building works by the defendant is well advised to seek interim relief in many cases. This has the advantage from his perspective of preventing the illegal operations and preserving the status quo until trial. Further, it obviates the risk discussed below of the defendant arguing at trial that because the claimant has stood by whilst the work has gone forward, possibly at great expense, the defendant should not be ordered to take the offending structure down. On the other hand, the claimant must if he is to be granted relief give an undertaking in damages, the effect of which is that if at trial the court decides the interim injunction should not have been granted the claimant may be ordered to pay the defendant the amount of any loss sustained by the defendant as a result of the grant of the injunction.[152] The grant of an interim injunction[153] can be regarded, in its simplest form, as a 'holding operation' until the action is heard at trial. As with other types of injunctions, interim injunctions may be sought to prevent a wrong before it occurs (*quia timet*); to prevent a wrong continuing (prohibitory); or to require the defendant to take some positive steps to remedy a wrong (mandatory). As a result, the grant or refusal of an interim injunction is a very important matter that can have a profound effect on both parties in practical and financial terms. It is proposed to examine first the general principles, secondly, the more limited circumstances in which an interim mandatory injunction will be granted, thirdly, the position as regards interim *quia timet* injunctions, fourthly, the situation where the grant of an interim injunction will effectively dispose of the case and, fifthly, the requirement of an undertaking in damages and when it will be enforced.

11.70 The application for an interim injunction is not, however, a mini-trial. The only evidence given to the court is by witness statement or affidavit and this will not be subjected to the rigours of cross-examination. Whilst this approach may seem deficient, it is consistent with the court's desire not to express an opinion on the merits of the case until the full action is heard, even though a defendant can ultimately be sent to prison for breaching the terms of an interim injunction.

---

[151] See CPR Part 25 for interim relief (including freezing orders) generally.
[152] See **11.85–11.90**.
[153] Formerly known as an 'interlocutory' injunction. The terminology was changed by the CPR in 1999.

General principles

11.71 The principles guiding the court's equitable discretion to grant an interim injunction are set out in *American Cyanamid Co v Ethicon Ltd*[154] by Lord Diplock. Lord Diplock set out a three-stage test:

(1)   Is there a serious issue to be tried?

(2)   Would damages be an adequate remedy for a party injured by the court's grant of, or failure to grant, an injunction?

(3)   Where does the 'balance of convenience' lie?

These principles, while of general application, should not be read as if they were set in stone[155] and it will be seen that they are subject to variations and may in some cases be entirely inappropriate. In any event, the '*American Cyanamid* Principles' rest upon the foundation of s 37(1) of the Supreme Court Act 1981, which allows the court to grant an injunction only where it is 'just and convenient to do so'.

Is there a serious issue to be tried?

11.72 Lord Diplock adopted a threshold test to separate the wheat from the chaff. In this instance, the application of a strict test is tempered by the level of inquiry that the court can undertake upon the evidence placed before it. Lord Diplock therefore rejected the view previously held of the need to show either 'a probability that the plaintiffs are entitled to relief' or a 'strong prima facie case that the right which he seeks to protect in fact exists'.[156] Instead, he continued:[157]

> 'The court no doubt must be satisfied that the claim is not frivolous or vexatious; in other words, that there is a serious issue to be tried.'

11.73 As to what these words mean Lord Diplock specifically rejected the idea of a percentage-based threshold test:[158]

> 'The purpose sought to be achieved by giving to the court discretion to grant such injunctions would be stultified if the discretion were clogged by a technical rule forbidding its exercise if upon that incomplete untested evidence the court evaluated the chances of the plaintiff's ultimate success in the action at 50 per cent or less, but permitting its exercise if the court evaluated his chances at more than 50 per cent.'

In general, therefore, this hurdle is fairly easily satisfied and all that has to be seen for a 'serious issue to be tried' is whether the claimant has prospects of success which exist both in substance and reality. Thus, a claimant will be unsuccessful where he relies on a cause of action unknown to English law, or a cause of action that is clearly unarguable on the facts presented.[159]

---

[154]   [1975] AC 396, HL.
[155]   *Cayne v Global Natural Resources Plc* [1984] 1 All ER 225, CA at 237 per May LJ.
[156]   [1975] AC 396 at 407G.
[157]   Ibid.
[158]   Ibid.
[159]   See *Mothercare Ltd v Robson Books Ltd* [1975] FSR 466 at 474; *Morning Star Co-operative Society Ltd v Express Newspapers Ltd* [1979] FSR 113.

An investigation as to the adequacy of damages

11.74 Damages can be an alternative method of giving relief to the wronged party. Therefore, once the court has established that there is a serious issue to be tried, the following inquiry is to be made, in four stages:[160]

'[i]   [T]he court should first consider whether, if the plaintiff were to succeed at trial in establishing his right to a permanent injunction, he would be adequately compensated by an award of damages for the loss he would have sustained as a result of the defendant's continuing to do what was sought to be enjoined between the time of the application and the time of trial.

[ii]   If damages in the measure recoverable at common law would be adequate remedy and the defendant would be in a financial position to pay them, no interlocutory injunction should normally be granted, however strong the plaintiff's claim appeared to be at that stage.

[iii] The court should then consider whether, on the contrary hypothesis that the defendant were to succeed at the trial in establishing his right to do that which was sought to be enjoined, he would be adequately compensated under the plaintiff's undertaking as to damages for the loss he would have sustained by being prevented from doing so between the time of the application and the time of the trial.

[iv]   If damages in the measure recoverable under such an undertaking would be an adequate remedy and the plaintiff would be in a financial position to pay them, there would be no reason upon this ground to refuse an interlocutory injunction.'

This approach of looking at the relevance of the availability of an adequate remedy in damages was confirmed by Lord Goff in *R v Secretary of State for Transport, ex parte Factortame Ltd (No 2)*.[161] So in *Gregory v Court Royal Ltd*[162] an interim injunction to restrain building works which were alleged by the claimants to be in breach of restrictive covenants was refused where the works were well advanced before proceedings were commenced and the further damage which the claimants would suffer between the date of the application and trial would be minimal. Further, damages would not be an adequate remedy for the defendants if the claimants failed to establish their case as they had already spent some £2m on development and any substantial delay in progress would seriously prejudice their financial position. There was no prospect of the claimants being able to pay any damages that might be awarded to the defendants. Accordingly there was less risk of injustice in refusing the injunction than granting it.

The 'balance of convenience'

11.75 This stage of the test applies only where a doubt exists as to the adequacy of the respective remedies in damages available to either party or both. Thus, by this stage, the court has examined the basic legal foundation of the cause of action and assessed the availability and adequacy of financial recompense. Assessing the 'balance of convenience', however, allows the court to step back and take the practical realities of the situation into account.

11.76 Unfortunately, the search for this balance of convenience is not aided by any hard and fast rules. The courts do not have a closed list of factors that should be taken into account. As such, any decisions as to the balance of convenience must be taken on

---

[160] *American Cyanamid Co v Ethicon Ltd* [1975] AC 396 at 408C–408E. Subdivisions [i] to [iv] have been inserted for clarity of exposition.

[161] [1991] 1 AC 603.

[162] [2002] EWHC 936 (Ch).

a case-by-case basis. Yet despite this obvious reluctance to fetter their equitable discretion, the courts have set out a number of guiding principles.

(1)   *The risk of injustice.* The balance to be ascertained is more fundamental and weighty than mere 'convenience' would suggest and should be considered against the background of s 37(1) of the Supreme Court Act 1981. This emphasis on injustice is confirmed by Lord Diplock in another case, *NWL Ltd v Woods*,[163] where he stated:

> 'In assessing whether what is compendiously called the balance of convenience lies in granting or refusing interlocutory injunctions in actions between parties of undoubted solvency the judge is engaged in weighing the respective risks that injustice may result from his deciding one way rather than the other at a state when the evidence is incomplete.'

(2)   The status quo.

> 'Where other factors appear to be evenly balanced it is a counsel of prudence to take such measures as are calculated *to preserve the status quo*.'[164]

As to when in time the 'status quo' applies, it was held in *Garden Cottage Foods Ltd v Milk Marketing Board*[165] that this meant the state of affairs immediately before the issue of the writ, ignoring minimal periods of time, unless the plaintiff is guilty of unreasonable delay.

(3)   *Special factors.*

> '[T]here may be many other special factors to be taken into consideration in the particular circumstances of individual cases.'[166]

There is some argument as to whether the exceptions, which will be discussed below,[167] to the *American Cyanamid* Principles can be incorporated within the 'special factors' hereto referred rather than forming specific principles for clearly distinguishable circumstances. It is submitted that if they were to be incorporated within the 'special factors' then the exceptions may well encompass the rule and this cannot have been what Lord Diplock intended.

(4)   *The merits of the case.*

> '[I]t may not be improper to take into account in tipping the balance the relative strength of each party's case as revealed by the affidavit evidence adduced on the hearing of the application. This however should be done only where it is apparent upon the facts disclosed by evidence as to which there is no credible dispute that the strength of one party's case is disproportionate to that of the other party.'[168]

---

[163]   [1979] 1 WLR 1294, HL at 1306G. See, also, for the choice of the course which will result in the least risk of injustice if it turns out to be wrong, *Zockoll Group Ltd v Mercury Communications Ltd* [1998] FSR 354; *Psychometric Services Ltd v Merant International Ltd* [2002] FSR 8.
[164]   *American Cyanamid v Ethicon Ltd* [1975] AC 396 at 408G per Lord Diplock.
[165]   [1984] AC 130, HL.
[166]   [1975] AC 396 at 409D per Lord Diplock.
[167]   See **11.78**.
[168]   [1975] AC 396 at 409B–409C per Lord Diplock.

The courts have generally been reluctant to give any greater prominence than that of 'tipping the balance' to the relative strengths of each party's case. However, in *Series 5 Software Ltd v Clarke*,[169] Laddie J did not approach this aspect as one of last resort. Like Lord Diplock, he held that the court must be able to come to a clear view as to the strength of each party's case on credible evidence, but once that was so, the view taken would immediately be a factor that the court could take into account when assessing the 'balance of convenience'.

While it may be expecting too much of the court not to look at, or form a view of, the relative strengths of each party's case, it is likely that courts will continue to be reluctant to express their decisions on this basis alone when dealing with cases which fall within the *American Cyanamid* Guidelines.

11.77 Based on the foregoing analysis and applying the *American Cyanamid* principles in the case of injunctions at the interim stage to prevent the construction of buildings which interfere with light, the court will, it is suggested, attach weight to (a) the strength of each party's case, (b) stage the works have reached at the date of the application, (c) the effect on the claimant of allowing the work to proceed, (d) the financial consequences to the defendant of halting the work until trial and (e) whether the claimant is likely to be good for any damages which the defendant may suffer as a result of the injunction, if the court decides that the claimant ought to pay such damages.[170]

The grant of mandatory interim injunctions

11.78 While the court has jurisdiction to grant a mandatory interim injunction, it is an exceptional form of relief. This is because the requirement that a positive act should be done to repair some omission or to restore the prior position by undoing some wrongful act, whilst still a 'holding operation', is a draconian requirement that may well have severe practical and financial consequences, resulting in injustice.

11.79 Consequently, the courts have adopted a different approach to these forms of interim injunctions as can be seen from *Shepherd Homes Ltd v Sandham*.[171] In *Nottingham Building Society v Eurodynamics Systems*[172] Chadwick J said:

> 'First, this being an interlocutory matter, the overriding consideration is which course is likely to involve the least risk of injustice if it turns out to be "wrong" in the sense described by Hoffmann J [ie granting an injunction to a party who fails to establish his right at the trial (or would fail if there was a trial) or alternatively, in failing to grant an injunction to a party who succeeds (or would succeed) at trial].

> Secondly, in considering whether to grant a mandatory injunction, the court must keep in mind that an order which requires a party to take some positive step at an interlocutory stage, may well carry a greater risk of injustice if it turns out to have been wrongly made than an order which merely prohibits action, thereby preserving the status quo.

> Thirdly, it is legitimate, where a mandatory injunction is sought, to consider whether the court does feel a high degree of assurance that the claimant will be able to establish his right at a trial. That is because the greater the degree of assurance the claimant will ultimately establish his right, the less will be the risk of injustice if the injunction is granted.

---

[169] [1995] 1 All ER 853.
[170] See in *Gregory v Court Royal Ltd* [2002] EWHC 936 (Ch).
[171] [1971] 1 Ch 340.
[172] [1993] FSR 468 at 474.

But, finally, even where the court is unable to feel any high degree of assurance that the claimant will establish his right, there may still be circumstances in which it is appropriate to grant a mandatory injunction at an interlocutory stage. Those circumstances will exist where the risk of injustice if [the] injunction is refused sufficiently outweigh the risk of injustice if it is granted.'

The approach of Chadwick J was approved in *Zockoll Group Ltd v Mercury Communications Ltd*.[173] For a case where the necessary 'high degree of assurance' was established, see *London and Manchester Assurance Co Ltd v O & H Construction Ltd and Another*.[174]

11.80 Although rare, mandatory interim injunctions have been granted to preserve, amongst other things, the claimant's rights to ancient lights. In both *Daniel v Ferguson*[175] and *Von Joel v Hornsey*[176] the defendants were required to remove the section of building works, erected after service of a writ, which obstructed the ancient lights pending trial of the action. It should be noted that the inequitable conduct, displayed by both defendants in trying to rush through their building works and thus make service of the writ ineffective, was clearly a factor which influenced the court's decision:

'It is right that buildings thus run up should be pulled down at once, without regard to what the result of the trial may be.'[177]

The grant of quia timet interim injunctions

11.81 The principles which govern the grant of an interim injunction to prevent a wrong before it occurs differ both in substance and terminology. Instead of the court assessing whether there is a serious issue to be tried, the fundamental question becomes whether there is a probability that damage will accrue to the claimant in the future. This has already been considered above at **11.67**. The level of probability required will, however, depend upon whether the claimant is seeking a prohibitory or mandatory order. It is clear that in relation to the latter there must be a 'very strong probability upon the facts that grave damage will accrue to him in the future'.[178]

11.82 Once this has been assessed, the normal inquiry into the adequacy of damages, if the court does not grant the *quia timet* injunction and the damage actually accrues, should be considered.

The situation where the grant or refusal of an interim injunction will dispose of the action

11.83 Where the grant or refusal of an interim injunction would finally dispose of the action the court may be more reluctant to grant such an injunction. This may occur either because, as a matter of law, there would be nothing left for the unsuccessful party's interest to proceed upon at trial, or looking at the commercial realities of the situation the court's decision to grant or refuse the injunction renders it uneconomic for the unsuccessful party to continue to pursue its case. In either event, the grant of the

---

[173]   [1998] FSR 354.
[174]   [1989] 2 EGLR 185.
[175]   [1891] 2 Ch 27.
[176]   [1895] 2 Ch 774.
[177]   *Daniel v Ferguson* [1891] 2 Ch 27 at 30 per Lindley LJ.
[178]   *Morris v Redland Bricks Ltd* [1970] AC 652, HL at 665G per Lord Upjohn.

interim injunction could not properly be regarded as a 'holding operation' and thus this is a type of case which falls outside of the *American Cyanamid* guidelines.

11.84 This was expressly confirmed by Lord Diplock in *NWL Ltd v Woods*[179] who went on to state that where this was the case:[180]

> '... the degree of likelihood that the plaintiff would have succeeded in establishing his right to an injunction if the action had gone to trial, is a factor to be brought into the balance by the judge in weighing the risks that injustice may result from his deciding the application one way rather than the other.'

However, the required strength of the case on the merits has not been defined with any consistency by the courts. While some cases have required 'an overwhelming case on the merits',[181] others have demanded only some assessment of the merits which show them to be 'more than merely a serious issue to be tried'.[182] Once again, the best touchstone is the level of potential injustice that would result from grant or refusal. One can expect that where the grant or refusal of the interim injunction would finally dispose of the action, the higher the potential for injustice and the more concerned the courts will be about the merits of either party's case.

The requirement for an undertaking in damages from the party in whose favour the interim injunction is granted, and when the undertaking will not be enforced

11.85 It is an almost invariable requirement of the grant of an interim injunction that the claimant gives an undertaking in damages, to safeguard the defendant if it subsequently transpires that the injunction should not have been granted.[183] The principles governing such undertakings were set out by Neill LJ in *Cheltenham and Gloucester Building Society v Ricketts*[184] as follows:

> 'From the authorities the following guidance can be extracted as to the enforcement of a cross-undertaking in damages.
>
> (1)   Save in special cases an undertaking as to damages is the price which the person asking for an interlocutory injunction has to pay for its grant. The court cannot compel an applicant to give an undertaking but it can refuse to grant an injunction unless he does.
>
> (2)   The undertaking, though described as an undertaking as to damages, does not found any cause of action. It does, however, enable the party enjoined to apply to the court for compensation if it is subsequently established that the interlocutory injunction should not have been granted.
>
> (3)   The undertaking is not given to the party enjoined but to the court.
>
> (4)   In a case where it is determined that the injunction should not have been granted the undertaking is likely to be enforced, though the court retains a discretion not to do so.
>
> (5)   The time at which the court should determine whether or not the interlocutory injunction should have been granted will vary from case to case. It is important to

---

179   [1979] 1 WLR 1294 at 1306D.
180   Ibid, at 1307B–1307C.
181   As in *Cayne v Global Natural Resources Plc* [1984] 1 All ER 225 per Everleigh LJ.
182   *Lansing Linde Ltd v Kerr* [1991] 1 All ER 418, CA.
183   *Smith v Day* (1882) 21 ChD 421.
184   [1993] 4 All ER 276, CA at 281d–282f.

underline the fact that the question whether the undertaking should be enforced is a separate question from the question whether the injunction should be discharged or continued.

(6)   In many cases injunctions will remain in being until the trial and in such cases the property of its original grant and the question of the enforcement of the undertaking will not be considered before the conclusion of the trial. Even then, as Lloyd LJ pointed out in *Financiera Avenida v Shiblaq* [1990] CA Transcript 973 the court may occasionally wish to postpone the question of enforcement to a later date.

(7)   Where an interlocutory injunction is discharged before the trial the court at the time of discharge is faced with a number of possibilities. (a) The court can determine forthwith that the undertaking as to damages should be enforced and can proceed at once to make an assessment of the damages. It seems probable that it will only be in rare cases that the court can take this course because the relevant evidence of damages is unlikely to be available. It is to be noted, however, that in *Columbia Pictures Industries Inc v Robinson* [1987] 3 All ER 338, [1987] Ch 38 Scott J was able, following the trial of an action, to make an immediate assessment of damages arising from the wrongful grant of an Anton Piller order. He pointed out that the evidence at the trial could not be relied on to justify ex post facto the making of an ex parte order if, at the time the order was made, it ought not to have been made (see [1987] 3 All ER 338 at 378, [1987] Ch 38 at 85). (b) The court may determine that the undertaking should be enforced but then direct an inquiry as to damages in which issues of causation and quantum will have to be considered. It is likely that the order will include directions as to pleadings and discovery in the inquiry. In the light of the decision of the Court of Appeal in *Norwest Holst Civil Engineering Ltd v Polysius Ltd* [1987] CA Transcript 644 the court should not order an inquiry as to damages and at the same time leave open for the tribunal at the inquiry to determine whether or not the undertaking should be enforced. A decision that the undertaking should be enforced is a precondition for the making of an order of an inquiry as to damages. (c) The court can adjourn the application for the enforcement of the undertaking to the trial or further order. (d) The court can determine forthwith that the undertaking is not to be enforced.

(8)   It seems that damages are awarded on a similar basis to that on which damages are awarded for breach of contract. This matter has not been fully explored in the English cases though it is to be noted that in *Air Express Ltd v Ansett Transport Industries (Operations) Ltd* (1979) 146 CLR 249 Aicken J in the High Court of Australia expressed the view that it would be seldom that it would be just and equitable that the unsuccessful plaintiff "should bear the burden of damages which were not foreseeable from circumstances known to him at the time". This passage suggests that the court in exercising its equitable jurisdiction would adopt similar principles to those relevant in a claim for breach of contract.'

11.86 In *Remm Construction (SA) Pty Ltd v Allco Newsteel Pty Ltd*[185] Mulligan J summarised the law, and it is thought that though the learned judge was applying the law of South Australia the same principles apply in England:

'It is necessary to consider principles which relate to injunctive relief of the nature here granted at the interlocutory stage, upon the basis of an undertaking in damages. As was observed by Kaye J in *Bond Brewing Holdings Ltd and ors v National Australian Bank Ltd and ors (No 2)* (1990) 8 ACLC 403 at p 406:

"… the requirement of an undertaking as to damages from a plaintiff seeking interlocutory intervention is for the purpose of safeguarding the defendant from being without remedy for damage suffered as a result of an interlocutory order which subsequently might be held ought not to have been made."

---

[185]   (1991) 56 SASR 515.

17. The party who gives the undertaking puts himself under the power of the Court, not merely in the suit but absolutely: *Newby v Harrison* (1861) 45 ER 889 per Turner LJ at p 890. As Turner LJ there acknowledges that power over such a party continues even if the proceedings have come to an end. The object of requiring an undertaking in damages was discussed in *Air Express* (supra). The only damages to which the party enjoined is entitled are those sustained by the injunction, per Gibbs J at p 312. Stephen J observed that the undertaking is made to the court, and not to the other party, and the court acquires powers to do justice between the parties which it would not otherwise possess, p 318. The undertaking is given as "the price" of obtaining an injunction: *Attorney-General v Albany Hotel Co* (1896) 2 Ch 696 per North J at p 699, *Air Express* (supra), *Southern Tableland Insurance Brokers Pty Ltd (In Liquidation) and Anor v Schomberg* (1986) 11 ACLR 337 and *Bond Brewing Holdings* (supra).

18. The damages to which the enjoined party is entitled must be sustained by reason of the injunction and not for any other reason: *Air Express* (supra). In that case Stephen J expressed that principle in this way, at p 320:

> "From this it can be seen that it will only be if damage is suffered because of the grant of the injunction, and would not have been suffered but for it, that the court should compensate a defendant who claims damages under the undertaking. Its grant must be shown to be the cause sine qua non of the damages complained of before the defendant can be entitled to be compensated for what turns out to be the erroneous grant by the court of the injunction against it. Only then will the defendant have suffered, from the grant of the injunction, such 'real harm' as Cussen J spoke of in *Finnigan's Case* what North J, in *Attorney-General v Albany Hotel Co* described as 'the damages which were really sustained'."

19. *Finnigan's case* is reported in (1922) VLR 819. Lastly, I mention that an inquiry as to damages will not be ordered and damages will not be assessed until either the party giving the undertaking has failed on the merits at the trial or it has been established before trial that the injunction should not have been granted in the first instance: *Ushers Brewery Ltd v PS King and Co (Finance) Ltd* (1972) 1 CL 148 per Plowman J at p 154.'

11.87 The court's discretion not to enforce an undertaking in damages has been exercised where, though it has held that an injunction should not have been granted, it considers that the conduct of the party injuncted was wrongful, or his case lacking in merit. In *Eliades v Lewis*[186] enforcement of the undertaking was refused on the basis of the unmeritorious conduct of the party injuncted. In *Lunn Poly Ltd v Liverpool and Lancashire Properties Ltd*[187] the cross-undertaking was not enforced where a landlord had illegally blocked a fire door serving a tenant's premises. The tenant had obtained an interim injunction but failed to uphold this at trial, the trial judge granting damages in lieu of an injunction. And in *Regan v Paul Properties DPF No 1 Ltd*[188] the claimant had been granted an interim injunction to restrain the construction of part of the upper storey of a block of flats which interfered with his right to light. The trial judge awarded damages rather than injunctive relief. He, however, declined to order enforcement of the claimant's undertaking for the following reasons:

---

[186]   [2005] EWHC 2966 (QB).
[187]   [2006] EWCA Civ 430 at [42] and [47]–[50].
[188]   [2006] EWHC 2052 (Ch). For the judgment at trial see [2006] EWHC 1941 (Ch) and for CA decision see [2007] Ch 135.

(1)   The defendants' actions had been unlawful and they had only reluctantly acknowledged the claimant's rights would be infringed just prior to the commencement of proceedings.

(2)   The claimant had acted in good faith and the interim injunction had only been held to be unjustified as at trial the court thought it right to award damages in lieu of an injunction. The circumstances were the same as in the case of *Lunn Poly Ltd v Liverpool and Lancashire Properties Ltd.*

(3)   To an extent the law governing the question as to whether a mandatory injunction should be granted in an infringement of light case had been unclear when the proceedings were commenced. The claimant would suffer greater hardship if the undertaking was enforced than if the defendants lost some of the profit on the development by reason of delay.

11.88   A factor also weighing in this decision was that in *Mortimer v Bailey*,[189] a case where a mandatory injunction was granted to procure the removal of a building erected in breach of a restrictive covenant, Jacob LJ had said at [41] that:

> 'Where there is doubt as to whether a restrictive covenant applies ... the prudent party will get the matter sorted out before starting building ...'

If the defendants had in accordance with this guidance sought to establish by proceedings of their own in advance of construction whether their works were lawful they would not have had the benefit of the claimant's undertaking in damages. It would be wrong to give them that benefit where the situation was reversed, and the action had been started by the injured party.

11.89   It is uncertain how much weight should be attached to this point. Although the court has jurisdiction to declare the parties' rights in advance of work starting it cannot, it is submitted, be right that in every case a developer should initiate such proceedings merely because his development may arguably infringe a private right, or lose the protection of an undertaking in damages if an interim injunction is sought. It appears more reasonable to give the failure to seek a declaration more weight where it is clear to the defendant that his actions will infringe the claimant's rights, but there is doubt as to whether a court would grant the claimant an injunction, having regard to the principles in *Shelfer v City of London Electric Lighting Co*[190] discussed at **11.94**. The jurisdiction of the court to grant a declaration in these circumstances is reasonably well established.[191] On appeal the issue of enforcement of the undertaking in damages did not arise as the Court of Appeal decided a permanent injunction should be granted.[192]

11.90   Nevertheless, in practice, the consequences of an undertaking can be serious. Claimants need to consider carefully whether by obtaining interim relief they may expose themselves to onerous liabilities, particularly when the effect of such relief is to hold up construction of a large commercial building, resulting in loss of rent, contractor's standing time and financing costs, all of which would certainly support a claim on the undertaking. The dilemma is compounded by the court's reluctance to

---

[189]   [2005] BLR 85.
[190]   [1895] 1 Ch 287 CA.
[191]   See *Greenwich NHS Trust v London & Quadrant Housing Trust* [1998] 3 All ER 437; *Well Barn Shoot v Shackleton* [2003] EWCA Civ 02.
[192]   [2006] 3 WLR 1231.

grant a final injunction where the claimant has not sought an interim injunction.[193] Clearly, an early assessment of the severity of the injury with expert advice is required. Recourse may also be had to the court's powers to order advance disclosure of documents.[194]

FINAL INJUNCTIONS

11.91 At trial, the court may award the claimant an injunction or decide, in the alternative, to award damages in addition to or in substitution for an injunction. The power to award such damages owes its origin to the Chancery Amendment Act 1858, known as Lord Cairns' Act. The original wording of s 2 of the 1858 Act was as follows:

> 'In all cases in which the Court of Chancery has jurisdiction to entertain an application for an injunction against any breach of any covenant, contract or agreement, or against the commission or continuance of any wrongful act, or for the specific performance of any covenant, contract, or agreement, it shall be lawful for the same court, if it shall think fit, to award damages to the party injured either in addition to or in substitution for such injunction or specific performance, and such damages may be assessed in such a manner as the court shall direct.'

11.92 The purpose of the Act was to enable the court to award damages rather than an injunction where it had power to grant an injunction but where an award of damages would be a more appropriate remedy. The Act itself was repealed, probably by inadvertence, but the courts have proceeded on the basis that they retain the powers it conferred.[195] The power is now enshrined in s 50 of the Supreme Court Act 1981:

> 'Where the Court of Appeal or the High Court has jurisdiction to entertain an application for an injunction or specific performance, it may award damages in addition to, or in substitution for, an injunction or specific performance.'

Section 38 of the County Courts Act 1984 makes corresponding provision in relation to county courts.

11.93 The effect of refusing an injunction would of course, in practice, enable the defendant to carry on with the wrongful act. Therefore, equitable damages are assessed on the basis that they compensate the claimant not only for the wrong he has suffered up to the date of trial, but also for the fact that he will, in practice, be losing his rights in perpetuity.[196] The principles governing the assessment of such damages are considered below, where the court has decided to award such damages in substitution for injunctive relief.

11.94 In deciding whether the appropriate remedy is damages or an injunction, the courts apply the principles below which were laid down in *Shelfer v City of London*

---

[193] See **11.111–11.113**.
[194] See CPR, r 31.16 and *Burrells Wharf Freeholds v Galliard Homes Ltd* [1999] CILL 1526.
[195] See *Leeds Industrial Co-operative Society v Slack* [1924] AC 851 at 862 per Viscount Finlay.
[196] See generally *Jaggard v Sawyer* [1995] 1 WLR 269; Jolowicz 'Damages in Equity: A study of Lord Cairns' Act' 1975 CLJ 224.

Electric Light Company,[197] (*'Shelfer'*) a case in which the claim related to nuisance by noise and vibration, arising out of the operation of a steam-powered power station. AL Smith LJ said:[198]

> 'In my opinion, it may be stated as a good working rule that–
>
> (1)   if the injury to the plaintiff's legal rights is small,
> (2)   and is one which is capable of being estimated in money,
> (3)   and is one which can be adequately compensated by a small money payment,
> (4)   and the case is one in which it would be oppressive to the defendant to grant an injunction
>
> then damages in substitution for an injunction may be given.
>
> There may also be cases in which, though the four above-mentioned requirements exist, the defendant by his conduct, as, for instance, hurrying up his building so as if possible to avoid an injunction, or otherwise acting with a reckless disregard of the plaintiff's rights, has disentitled himself from asking that damages may be assessed in substitution for an injunction.
>
> It is impossible to lay down any rule as to what, under the differing circumstances of each case, constitutes either a small injury, or one that can be estimated in money, or what is a small money payment, or an adequate compensation, or what would be oppressive to the defendant. This must be left to the good sense of the Tribunal which deals with each case as it comes up for adjudication. For instance, an injury to the plaintiff's legal right to a window and a cottage represented by £15 might well be held not to be small but considerable; whereas a similar injury to a warehouse or other large building represented by ten times that amount might be held to be inconsiderable. Each case must be decided upon its own facts; but to escape the rule it must be brought within the exception. In the present case, it appears to me that the injury to the plaintiff is certainly not small, nor is it in my judgment capable of being estimated in money, or of being adequately compensated by a small money payment.'

11.95   This statement of the law has generally, been adopted in subsequent cases. In *Colls v Home and Colonial Stores*[199] (*'Colls'*) Lord Lindley referred to it with approval, citing it as a case in which it was explained that the general rule that where a legal right is continuously infringed an injunction to protect it ought to be granted was subject to qualification. The words of AL Smith LJ have frequently been quoted subsequently with approval, and applied.[200] However, other authoritative views have been expressed. These differ from those of AL Smith LJ in two respects, more of emphasis than substance. First, AL Smith LJ expressed himself in terms which suggest that unless the tests he laid down were satisfied, an injunction ought to be granted. However, in *Colls*, Lord Macnaughten took the view that the court should incline towards the grant of damages in lieu of an injunction unless there were specific factors pointing towards the grant of an injunction:

> 'In some cases, of course, an injunction is necessary – if, for instance, the injury cannot fairly be compensated by money – if the defendant has acted in a high-handed manner – if he has endeavoured to steal a march on the plaintiff or to evade the jurisdiction of the court. In all these cases an injunction is necessary, in order to do justice to the plaintiff and as a warning

---

[197]   [1895] 1 Ch 287.
[198]   [1895] 1 Ch 322 at 323.
[199]   [1904] AC 179.
[200]   *Slack v Leeds Industrial Co-operative Society* [1924] 2 Ch 475; *Price v Hilditch* [1930] 1 Ch 500; *Pugh v Howells* (1984) 48 P&CR 298; *Deakins v Hookings* [1994] 1 EGLR 190; *Jaggard v Sawyer* [1995] 2 All ER 189, CA; *Gooden v Ketley* [1996] EGCS 47, CA.

to others. But if there is really a question as to whether the obstruction is legal or not, and if the defendant has acted fairly and not in an unneighbourly spirit, I am disposed to think that the court ought to incline to damages rather than an injunction.'

11.96 In *Kine v Jolly*[201] in which a mandatory injunction to remove part of a house was granted at first instance, but overturned on appeal, Vaughan-Williams LJ somewhat enigmatically stated:[202]

> 'I propose to apply either the test laid down by Lord Macnaghten in *Colls v Home and Colonial Stores Ltd* or that laid down by AL Smith LJ in his judgment in *Shelfer v City of London Electric Lighting Company.*'

He went on to hold that it was impossible to say that there ought to be any injunction upon the ground that the defendant has acted in a high-handed manner, or has shown a desire to steal a march on the plaintiff, or to evade the jurisdiction of the court. He stated that both parties had acted honestly in accordance with what they believed and not unreasonably. On the other hand, Cozens-Hardy LJ thought that 'the tendency of the speeches in the House of Lords in *Colls v Home and Colonial Stores Ltd* is to go a little further than was done in *Shelfer v City of London Electric Lighting Co*' and that, as a general rule, the court ought to be less free in granting mandatory injunctions than it was previously.[203] The third member of the court, Romer LJ, delivered a dissenting judgment.

11.97 In *Fishenden v Higgs and Hill Ltd*[204] ('*Fishenden*') the Court of Appeal expressed the view that the *Shelfer* case did not lay down rigid rules. Lord Hanworth MR said that the rules in the *Shelfer* case should be read together with the later cases of *Colls* and *Kine v Jolly*, and that the court should incline against an injunction if possible. Romer LJ took the view that AL Smith LJ did not intend to say and did not in fact say that in all cases where the conditions he laid down were not satisfied an injunction should be granted. Maugham LJ indicated disapproval of AL Smith LJ's 'good working rule'. In *Fishenden* the loss of light resulting from the defendant's proposed building was certainly substantial.[205] This gave support to the argument that even where the injury was significant the court would refuse an injunction.

11.98 The court is more disposed to grant a prohibitory than a mandatory injunction, although the reluctance to grant an injunction of the latter kind is less marked than at the interim stage since all the facts will be known, hence the risk of injustice inherent in the grant of a mandatory injunction will not be present.

11.99 Thus in *Redland Bricks Ltd v Morris*[206] the plaintiff complained of the defendant's excavation on neighbouring land which had rendered the plaintiff's land unstable. The cost of restoring the support to the plaintiff's land was £30,000, and the value of that land £12,000. The House of Lords held that an injunction ought not to be granted against the defendant requiring it to carry out works of this extent, although the judge would have been justified in imposing on the defendants an obligation to do some

---

[201] [1905] 1 Ch 480.
[202] Ibid, at 495.
[203] [1905] 1 Ch 480 at 504.
[204] (1935) 153 LT 128.
[205] The light contours showing the loss of well-lit areas within the plaintiff's premises from the defendant's development are reproduced in J Swarbrick *Easements of Light* (BT Batsford Ltd, 1938) at pp 48 and 49, 56 and 57.
[206] [1970] AC 652.

reasonable and not too expensive works which might have a reasonable chance of preventing further damage. Lord Upjohn said:[207]

> '1. A mandatory injunction can only be granted where the plaintiff shows a very strong probability on the facts that grave damage will accrue to him in the future ... It is a jurisdiction to be exercised sparingly and with caution, but in the proper case, unhesitatingly.
> 2. Damages will not be a sufficient or adequate remedy if such damage does happen ...
> 3. Unlike the case where a negative injunction is granted to prevent the continuance or recurrence of a wrongful act the question of the cost to the defendant to do works to prevent or lessen the likelihood of a future apprehended wrong must be an element to be taken into account: (a) where the defendant has acted without regard to his neighbour's rights, or has tried to steal a march on him or has tried to evade the jurisdiction of the court or to sum it up, has acted wantonly and quite unreasonably in relation to his neighbour he may be ordered to repair his wanton and unreasonable acts by doing positive work to restore the status quo even if the expense to him is out of all proportion to the advantage thereby accruing to the plaintiff ... (b) but where the defendant has acted reasonably, although in the event wrongly, the cost of remedying by positive action his earlier activities is most important for two reasons. First, because no legal wrong has yet occurred (for which he has not been recompensed at law and in equity) and, in spite of gloomy expert opinion, may never occur or possibly only on a much smaller scale than anticipated. Secondly, because if ultimately heavy damage does occur the plaintiff is in no way prejudiced by his action at law and all his consequential remedies in equity.'

11.100 In the context of rights to light, the issues as to the grant or refusal of an injunction at trial will be as follows:

(1) If the claimant has applied for and obtained an interim injunction restraining the infringing development, should a final injunction to this same effect be granted?

(2) If the claimant has either not applied for or been refused such an interim injunction, should a mandatory injunction to order the removal of the infringing development be granted?

11.101 Despite the dicta of Lord Macnaughten in *Colls*, and the doubts expressed as to their applicability in *Fishenden*, the *Shelfer* guidelines continued to be applied both in rights of light cases and in cases where the issue arose whether to grant an injunction to require removal of a building which interfered with some other type of easement or had been erected in breach of restrictive covenants. The following factors were regarded as of significance:

(1) the extent of the injury to the claimant;

(2) whether there has been an interim injunction applied for or granted; and

(3) the defendant's conduct.

11.102 The decisions exhibited some reluctance to order completed buildings to be pulled down, at least where the defendant has acted in good faith and not so as to attempt to steal a march on the claimant. So, in *Wrotham Park Estate Co Ltd v Parkside*

---

[207] Ibid.

Homes Ltd,[208] a mandatory injunction was sought to secure the demolition of houses constructed in breach of a restrictive covenant. The court refused to grant a mandatory injunction, Brightman J saying:[209]

> 'It would in my opinion be an unpardonable waste of much needed houses to direct that they now be pulled down ... no damage of a financial nature has been done to the plaintiffs by the breach of the layout stipulation. The plaintiff's use of the Wrotham Park Estate has not been and will not be impeded. It is totally unnecessary to demolish the houses in order to preserve the integrity of the restrictive covenants imposed on the rest of area 14.'

11.103 In *Bracewell v Appleby*[210] when both the first and second factors came into play the issue arose as to whether a mandatory injunction should be granted preventing future use of a right of way which the defendant had wrongfully used for access to a new house, which had not been fully constructed at the date the plaintiff's rights were asserted, but which was completed and inhabited at the date of trial. The court refused an injunction on the ground that it would have the effect of rendering the house uninhabitable. The plaintiff had not sought an injunction until the house was actually constructed.

11.104 In the earlier case of *National Provincial Plate Glass Insurance Co v Prudential Assurance Company*,[211] a rights of light case, a mandatory injunction was refused on the grounds that the infringing building would not seriously affect the occupation of the plaintiff's house, and that the injury done to the plaintiffs was done by an integral part of a very important building scheme, and that a portion of that scheme actually benefited the plaintiff. In *Snell & Prideaux Ltd v Dutton Mirrors Ltd*[212] again the basis for refusal of a mandatory injunction to remove an obstruction to a right of way was related to the failure by the plaintiff to seek an interim injunction, despite being given an opportunity to do so, before the offending building works were carried out. The court took into account that the defendants were acting in good faith, and the fact that the plaintiffs had an alternative access to their building from the front, and had made virtually no use of the right of way obstructed for many years.

11.105 On the other hand, in other cases the court has been prepared to grant a mandatory injunction at trial to compel the removal of the infringing building. In *Smith v Smith*[213] the plaintiff raised a wall from 9 ft 6 ins to 26 ft 8 ins about 8 ft from the plaintiff's windows, despite protests by the plaintiff. The plaintiff claimed that the erection of the wall had darkened his rooms, especially the kitchen and scullery, and his workshop which was rendered useless for the work of a cabinet maker and upholsterer. He adduced evidence that the rooms facing the party wall were so darkened that they could scarcely be used except by artificial light; that the workshop was rendered almost useless for its purpose; that the house had become almost uninhabitable; that the health of some of the inmates had been affected and the plaintiff's wife and children had been obliged to leave. The main defence was delay and acquiescence. The court dismissed the defence. Sir George Jessell MR said:

---

[208] [1974] 1 WLR 798.
[209] Ibid, at 811B.
[210] [1975] 1 Ch 408.
[211] (1877) 6 ChD 757.
[212] [1995] 1 EGLR 259.
[213] (1875) LR 20 Eq 500.

'Without laying down any absolute rule, in the first place it is of great importance to see if the defendant knew he was doing wrong, and was taking his chance about being disturbed in doing it.

The next point for consideration is the materiality of the injury to the plaintiff … but that alone was not sufficient; all the circumstances of the case must be taken into consideration, not only the injury to the plaintiff but also the amount which has been laid out by the defendant.

In the present case the injury was most serious to the plaintiff, and he could not be compensated without the defendant buying the house, also as regards the defendant I am not satisfied that any considerable sum has been laid out upon his building. Again the plaintiff was occupier of the house, so that it was a personal injury to him …'

Interestingly, the order of the court provided that if there was a dispute as to whether the defendant had pulled down a sufficient extent of the wall, it was to be referred to a named surveyor.

11.106 In *Pugh v Howells*[214] the defendants built a two-storey extension to their house, next door to the plaintiff's house, thereby affecting the light to the plaintiffs' kitchen. When the plaintiffs observed that the defendants were carrying out work their solicitors wrote to the defendants' solicitors asking them to disclose any plans. The reply was unhelpful and the defendants completed the extension to roof level over a bank holiday weekend. The court of first instance refused an injunction, and awarded the plaintiffs £500 damages in lieu. The Court of Appeal granted a mandatory injunction for removal of that part of the extension above ground floor level, on the ground, first, that the defendants' conduct, in proceeding in the teeth of complaints by the plaintiffs and advice from their own expert was such as to merit serious criticism. Further, that it was not possible to say that the injury to the plaintiffs' rights was insignificant. Similarly, in *Cudmore-Ray v Pajouheshnia*,[215] a mandatory injunction was granted when the defendant had hurried up the building works and acted with reckless disregard for the plaintiff's rights.

11.107 In *Deakins v Hookings*,[216] another case concerning an extension to a property which affected the plaintiff's house, in which she lived, a mandatory injunction was granted on the ground that the injury to the plaintiff was significant, since the rooms affected formed part of her house. In *Daniells v Mendonca*[217] the grant of a mandatory injunction to require demolition of works contravening the London Building Acts (Amendment) Act 1939, Part VI was upheld on appeal, applying the *Shelfer* guidelines.

11.108 In *Jaggard v Sawyer*,[218] another case involving the construction of a house in breach of a restrictive covenant, the court refused a mandatory injunction to remove the house, and awarded damages in lieu. The Court of Appeal approved the *Shelfer* guidelines. Millett LJ said:[219]

---

[214]   (1984) 48 P&CR 298, CA.
[215]   [1993] CLY 4040.
[216]   [1994] 1 EGLR 190.
[217]   (1999) 78 P & CR 401
[218]   [1995] 1 WLR 269.
[219]   Ibid at 287H.

'Laid down just 100 years ago, AL Smith LJ's check-list has stood the test of time: but it needs to be remembered that it is only a working rule and does not purport to be an exhaustive statement of the circumstances in which damages may be awarded instead of an injunction.'

Bingham LJ also referred to the 'good working rule' with approval.[220] It was held that the injury to the plaintiff's rights was small, that it could be adequately compensated by a small money payment, and that it would be oppressive to the defendant to grant an injunction. It was relevant also that the plaintiff had not sought an interim injunction, and that the defendants had not acted in blatant and calculated disregard of the plaintiff's rights.

11.109 In *Jaggard v Sawyer* the power to grant damages in substitution for an injunction was held to extend to cases of trespass to land, such as oversailing by cranes. Suggestions in previous cases to the effect that there was no power to grant damages in lieu of an injunction in such cases, as trespass was actionable without proof of damage, were disapproved.[221] The rule that a landowner whose title is not in issue is entitled to an injunction as of right to restrain trespass no longer applies. So in *Gooden v Ketley*,[222] a case of trespass by building works, the plaintiff sought the removal of a manhole, drains and wall, constructed when the defendant built three blocks of flats on his land and, it was alleged and found, constituted trespass on the plaintiff's land. It was held that a mandatory injunction should be refused, on the ground that the case was one where the injury to the plaintiff's legal right was small, it was capable of being estimated in money, and could adequately be compensated by a small money payment. Further, the case was one in which it would be oppressive to the defendant to grant an injunction. The court further held that in considering oppression, there was a range of cases to be considered, at one end of which the defendant might have acted openly and in good faith and in ignorance of the plaintiff's rights, and at the other end in full knowledge that he was invading the plaintiff's rights and hoping to present the plaintiff with a fait accompli. In the instant case, whilst the defendant had acted deliberately, it was not an appropriate one for the grant of an injunction, although an award of aggravated damages was upheld.

11.110 However, in *Gafford v Graham*,[223] a case of building in breach of a restrictive covenant, an injunction to have the offending structure removed was refused both on the ground of hardship and on the ground that the owner of the dominant tenement had, with full knowledge of his rights, omitted to seek an interim injunction, even though the defendant's conduct had shown blatant and calculated disregard for the plaintiff's rights. The Court of Appeal recognised that the injury to the plaintiff's rights was not small. However, the decision was justified by reference to the fact that the plaintiff had shown willingness to accept compensation. The decision seemed to mark a possible departure from the guidelines, at least where the claimant had either failed to act to seek an interim injunction or indicated a willingness to accept a financial payment for release of his rights.

---

[220] Ibid at 278B.
[221] Ibid at 280D–H (Sir Thomas Bingham) and at 284F (Millet LJ). The 'oversailing' cases included *Woollerton and Wilson Ltd v Richard Costain Ltd* [1970] 1 WLR 411; *John Trenberth v National Westminster Bank Ltd* (1979)39 P&CR 104; *Anchor Brewhouse Developments Ltd v Berkeley House (Docklands Developments) Ltd* [1987] 2 EGLR 173.
[222] [1996] EGCS 47.
[223] (1998) 77 P&CR 73.

11.111 The tendency of the courts to refuse a final injunction for the latter two reasons had appeared in the earlier case of *Blue Town Investments v Higgs & Hill*[224] where it was held that these factors were decisive against the grant of a final injunction (the plaintiff refused an offer by the court to grant an interim injunction which would have had the effect of imposing an undertaking in damages as the price of such an injunction). Although in *Oxy Electric v Zainuddin*[225] Hoffmann J criticised the *Blue Town* decision, he explained his criticism when giving judgment in *Snell & Prideaux Ltd v Dutton Mirrors Ltd*[226] in the following terms:

> 'Finally on the remedy, I should mention that Mr West, in submitting that his client should be granted a mandatory injunction, relied upon a decision of my own in *Oxy Electric Ltd v Zainuddin* [1991] 1 WLR 115 as support for the proposition that the fact that the plaintiffs did not apply for an interlocutory injunction was immaterial to whether they should be granted a final one at the trial. That case goes no further than deciding that failure to apply for an interlocutory injunction is not a reason for striking out the action as frivolous and vexatious. It by no means follows that it is not a matter to which regard may be had in deciding whether a final injunction should be granted. In this case, it was quite clear that delaying the commencement of the works on the defendants' land until this action had been determined was going to involve a risk of financial loss to the defendant. The question was, who should bear the risk of that financial loss if their claim turned out to be wrong? The defendants offered the plaintiffs the opportunity of preserving the status quo on condition that they were willing to give a cross-undertaking which would impose that risk upon them. That the plaintiffs declined to do. In those circumstances, the defendants, being advised that they had an arguable case, went ahead and averted the loss by going forward with the building. In my judgment, that was not an unreasonable thing for them to do. In those circumstances, I think it would be quite wrong to penalise them by ordering their building to be torn down.'

11.112 It seems, however, clear that the suggestion in *Gafford v Graham* that failure to apply for an interim injunction *automatically* disentitles the claimant from a final injunction is unlikely to have survived *Mortimer v Bailey*.[227] In that case a final injunction was granted to remove a building erected in breach of a restrictive covenant. There was evidence of substantial damage to the covenant holder's interest and they had albeit belatedly applied for but been refused an interim injunction. The Court of Appeal distinguished *Gafford v Graham* on the grounds that in that case the plaintiff had stood by and had been willing to accept a cash sum. But Peter Gibson LJ, with whom the other members of the court agreed, also said at para 29 of the report:

> 'For my part, I own to some doubt as to whether it is appropriate to say that a person who does not proceed for an interlocutory injunction when he knows that a building is being erected in breach of covenant, but who has made clear his intention to object to the breach, should generally be debarred from claiming a final injunction to pull down the building. There may be some circumstances in which a claimant would not be able to take the risk of seeking an interim injunction He would need to satisfy the *American Cyanamid* test and would have to provide an undertaking in damages. It may be entirely reasonable for the claimant, having put the defendant on notice, to proceed to trial rather than take the risk of expending money wastefully by seeking interim relief.'

11.113 Peter Gibson LJ did, however, recognise that not seeking an interim injunction was a factor which could be taken into account in weighing in the balance whether a

---

[224]   [1990] 2 All ER 897.
[225]   [1990] 2 All ER 902.
[226]   [1995] 1 EGLR 259.
[227]   [2005] BLR 85.

final injunction should be granted. But in *Jacklin and another v Chief Constable of West Yorkshire*[228] the Court of Appeal upheld the grant of a mandatory injunction to remove obstructions from a right of way despite the claimant's failure to seek an interim injunction and delaying bringing proceedings for more than 3 years. The Court held that for an injunction to be refused, all four criteria in *Shelfer* had to be satisfied. The appellant had failed to demonstrate that the grant of an injunction would be oppressive, the fourth criterion.

11.114 Fresh impetus to the argument that injunction would be inappropriate in rights of light cases, at least where commercial premises were involved, was given by *Midtown v City of London Real Property Co*[229] ('*Midtown*'). In *Midtown* a prohibitory injunction was sought by the landlord and tenant of a commercial building used as solicitors' offices to restrain the proposed redevelopment of a site across the road which admittedly would greatly reduce the light received through its windows. The claim for an injunction failed. As regards the landlord, it was held by Peter Smith J that (i) it was only interested in the property from a money making point of view, (ii) there was no present loss due to the length of the lease, (iii) it had redevelopment proposals of its own, and (iv) it had rebuffed efforts at negotiation. The tenant's claim failed because it could not demonstrate any real disadvantage by having to work with artificial light.

11.115 The judgments in *Jaggard v Sawyer* were regarded by Peter Smith J in *Midtown* as 'establish[ing] a willingness on the part of the courts to depart from the strict requirements of the four requirements set out in *Shelfer* in an appropriate case'.[230] On that basis he felt free to refuse relief to the claimants.

11.116 However, more recently, in *Regan v Paul Properties DPF No 1 Ltd*[231] the Court of Appeal reaffirmed the application of the *Shelfer* guidelines. At first instance Stephen Smith QC accepted Mr Regan's contention. In particular, his lounge would be reduced from 67% well lit to about 42–45%. Mr Regan used his lounge for reading, painting and model-making all of which would be affected. On the other hand, the injury to the value of his maisonette was only about 2–2.5% of its value. The injury to the defendants if they could not go ahead was significant, reducing the value of the truncated penthouse to £300,000 from £450,000. There would be additional building costs of between £12,000 and £35,000. Applying the guidelines laid down in *Shelfer*, the judge considered the injury to Mr Regan's legal rights small, capable of being estimated in monetary terms, and capable of being adequately compensated for by a small monetary payment and that the grant of injunctive relief would be oppressive. He also considered and adopted a suggestion of Lord Macnaughten in *Colls* and taken up in *Fishenden* to the effect that injunctions should be less readily granted in rights of light cases. He held that the burden was on Mr Regan to justify the grant of an injunction, which he had failed to do. He awarded damages to be assessed and refused an injunction.

11.117 In the Court of Appeal the decision was reversed. Giving the only judgment, Mummery LJ reaffirmed the authority of *Shelfer* and rejected the argument based on the dicta of Lord Macnaughten in *Colls* that the court should be reluctant to grant injunctions in rights of light cases. He pointed out that Lord Macnaughten prefaced what he described as *practical suggestions* with the comment that he did not put them forward as carrying any authority. Nor did he comment adversely on *Shelfer*. Later

---

[228] [2007] EWCA Civ 181.
[229] [2005] 1 EGLR 65.
[230] See *Midtown* at [73].
[231] [2007] Ch 135.

judges who had suggested that he intended to cast doubt on *Shelfer* were in error. Further, the suggestion that Lord Macnaughten intended to lay down a rule that injunctions would be less readily granted in rights of light cases was expressly denied by the Court of Appeal in *Slack v Leeds Industrial Co-operative Society Ltd*.[232] Mummery LJ held that later cases, including *Jaggard v Sawyer* did not have the effect of placing the onus on a claimant to persuade the court that he should not be left to his remedy in damages. Since the judge had applied the wrong test, the Court of Appeal was free to come to its own decision on the merits. He held that the injury to Mr Regan was significant, in terms of loss of amenity, and that the injury to the value of his maisonette was more than could be compensated by a small money payment. Further, the amount of damages which he would be entitled to in lieu of an injunction would be substantial, as it would be linked to the value of the penthouse.

11.118 On the question of whether it would be oppressive to grant an injunction, Mummery LJ said that the defendants had taken a calculated risk in proceeding with the works despite Mr Regan's protests, and could not complain about the consequences. It was not therefore oppressive. The same approach appears to have been adopted in the slightly later case of *Jacklin and another v Chief Constable of West Yorkshire*.[233]

11.119 *Regan* establishes that the *Shelfer* guidelines still apply, and that there is no principle that injunctions are less readily granted in rights of light cases. It also suggests that where the injury is to the claimant's home, the court will readily grant a mandatory as well as a prohibitory injunction provided he has acted promptly and the defendant has chosen to ignore his protests. A question left unanswered is the status of *Midtown*, ignored by Mummery LJ. It seems reasonably clear it cannot be relied on as establishing any general propositions.

11.120 The terms of an injunction are a matter of the court's discretion. In the drafting of an injunction, it must be remembered that the remedies for breach of the terms of an injunction are by way of sequestration and committal for contempt of court. It is therefore important that the order clearly sets out what the defendant is required to abstain from doing, or to do. In the case of a prohibitory injunction, the injunction ought to make it clear what the defendant is prohibited from doing. Where the prohibition on building is partial only, a set of drawings defining the limits within which works may be carried out in terms of height, width and distance from the dominant property may be attached to the order. In the case of a prohibitory injunction, it was said by Lord Macnaughten in *Colls*,[234] that the order should be in general terms restraining the defendant from erecting any building so as to cause a nuisance or illegal obstruction to the plaintiff's ancient windows. He also suggested that if the act came to trial before the defendant's building was completed, there should be liberty to the plaintiff to apply for a further mandatory injunction or damages within a fixed time after the building was completed. This was intended to meet the case, presumably, where it is not clear whether the building as completed will constitute an actionable interference. Examination of orders made in decided cases show that these suggestions have been followed.[235] Modification of the standard form may be required to take account of those parts of a proposed new building which are uncontroversial. Alternatively, it may be in some cases appropriate to define the outline of the building which is permitted.

---

[232] (1924) 2 Ch 475.
[233] [2007] EWCA Civ 181.
[234] [1904] AC 179 at 194.
[235] See, eg, *Higgins v Betts* [1905] 2 Ch 210 at 218; *Andrews v Waite* [1907] 2 Ch 500 at 510–511.

11.121 In the case of mandatory injunctions, the court will generally refuse to grant an injunction in terms which require constant supervision by the court.[236] It is therefore important to define precisely the extent of the defendant's obligations. One possible solution in the case of uncertainty is for the order to provide for reference to a surveyor or other expert.[237] Alternatively, the order may be framed by reference to a plan showing the area to be demolished. It may be appropriate to suspend the operation of an injunction for a reasonable period to avoid hardship to the defendant or occupiers of the building, and the time for compliance should be specified in the order, and should be reasonable having regard to all the circumstances, including the need to arrange contractors, obtain statutory permissions, etc. It would be highly unusual for the operation of an injunction not to be suspended pending appeal. Normally, this is done by inserting in the order a provision that provided a notice of appeal is entered within a certain time the operation of the injunction is to be suspended until final determination of the appeal.

THE AWARD OF DAMAGES IN ADDITION TO OR IN SUBSTITUTION FOR AN INJUNCTION

11.122 Such damages are, as already explained,[238] awarded in addition to or in lieu of injunctions, under powers originally conferred by the Chancery Amendment Act 1858, s 2, known as Lord Cairns' Act.[239] They can be awarded only where the claimant is entitled to claim an injunction. It is clear that the date at which the claimant must establish his entitlement to an injunction is the date of commencement of the proceedings. In *Holland v Worley*[240] Pearson J, having read s 2 of the Chancery Amendment Act 1858, said:

> 'It only arises when the Court of Chancery has jurisdiction to grant an injunction. It can only apply to those cases in which the court could have granted an injunction, at all events at the time of the filing of the Bill.'

That this is the position has been confirmed in *Jaggard v Sawyer*:[241]

> '(4) The power to award damages under Lord Cairns' Act arises whenever the court "has jurisdiction to entertain an application" for an injunction or specific performance. This question must be determined as at the date of the writ. If the court would then have had jurisdiction to grant an injunction, it has jurisdiction to award damages instead. When the court comes to consider whether to grant an injunction or award damages instead, of course, it must do so by reference to the circumstances as they exist at the date of the hearing.
>
> (5) The former question is effectively one of jurisdiction. The question is whether, at the date of the writ, the court *could* have granted an injunction, not whether it *would* have done (see *City of London Brewery Co v Tennant* (1873) LR 9 Ch App 212). Russell LJ put it neatly in *Hooper v Rogers* [1974] 3 All ER 417 at 419, [1975] Ch 43 at 48, when he said that the question was "whether ... the judge could have (however unwisely ...) made a mandatory order". There have been numerous cases where damages under Lord Cairns' Act were refused because at the date of the writ it was impossible to

---

[236] *Co-op Insurance Society Ltd v Argyll Stores (Holdings) Ltd* [1997] 3 All ER 297, HL.
[237] As in *Smith v Smith* (1875) LR 20 Eq 500 at 505.
[238] See **11.92**.
[239] See **11.91**.
[240] (1884) 26 ChD 578.
[241] [1995] 1 WLR 269 at 284H per Millett LJ.

grant an injunction or specific performance: for one well-known example, see *Lavery v Pursell* (1888) 39 Ch D 508. The recent case of *Surrey CC v Bredero Homes Ltd* [1993] 3 All ER 705, [1993] 1 WLR 1361 appears to have been a case of this character.'

11.123 An example of the application of this rule is provided by *Fritz v Hobson*.[242] Equitable damages were granted notwithstanding that subsequent to the commencement of proceedings the nuisance in question had been abated. The plaintiff's failure to apply for or obtain an interim injunction, which might otherwise be held to be a factor which would prevent him being awarded an injunction at trial, is not a bar to his claiming equitable damages as such.

11.124 The claimant is awarded a sum equivalent to that which he would notionally have agreed to accept in reasonable negotiations for the release of his right before proceedings were commenced. The compensation is intended to cover not only past, but also future wrongs, so that the claimant's rights are in effect extinguished. In all these cases, damages were awarded by reference to the sum, which the claimant would notionally have accepted for a release or modification of his rights. The relevant date is (in the case of covenants against building) a date before the building works were started. The court must put itself in the position of the parties as at that time, although it is permissible, at least in some circumstances, to have regard to what has happened subsequently: see *Attorney-General v Blake*[243] and *Amec Developments Ltd v Jury's Hotel Management (UK) Ltd*.[244] Damages would only be nominal if for some reason there was never any prospect of the claimant obtaining an injunction, as where the wrongdoer had parted with the land burdened by the covenant before proceedings were started, and the current owners were not joined as parties to the action. In *Surrey County Council v Bredero Homes Ltd*[245] the defendant developed a housing estate more intensively than permitted by restrictive covenants in the transfers to it. The plaintiff covenantees took no steps to restrain this development by way of claim for an injunction or specific performance. After the defendant had disposed of all the houses, the covenantees commenced claims for damages, based on a sum equal to the payment that might have been extracted from the defendant in return for agreed modifications to the covenants so as to authorise the more profitable development which had in fact been carried out. It was held that the plaintiffs were entitled only to nominal damages, since by the time the action had commenced there was no prospect of the plaintiffs being awarded equitable relief. This decision has been (and it is submitted rightly) criticised as allowing a defendant to profit from his own wrong. It is thought that following *Attorney-General v Blake* it would not now be followed. Clearly, if the claimant at the time he started proceedings is no longer the dominant owner at the time those proceedings are commenced, he could not have any prospect of claiming any relief apart from damages for the loss of business and discomfort he suffered from the infringement of light whilst he was in occupation. Equally, if the right to light arose under a deed, and the defendant is not at the date of the proceedings the owner of the servient land, there would be no prospect of an injunction, and hence no claim except to common law damages. Where the claimant claims a *quia timet* injunction, there is jurisdiction to award equitable damages, but such damages will be awarded solely in respect of the damage to be sustained in the future by injuries which the injunction, if granted, would have prevented.[246]

---

[242] (1880) 14 ChD 542.
[243] [2001] 1 AC 268. The principle of the award of such damages was explained by Lord Nicholls at 281G–H.
[244] (2000) 82 P&CR 286.
[245] [1993] 3 All ER 705, CA.
[246] *Leeds Industrial Co-operative Society v Slack* [1924] AC 851.

11.125 Equitable damages are to compensate the claimant for all loss, past and prospective.[247] Past loss would cover matters which would form the subject of a claim at common law, for example, discomfort and injury to business. In the case of trespasses, a defendant can be ordered to pay daily damages representing the value to the defendant of the wrongful use.[248] But where as in the case of infringement of light the infringement is permanent the better view seems to be that the court, if it refuses an injunction, will award global damages for both past loss and prospective loss, without differentiation.

11.126 The method of calculation of damages, where an injunction has not been granted, was summarised by Millett LJ in *Jaggard v Sawyer*:[249]

> 'Prima facie the measure of damages in either case for breach of a covenant not to build a house on neighbouring land is the diminution in the value of the plaintiff's land occasioned by the breach. One element in the value of the plaintiff's land immediately before the breach is attributable to his ability to obtain an injunction to prevent the building. Clearly a defendant who wished to build would pay for the release of the covenant, but only so long as the court could still protect it by the grant of an injunction. The proviso is important. It is the ability to claim an injunction which gives the benefit of the covenant much of its value. If the plaintiff delays proceedings until it is no longer possible for him to obtain an injunction, he destroys his own bargaining position and devalues his right. The unavailability of the remedy of injunction at one and the same time deprives the court of jurisdiction to award damages under the Act and removes the basis for awarding substantial damages at common law. For this reason, I take the view that damages can be awarded at common law in accordance with the approach adopted in *Wrotham Park*, but in practice only in the circumstances in which they could also be awarded under the Act.'

11.127 The actual method of calculation was described thus by Sir Thomas Bingham MR:

> '[The trial judge] valued the right at what a reasonable seller would sell it for. In situations of this kind a plaintiff should not be treated as eager to sell, which he very probably is not. But the court will not value the right at the ransom price which a very reluctant plaintiff might put on it. I see no error in the judge's approach to this aspect.'

The approach in *Jaggard v Sawyer* has subsequently received support from the Court of Appeal decision in *Gafford v Graham*[250] and *Lunn Poly Ltd v Liverpool and Lancashire Properties v Ltd*.[251]

11.128 Damages, therefore, fall to be assessed by reference to the amount which the dominant owner could reasonably have expected to receive for their release, discounting any ransom element. The same approach had been adopted in *Bracewell v Appleby*,[252] a case relating to a right of way where Graham J said:

> '... I think that for the purpose of estimating damages they [i e the plaintiffs] and the other servient owners in Hill Road, albeit reluctant, must be treated as being willing to accept a fair price for the right of way in question and must not be treated as if they were in the

---

[247]   *Fritz v Hobson* (1880) 14 ChD 542.
[248]   *Whitwham v Westminster Brymbo Coal Company* [1896] 2 Ch 538.
[249]   [1995] 1 WLR 269 at 291F.
[250]   (1998) 77 P&CR 73.
[251]   [2006] EWCA Civ 430 at [17] ff.
[252]   [1975] 1 All ER 993.

extremely powerful bargaining position which an interlocutory injunction would have given them if it had been obtained before the Defendant started operations and incurred expense.'

11.129 The decided cases give some guidance as to the amount of awards. The most usual starting point is to consider the profit which the defendant has made as a result of the wrongful act, and make an award which reflects a part of this profit, on the ground that the defendant would notionally have been prepared to give up some profit element in order to secure his objective. In *Bracewell v Appleby*, the defendant had built a house on a plot of land. Access to the house could be gained only down a private road, but the defendant had no right to use the private road for such purposes. The court assessed the likely net value of the house at £5,000. The defendant was not a professional developer, and had built the house for his own occupation. The court concluded that he would have been prepared to pay a substantial sum for the privilege of doing so, and awarded damages of £2,000. In *Wrotham Park Estate Co Limited v Parkside Homes Limited*,[253] a case concerning a breach of a restrictive covenant by the construction of a house, the sum awarded amounted to approximately 5% of the benefit obtained by the defendant. In *Jaggard v Sawyer*, the basis of the calculations is not apparent from the report. In *Tamares (Vincent Square) Ltd v Fairpoint Properties (Vincent Square) Ltd*[254] the court accepted that the measure of damages was the greater of (a) damages for loss of amenity and (b) damages to compensate for loss of the ability to obtain an injunction. The court received evidence from valuers who estimated the profit from the infringing part of the development as between £163,000 (claimants) and £186,000 (defendants). The judge, Gabriel Moss QC, applying the guidance in *Carr-Saunders v Dick McNeil Associates Limited* (see **11.132**), as well as the cases cited above awarded £50,000, roughly one-third of the profit, based on what would have been agreed in the hypothetical negotiation.

11.130 The starting point is sometimes the one-third figure which, in the compulsory purchase case of *Stokes v Cambridge Corporation*,[255] was applied to assess the percentage of the developer's profit which the holder of a ransom strip would seek as a condition of releasing the strip. The analogy is not perfect, because in the *Stokes* case it was assumed that an inducement to the holder of the ransom strip would be that its own land would benefit from the development, which can seldom be the case in a rights to light situation. It is in any event difficult to apply the principle where the infringing development is of no direct financial benefit to the defendant, for example, if it is part of his residence, or where indeed the infringing development actually involves the defendant incurring a loss. The size of the award should not be so large that the development would not have taken place had such a sum been payable.[256]

11.131 A further point is that, in rights to light cases, it is seldom that the true comparison is between the defendant's site undeveloped and developed, as opposed to a comparison between the defendant's site with the existing building and with a reduced or reconfigured building so as to avoid infringing the claimant's right. Defendants not infrequently argue that had the claimant proved unreasonable in negotiations it would have been open to them to redesign their building so as to avoid infringing the light, without any loss of floor space or architectural charm, and hence the amount that the

---

[253]   [1974] 2 All ER 321.
[254]   [2007] EWHC 212 (Ch).
[255]   (1961) 13 P&CR 77.
[256]   *Tamares (Vincent Square) Ltd v Fairpoint Properties (Vincent Square) Ltd* [2007] EWHC 212 (Ch). For the decision on liability see (2006) 41 EG 226.

claimant should be looking for is minimal. Where the there is no evidence of the amount of the likely profit the court can do its best by awarding a suitable multiple of the damages for loss of amenity.[257]

11.132 The court, in assessing the damages, will generally be assisted by expert valuation evidence, directed to the question of the benefit achieved by the defendant as a result of the infringement.[258] An alternative approach to calculation of such damages but using the same principle was adopted in *Carr-Saunders v Dick McNeil Associates Limited*.[259] Millett J awarded damages for obstruction to light on the same general principles but calculated them differently. He said:[260]

> 'I am entitled to take into account not only the loss of light and the loss of amenity generally, due to such factors as loss of sky visibility, the impression that the building at the rear is now closer than it was (though that is an optical illusion), the loss of sunlight and other such matters, in short, the general deteriorating quality of the environment. Also I have to bear in mind the fact that in any negotiations between the Plaintiff and the Defendants the Plaintiff would certainly not be satisfied with the £3,000 which Mr Anstey considers appropriate. He would have a bargaining position because, unless he were bought out, the Defendants would be inhibited in their development. In *Wrotham Park Estate Co Limited v Parkside Homes Limited* this approach was applied to the award of damages for breach of restrictive covenant; and in *Bracewell v Appleby* it was applied to damages for obstruction to a right of way. In my judgment the same approach ought to be adopted where damages are awarded, in lieu of a mandatory injunction, for the interruption of the right to light to ancient windows ...
>
> Accordingly I am entitled to take account of the servient owner's bargaining position and the amount of profit which the Defendants would look to in the development of their site. I have no evidence of the amount of profit which the Defendants are expected to make from their development ... but I have evidence of the general loss of amenity. To that extent, it seems to me that the Court is entitled to approach the question on the basis that damages are awarded in lieu of an injunction, and not merely in compensation for the loss of the actual legal right. If the mandatory injunction had been granted, the building would have been pulled down and the Plaintiff would have been restored not only to its direct light, but also to sky visibility, a pleasant view of brickwork and a sloping roof, sunlight and so on.
>
> I have little material to guide me, except the £3,000 or thereabouts must be the absolute minimum figure. Doing the best I can and taking into account, I hope, all of the considerations which have been pressed on me by both sides, of the evidence that I have heard and, indeed, of my own view, I award general damages of £8,000.'

11.133 The importance of this case is that:

(1)   damages were assessed by reference to what was in effect a multiplier of the actual loss, rather than by reference to a percentage of the profit that the defendant made;

(2)   damages were assessed by reference to loss of amenity, as well as to financial loss.

It is not entirely clear whether Millett J was treating the plaintiff as entitled to have his damages assessed as including a ransom element. If so, the decision would be

---

[257] Ibid.
[258] See, eg, *Gafford v Graham* (1998) 77 P&CR 73.
[259] [1986] 2 All ER 888.
[260] Ibid, at 896b.

inconsistent with *Bracewell v Appleby*, and Millett J's own later judgment in *Jaggard v Sawyer* (where, however, *Carr-Saunders v Dick McNeil Associates* was not cited). Given the judge's citation of *Bracewell v Appleby*, it seems unlikely that he intended to adopt a different approach, however. On this basis, *Carr-Saunders* can be regarded as simply another approach to the assessment of damages in the way pointed by earlier cases, and approved in *Jaggard v Sawyer*.

11.134 These are not the only possible methods of calculating equitable damages. In *Gafford v Graham*[261] an award was made based on the diminution in value of the plaintiff's property, on the basis that this would have been reflected in the sum which might reasonably have been demanded as a quid pro quo for relaxing the covenant. In *Marine and General Mutual Life Assurance Society v St James' Real Estate Co Ltd*[262] the court had regard to a settlement of a claim between the defendant and a neighbouring dominant owner.

DECLARATORY RELIEF

11.135 The court has power at trial to declare the respective rights of the parties. Declaratory relief may be appropriate where it is important to establish the parties' rights for the future. Examples would include:

(1)   where disputed questions relating to a rights to light deed have been resolved;

(2)   where disputed questions as to the rights enjoyed by one party under an agreement, or by virtue of an easement, have been resolved;

(3)   where disputed questions as to whether such rights have been lost by abandonment or delay have been resolved.[263]

More generally, it is often prudent to include a claim for declaratory relief where the primary issues relate to damages and an injunction, so as to establish the entitlement to light in the future.

11.136 Historically, the general power to grant declarations was reserved to the Courts of Equity, having first been conferred by the Court of Chancery Act 1850, s 14. Until 1883, courts would only grant declarations ancillary to claims for other relief, but it has since then been possible to claim a declaration as a free-standing remedy.[264] However, the jurisdiction of the court will be exercised in general only in relation to legal rights, subsisting in future, of the parties represented in the litigation. Further, those whose rights are not affected have no locus standi to seek a declaration.[265]

11.137 A further limitation is that the court will not grant a declaration in relation to rights which may arise in the future, but which depend on a contingency which may or may not happen and are to that extent hypothetical. However, where the right depends on a contingency which is practically certain to occur, the right is for the purposes of

---

[261]   (1998) 77 P&CR 73.
[262]   [1991] 2 EGLR 178.
[263]   See, eg, *Ankerson v Connolly* [1906] 2 Ch 544, affirmed [1907] 1 Ch 678, CA.
[264]   See RSC Ord 15, r 16, in Sch 1 to the CPR.
[265]   See, eg, *Meadows Indemnity Co Ltd v Insurance Corporation of Ireland plc* [1989] 2 Lloyd's Rep 298, CA. But see *Re S* [1995] 3 All ER 290, CA.

declaratory relief regarded as a future right and not hypothetical.[266] Further, the court will not grant a declaration if its effect would be to open the floodgate to numerous similar claims, for example, as to whether a party is entitled to terminate a contract.[267]

11.138 There was formerly believed to be a rule that the court would not grant a declaration when giving judgment by consent or without trial, for example, where there was judgment in default of defence or notice of intention to defend. It has, however, been stated that this is simply a rule of practice, and the court will grant a declaration where the undefended claim is for a breach of contract and it would not otherwise be clear that the contract is at an end by reason of the defendant's repudiation.[268] There seems no reason in principle why the same position should not apply in relation to rights to light. In *Greenwich Healthcare NHS Trust v London & Quadrant Housing Trust and Others*,[269] where the issue concerned whether a proposed realignment of a road would interfere with a right of way, and, importantly, whether an injunction or damages would be granted, Lightman J held that there was jurisdiction to grant appropriate declaratory relief:

> 'The question now arises whether I can grant a declaration that if the plaintiff proceeds with the development the defendants have no entitlement to an injunction or damages in respect of any breach of the restrictive covenant but that their rights (if any) are limited to a claim for compensation in proceedings before the Lands Tribunal; and that the defendants have no entitlement to an injunction in respect of any interference with the right of way, but their remedy (if any) is limited to an award of damages.

> In *F v West Berkshire Health Authority (Mental Health Act Commission intervening)* [1989] 2 All ER 545 at 570, [1990] 2 AC 1 at 81 Lord Goff pointed to the width of the jurisdiction conferred on the court by RSC Ord 15, r 16 to grant binding declarations of rights, and the three conditions to be satisfied if that jurisdiction is to be exercised. These conditions are that the question under consideration is a real question; that the person seeking the declaration has a real interest; and that there has been proper argument. In *Camilla Cotton Oil Co v Granadex SA, Shawnee Processors Inc v Granadex SA* [1976] 2 Lloyd's Rep 10 at 14 Lord Wilberforce said that special circumstances may justify the grant of a declaration that a person is not liable in an existing or possible action, and that careful scrutiny is required before such a declaration is granted, most particularly as to the utility of such a negative declaration. In *Patten v Burke Publishing Co Ltd* [1991] 2 All ER 821, [1991] 1 WLR 541 Millett J emphasised the importance of the consideration whether the paramount duty of the court to do the fullest justice to the plaintiff to which he is entitled can be fulfilled without such a grant of a declaration.

> In this case there is a real question whether the defendants have a right to an injunction or damages in respect of the restrictive covenant and to an injunction in respect of the easement; the plaintiff has a very real interest in obtaining the declarations sought; and I have heard full argument. Further the grant of a negative declaration that the plaintiff is not exposed to possible action seeking such relief is a matter of the highest utility since it is the precondition to the ability of the plaintiff to secure the building of a new modern national health service hospital and the provision of national health care services. Justice to the plaintiff cannot be done without the grant of this relief.

> I am quite satisfied that I have jurisdiction to grant the declarations sought and that I should do so. One special feature of this case is that the declarations sought extend to the entitlement of the defendants, not to proprietary rights e g to easement or the benefit of

---

266 *Powell and Thomas v Evan Jones & Co* [1905] 1 KB 11; *Re S* [1995] 3 All ER 290, CA.
267 *Midland Land Reclamation Ltd and Leicestershire County Council v Warren Energy Ltd* [1997] CILL 1222.
268 *Patten v Burke Publishing Co Ltd* [1991] 2 All ER 821.
269 [1998] 3 All ER 437.

restrictive covenants, but to their entitlement to the equitable remedy of injunction. The jurisdiction of the court to grant declarations must extend to entitlement both to proprietary rights and to particular remedies. The circumstances in which the discretion may be properly exercisable in case of declarations as to entitlement to particular remedies may be rare, but circumstances may exist when a declaration eg that a defendant is not entitled to specific performance, rectification or an injunction, is necessary if a period of damaging (or indeed paralysing) uncertainty is to be avoided and indeed the occasion for an unwarranted ransom demand is to be removed.'

11.139 In *Well Barn Shoot Ltd v Shackleton*[270] the Court of Appeal upheld the grant of declaratory relief related to use of a private right of way for development purposes, on the ground that this was better than leaving the matter in a state of legal uncertainty. Despite the width of the jurisdiction, the limitations on the court's grant of declaratory relief can be important in two situations in particular. First, where a potential developer is contemplating the purchase of a site, overlooked by buildings with windows which may enjoy prescriptive rights to light, there is no readily available way of trying the issue whether, if the purchase proceeds, the development will be possible without running into rights to light difficulties. The developer will have no interest in land capable of giving him locus standi unless and until his purchase proceeds and the court is unlikely to be prepared to assist a *prospective* purchaser with a declaration. Secondly, the court is unlikely to be prepared to entertain a claim for a declaration as to light unless there is some substantive issue between the parties. Therefore, a dominant owner who wishes to ensure that his title to ancient lights is secure has no readily available method of confirming this.[271]

11.140 The court may grant final, but not interim, declaratory relief against the Crown.[272]

---

[270] [2003] EWCA Civ 02.
[271] Although the servient owner can of course call the dominant owner's rights into question by a light obstruction notice under the Rights of Light Act 1959; see Chapter 8.
[272] Crown Proceedings Act 1947, s 21.

Chapter 12

MEASUREMENT AND VALUATION OF LIGHT

METHODS OF MEASUREMENT

Percy Waldram

12.1 In September 1928, Percy Waldram, the well-known light expert, gave a paper entitled *Daylight and Public Health* to the Commission Internationale de L'Eclairage. In that paper, he reminded his audience that:

> ' . . . the "ancient light" law of England, which gives the owner of windows over 20 years old an indefeasible right to an adequate access of light and air, is often quoted as a piece of comparatively modern legislative interference with commercial development. It is however as old as English law, and that was copied direct from Roman law.'

12.2 In his summing up, he drew attention to the most important aspects as to why loss of light should be measured when he stated:

> '(a) that positions from which no sky at all is visible at table height are inadequately lit for ordinary purposes, such as continued clerical work, and
>
> (b) that it is undesirable that rooms should be constructed, or used for habitancy, or for clerical or other ordinary work over long periods, unless they have at least some sky visible from table height over some reasonable portion of their area.'

12.3 He also urged the members to be wary of the claims that 'whitened obstructions, light walls and ceilings and other expedients for mitigating gloom' worked when the surfaces became dirty and no longer operated with any benefit, especially on dull days. Indeed, in earlier papers, Percy Waldram categorically stressed that the human eye cannot be trusted when dealing with light levels. He gave as an example the fact that light in any ordinary room lit by windows from one side only falls away very quickly indeed as the distance from the window increases, for the amount of visible sky decreases very rapidly. Yet the human eye is not necessarily aware of this.

12.4 In summary, Percy Waldram highlighted three main points:

(1) for healthy living, man must have, and is legally entitled to have, an adequately lit room;

(2) light must be direct from the sky, and not from artificial light or from reflected surfaces; and

(3) the human eye cannot be trusted for measuring light.

What is meant by light in rights to light terms?

12.5   In a room, light is normally found consisting of three parts, namely:

(1)   sunlight;

(2)   artificial light; and

(3)   skylight or what is often referred to as daylight.

Sunlight is not relevant in most rights to light cases, and, clearly, artificial light must also have no place. An argument is often voiced that artificial lighting should be taken into account because when there are deep plan offices it is clearly impossible to rely upon daylight. This point was considered in *Midtown Ltd v City of London Real Property Company Ltd*[1] and is discussed further in Chapter 3.

12.6   It is daylight which is relevant, but daylight consists of three components:

(1)   the externally reflected component;

(2)   the internally reflected component; and

(3)   the sky component.

The absolute level of daylight at a point in a room is the result of many stages of attenuation and reflection. Indeed, to predict it accurately requires an intricate calculation, normally based upon the standard method of calculating the ratio of internal illuminants to external illuminants under a simple sky brightness pattern. This ratio is called the daylight factor.

12.7   The externally reflected component consists of light reflected from adjoining buildings, obstructions or other objects, and obviously can vary considerably. The second component, being the internally reflected component, comprises light received within a room from the walls, ceilings, floors and objects in the room in question and, similarly, can vary tremendously depending on decorative preferences. However, the third component, known as the sky component, comprises light direct from the sky and this can be measured accurately based upon an agreed standard. The uncertainty of external and internal reflection becomes irrelevant in rights to light calculations because it is ignored and, instead, the calculations are based on a sky of uniform brightness. All glazing is ignored and, generally, the framework to windows. It is the sky through the apertures or unglazed openings which counts.

12.8   Clearly, there can be a wide variation in the amount of light from the sky at any one time, whether it is sunny or cloudy, whether external buildings are glazed or in dark bricks, or ceilings are black or white, and for all these reasons light meters cannot be used in assessing rights to light claims. Indeed, light meters are of value only for moments in time, for example, when photographs are being taken or when deciding whether a cricket match should continue or not. They are never used in determining whether a room has lost light.

---

[1]   [2005] EWHC 33 Ch, [2005] 1 EGLR 65.

12.9   It was the work of Percy Waldram, and his father before him, which led to a standard being adopted for a uniform sky. Imagine a man lying on his back in the middle of a field with nothing on the horizon. In a theoretical sense, he has a dome of sky over his head, touching the horizon on all sides (see Figure 12.1). In order to make any calculations with regard to skylight penetration, there has to be an assumption of uniform sky brightness or luminance coming from this dome of sky.

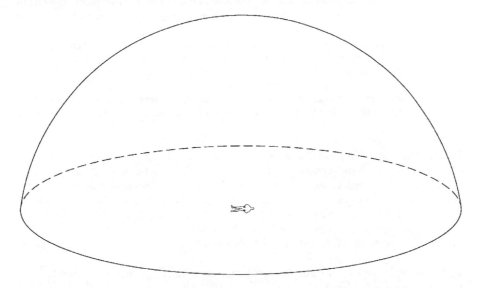

Figure 12.1: The dome of the sky

12.10   Sky brightness varies unpredictably in temperate climates. It depends on the height of the sun above the horizon and on the various cloud formations. The amount of light in a room lit by daylight is proportional to sky brightness. The intensity of light coming from a window varies with time unpredictably and over a wide range of conditions. A standard had to be set and the figure of 500 foot candles illumination was adopted by the National Physical Laboratory in 1928 as being the average condition of sky brightness found in towns in Great Britain over the greater part of winter days, over long periods in late autumn and early spring, over substantial but less lengthy periods in early autumn and late spring, and on wet days in summer. It was felt that over these periods and, therefore, over a great part of the year, reasonable people would normally expect to have adequate light for ordinary purposes.

12.11   On 5 March 1928, Percy Waldram's paper *The Estimation of Damage in Ancient Lights Disputes* was read at the Surveyors Institution and he confirmed:

> ' . . . the brightness of the sky on such a moderately dull day has been standardised, at least for this country, by the National Physical Laboratory at 500 foot candles, ie such a sky brightness as would cause a white card open to a complete hemisphere of sky (as when laid on a flat roof higher than all surrounding buildings) to be as bright as it would be were it exposed to a measured illumination of 500 foot candles; or when exposed to half a hemisphere of sky (as when laid upon the cill of an unobstructed window) to be as bright as it would be were it exposed to a measured illumination of 250 foot candles.'

The maximum light coming from the sky as you lie in a field is therefore 500 foot candles; 500 foot candles is 500 lumens per square foot (or approximately 500 lux).

What is being measured?

12.12 Percy Waldram and his father spent considerable time in 1912 measuring and valuing daylight illumination in public and private buildings and came to the conclusion that:

> ' . . . for ordinary purposes, comparable with clerical work, the natural illumination at which average reasonable persons would consistently grumble was that which represented 1/250 (0.4%) of the outside illumination which would fall on a window cill from an unobstructed quartersphere of sky, of the same brightness as that of the patch of sky which illuminated the position under consideration. This grumble point is, of course, the same as 1/500 or 0.2% of the light which would fall from an unobstructed hemisphere of uniform sky onto a flat roof.'

Indeed, this quotation from *The Illuminating Engineer* of April/May 1923 went on to confirm that this basic conclusion had 'survived the drastic test of many closely contested ancient light cases'. In other words, the grumble point was agreed as 0.2% which equals one foot candle or one lumen per square foot. A lumen per square foot is a measure of illumination equal to that provided by a candle one foot away from you, providing enough light to read a newspaper. Thus one lumen per square foot or one foot candle has become the standard by which rights to light is measured within a room.

12.13 In 1932, the Commission Internationale de L'Eclairage met at Cambridge and resolved three further issues:

> '(1) that the use of contour lines be adopted . . . in all questions;
> (2)   that table height should be regarded as 85cm (ie 850mm or at that time, taken in imperial, as 2 ft 9 in); and
> (3)   that less than 0.2 per cent daylight should be regarded as inadequate for work involving visual discrimination.'

There was an appreciation that 0.2% was the barest minimum, but recognising that there should normally be more lumens per square foot available even directly from the sky, without taking into account the additional benefit of reflected light both external and internal.

12.14 With the basic criteria above, the measurement being ascertained is the loss of light which will occur between the existing 0.2% contour in any given room and the position of the 0.2% contour when the development outside the room is constructed.

How is it measured?

12.15 As a result of 'an enormous amount of uncongenial work', Percy Waldram devised a method in the 1920s in which the three dimensions needed in order to measure light were translated into two dimensions. He produced what is called the Waldram diagram based upon the principles of Mercator's projection. Waldram concluded that:

> '... the adjusted flat projection of the quartersphere of sky which affords the light received by an unobstructed window cill . . . in which all the angular scales are so adjusted that the area of sky represented by one square inch anywhere onto a diagram so adjusted has precisely the same lighting value.'

If such a diagram is drawn 20 in x 10 in or 200 sq in in area, every square inch of sky projected onto it will represent 0.5% of the daylight to sill ratio.

12.16 Figure 12.2 shows a Waldram diagram based on an unglazed aperture, ie disregarding the glazing bars and frame of the actual window.[2] Waldram sums up the benefit of his diagram saying:

'. . . from the worst lit positions in the given interiors, or from any number of doubtful positions, the sky visible through the window, windows or skylight over any obstructions which may be present is plotted by its angular co-ordinates on a suitable measuring diagram, representing the quartersphere of visible sky. The divisions [of the diagram] are so adjusted as to represent by the area any piece of the visible sky its power of illuminating a surface at the point under consideration. This plotting can usually be done from the plans and sections . . .'

12.17 Before translating information onto a Waldram diagram, it is necessary to have as full and as precise details as possible of all relevant buildings on the site and adjoining sites. When acting for a developer this involves accurate dimensions of the bulk of the existing building on the site which is soon to be demolished. Similar details are required for the new building proposed for the site and its exact positioning relative to the existing building. It is the bulk that is significant and details of windows, doors, etc are not relevant. Each adjoining owner's building must be positioned in exact relationship to the existing building and the building proposed. Details are needed of the size of every window, or aperture which obtains light, and the thickness of the structural walls. The size of the rooms behind the apertures is also of importance. Indeed, when acting for a developer it may well be impossible to obtain access to adjoining owners' buildings. The developer may not wish to communicate with adjoining owners, and therefore presumptions must be made on the actual room sizes behind the windows. When considering whether or not loss is likely to be actionable room sizes are vitally important, and indeed possible alternative room layouts need consideration. This also affects the valuation. This is dealt with later in this chapter at **12.37**.

12.18 When analysing each adjoining building in turn, it must be remembered that the developer's building and other adjoining owners' buildings may not be the only buildings which affect the light penetration. There could be other buildings adjoining which cut out light such as, in London, Tower 42 (formerly the NatWest tower), the Canary Wharf tower or Centre Point. Any building which is visible from an adjoining owner's property from rooms likely to be affected must be plotted on the analysis.

12.19 Land surveyors are often used to produce the data required for an accurate study and they are equipped with modern technology to assess heights of buildings and their positions. Ordnance Survey maps can be invaluable.

12.20 When the data is collected, a plan, sections and elevations of the respective buildings need to be drawn to scale before being plotted on the Waldram diagram. First, a grid system is set up in every room likely to be affected by the new development. The grid is positioned at 850 mm above floor level, or at the working plane, all as agreed in 1932. Then it is necessary to find the position of the 0.2% contour based upon the

---

2   Cf Chapter 4 at **4.16**.

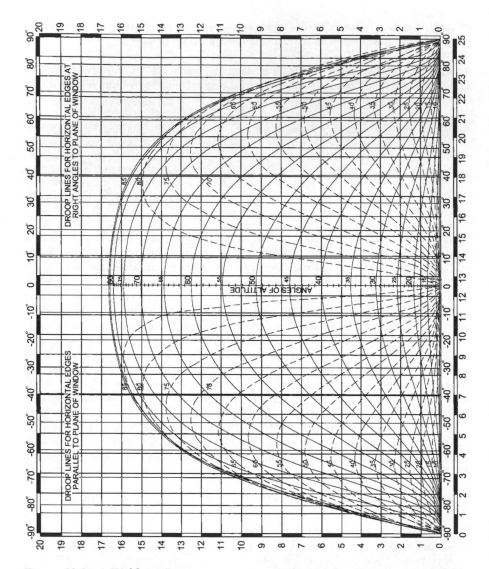

Figure 12.2: A Waldram Diagram

existing building which stands on the site. Having discovered this, the same exercise is carried out to ascertain where the 0.2% contour will move to in each room once the new building is constructed.

12.21 Figure 12.3 shows in plan a room with one window and the site next door. The existing building on the site is shown shaded and the proposed new building in solid dashed outline. A point is chosen on the grid where it is anticipated that the existing 0.2% contour will be. Using a protractor, the angles to the window reveals are measured in each direction with the '0' position of the protractor based on the reference point. The window reveals are then transferred to the Waldram diagram. The angles of every corner of every relevant obstruction outside the window are also measured and transferred to the Waldram diagram. This would include Centre Point or the Canary

Wharf tower if they were visible and affected the calculation. The Waldram diagram will have a number of vertical lines on it defining these angles.

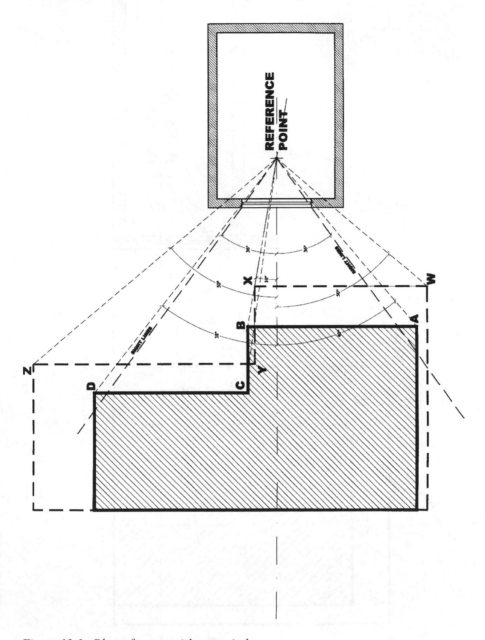

Figure 12.3: Plan of room with one window

12.22 The same exercise is carried out in section as shown at Figure 12.4. Here the existing building is shown shaded for easy reference. Care must be taken to draw in the correct angle relating to each specific corner or projection of the building prior to transferring it onto the Waldram diagram. Again, all buildings which could possibly affect the light entering the window must be recorded.

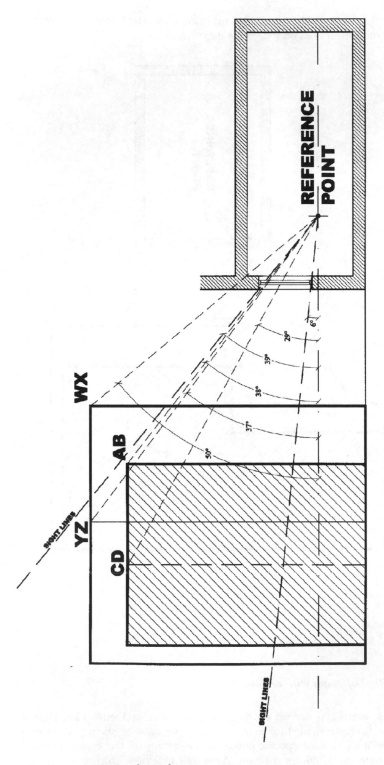

Figure 12.4: Section through room

12.23 Figure 12.5 shows a completed Waldram diagram with the outline of the window and the existing adjoining building. It is then possible to ascertain how much of the sky remains visible. Is it 0.2%? Figure 12.5 shows more than 0.2% remaining and therefore another reference point further back in the room must be chosen and the process repeated until only 0.2% remains visible through the window. The process has to be repeated often enough to allow for the entire 'as existing' contour to be drawn in as all the points of reference of 0.2% are joined together. The process is then repeated in exactly the same way to draw in the 'as proposed' contour but anticipating that it is likely to have moved closer to the window (see Figure 12.6). On plan, the result is shown in Figure 12.7. The shaded area was 'in darkness' when the existing building stood on the site. The hatched area shows the additional area which will now be in darkness with the new building in position.

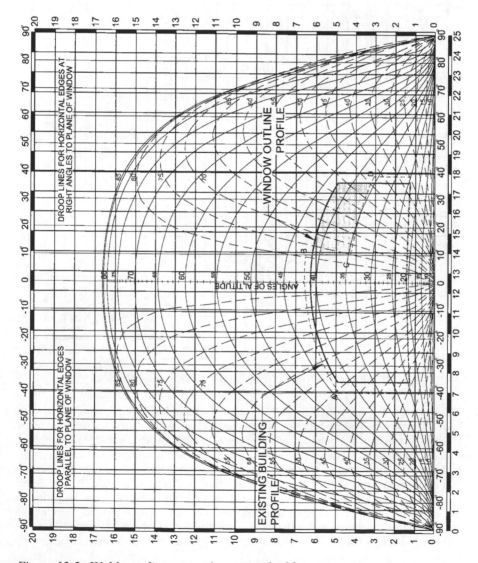

Figure 12.5: Waldram diagram with existing building

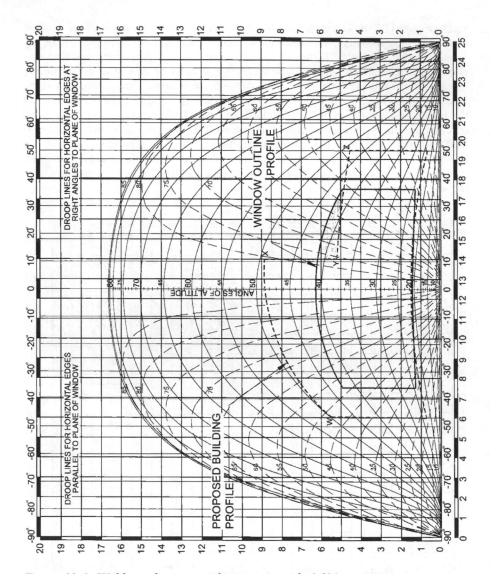

Figure 12.6: Waldram diagram with approximately 0.2% remaining

12.24 Sometimes, rights to light deeds have to be considered when measuring loss of light to a property. A deed between two parties may allow the developer to build a new building to a certain height and profile and the adjoining owner is not able to complain. It is only if the developer wishes to build a building which transgresses these controls that an assessment needs to be made. Instead of assessing the contour with the existing building standing on the site, the 'existing building' has to be assumed to be a building of the height and profile set out on the deed. This is what is plotted first on the Waldram diagram prior to the new building being plotted. The first contour plotted, therefore, is for the allowed building under the deed prior to plotting the 0.2% contour for the proposed building. The interpretation of rights to light deeds is considered in Chapter 9.

12.25 The development of more advanced computers has allowed for software to be written taking away the tedium of preparing Waldram diagrams. The software is based

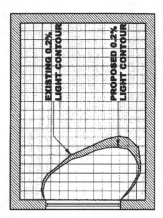

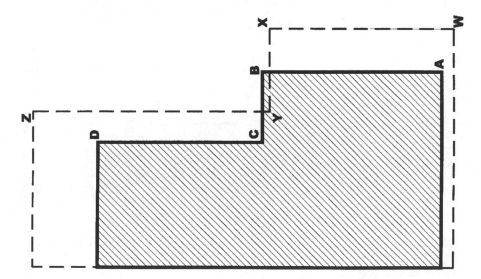

Figure 12.7: Plan showing loss hatched

upon the principles of trigonometry and allows for immense flexibility when a developer is designing a new building. Once all base data has been put into a computer, the software can analyse a variety of possible schemes for the site and the developer can decide what kind of risk he might want to take. Rights to light advisers work closely with architects to produce what is anticipated to be an acceptable scheme. (This has the additional benefit of providing information such that daylighting and sunlighting analyses for planning can also be prepared.)

12.26 A very rough and ready method of starting gauging where the light contour might fall can be undertaken using what is called the 'no-sky line'. Where there are two close parallel buildings, this is a good initial ready-reckoner. See Figure 12.8 where the no-sky line passes under the head of the adjoining owner's window from the working plane and over the top of the building standing immediately alongside. On the working plane, you can see how there is light on the side of the line closest to the window and no light behind it. Indeed, Percy Waldram advised that the no-sky line lies at about 0.1% or 0.15%. When setting off to find the 0.2% contour, therefore, it is important to start in front of this line closer to the window.

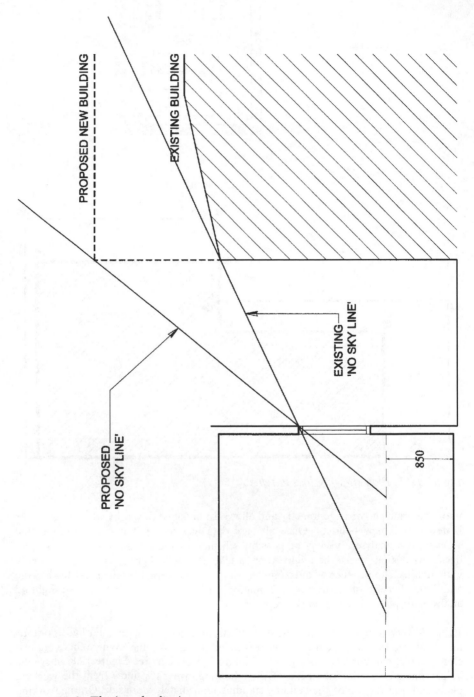

Figure 12.8: The 'no sky line'

12.27 Although in early rights to light cases, the 45° angle has been cited as relevant, it has no basis or validity in rights to light work. Figure 12.9 shows in two simple pictures how irrelevant it is. This is whether the line is taken from the sill of the lowest window or through the head. The boardroom shown will be badly lit but the bathroom will be well lit – it is the room shape and size which is significant.

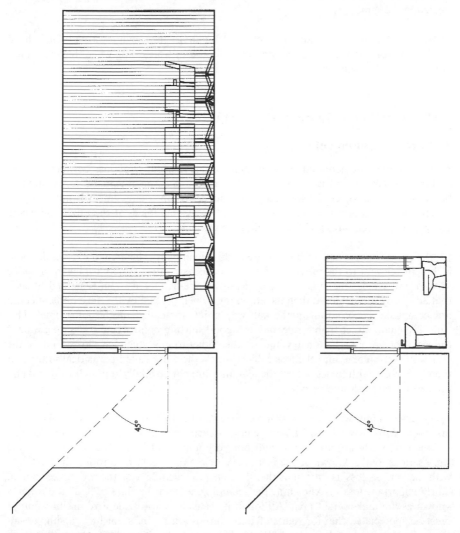

Figure 12.9: The 45° angle

12.28 Research is necessary to provide background data on the siting of old buildings, window positions, and when buildings were demolished. The use of aerial photographs can be invaluable. During the last 30 years, a number of major companies have specialised in aerial photography, including the Ordnance Survey. In addition, planning authorities, the British Library, and local authority libraries can all be of assistance.

12.29 There are some key factors with regard to developments which can assist in maintaining light penetration or positively inhibit it. Developers should be aware that providing balconies to new buildings can not only have an impact on adjoining buildings but will dramatically cut down light penetration into their own building. Low head heights, narrow and small windows and deep cheeks to mansards also inhibit light penetration. It is not beneficial to adjoining owners for a developer to raise enclosing parapet walls to roof areas – railings are better. Brise soleil are considered solid obstructions when rights to light analyses are being undertaken, and glass canopies are treated in the same way.

12.30 It is helpful when adjoining owners' buildings have windows with high head heights and roof lights. The Georgians knew what they were doing when they built their houses with taller windows at the lower floor levels.

VALUATION OF LOSS OF LIGHT

The area measurement

12.31 The measurements undertaken above produce an area of loss between the old and the new contour positions. However, before any assessment is made, any gain must be off set against losses. This is accepted practice within rooms, but it is not accepted practice to off set gains at one end of a building against losses at the other end where completely different areas of the building are affected.

12.32 The size and shape of a room are highly significant. The area of the whole room is directly relevant to the outcome and must be assessed first. Reference has been made to what was called 'the 50/50 rule'. Basically, if one-half of a room remained lit such that adequacy was achieved then the adjoining owner affected by the development could not complain. The contour at the half-way point was called the 'grumble line'. This 'rule' is a guide rather than a rule, but, is a good starting point when assessing a room.[3] Indeed, if one room is actionably injured, then other rooms which have losses only at the rear would also come into the loss calculations – these are called parasitical injuries. If there are rooms with losses only at the rear, they are not normally actionably injured and no compensation should be paid.

12.33 Each room, whatever its shape or size can be divided into four. John Anstey in his book *Anstey's Rights of Light*[4] refers to each 25% in turn as 'very serious loss, serious loss, fairly important loss and not very important loss'. The first area of the 'very serious loss' is known as the front zone or the front 25% of a room; the next 25% with the 'serious loss' is known as the first zone; the next 25% of the room, the zone of 'fairly important loss', is known as the second zone; and the final 25% of the room is known as the makeweight area. Although it seems easy to divide a room into four, it must be appreciated that for rights of light purposes a room is not lit in a simple way. First, a room is unlikely to be 100% lit. It is normally about 98.5% lit as there will almost inevitably be unlit areas in the corners immediately to the left and right of a window. This clearly affects the calculation. Indeed, it is possible to obtain a shaft of light passing through a window and lighting one side portion only of a room to the back wall. Figure 12.10 shows the 25% front zone actually to the side and back of the room! Consideration must also be given to possible different layouts in a building. Cellular offices are a perfectly valid alternative to open plan areas.

---

3   See *Regan v Paul Properties & Ors* [2006] EWCA Civ 1319.
4   Updated by Lance Harris; *Anstey's Rights of Light* (RICS Books, 4th edn, 2006).

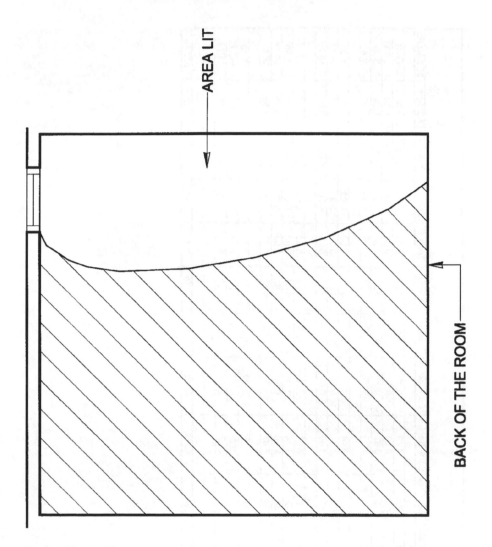

Figure 12.10: The zoning peculiarity

12.34 In any analysis, good light should be present for at least 25% of a room. If light is lost from this area the matter is serious as there is 'very serious loss'. Any loss within this area is multiplied by 1.5 so the area is always increased to account for the significant damage. The area of the room between 50% and 25% well lit is considered a standard area and is called the first zone loss. There is no multiplication to enhance the area of recorded loss but all other measurements are equated to this first zone. The area between 50% and 75% could be argued as being an area not actionable in itself, but actionable if it forms part of a loss in the front 50% of the room. The area calculated is therefore taken as one-half and the loss multiplied by 0.5. The rear or makeweight part of the room is taken at one-quarter the area, so the multiplication factor is 0.25.

12.35 Figure 12.11 shows a typical analysis of a number of floors in a building and the analysis of loss equating all the areas to the equivalent of the first zone loss. This table is utilised in all rights to light assessments and is known therefore as the Equivalent First Zone ('EFZ') table.

Rights of Light Calculations
EFZ Table - Existing and Proposed

Room Ref	Floor	Room Area (Sq.M.)	1/4 Room Area	0.2% Before	0.2% After	Loss	Front	Zone 1	Zone 2	MWT	EFZ Sq.M.	EFZ Sq.Ft.
ROOM-00-01	0	8.81	2.20	0.73	0.02	0.71	0.71	0.00	0.00	0.00	1.06	11.41
ROOM-00-02	0	12.72	3.18	0.83	0.44	0.39	0.39	0.00	0.00	0.00	0.59	6.35
ROOM-00-03	0	17.73	4.43	0.57	0.37	0.20	0.20	0.00	0.00	0.00	0.30	3.23
ROOM-00-04	0	16.14	4.03	0.71	0.69	0.03	0.03	0.00	0.00	0.00	0.04	0.43
ROOM-01-01	1	11.26	2.82	0.91	0.79	0.12	0.12	0.00	0.00	0.00	0.18	1.94
ROOM-01-02	1	19.05	4.76	1.40	0.37	1.03	1.03	0.00	0.00	0.00	1.54	16.58
ROOM-01-03	1	16.74	4.18	1.69	0.68	1.00	1.00	0.00	0.00	0.00	1.51	16.25
ROOM-02-01	2	27.67	6.92	3.87	2.30	1.58	1.58	0.00	0.00	0.00	2.37	25.51
ROOM-02-02	2	20.46	5.12	1.14	1.06	0.09	0.09	0.00	0.00	0.00	0.13	1.40
ROOM-02-03	2	16.89	4.22	2.10	0.48	1.62	1.62	0.00	0.00	0.00	2.43	26.16
ROOM-02-04	2	40.29	10.07	9.82	3.84	5.98	5.98	0.00	0.00	0.00	8.98	96.66
ROOM-03-01	3	22.57	5.64	17.25	15.77	1.49	0.00	0.00	1.16	0.33	0.66	7.10
ROOM-03-02	3	72.14	18.04	26.88	15.03	11.85	3.00	8.85	0.00	0.00	13.35	143.70
ROOM-03-03	3	6.92	1.73	4.48	2.88	1.60	0.00	0.58	1.02	0.00	1.09	11.73
Totals:		309.39	77.34	72.38	44.72	27.69	15.75	9.43	2.18	0.33	34.23	368.45

Figure 12.11: A typical EFZ table

12.36 The weighting does, however, change depending on the circumstances of the particular case. When the loss is actionable, ie in the front or first zone, then any makeweight loss is promoted to the second zone and receives a 0.5 weighting rather than a 0.25 weighting. However, when losses are not actionable in some parts of a building, then any second zone loss is demoted and receives a 0.25 weighting rather than a 0.5 weighting, and the totals are then added in to other losses in other parts of the building which are actionable.

Valuation

12.37 First, a decision must be taken as to what proportion of the rent of the affected property could be said to be being paid for the amount of light penetrating the property. This has been a matter of debate over many years but in major city centres, particularly where higher rents are involved, it is felt currently that no more than £5 per square foot of the annual rent represents the value of light. There is still considerable argument about how much of the rent should be taken in every case. It is worth viewing John Anstey's book on rights to light where he gives a number of alternative graphs which conclude that it is a matter for the two experts to agree at the beginning. Local letting agents should be able to provide evidence of local rental levels as a starting point.

12.38 Valuation advice is important, particularly when deciding upon an appropriate Years' Purchase ('YP') yield since this is the final part of the process to produce the capital figure relating to the damage. The rental figure for the light is multiplied by the EFZ and then the YP. The valuer advising must be told that rights to light injuries are valued on the basis of a freeholder in possession, even if the property is an investment property, and even though there may be several subsidiary interests in the dominant tenement which have to be taken into account. The value of the rights to light injury depends upon the unexpired term of the leases and also whether landlords have retained all rights of light to themselves.

12.39 As a simple example, consider a freeholder with a headlessee who has 7 years remaining on his lease and a sub-tenant with 4 years. Let us assume the loss is 500 sq ft and the element of rent relating to light is £5 per square foot per annum. The annual rent is therefore £2,500. Assuming the appropriate yield is 6% (and so the YP multiplier is approximately 16.5), the capitalised figure is £41,250. The sub-tenant has 4 years to go before the end of the term of this sub-lease and the head lessee 7 years to run. The total sum of £41,250 must be divided equitably between the three parties. Let us now consider that from a valuer's point of view, using Parry's 'Valuation Tables'. Within Parry's tables is the 'Present Value of £1 per annum' table. This sets out the capitalisation factors to be applied to the annual income stream at various rates of return. (They assume rental income receivable annually in arrears but are still used in some areas of valuation including rights to light.)

12.40 The perpetuity figure at 6% is actually 16.6667 and therefore the true payment is £41,666.75 to be divided between the parties. For the sub-tenant with 4 years to run, the 6% column for 4 years has a YP of 3.4651. The headleaseholder with 7 years has a YP of 5.5824 and from this must be deducted the tenant's 3.4651 to give 2.1173. The freeholder has the remainder which is 16.6667 minus 5.5824 to give 11.0843. The sub-tenant therefore gets £8,662.52 (20.79%), the headleaseholder £5,291.68 (12.70%) and the freeholder £27,712.55 (66.51%). (If there had been any rent review in either the headleaseholder's term or the sub-tenant's term, then the YP calculation would reflect only the period to the next rent review because the loss of light should be taken into account at that review.)

12.41 In rights to light discussions, the sum of £41,666.75 is referred to as the 'book value'. All parties should be satisfied with their proportion but remember that the YP can change depending on when the valuation is carried out and, although most sums are agreed prior to the damage occurring, the loss should really be valued at the exact point in time when damage accrues.

APPLYING THE LAW

12.42 It has been stated earlier that the size and shape of a room is of great importance when assessing loss of light and how serious it is. To reiterate, it is generally agreed that provided more than 50% of a room remains lit in commercial properties, then there is no injury and no action. However, when the amount of space lit falls below 50%, then there is potentially actionable damage.

12.43 This cannot be taken as a guide when dealing with residential properties. It is clear that judges are inclined to side with the adjoining owner whose light is damaged, particularly when a developer can be seen to be making profit from a scheme. It seems from the cases before the courts that even rooms lit to 55% may not be adequately lit.

12.44 In commercial properties, an affected adjoining owner, who has rooms damaged such that less than 50% remains well lit, can then claim for other rooms which might be damaged only in the rear portion. This comes under the heading of parasitical injuries. Parasitical injuries are also relevant when a developer has to pay well over book value when paying damages. This arises because the adjoining owner or dominant owner has the basic right to obtain an injunction.

12.45 It is impossible to be sure when an adjoining owner would obtain an injunction relating to commercial adjoining premises. However, it must be remembered that if a room is already poorly lit, ie to only 25% or less, then any reduction in the light to this area would almost inevitably be regarded as a serious loss, and a plain case for an injunction. Even if the damage is relatively minor, the available light is held to be invaluable because there is so little of it, and any developer could be in jeopardy by reducing penetration further.[5]

12.46 The book value can be enhanced not just by one-and-a-half times its value but to whatever sum the adjoining owner might ask for, although this is normally by up to three or four times the book value. The adjoining owner has the ability to seek an injunction and is in a powerful position. The courts have on many occasions affirmed that they will not countenance a wrongdoer effectively compulsorily purchasing the right of the dominant owner.[6] This is when what could be called the 'wayleave' principle comes into operation. Basically, it is no longer satisfactory to look at the area of loss in the adjoining owner's building and try to ascertain an enhancement factor. The only sensible way of reaching any kind of negotiated settlement is for some sharing of the developer's profit to be agreed.[7]

---

[5] For the principles giving the grant of injunctions, see Chapter 11 at **11.69–11.121**.

[6] See, eg, *Anchor Brewhouse Developments Ltd v Berkeley Homes (Docklands Developments) Ltd* [1987] 2 EGLR 173; *London & Manchester Assurance Co Ltd v O & H Construction Co Ltd* [1989] 2 EGLR 185; *Deakins v Hookings* [1994] 1 EGLR 190.

[7] For the principles on when the court awards damages in lieu of an injunction, see Chapter 11 at **11.122–11.134**.

12.47 The developer, who is raising his building to a greater extent than a previous building, is benefiting from the value of the extra floor space. It is the value of this additional extra floor space which the developer could not realise if the adjoining owner obtained an injunction, which may have to be shared in profit terms with the adjoining owner (or owners if there are more than one). An analysis is made of this additional floor space which is then valued to ascertain the profit level for the developer. Building costs must be taken into consideration but the final profit element could be shared, if there is extremely serious damage, on a 50/50 basis between the badly affected adjoining owner and the developer.

12.48 In the case of deeds with restrictive covenants, similarly the adjoining owner could end up with half of the profit of the extra floor space which can be built only if the restrictive covenant is released. Indeed, the adjoining owner may even ask for other benefits and is clearly in an extremely strong position.

Chapter 13

RIGHTS TO LIGHT AND PLANNING LAW

SUMMARY

13.1 This chapter examines the relationship between rights to light and planning law, as established under the Planning Acts, which regulate development, including building works. Generally, planning provision is required for such works. Planning permission is granted by public authorities, normally local planning authorities ('LPAs').[1]

13.2 In deciding whether to grant planning permission, LPAs are guided by policies including ones which are designed to protect sunlight, daylight and views. Such criteria are both wider and narrower than those governing rights to light. Wider in that view and direct sunlight are considered, narrower in that planning law does not directly protect private rights, and cannot be invoked directly by an aggrieved landowner to restrain his neighbour from infringing his rights to light. In terms of planning law the action which a dominant owner who believes that proposed development of nearby property will interfere with his rights of light can take depends on how far he can show the proposed development, in addition to interfering with his light, will contravene relevant planning policies. Essentially there are two routes open to him. First, he may seek to persuade the LPA to refuse planning permission on the grounds that to grant it would contravene the LPA's or Central Government planning policies to protect such matters as amenities, views and privacy from overlooking. Secondly, if the LPA nevertheless grants permission, he may seek to challenge the grant of such permission by judicial review.[2] Planning law is concerned with public rights and duties, and the decision whether to grant or refuse permission is taken by the LPA in the public interest. Accordingly, in deciding such issues, the LPA will not be directly concerned as to the existence or extent of private rights of light. This point is examined in more detail below.

13.3 It is perhaps worth emphasising at the outset of the discussion two points which non-experts frequently find confusing:

(1) the grant of planning permission does *not* grant protection from private law claims for infringement of rights to light;[3]

(2) the criteria generally applied in deciding whether to grant or refuse planning provision are *not* the same as those used by the courts in deciding whether a right to light has been infringed.

---

[1]   Local planning authorities are defined in Part I of the Town and Country Planning Act 1990 and in s 37 of the Planning and Compensation Act 2004 as regards England, and s 78 of the same Act as regards Wales. This Act introduced a new scheme of development plans, which includes various levels of local authorities and certain other designated bodies. In certain cases the Secretary of State grants permission, eg, on appeal against a refusal of permission (see below).

[2]   For the procedure to be followed on Judicial Review see the Civil Procedure Rules 1998, SI 1998/3132 ('CPR'), Part 54.

[3]   *Hunter v Canary Wharf Ltd* [1997] AC 655 at 710D.

THE EXTENT TO WHICH LIGHT IS PROTECTED BY PLANNING LAW AND POLICIES

13.4   Development of land is regulated by the provisions of the Planning Acts.[4] Under this legislation, development as defined in s 55 of the Town and Country Planning Act 1990 ('the 1990 Act') may be carried out only if planning permission has been granted[5] by the LPA or the Secretary of State.[6] LPAs are certain designated local authorities. 'Development' is defined as including building and engineering operations.[7] Such development is termed 'operational development', in contra-distinction to development involving change of use. Although under the 1990 Act it is in principle necessary to apply for and obtain planning permission for any development of land this requirement is in practice relaxed. Under the Town and Country Planning (General Permitted Development) Order 1995,[8] planning permission is granted without the need for an application for certain types of development including works of enlargement, improvement or other alteration of a dwelling-house (subject to certain limitations) and for other specified building operations including works reasonably necessary for the purposes of agriculture within an agricultural unit (Part VI) and the alteration and extension within certain limits of an industrial building or warehouse. And, under the Town and Country Planning (Use Classes) Order 1987,[9] certain changes in the use of land are deemed not to involve material changes of use and hence do not require planning permission.

13.5   The decision whether to grant or refuse planning permission is one for the LPA, or in certain cases the Secretary of State.[10] Where planning permission is refused, an appeal lies in accordance with regulations either to the Secretary of State or to a person appointed by him. From thence, an appeal may lie to the High Court on a point of law.[11] A general account of planning law is beyond the scope of the present work.[12]

13.6   In deciding whether to grant or refuse planning permission, the LPA must normally apply the provisions of the development plan[13] unless material considerations indicate otherwise. The development plan is the plan prepared by the LPA under its statutory duties under the Planning Acts and the Planning and Compulsory Purchase Act 2004. The responsibility for preparing development plans has historically been laid on various local authorities. There is, for example, no development plan covering the whole of England and Wales. Various changes in local authority organisation,

---

[4]   Comprising the Town and Country Planning Act 1990, the Planning (Listed Buildings and Conservation Areas) Act 1990, the Planning (Consequential Provisions) Act 1990 and the Planning (Hazardous Substances) Act 1990. See Town and Country Planning Act 1990, s 336. In addition, important changes to the methods of preparation of and content of development plans are embodied in the Planning and Compulsory Purchase Act 2004.

[5]   Under s 57 of the Town and Country Planning Act 1990.

[6]   For the provisions governing the grant of permission by local planning authorities, see Town and Country Planning Act 1990, ss 70–72; in the case of the Secretary of State, see ss 77–79. The Secretary of State also has the power to provide for the grant of planning permission by development order by virtue of s 59.

[7]   See Town and Country Planning Act 1990, s 55(1).

[8]   SI 1995/418.

[9]   SI 1987/764, as amended by the Town and Country Planning (Use Classes) (Amendment) Order 2005, SI 2005/84.

[10]   See Town and Country Planning Act 1990, ss 77–79.

[11]   Ibid, s 288.

[12]   The most comprehensive work is the *Encyclopedia of Planning Law* (Sweet & Maxwell).

[13]   Planning and Compulsory Purchase Act 2004, s 38(6). The expression 'development plan' is defined in s 336 of the Town and Country Planning Act 1990, which refers to s 38 of the Planning and Compulsory Purchase Act 2004.

devolution of some governmental functions to Wales and Scotland, and the differing paces with which each local authority has proceeded with the preparation and revision of plans mean that there is now something of a patchwork of approved plans in different areas. The Planning and Compulsory Purchase Act 2004 ('the 2004 Act') repealed Part II of the 1990 Act and introduced prospectively a new system under which the former structure plans, local plans and unitary development plans are replaced with local development documents ('LDDs'). This system is supplemented by regional spatial strategies ('RSSs') prepared by regional planning bodies ('RPBs') under Part 1 of the 2004 Act. The RSS embodies the policies of the Secretary of State in relation to each region The planning regime in Wales is similar but dealt with in a separate part of the 2004 Act, Part 6. There is to be only one spatial plan for Wales, the Wales Spatial Plan. In principle, approved plans are likely to comprise either:

(1)   a unitary development plan ('UDP') for the area in question; or

(2)   a local plan or plans; or

(3)   the structure plan;

(4)   (for any area in Greater London) the spatial development strategy and the development plan documents (taken as a whole) which have been adopted or approved in relation to that area;

(5)   elsewhere in England, the regional spatial strategy and the development plan documents (taken as a whole) which have been adopted or approved in relation to that area;

(6)   for the purposes of any area in Wales, the local development plan adopted or approved in relation to that area.[14]

LPAs, and the Secretary of State on appeal, must also take account of central government policy, as embodied in official statements and planning policy guidance notes ('PPGs'),[15] planning policy statements ('PPSs') and guidance relating to specific topics and areas.

THE RELEVANCE OF RIGHTS TO LIGHT IN THE DECISION-MAKING PROCESS

13.7   The general rule is that since planning powers are to be exercised in the public interest, private rights (or the absence thereof) are not directly relevant to decisions as to their exercise. On the general principle, the basic position is usefully set out in a government publication, annexed to PPS 1,[16] issued by the Office of the Deputy Prime Minister entitled *The Planning System: General Principles*. This states:[17]

> 'The Planning system does not exist to protect the private interests of one person against the activities of another, although private interests may coincide with the public interest in some

---

[14]   See Planning and Compulsory Purchase Act 2004, s 62.
[15]   See, generally, [1999] JPL 568.
[16]   *Planning Policy Statement 1: Delivering Sustainable Development* (Office of the Deputy Prime Minister, 2005).
[17]   At para 29.

cases . . . The basic question is not whether owners and occupiers of neighbouring properties would experience financial or other loss from a particular development, but whether the proposal would unacceptably affect amenities and the existing use of land and buildings which ought to be protected in the public interest.'

This view is applied by the courts and illustrated by *Brewer v Secretary of State for the Environment*[18] where the court held that the existence or absence of private rights of light was not a material consideration in determining a planning application. This case is discussed in more detail below.

13.8 It would appear at first glance to follow that the concerns of private individuals with private rights such as easements which may be affected by a proposed new building for which planning permission is being sought, but are unrelated to planning considerations, are not matters which the LPA should take account of when deciding whether to grant or refuse permission. This is undoubtedly true in the sense that the LPA should not refuse permission simply to protect a private easement. However, there are two ways in which the existence of such interests may indirectly influence the planning process.

13.9 First, the development plan will almost invariably include policies designed to enhance the environment and to protect the amenities of residents against unsuitable development. Policies designed to protect sunlight, daylight and privacy are almost universal. Local plans will often incorporate, by reference, standards derived from *Site Layout Planning for Daylight and Sunlight: A guide to good practice*,[19] a document issued by the Building Research Establishment ('BRE'). A dominant owner may therefore seek to urge on the LPA that the grant of a particular application for development may contravene the development plan, if it would leave his property with insufficient sunlight or daylight, or otherwise interfere with his amenities having regard to the standards in the development plan. In the event the LPA grants such permission he may seek to challenge it by way of application for permission to apply for judicial review on the grounds of failure to apply the development plan and any other relevant policies which constitute material considerations. It is, however, not a universal rule that the decision need refer to each material policy in order to establish that regard has been had to it. It is assumed that a policy has been taken into account unless the circumstances suggest it may have been overlooked.[20] Policies must be interpreted properly, and if proper regard has not been had to the policy the decision will be quashed unless the court decides exceptionally that the failure has not affected the outcome.[21]

13.10 The LPA is required to give reasons for the grant of permission by virtue of the Town and Country Planning (General Development Procedure) Order 1995[22] and the reasons must be clear, concise, full and specify all policies and proposals in the development plan relevant to the decision. Where reasons are given the court will normally accept them as giving a faithful account of the factors taken into account unless they are challenged for lack of good faith or there is no evidence to support them. Where no reasons are given the court will ascertain the reasons by extrinsic evidence and

---

18   [1998] JPL 480.
19   See **13.26** et seq.
20   *Boulevard Land Ltd v Secretary of State for the Environment* [1998] JPL 983.
21   *R v Derbyshire County Council ex parte Woods* [1997] JPL 958; *Simplex GE (Holdings) Ltd v Secretary of State for the Environment* [1988] 3 PLR 25; *Gransden v Secretary of State for the Environment* [1986] JPL 519.
22   SI 1995/419. See art 22(1) as substituted by SI 2003/2047.

will usually assume that the officers' report to the committee contains the reasons. As David Keene QC said in *R v Canterbury City Council ex parte SpringImage Ltd*:[23]

> '... it is very difficult to know the reasoning process of such a body when they decide to grant permission. One should, therefore, be slow to attribute the reasoning of an officer's report to the Committee. On the other hand, it is to be assumed that such a Committee take into account that officer's report and attach weight to it, especially since the officers are professionally qualified and the members in most cases probably are not.'

13.11 It is even possible that in an extreme case failure to take account of loss of light or privacy might amount to a breach of Art 8 of the European Convention on Human Rights. The existence of severe loss of privacy is undoubtedly a matter which could give rise to a potential claim for breach of human rights under Art 8. In *Cummins v Camden London Borough Council*[24] Ouseley J held that:

> 'It is inconceivable that overshadowing or overlooking the playground attached to a block of flats could constitute a want of respect for home or family life; a less attractive view from the windows of one flat cannot do so either. The claim is not made that the effect of the grant of planning permission would be to create some overlooking of the domestic accommodation which would interfere with the normal level of privacy which someone in a Central London block of flats could expect to enjoy. Accordingly, no civil rights of the Fifth Claimant were engaged or determined.'

13.12 In *R v Ipswich Borough Council ex parte Malster*[25] an application for judicial review of the grant of planning permission for redevelopment of the north stand of a football club was made. The applicant's house near the stadium would suffer a degree of loss of sunlight from construction of the new stand. The applicant relied on three grounds, failure to commission an environmental impact assessment, failure to apply the policies in the development plan, and the severity of the loss of light resulting in an infringement of his Art 8 rights. The application failed. Effects of development on individual properties' amenities did not amount to a significant effect on the environment requiring an environmental impact assessment. The planning policies relied on by the applicant were not applicable except in solely residential areas. Finally, as regards Art 8, the court recognised that Art 8 might be engaged in the case of severe environmental pollution. However, the applicant's case did not meet that test.

13.13 In any event the interference was justified under Art 8(2). The effect of the decisions appears to be that it appears that interference with light or loss of privacy of residential accommodation might in principle involve breach of the Convention right and lead to the grant of permission being quashed, but only in highly unusual situations.

13.14 The second way in which private rights may influence planning decisions lies in the readiness of the courts to accept that such rights may amount to material considerations in some cases. Indeed, the material considerations may extend more widely. So in *Wood-Robinson v Secretary of State for the Environment*[26] the LPA refused permission for the erection of a house in the grounds of a block of flats, on the ground that it would spoil the residents' views. The developer appealed unsuccessfully to a planning inspector and to the High Court. Its argument was that private interests (ie the residents' view) were irrelevant to planning. The court held that whether protection of

---

23   [1993] 3 PLR 58 at 69.
24   [2001] EWHC Admin 1116.
25   [2001] EWHC Admin 711; [2002] PLCR 14.
26   [1998] JPL 976.

the view in the public interest was a legitimate planning consideration was for the decision-maker (ie the inspector) to decide. Note that the residents could not have sued the developer for blocking their view once the house had been erected, since there is no common law right to a view.

13.15 This decision is consistent with cases which established that an LPA can refuse planning permission for development that would harm purely private amenities whether amounting to legal rights or not, provided there is a planning purpose of other special consideration involved.[27] Courts have upheld:

(1)   restrictions on development round a radio telescope to prevent interference (*Stringer v Minister of Housing and Local Government*);[28]

(2)   a refusal of permission for a concrete plant that would harm a nearby precision engineering factory through dust (*RMC Management Services v Secretary of State for the Environment*);[29]

(3)   a refusal of permission for conversion of a house into two flats, resulting in each occupier suffering noise disturbance from the other (*London Borough of Newham v Secretary of State for the Environment*);[30]

(4)   refusal of permission for retention of a house whose wrong siting was detrimental to another house (*Barratt Developments (Eastern) Ltd v Secretary of State for the Environment*).[31]

13.16 However, in *Brewer v Secretary of State for the Environment*[32] the would-be developer sought to rely on the *absence* of a common law right to light as a ground for granting planning permission. A planning inspector granted permission on appeal. He found that the proposed development (a house extension) would substantially harm the light received by the windows of an adjacent property.

13.17 However, he accepted that because the developer proposed to register a light obstruction notice against the adjacent property,[33] the effect of which (if unchallenged for the necessary period) would be to prevent the adjacent owner asserting a right to light, this harm was not relevant. The court overturned the decision and held that the inspector had been wrong to take the presence or absence of a common law right to light into account. A similar approach was adopted in *R v Solihull Borough Council ex parte Berkswell Parish Council*[34] where the court declined to set aside the grant of planning permission for failure to have regard to the protection of certain hedgerows under a local enclosure Act.

13.18 There is a further way in which the planning process may be relevant to private rights indirectly. LPAs are obliged to maintain a register of planning applications and decisions under s 69 of the 1990 Act and the Town and Country Planning (General

---

27   See *Great Portland Estates plc v Westminster City Council* [1985] AC 661.
28   [1971] 1 All ER 65.
29   (1972) 222 EG 1593.
30   [1986] JPL 607.
31   [1982] JPL 648.
32   [1988] JPL 480.
33   For light and obstructing notices and their effect, see **7.10–7.21** and **8.31**.
34   (1998) 77 P&CR 312.

Development Procedure) Order 1995.[35] The same Order, by Art 6, requires notice of application for permission to be given to owners[36] and tenants of the land apart from the applicant and Art 8 requires applications for permission to be given publicly, the precise extent of which differs depending on the type of application. The existence of such sources of information may be relevant in deciding whether a dominant owner has acted promptly where he seeks an interim or final injunction, particularly a mandatory injunction to compel the wrongdoer to demolish a building already erected.

THE EFFECT OF PLANNING PERMISSION ON PRE-EXISTING RIGHTS OF LIGHT

13.19 The effect of the grant of planning permission for the erection or alteration of a building which when erected or altered will infringe established rights to light is not to deprive the dominant owners of their existing private law rights or confer immunity from claims for nuisance. So in *Hunter v Canary Wharf Ltd*[37] Lord Hoffmann said:[38]

> ' . . . I am not suggesting that a grant of planning permission should be a defence to anything which is an actionable nuisance under the existing law. It would, I think, be wrong to allow the private rights of third parties to be taken away by a permission granted by the planning authority to the developer.'

13.20 *Wheeler v JJ Saunders Ltd*[39] illustrates this principle. Planning permission was granted for a pig farm, the operation of which caused nuisance to an adjoining owner through smells. The adjoining owner brought legal proceedings to restrain it. The owner of the pig farm argued that the effect of the grant of planning permission was to authorise that which would otherwise have been a nuisance, and hence that the plaintiff had been deprived of a right of action in respect of it. He relied on the decision in *Gillingham Borough Council v Medway (Chatham) Dock Co Ltd*.[40]

13.21 In an earlier case, *Allen v Gulf Oil Refining Ltd*,[41] the Court of Appeal was concerned with a nuisance that arose from an oil refinery built with statutory permission. The court held that a planning authority had no jurisdiction to authorise nuisance save insofar as it had the statutory power to permit the change of the character of the neighbourhood. However, in the *Gillingham Borough Council* case, the Court of Appeal distinguished *Allen* in which planning permission for the development of a commercial port had resulted in the use of roads in the neighbourhood by heavy goods vehicles 24 hours a day. The court held that the planning permission was not a licence to cause nuisance, but where the permission relates to development or change of use then the question of nuisance falls to be decided with reference to the neighbourhood with that use or development and not by reference to the neighbourhood as it previously existed.

13.22 In *Wheeler*, reliance was placed by the defendant on the *Gillingham Borough Council* case. The Court of Appeal, however, held that in the *Wheeler* case the grant of

---

[35]   SI 1995/419.
[36]   Defined in s 65(2) of the Town and Country Planning Act 1990.
[37]   [1997] AC 655, HL.
[38]   Ibid, at 710D.
[39]   [1995] 2 All ER 697, CA.
[40]   [1993] QB 343.
[41]   [1981] AC 1001.

planning permission had not changed the character of the neighbourhood, since the defendant's farm had, prior to the planning permission, been used for pig breeding, although on a different part of the farm property. The same must presumably be true in relation to rights of light, as the standard of light to which the easement gives the right does not vary with the locality.[42]

13.23 In *Greenwich Health Care NHS Trust v London and Quadrant Housing Trust*[43] the court granted declaratory relief to the effect that an injunction would not be available to restrain an interference with an easement because the proposed development was 'necessary to achieve an object of substantial public and local importance and value'. The case probably does not support the proposition that the grant of planning permission for such a project will prevent the owner of easements affected from seeking an inspection. There was in that case no opposition to the development, and the decision can be justified on other grounds.

13.24 It appears, therefore, that the law as it stands at present may be summarised as follows:

(1)   The grant of planning permission does not directly affect private rights, whether to light or other rights.

(2)   The grant of planning permission does not authorise a nuisance.

(3)   Insofar as the *character of the neighbourhood* is relevant in deciding whether a nuisance has occurred, the effect of the grant of permission may be relevant, insofar as it leads to a change in the character of the area.[44] This is, however, unlikely to affect rights of light.

13.25 Where an aggrieved dominant owner wishes to challenge the grant of permission this may be done by application for judicial review, governed by CPR Part 54. A general account of this is beyond the scope of this work, and the reader should consult the Civil Court Service. One point of general importance is the need for applicants to act promptly and in any event not later than 3 months after the grounds for making the claim first arose (CPR, r 54.5). In the case of planning permission, time runs from the date of grant.[45] The date on which the applicant first became aware of the decision is not relevant, although lack of awareness may induce the court to grant an extension of time.

CURRENT PLANNING POLICIES RELATING TO LIGHT

13.26 There are no national planning policies specifically related to the protection of light to existing buildings. But, as already noted, LPAs will usually incorporate policies in the local plan aimed to protect sunlight, daylight and privacy from overlooking. The most common criteria used are those in the BRE publication first published in 1991[46] – *Site Layout Planning for Daylight and Sunlight: A Guide to Good Practice*[47] ('the BRE

---

[42]   *Hortons' Estate Ltd v James Beattie Ltd* [1927] 1 Ch 75.
[43]   [1998] 3 All ER 437.
[44]   See the comment on the *Wheeler* case at [1995] JPL 619 at 632.
[45]   *R v Hammersmith and Fulham LBC ex parte Burkett* [2002] 1 WLR 1593.
[46]   Reprinted 2005 with minor corrections.
[47]   British Standard BS8206: Part 2, 1992.

document'). This in turn incorporates references to a document published by the British Standards Institution – *Code of Practice for daylighting* ('the Code of Practice'). The BRE has also published *Design with Innovative Daylighting* (1996) which is concerned with the design of new development to maximise the benefits of daylight rather than protection of existing buildings. A brief overview of the BRE document and the Code of Practice will be given, but more detailed application is likely to require expert input from a specialist rights of light surveyor.

13.27 Dealing first with the Code of Practice, its purpose is stated in the Foreword as being 'intended to enhance the well being and satisfaction of people in buildings'. It cautions that 'careful judgment should be exercised when using the criteria for other purposes, particularly town planning control'.

13.28 Paragraph 4 of the Code of Practice states that unless an activity requires the exclusion of daylight, a view out-of-doors should be provided irrespective of its quality. Paragraph 5 states that sunlight should be admitted unless it is likely to cause thermal or visual discomfort to the users, or deterioration of materials. It is stated that in 'interiors in which the occupants have a reasonable expectation of direct sunlight should receive at least 25 per cent of probable sunlight hours'. Probable sunlight hours are the number of hours annually during which the sun shines on unobstructed ground taking cloudiness into account. The Code of Practice further states that 5% of probable sunlight hours should be received during the winter months. Paragraph 5 continues by suggesting that the general illumination from skylight should be such that there is no excessive contrast between the interior and the view outside, and that if electric lighting is not normally to be used during daytime the average daylight factor should be not less than 5%. If electric lighting is to be used during the daytime, the average daylight factor should not be less than 2%. These criteria apply where a predominantly day-lit appearance is required. The Code of Practice further suggests that even if a predominantly day-lit appearance is not required in dwellings, it is recommended that the average daylight factor be at least 1% in bedrooms, 1.5% in living rooms and 2% in kitchens.

13.29 Paragraph 6 of the Code of Practice states that in relation to task lighting the principles of lighting design using daylight are the same as those for electric lighting. It is necessary both to achieve a given level of illumination and to take account of the circumstances that determine its quality.

13.30 The Code of Practice lists recommended minimum proportions of glazing the view in deep side-lit rooms. It also lists recommended illuminances in an appendix, and contains sections on the design of supplementary electric lighting, sunlight shading, energy efficiency and conservation of materials.

13.31 Although the Code of Practice is aimed at the design of new buildings, its principles can be adapted to an assessment of the qualitative impact on existing properties of new development. In particular, para 5 of the Code of Practice could be used to assess what would be acceptable in terms of loss of sunlight and illumination.

13.32 The BRE document is designed to prescribe good practice on the layout plans of new development to achieve daylight and sunlight. Paragraph 2 deals with daylight to existing buildings, and the impact of new development. It states that:

'... if any part of a new building or extension ... suspends an angle of more than 25 to the horizontal, then the diffused daylighting of the existing building may be adversely affected. This will be the case if either the vertical sky component ... is less than 27% and less than

0.8 times its former value; or the area of the working plan in a room which can receive direct skylight is reduced to less than 0.8 times its former value.'

This deals with the design of new development in relation to sunlight. The document makes recommendations concerning the preservation of sunlight to existing buildings. Diagrams and calculation methods are contained in the appendix.

13.33 Part 2 deals with light from the sky. Paragraph 2.1 deals with new development. It recommends that to prevent obstruction of daylight to the new building it should be positioned so that taking a plane 2 m above ground level within it the angle from the horizontal to the top of the existing building should not exceed 25°. Paragraph 2.2 deals with existing buildings. It recommends the use of a modified form of the procedure adopted for new buildings to find out whether an existing building still receives enough skylight. The angle to the horizontal subtended by the new development at the level of the centre of the lowest window should be measured. If this is less than 25° for the whole of the development then it is unlikely to have a substantial effect on the diffuse skylight enjoyed by the existing building. Where the angle is greater the loss can be calculated using the skylight indicator (Appendix A) or the Waldram Diagram (Appendix B). If the vertical sky component is greater than 27% enough skylight should still be reaching the existing building. If it is both less than this and less than 0.8 times the former value, the occupants of the existing building will notice the reduction in the amount of skylight. The paragraph discusses the interrelationship between the loss of skylight and rights to light. It states that 'none of the guidelines here is intended to replace, or be a means of satisfying, the legal requirements contained in rights-to-light law'. It continues by suggesting that it is usually true that if the guidelines here are satisfied then a new development will not infringe rights to light. But this is not always true, particularly if the existing building is unusually deep or has especially small or low windows. Appendix E contains a brief overview of the law relating to rights to light.

13.34 Part 3 deals with sunlight. Paragraph 3.1 deals with the design of new buildings, bringing in the Code of Practice. The standard for adequate sunlight it adopts involves two elements. The first is whether at least one main window wall faces within 90° of due south and the second is whether on this wall all points on a line 2 m above ground level are within 4 m (measured sideways) of a point which receives at least a quarter of annual probable sunlight hours, including at least 5% of annual probable sunlight hours during the winter months between 21 September and 21 March.

13.35 Paragraph 3.2 covers existing buildings and suggests applying the same standard to decide whether a new building is so designed as to safeguard the access to sunlight of the existing building in question. Access to sunlight should be checked for the main window in each room facing within 90° of due south. If the available sunlight would be both less than this amount and less than 0.8 times the former value either over the whole year or the winter months the occupants of the building will notice the loss of sunlight.

13.36 Paragraph 3.3 deals with gardens and open spaces, and lays down criteria to protect against loss of sunlight. The methodology is based on a sunlight-on-ground indicator (Appendix G). It is suggested that no more than two-fifths and preferably no more than a quarter of any amenity area should be prevented by buildings from receiving any sunlight at all on 21 March. The effect of trees and shrubs is discussed. The effect of high hedges is now regulated by statute with its own set of standards, also prepared by BRE, and these are discussed in Chapter 16.

13.37 Part 4 of the document refers to passive solar design. Where new development would overshadow existing buildings which rely on passive solar design this should be minimised in various ways. Part 5 deals with briefly with view, privacy, security, enclosure, microclimate and solar dazzle.

Chapter 14

CONVEYANCING ISSUES WHICH AFFECT RIGHTS TO LIGHT

INTRODUCTION

14.1   In this chapter conveyancing issues which affect rights of light will be considered under the following headings:

(1)   Rights of light and registered titles.
    (a)   Where titles were registered and dealings took place before 13 October 2003.
    (b)   Where titles were registered and dealings took place after 13 October 2003.[1]

(2)   Rights of light and unregistered titles.

(3)   Landlord and tenant issues where rights of light are material.

(4)   Searches and inquiries.

(5)   Other general matters.

RIGHTS OF LIGHT AND REGISTERED TITLES

Where titles were registered and dealings took place before 13 October 2003

The dominant land

14.2   The easement of light was treated in the same way as any other easement by the Land Registry. On first registration, benefit of an easement passed as a right which appertained or was reputed to appertain to the land which was to be registered and no mention of the benefit was required to be made on the property register of the dominant land.[2] This principle applied whatever the class of title registered. Following registration, under the Land Registration Rules 1925 ('LRR 1925'),[3] r 252 the dominant owner could apply to have the benefit of the easement expressly noted on his title. If

---

[1]   Note: the significance of the distinction between the two periods at (a) and (b) is because of the commencement of the Land Registration Act 2002 ('LRA 2002') on 13 October 2003. There are some transitional provisions relevant to rights of light in Sch 12 to that Act; see paras 8, 9 and 10 thereof. See **14.12** for specific examples where these transitional provisions apply. In view of the fact that there will continue to be titles to which the 'old' law applies for a while to come, this chapter starts by looking at those titles where it is necessary to consider that law; e g in order to understand why entries are, or are not on the register where the relevant disposition or entries were made before 13 October 2003.

[2]   Sections 5 and 72 of the Land Registration Act 1925 ('LRA 1925'); r 251 of the Land Registration Rules 1925 ('LRR 1925').

[3]   SI 1925/1093.

such an application was made, the district land registry notified those affected by the easement, being the registered proprietors and others interested in the potentially servient land where it was registered.[4] If the servient land was unregistered, the dominant owner served notice on the person who was in possession. In practice, not many registered proprietors of dominant land applied for the benefit of the easement of light to be placed on their title.

14.3   Thus, *on first registration*, it was not necessary to make an express application for the benefit of the easement of light to be noted on the title for that easement to be effective post registration. The right, if appearing from the document of title to exist as a legal easement, was entered on the property register. In practice, it was only where there was an express grant of a right to light that the Registry made such an entry. On the subsequent transfer of the title to the dominant land, the right passed whether or not it was noted on the register.[5]

14.4   But where the title to the dominant land was already registered, an easement of light granted by deed, or in a transfer of land, took effect as a legal easement *only* if it was registered as appurtenant to the registered title of the dominant land.[6] This also required the Registry to serve notice on the servient land owner and for the burden of the easement to be noted on the register of that title.[7] In the case of a grant by deed (without any transfer), this required the servient owner to produce his Land Certificate for this to be done. If unregistered, the owner of the servient land had to deduce his title to show the ability to make the grant.

The servient land

14.5   As regards the burden of an easement, the position was as follows:

(1)   Where an easement had been expressly granted, was shown on the title deeds, and on first registration appeared adversely to affect the servient land which was to be registered, an entry on the charges register of the title to that land of that easement was made.[8] In practice, the Registry always made such an entry notwithstanding their status as overriding interests as described at (2) below.[9]

(2)   Legal easements (which includes a right to light) were within the class of overriding interests defined by s 70(1)(a) of the Land Registration Act 1925 ('LRA 1925'). Therefore, they took effect and bound the servient land even if they were not noted on the charges register of the title to that land.[10] In practice, because of the way in which the Registry made the entry under its practice set out in (1) above, there are few titles where express grants were not set out on the face of the register.[11]

---

4   LRR 1925, rr 252 and 253.
5   LRA 1925, ss 20, 23 and 72.
6   Ibid, s 19.
7   Ibid.
8   LRA 1925, s 70(2).
9   See *Re Dances Way Hayling Island* [1962] Ch 490.
10   LRR 1925, r 258.
11   By virtue of Sch 12, para 9 to LRA 2002, the status of legal easements to which the terms of s 70(1)(a) applied was preserved. There is no time-limit to this preservation.

Both dominant and servient land; no express grant

14.6   What, however, was the position on registered land where a right to light was not the subject of an express grant by deed? In such cases, the status of easement as overriding interests led to confusion. This is because in the case of non-apparent easements – of which light is a prime example – there is no evidence on the ground, and no evidence on the register to indicate whether any right to light exists for or against any particular title. The next three paragraphs deal with this problem.

Both dominant and servient titles – express agreements relating to rights to light not completed by deed, creating equitable easements

14.7   These were minor interests, unless they qualified as overriding interests. As regards the protection of the interest of the parties under equitable easements created by agreements regulating light or restricting it,[12] the sensible course in all cases was to ensure that all parties applied to have the benefit or burden of any such agreement noted on the register of titles of the land affected. In the case of restrictive agreements which amount to covenants, this had to be done as regards the land burdened, for otherwise the successor to the covenantor took free from such interests which were not protected by registration.[13]

14.8   In the case of equitable easements which might be enforceable as overriding interests, no entry needed be made of them on the register. There were two instances where such equitable easements ranked as overriding interests. First, where they fell within s 70(1)(g) of LRA 1925, being the rights of persons in actual occupation of the land (or in receipt of the rents and profits thereof) save where inquiry is made of such persons and the rights are not disclosed.[14] In the case of a right to light created by an agreement not made under seal, it was easy to see how the benefit of the right under the agreement could be part and parcel of the rights of the person in actual occupation of the dominant land, but less easy to see how that right extended to protect the servient owner. However, it could be said that as the right to light is a right which can extend over other land, there is no reason why the servient owner should not be bound, just as the rights of the occupying tenant-in-common may bind third parties.[15] Secondly, equitable easements which were an adverse right, privilege or appurtenance occupied or enjoyed with land might be overriding interests under LRA 1925, s 70(1)(a) by virtue of LRR 1925, r 278 and the decision in *Celsteel v Alton House Holdings Ltd.*[16] However, in that authority the court's finding on the extent of overriding interests related only to a right of way, and it was open to question whether the easement of light should fall within this category of interests.

---

[12]   See Chapter 9.
[13]   LRA 1925, ss 20 and 50.
[14]   For a full discussion of the new law on interests which override under LRA 2002 with a comparison to the law before 13 October 2003, and with reference to the transitional provisions, see *Ruoff & Roper: Registered Conveyancing*, ch 10. See **14.12** for the way in which such overriding interests are treated under the new law after 13 October 2003.
[15]   *Williams & Glyn's Bank v Boland* [1981] AC 487; *Ferrishurst Ltd v Wallcite Ltd and Another* [1999] 2 WLR 667.
[16]   [1985] 2 All ER 562.

14.9   Where protection as a minor interest against the servient owner's title was not possible (because he would not produce his Land Certificate for the noting of the entry of the agreement), the agreement could be protected by a caution against dealings against that title.[17]

Both dominant and servient titles – easements of light created by implication

14.10   Where the title of land is registered, an easement of light may be acquired by virtue of the doctrine of non-derogation from grant and LPA 1925, s 62, as if the title to the land was not registered.[18] Section 19(3) of LRA 1925 applies the 'general words' implied in conveyances to transfers of registered land.[19] No express entry on the register of either the dominant or the servient title was, therefore, necessary. Under LRR 1925, r 258, these rights took effect as overriding interests. This caused uncertainty in practice as it was necessary to look behind the register at the history of the two titles to ascertain: (i) when the titles were sold off; and (ii) what apertures or other means of enjoyment of light were in existence at that time. In addition, where an easement of light can arise by estoppel or by common intention of the parties,[20] some individual 'digging' will be needed to establish the right. Only where the dominant owner made application for a right to light created by implication and only where the servient owner was duly notified and where the Registrar was satisfied as to the legal origin and existence of the right, was it noted as appurtenant to the dominant title and as a burden on the servient title.[21]

Both dominant and servient titles – prescriptive rights

14.11   In cases where rights to light are not the subject of an express or implied grant, but rely for their existence upon enjoyment under the various ways in which such rights can be acquired by prescription, such rights could be enjoyed as overriding interests, just as if they were expressly or impliedly granted.[22] But as regards the servient land, because the prescriptive right claimed is inchoate until declared by a court, the Land Registry (subject to what is said below) declined to make an entry of the right claimed on the servient title unless there was an order declaring the right to light to be appurtenant to the dominant title and against the servient title.[23] In such cases, the Registry entered the terms of the right declared against the servient title and, if application was made, noted the benefit of the right on the dominant title. In cases where no court order had been obtained, it was open to claimants to seek the entry of the right against the servient title under LRR 1925, r 250.[24] This required proof of the existence and acquisition of the right and, in practice, was difficult to achieve. In any such application, the Registry served notice of the application on the servient registered proprietor and other interested parties (under LRR 1925, r 253) and, if no objection was received, the entry of the right was made on the charges register of the servient title. If objection was received, the Registry might decline to make the entry, or might enter the right as a claimed one only.[25] As a matter of experience, it is difficult in many claims to rights to

---

[17]   LRA 1925, ss 54 and 59(2).
[18]   LRA 1925, s 20(1).
[19]   For grants of rights to light by implication, see Chapter 5 at **5.10** et seq.
[20]   See Chapter 5 at **5.4** and **5.34**.
[21]   See LRR 1925, rr 252 and 253.
[22]   Ibid, r 258.
[23]   See LRR 1925, r 302.
[24]   Pursuant to s 75(5) of LRA 1925.
[25]   The latter is made under s 70(3) of LRA 1925.

light to establish the right (other than in clear cases) to the satisfaction of the Registry without an order of the court. This is an instance where if an entry is to be made, the servient owner is obliged to produce his land or charge certificate.[26]

TRANSITIONAL PROVISIONS

14.12 These are contained in Sch 12, paras 8, 9 and 10 to LRA 2002 and provide as follows:

(1)   Schedule 12, para 8:

> 'Schedule 3 has effect with the insertion after paragraph 2 of—
>
> "2A(1) An interest which, immediately before the coming into force of this Schedule, was an overriding interest under section 70(1)(g) of the Land Registration Act 1925 by virtue of a person's receipt of rents and profits, except for an interest of a person of whom inquiry was made before the disposition and who failed to disclose the right when he could reasonably have been expected to do so.
>
> (2) Sub-paragraph (1) does not apply to an interest if at any time since the coming into force of this Schedule it has been an interest which, had the Land Registration Act 1925 (c. 21) continued in force, would not have been an overriding interest under section 70(1)(g) of that Act by virtue of a person's receipt of rents and profits."'

Easements which under the old law were overriding interests within s 70(1)(g) of LRA 1925 (see 14.8) may be capable of continuing as an interest which overrides under Sch 3, para 2A to LRA 2002. This will only apply to the benefit of an easement (in this case) of light.

(2)   Schedule 12, para 9:

> '(1) This paragraph applies to an easement or profit a prendre which was an overriding interest in relation to a registered estate immediately before the coming into force of Schedule 3, but which would not fall within paragraph 3 of that Schedule if created after the coming into force of that Schedule.
>
> (2) In relation to an interest to which this paragraph applies, Schedule 3 has effect as if the interest were not excluded from paragraph 3.'

This preserves the effect of legal easements formerly treated as overriding interests within s 70(1)(a) of LRA 1925; see **14.5(2)**.

(3)   Schedule 12, para 10:

> 'For the period of three years beginning with the day on which Schedule 3 comes into force, paragraph 3 of the Schedule has effect with the omission of the exception.'

This provides for a temporary exception to the requirement of proof of user within one year of the date of a disposition contained in Sch 3, para 3(2) to LRA 2002. The exception lasted until 13 October 2006. It is unlikely that the

---

[26]   LRA 1925, s 64(1).

requirement of user will apply to many rights of light cases as without user it is questionable whether the right exists: see Chapter 6. But it is conceivable that an aperture may be obscured (for some reason) and the intending purchaser may be unaware of it and it may not be discoverable on a reasonably careful inspection of the land. Until 13 October 2006 the requirement for use was not required and in the circumstances just stated the easement did not override. After that date the proof of user within one year of the disposition will be a relevant fact and subject to the purchaser's knowledge and what would have been revealed on a reasonably careful inspection, the interest will override. It is suggested that in the vast majority of cases where apertures exist and enjoy light such light will be an interest which overrides: see **14.14**. As is pointed out a **14.14(3)** the purchaser should apply for the entry of a notice referring to the right of light under r 74(1) of the Land Registration Rules 2003[27] ('LRR 2003'), that being preferable to relying on the terms of the rules which determine whether or not interests override.

Where titles have been registered and dealings take place after 13 October 2003

14.13 In respect of dispositions and dealings with the registered land after 13 October 2003, there are two main events to consider. First, first registration and secondly, subsequent dispositions. For the detail of the law see *Ruoff & Roper: Registered Conveyancing.*[28] In respect of both first registrations and subsequent dispositions, it is necessary to consider: (i) express grants; (ii) implied grants whether under the doctrine of *Wheeldon v Burrows*[29] or s 62 of the Law of Property Act 1925; (iii) prescription and lost modern grant and Prescription Act 1832 cases; and finally (iv) Orders of the Court.

First registration

14.14

(1) *Express grants.*
      In the case of an express grant, a legal interest will be an interest which overrides under Sch 1, para 3 to LRA 2002. Therefore, in theory, a grant does not have to be noted on the register to both the dominant and servient land. However, it is preferable to note that such a legal interest is granted on both the dominant and the servient land. This is because of the duty to disclose such interests under LRR 2003, r 28 on first registration. Reference should also be made here to forms FR1 and D1. In addition, in practice, the Land Registry will note such express grants of easements under s 37(1) of LRA 2002. The power to note against the servient title is made under s 27(2)(d) and (e) and s 38 of LRA 2002.

(2) *Implied grants.*
      These will override Sch 1, para 3 to LRA 2002 and also reference should be made to LRR 2003, r 74 and in particular r 74(3) where the owner of the dominant tenement may apply for the entry of the implied easement.

(3) *Prescriptive rights.*

---

[27]   SI 2003/1417.
[28]   See also C Harpum and J Bignell *Registered Land: The New Law: A Guide to the Land Registration Act 2002* (Jordans, 2002) ('Harpum & Bignell').
[29]   (1879) 12 ChD 31.

These rights may not be regarded as a legal easement properly so called if they are in the process of being acquired. However, in practice, the preferable course is to apply under r 74 of LRR 2003 setting out in a statutory declaration to be annexed to Form AP1 the basis on which the claim to the right of light is made. In respect of such applications and in respect of applications for the entry of implied grants, the Registry will serve notice on the servient owner and if no objection is made it will be noted on the servient owner's land under ss 27 and 38 of LRA 2002. If there is an objection by the servient owner, the proper procedure is to refer the dispute to the Adjudicator under s 73.[30]

(4) *Orders of the Court.*
Orders declaring the existence, or non-existence of rights of light should be noted against the titles affected under r 74. The Order should make specific provision for this and for the entry of any other terms which require noting on the dominant or servient titles. Where a title is unregistered the owner should ensure that a copy of the Order is kept with the documents of title.

Registered dispositions

14.15

(1) *Express grants.*
The benefit of express grants should be registered and whilst such a legal easement is capable of being an interest which overrides under Sch 3, paras 2 and 3 of LRA 2002, the preferable course is to ensure registration. The use of Form AP1 is suggested here and in view of the fact that there is an express grant, the grantor should not be able to dispute the entry of the burden of the ground on his title. In any case of an express grant, it is, therefore, the grantor who should be required to submit his title (if registered) to the Land Registry for updating so that the entry of the grant is shown as a burden on the Charges Register to his title.

(2) *Implied grants.*
As with express grants these can also be interests which override under Sch 3. Also, as with express grants, it is preferable to note the benefit under LRR 2003, r 74 using Form AP1. As before, in the case of an implied grant under s 62 of LRA 2002 or under the doctrine of *Wheeldon v Burrows*,[31] the former common vendor should accede to the entry of the burden of the grant on his title and should, therefore, supply his register with Form AP1 for updating. If, however, there is a dispute for some reason, the servient owner is entitled to object and place his dispute in front of the Adjudicator under s 73 of LRA 2002. If the right which is the subject of the implied grant is subject to some doubt or difficulty, the Registry may enter that as a 'claimed right' – which does not guarantee its validity.[32]

(3) *Prescriptive rights.*
These can be interests which override under Sch 3 to LRA 2002. The preferable course, however, is to apply to enter the benefit of such rights on the dominant

---

[30] See Harpum and Bignell, [8.50] and [8.51]. Note that the time for objections will be stated on the notification to the servient owner sent by the Land Registry and generally the time expires at 12 noon on the fifteenth business day after the date of the issue of the notice by the Land Registry: see LRR 2003, r 197(2).
[31] (1879) 12 ChD 31.
[32] See Harpum and Bignell, [8.50].

tenement under r 74 of LRR 2003 using Form AP1. As before, service of such an application will be made on the servient tenement and, if there is no objection, the entry will be registered against the servient tenement on the Charges Register under s 38 of LRA 2002. Also as before, if there is an objection by the servient owner, that dispute may be referred to the Adjudicator under s 73 of LRA 2002. If there is some uncertainty over the existence of the right or the scope of the right, it may be noted as a claimed right.[33]

(4)   *Agreements as to rights of light and air, etc.*
       It is possible to note these agreements either on first registration under LRR 2003, r 36 or where there are subsequent dispositions of the title to note them on the register under r 76. It is, of course, important to note that if agreements are in the form of covenants (see **14.16** and Chapter 9) these must be entered on the burdened land in order for such restrictive covenants to bind successors in title of the original covenantor.

(5)   If the burdened land is unregistered, the dominant owner as the owner of a registered estate who claims the benefit of a legal easement (of light) which has been expressly granted over an unregistered estate may apply for it to be registered as appurtenant to his estate. The application must be accompanied by the grant and evidence of the grantor's title to the unregistered estate. In this context the reference to an express grant does not include a grant as a result of the operation of s 62 of the Law of Property Act 1925, or seemingly an implied grant under the doctrine of *Wheeldon v Burrows*.[34] In such cases, it is, therefore, possible to ensure that the benefit of the easement is properly registered against the benefited land. As regards the unregistered servient land, the deed of grant must, of course, be retained with the title deeds and produced (when first registration occurs) as part of the abstract, or epitome, of title deduced (see r 73 of LRR 2003).

(6)   *Orders of the Court.*
       Orders declaring the existence, or non-existence of rights of light should be noted against the titles affected under r 74. The Order should make specific provision for this and for the entry of any other terms which require noting on the dominant or servient titles. Where a title is unregistered the owner should ensure that a copy of the Order is kept with the documents of title.

PRACTICAL POINTS ARISING UNDER LRA 2002

14.16 There are some short practical points which can be made at the conclusion of this chapter.

(1)   Unregistered rights should be disclosed wherever possible and steps should be taken to ensure that they are noted on the register of both the dominant and servient titles. The duty of disclosure is, of course, an important one and this therefore means that it is preferable as part and parcel of disclosure to make application for the entry of the easement of light either on first registration or on the relevant disposition.

---

[33] See Harpum and Bignell, [8.50].
[34] (1879) 12 Ch D 31. See also s 37(7) of LRA 2002. For a recent case where s 62 applied to a right of way between adjoining owners (in the context of the Leasehold Reform Act 1967) see *Kent & Anor v Kavanagh & Anor* [2006] EWCA Civ 162.

(2) When making an application for the registration of unregistered interest, particularly using Form AP1 when it is sought to register a prescriptive easement of light under r 74, the statutory declaration should be carefully drawn so as to reflect the true facts of the case. It is suggested that the more detailed the evidence the better the prospect of the registration succeeding and also the better the prospect of any objection being resisted. It is important to note that if there is a dispute about the application, the disputed application will be heard by the Adjudicator to the Land Registry. That is another reason why care should be taken with the statutory declaration in support of Form AP1.

(3) Notwithstanding the above, because many prescriptive rights of light or those which have been acquired by an implied grant will not be apparent on the face of the Register, the Register will not, therefore, always be a mirror of the true position as to rights of light if prescriptive or implied rights of light exist. This is particularly important when advisers are carrying out searches on behalf of intended purchasers. Reports on title should make it clear what steps (if any) have been taken to check whether or not prescriptive claims to light exist for or against the subject property. In the context of acquisitions, particularly of investment or development property, it will be prudent to engage rights of light surveyors at an early stage in order to identify any rights of light issues which may be relevant to the acquisition or the development. Site inspections are vitally important with all advisers present. In conjunction with this, a search of the *local* Land Charges Register to ascertain whether there are any light obstruction notices will also be mandatory. It is important to recognise that light obstruction notices will only be on the local Land Charges Register and will not be on the registers maintained by the Land Registry either under LRA 2002 or under the Land Charges Act 1972.

(4) Pre-contract inquiries and requisitions should be carefully drawn to ensure that rights of light issues and in particular inquiries should ask whether notices under the Rights of Light Act 1959 have been served or received. The standard forms should be modified as necessary to ensure that the right questions are asked.

RIGHTS TO LIGHT AND UNREGISTERED TITLES

14.17 With the increase in registered titles and the obligation to register now universal, such titles are becoming rarer. No specific conveyancing issues arise, save that it is customary to draw a counterpart or copy of any agreement granting an easement of light so that all parties have counterparts or copies to keep with their documents of title. As regards agreements restricting the use of light or building which may be treated as restrictive covenants, these must be registered as Class D(ii) Land Charges, in the name of the estate owner of the land burdened, in order to bind a successor owner of that land.[35] An equitable (as opposed to a legal) easement must be registered as a Class D(iii) Land Charge to be valid.[36] In either case, if unregistered, they will not bind a purchaser of the legal estate for money or money's worth.[37] Unless, so registered, such interests will not be entered on the title of the land affected on first registration.

14.18 Orders of the Court declaring the existence, or non-existence of rights of light should be kept with the documents of title. Note that some forms of Order may require

---

[35] Land Charges Act 1972, s 2(5); and see Chapter 9 at **9.30**.
[36] Ibid, s 2(5).
[37] Ibid, s 4(6).

registration as a Class D(ii) Land Charge against the estate owner of the burdened land if the terms effectively impose a restrictive obligation; see above.

14.19 In view of the practice of the Registry on first registration (see above), the evidence of grants, agreements and Orders must be kept in such a way that the appropriate entries can be made on the new title on first registration when the title is produced.

LANDLORD AND TENANT ISSUES

14.20 Attention is drawn to Chapter 6 at **6.30** as to the ability of tenants to prescribe both for and against their landlords and third parties.

In summary, a well-drawn lease should:

(1)   reserve all light to the landlord;

(2)   give the landlord the right to build on any adjoining or neighbouring land as he pleases; this right can be expressed widely so as to encompass land not within the ownership of the landlord, but to have such an effect the terms must be clearly in favour of such a construction.[38]

(3)   prohibit the tenant from enjoying any light other than by consent of the landlord;

(4)   prohibit the tenant from making any agreement regarding light without the consent of the landlord;

(5)   oblige the tenant to inform the landlord of all notices (eg light obstruction notices) and of any attempted infringement of light coming to the demised premises;

(6)   prohibit the tenant from stopping up any windows.

SEARCHES AND INQUIRIES

14.21 The following searches are material in the context of conveying land where the right to light may be material:

(1)   Searches of adjoining registered titles for any easements, the benefit of which is claimed or to which that title may be subject. This is useful if there is doubt over one's own title and the rights for and against it.

(2)   In unregistered titles, searches of the Land Charges Register against the names of successive estate owners to establish whether any entries reveal adverse Class D(ii) entries protecting restrictive deeds or agreements.

---

[38]   See *Paragon Finance v CLRP Co* [2002] 1 EGLR 97.

(3) Searches of the local Land Charges register to reveal whether any light obstruction notices have been registered.[39] Both the property being acquired *and* adjoining properties should be within this search. Note that properties may be located within different registering authorities and more than one register may, therefore, have to be searched. Proper inquiries in pre-contract inquiries and a specific question as to whether any notices have been received under the Rights of Light Act 1959 will be prudent; see Chapter 8 at **8.31** et seq.

14.22 The importance of disclosing any documents relating to light and the results of any searches cannot be over-emphasised, and that requires careful management of such documents within unregistered titles in particular.[40]

14.23 Although not strictly a matter of conveyancing, management surveyors and others concerned with large buildings should maintain records of all elevations and plans and ideally photographic records of the dominant building and servient buildings, with views from windows which may be considered vulnerable if adjoining buildings are developed. In the context of abandonment,[41] where the position of apertures is altered in both the horizontal and vertical plane, such evidence may be vital. Photographic evidence taken to show adjoining buildings can also be vital when assessing interference after such buildings have been demolished and a 'before' and 'after' assessment of loss of light is required.

GENERAL CONVEYANCING POINTS IN BOTH REGISTERED AND UNREGISTERED TITLES

14.24 Consideration must always be given in any title where agreements (whether or not executed under seal) relating to the use and enjoyment of light appear to affect the title whether the agreements are restrictive or permissive.[42] Agreements which have a restrictive effect must always be registered against the burdened land in order to bind successors in title of the covenantor; see **14.15(4)** and **14.17** above.

14.25 As to general words,[43] it is usual to exclude any implied grant of rights to light under s 62 of the Law of Property Act 1925. In registered titles such implied grants must be excluded expressly for otherwise they will pass under s 11(3) (first registration) or s 27 of LRA 2002 (dispositions).[44] Likewise, the exclusion of any implied grant of rights (former quasi-easements) arising under the principle of non-derogation from grant is customary by reserving rights to light to the vendor, or lessor.[45]

Note that a reservation is not a 'consent' under s 3 of the Prescription Act 1832: see **6.25**.

---

[39] See Chapter 7 at **7.10–7.14** and Chapter 8 at **8.31–8.37**.
[40] See *Cemp Properties (UK) Ltd v Dentsply Research and Development Corporation (No 1)* [1989] 2 EGLR 192 for the consequences of the failure to observe these rules.
[41] See Chapter 8.
[42] See Chapter 9.
[43] See Chapter 5.
[44] See s 27(7) of LRA 2002.
[45] The importance of expressly reserving rights which would otherwise pass is demonstrated in the recent authority of *Kent & Anor v Kavanagh & Anor* [2006] EWCA Civ 162. See Ruoff & Roper, at 36.023. Express notice of implied or prescriptive grants can be made under r 74 of LRR 2003.

PROPOSALS FOR REFORM

14.26 The Law Commission is currently (April 2007) engaged on a programme which is considering the reform of easements and covenants. For up-to-date information on progress see www.lawcom.gov.uk.

Chapter 15

HUMAN RIGHTS

INTRODUCTION

15.1 The entry into force of the Human Rights Act 1998 ('HRA 1998') on 2 October 2000 was a significant event in the development of English law. HRA 1998 gave domestic force to various rights in the European Convention on Human Rights ('the Convention'). It has been classed as a constitutional statute.[1] It has heralded far-reaching changes for several areas of English law. However, its impact in the sphere of the law of property has been decidedly mixed. The continued development of the jurisprudence on Art 8 of, and Art 1 of the First Protocol ('A1P1') to, the Convention at the level of the European Court of Human Rights ('the Strasbourg Court') in, for example, *Connors v United Kingdom*[2] and *Pye v United Kingdom*[3] must be contrasted with decisions on the domestic level in cases such as *Harrow LBC v Qazi*[4] and *Kay v Lambeth LBC*.[5]

15.2 At the date of writing, there had not been any case at either the domestic or the Strasbourg level giving substantive consideration to the compatibility of the domestic law on rights of light with the Convention. In *Midtown Ltd v City of London Real Property Company Ltd*[6] the compatibility of s 237 of the Town and Country Planning Act 1990 ('the 1990 Act') with A1P1 was fully argued, but Peter Smith J found it unnecessary to decide the point. Aside from this, there has been no judicial consideration of the compatibility of the domestic law in this area with the Convention. What follows must, therefore, be seen only as an assessment of the potential issues that could arise in this area.

15.3 The domestic law on rights of light would appear potentially to raise issues under three provisions of the Convention: Art 8, Art 14 and A1P1. Before examining the operation and application of these provisions, some general points about HRA 1998 should be made.

---

1   *Thoburn v Sunderland City Council* [2003] 1 QB 151 at 186G, para 62 per Laws LJ.
2   (2004) 40 EHRR 189.
3   [2005] 3 EGLR 1.
4   [2004] 1 AC 983.
5   [2006] 2 AC 465. See, however, *Beaulane Properties Ltd v Palmer* [2006] Ch 79, which anticipated the decision of the Strasbourg Court in *JA Pye v United Kingdom* in its assessment of the incompatibility of the pre-Land Registration Act 2002 regime of adverse possession with A1P1.
6   [2005] 1 EGLR 65.

HRA 1998

15.4   In a number of respects, HRA 1998 contains novel mechanisms with respect to enforcement and remedies. The main provisions of interest for present purposes are ss 3, 4 and 6.

15.5   Section 3 of HRA 1998 introduces a powerful interpretative obligation. It provides that 'so far as it is possible to do so, primary legislation and subordinate legislation must be read and given effect in a way which is compatible with the Convention rights'. This approach is borrowed from the *Marleasing* doctrine in European Community Law.[7] Unless the legislation would otherwise be in breach of the Convention, s 3 can be ignored, so courts should always first ascertain whether, absent s 3, there would be any breach of the Convention: *Poplar Housing and Regeneration Community Association Limited v Donoghue*.[8] As Lord Hoffmann stated in *Oxfordshire County Council v Oxford City Council*:[9]

> 'Before a court has to resort to section 3, it must first decide that an ordinary reading of the statute would be inconsistent with Convention rights.'

15.6   The leading case on the s 3 interpretative obligation is a property case, *Ghaidan v Godin-Mendoza*.[10] It concerned the succession of a statutory tenancy to the surviving member of a same-sex couple following the death of the other partner. The following points may be noted from the judgments of their Lordships (Lord Millett dissenting):

(1)   No ambiguity is necessary in the legislation being interpreted in order to engage s 3.

(2)   The only limit on the courts' function under s 3 is what is 'possible'.

(3)   Section 3(1) implies a stronger and more radical obligation than to adopt a purposive interpretation in the light of the Convention.

(4)   Parliament could not, however, have intended that the courts adopt a meaning inconsistent with a fundamental feature of the legislation.

(5)   Parliament had not intended courts to make decisions for which they were not equipped. There might be several ways of making a provision Convention-compliant, and the choice might involve issues calling for legislative deliberation.

(6)   The key to what it is possible for the courts to imply into legislation without crossing the border from interpretation to amendment lies in the careful consideration of the essential principles and scope of the legislation being interpreted.

(7)   Section 3 was the prime remedial measure and resort to a s 4 declaration of incompatibility must always be a last resort. In practical terms, there is a strong rebuttable presumption in favour of an interpretation consistent with Convention rights.

---

[7]   Case C-106/89 *Marleasing SA v La Comercial Internacional de Alimentacion SA* [1990] ECR I-4135.
[8]   [2002] 1 QB 48 at 72H, para 75 per Lord Woolf CJ.
[9]   [2006] 2 AC 674 at 700A, para 59.
[10]   [2004] 2 AC 557.

(8) The obligation under s 3 applies not only to the courts but is of general application.

15.7 Section 4 of HRA 1998 provides that a court considering the compatibility with the Convention of a provision of primary or secondary legislation, if satisfied that it is incompatible with a Convention right (and, where considering a provision of secondary legislation, that the empowering primary legislation prevents removal of the incompatibility), may make a declaration of that incompatibility. The operation of s 4 was considered in *Ghaidan*. In comparison with s 3, the s 4 declaration of incompatibility is to be considered as 'an exceptional course'.[11]

15.8 Section 6(1) of HRA 1998 provides that it is unlawful for a public authority to act in a way which is incompatible with a Convention right. By s 6(3) 'public authority' expressly includes a court or tribunal. Detailed consideration has been given to the definition of 'public authority' in *Aston Cantlow and Wilmcote with Billesley Parochial Church Council v Wallbank*.[12] A distinction was there drawn between public authorities which are public authorities for all purposes, and those organisations which act as public authorities for the discharge of some only of their functions. The former have been termed 'core public authorities', whilst the latter are known as 'hybrid public authorities'. The modern tendency of traditional public authorities, particularly local authorities, to outsource the provision of their services has raised difficult questions as to the scope of protection of Convention rights offered where public services are provided by a private sector organisation.[13] The important point to note is that, through the inclusion of courts and tribunals within the definition of 'public authority', disputes between private parties which touch on Convention issues can be raised before the courts.

15.9 A general point that should be made about potential interferences with Convention rights is that these may be established at any stage; there would be no need to wait until the acquisition of a right to light at the expiry of the 20-year prescription period in s 3 of the Prescription Act 1832. Thus the requirements for a breach of Art 8 or A1P1 could, in theory at least, be made out in advance of such a right being acquired if a sufficient interference with those Convention rights occurred (eg through the planning process looking at the merits of particular development).

PROTECTION OF PRIVATE AND FAMILY LIFE AND THE HOME

15.10 Article 8 of the Convention states:

'1. Everyone has the right to respect for his private and family life, his home and correspondence.

2. There shall be no interference by a public authority with the exercise of this right except such as is in accordance with the law and is necessary in a democratic society in the interests of national security, public safety or the economic well being of the country, for the prevention of disorder or crime, for the protection of health or morals, or for the protection of the rights and freedoms of others.'

---

[11] Per Lord Steyn at 577E, para 50.
[12] [2004] 1 AC 546.
[13] See, eg, *Johnson v Havering LBC* [2007] EWCA Civ 26.

15.11 Recent case-law of the Strasbourg Court has confirmed the potentially wide scope of Art 8 in relation to interference with a person's home. The spatial and environmental dimension to Art 8 would appear to provide a basis for challenges to interferences with rights to light.

15.12 As an initial point, it should be noted that 'home' is an autonomous concept under the Convention.[14] As such, it has been interpreted to extend to business as well as domestic premises.[15] Furthermore, the notion of private life extends to include activities of a business or professional nature, since it is partly through the course of such activities that people establish and maintain relationships with others.[16] This is an important principle, since it means that the protection granted by Art 8 potentially extends to both commercial and residential premises. Thus, interferences with rights of light in the context of commercial premises may engage the protections of Art 8.

15.13 There is no right to general protection of the environment as such in the Convention.[17] However, severe environmental pollution may affect individuals' well-being and prevent them from enjoying their homes in such a way as to affect their private and family life adversely without seriously endangering their health.[18] In *Powell and Rayner v United Kingdom*[19] the Strasbourg Court held that the quality of the applicant's private life and the scope for enjoying the amenities of his home had been adversely affected by the noise generated by aircraft using Heathrow Airport. In that case, the Court held that the interference was justified because noise abatement measures had been taken by the government. National authorities were accorded a broad margin of appreciation in such matters. The case is important nevertheless because it establishes that a breach of Art 8 can flow from nuisance, such as excessive noise. It also reaffirms the principle that Art 8 imposes positive obligations on the state to take reasonable and appropriate measures to safeguard the rights protected thereunder.[20] It is notable that in *Hatton v United Kingdom*,[21] a later case involving consideration of the impact of night flights at Heathrow, the Strasbourg Court found, by a majority, a breach of the UK's positive obligations under Art 8. Although a fair balance had to be struck between the rights of individuals and the interests of the wider community:

> '... in the particularly sensitive field of environmental protection, mere reference to the economic well-being of the country is not sufficient to outweigh the rights and freedoms of others ... It considers that States are required to minimise, as far as possible, the interference with these rights, by trying to find alternative solutions and by generally seeking to achieve their aims in the least onerous way as regards human rights. In order to do that, a proper and complete investigation and study with the aim of finding the best possible solution which will, in reality, strike the right balance should precede the relevant project.'

15.14 In three more recent cases, the Strasbourg Court has developed the principle in *Hatton*. In *Taskin v Turkey*[22] the applicants claimed to suffer from the environmental effects of the construction and operation of a gold mine, in particular dangers from the use of cyanide and noise pollution. The applicants challenged both the substantive

---

14   See *Buckley v United Kingdom* (1996) 23 EHRR 101.
15   See *Niemitz v Germany* (1992) 16 EHRR 97 at 112, para 30.
16   Ibid, at 111, paras 29–30.
17   See *Kyrtatos v Greece* (2005) 40 EHRR 16.
18   See *Lopez Ostra v Spain* (1994) 20 EHRR 277.
19   (1990) 12 EHRR 355.
20   See *Guerra v Italy* (1998) 26 EHRR 357.
21   (2002) 34 EHRR 1.
22   (2006) 42 EHRR 50.

decision to permit the use of cyanide as well as the procedures which had accompanied the decision-making process. The Strasbourg Court identified three important aspects of the decision-making process that were required in order for any interference with Art 8 rights to be fair:

(1) there must be appropriate investigations and studies in order to allow for the prediction and evaluation in advance of the effects of impugned activities;

(2) the public had to have access to the conclusions of such studies and to information that would enable members of the public to assess the danger to which they were exposed; and

(3) the individuals concerned must be able to appeal to the courts where they considered that their interests or comments had not been given sufficient weight in the decision-making process.

15.15 The Strasbourg Court found an unjustified violation of Art 8. In *Moreno Gomez v Spain*[23] the Strasbourg Court found a breach of Art 8 where the Spanish Government had violated the applicant's right to respect for her home by making it impossible for her to sleep because of excessive noise levels. A city council had granted a new licence for a discotheque, notwithstanding that it was in an area which had already been classified as 'acoustically saturated'.[24] The Court recalled that Art 8 protected not only concrete or physical breaches of someone's home, but also 'those that are not concrete or physical, such as noise, emissions, smells or other forms of interference'.

15.16 *Fadeyeva v Russia*[25] concerned a claim that the Russian state had failed to protect the applicant's private life and home from severe environmental pollution where it had failed to resettle her outside an industrial zone surrounding Russia's largest iron smelter. She had suffered ill health which she claimed was linked to the plant. The Court found a violation of Art 8. It recalled that the adverse effects of environmental pollution had to reach a minimum level of severity. The assessment of this level was relative and depended on all the circumstances of the case, such as the intensity and duration of the nuisance, its physical and mental effects. The general environmental context also had to be taken into account.

15.17 On the domestic level, the question whether the impact of development on sunlight and daylight, together with overshadowing, engaged the protection of Art 8 was considered in *Lough v First Secretary of State*.[26] Although not involving any rights to light per se, the case is of interest because of the extension of the *Lopez Ostra* doctrine to cases of interference with sunlight and daylight. Pill LJ stated:[27]

> 'Not every loss of amenity involves a breach of article 8(1). The degree of seriousness required to trigger lack of respect for the home will depend on the circumstances but it must be substantial.'

---

[23]   (2005) 41 EHRR 40.
[24]   One of the effects in Spanish law of an area being designated an 'acoustically saturated zone' was that there was a ban on new activities, such as discotheques and nightclubs.
[25]   Application no 55723/00, judgment 9 June 2005.
[26]   [2004] 1 WLR 2557.
[27]   Ibid, at 2573, para 43.

15.18 At issue in *R (on the application of Malster) v Ipswich Borough Council*[28] was the effect of the redevelopment of the North Stand of Ipswich Town Football Club on levels of daylight and sunlight received by neighbouring properties. Sullivan J accepted, following *Lopez Ostra*, that severe environmental pollution might result in a breach of Art 8. However, it was doubtful that the shadowing effect of the new development on the claimant's garden crossed that threshold, given that the Council's own standards for daylight and sunlight were not infringed. However, even if the threshold had been crossed, Sullivan J recalled that the protection of rights under Art 8 was not absolute. A balancing exercise had to be undertaken between the claimant's rights to enjoy her garden and the public interest in the redevelopment of an outmoded stand and the provision of new sporting facilities. This is what the Council had done. There was accordingly no breach of Art 8.

15.19 Where the domestic legislature has struck a balance between competing interests through a particular statutory scheme, this may satisfy the Art 8(2) balancing exercise.[29] Finally, in *Dennis v Ministry of Defence*[30] although Buckley J decided the case on the basis of the law of nuisance, had he been required to do so he would have held that the effect of noise from Harrier fighter jets on the claimant's estate constituted an interference with Art 8 and A1P1 rights. Similarly, in *Andrews v Reading BC*[31] an Art 8 claim in relation to excessive traffic noise caused by a traffic regulation order succeeded.

15.20 These cases would suggest that:

(1)   Art 8 can be engaged by interferences with daylight and sunlight;

(2)   accordingly, interferences with rights to light may also raise Art 8 issues;

(3)   however, to constitute a breach of Art 8(1), any interference occurring must be severe;

(4)   no such case has yet come before the courts;

(5)   even if a breach of Art 8(1) did occur, a balancing exercise between public and private interests would be required; and

(6)   this could potentially find any interference justified.

PROTECTION OF PROPERTY RIGHTS

15.21 A1P1 states:

> 'Every natural or legal person is entitled to the peaceful enjoyment of his possessions. No one shall be deprived of his possessions except in the public interest and subject to conditions provided for by law and by the general principles of international law.

---

28   [2002] PLCR 14.
29   See *Marcic v Thames Water Utilities Ltd* [2004] 2 AC 42.
30   [2003] 2 EGLR 121.
31   [2005] EWHC 256.

The preceding provisions shall not, however, in any way impair the right of a State to enforce such laws as it deems necessary to control the use of property in accordance with the general interest or to secure the payment of taxes or other contributions or penalties.'

15.22 It is well established that A1P1 contains three distinct rules. In *Sporrong and Lönnroth v Sweden* the Strasbourg Court held as follows:[32]

'The first rule, which is of a general nature, enounces [*sic*] the principle of peaceful enjoyment of property; it is set out in the first sentence of the first paragraph. The second rule covers deprivation of possessions and subjects it to certain conditions; it appears in the second sentence of the same paragraph. The third rule recognises that the States are entitled, amongst other things, to control the use of property in accordance with the general interest, by enforcing such laws as they deem necessary for the purpose; it is contained in the second paragraph.'

15.23 The three rules are not distinct in the sense of being unconnected; the second and third rules are concerned with particular instances of the first general principle, and must be construed in the light of it.[33]

15.24 It is well established under the case-law of the Strasbourg Court and the now defunct European Commission of Human Rights ('the Commission'),[34] that serious interference with the enjoyment of property[35] can potentially fall within the scope of A1P1. However, as the Commission noted in *Powell and Rayner v United Kingdom*,[36] A1P1 is 'mainly concerned with the arbitrary confiscation of property and does not, in principle, guarantee the right to peaceful enjoyment of possessions in a pleasant environment'. The Strasbourg Court and the Commission have tended to require an adverse impact on the economic value of possessions before accepting that there has been interference. In *Rayner*, the Commission stated that 'aircraft nuisance of considerable importance both as to level and frequency may seriously affect the value of real property or even render it unsaleable and thus amount to a partial taking of property'. However, in that case, there was no proof that the value of the property had been significantly affected such that the applicant could be said to have borne a disproportionate burden amounting to a partial taking of property. Accordingly, no compensation was necessary and there was no violation. Where serious interferences with rights to light occur, this should not be difficult to establish.

15.25 Not every interference with property rights will amount to an interference for the purposes of A1P1. The wording in *Rayner* suggests that a minimum level of severity is required. This is in keeping with the jurisprudence on Art 8. In *Vearncombe v United Kingdom and Germany*[37] the construction of a shooting range did not create a sufficiently serious interference to amount to a breach of A1P1.

15.26 There is no specific authority on interference with rights to light and A1P1. An analogous type of case, where the Strasbourg Court and the Commission have found

---

[32] (1982) 5 EHRR 35 at para 61.
[33] See *James v United Kingdom* (1986) 8 EHRR 123 at para 37.
[34] This body of case-law must be taken into account by the UK courts in determining a human rights question: HRA 1998, s 2.
[35] The Convention concept of 'possessions' is a broad one. It includes land and leases but is much wider, including contractual rights, shares, patents and debts (see, eg, *Tre Traktörer AB v Sweden* (1989) 13 EHRR 309).
[36] (1986) 9 EHRR 375 at 378. See, to similar effect, *S v France 65 DR 250* at 251.
[37] 59 DR 186 at 196.

that there had been interference within A1P1, is noise nuisance. In *Baggs v UK*[38] the Commission declared admissible a complaint that noise nuisance which was severe and frequent and which had a potential impact on the economic value of the property could amount to an interference with possessions within the scope of A1P1. It is therefore anticipated that serious interference with the amount of light that reaches another's property is likely to satisfy the requirement of interference with possessions within A1P1 where an adverse impact on the economic value of property can be established.

15.27 It should be noted that A1P1 does not affect the ascription and identification of property rights which the Strasbourg Court and the Commission have considered being a matter for national courts.[39] However, this limitation is unlikely to affect the application of A1P1 to rights of light. The courts are likely to focus on the interference with the enjoyment of the dominant tenement; not the process of acquisition of rights to light by prescription. It follows from this that A1P1 may well be relevant in circumstances where no right to light has crystallised by the expiry of the 20-year prescription period.

15.28 Interference with enjoyment of property is simply the starting point for establishing a breach of A1P1. A claim will fail if it can be established that the interference can be justified because the law strikes a fair balance between the rights of the state and the individual. The text of A1P1 and the general approach adopted by the Strasbourg Court gives a wide ambit to states to justify interference. The extent of the interference is highly relevant. Generally speaking, interference with rights to light is at the lower end of the scale of interferences with property under A1P1, which is more commonly associated with the confiscation or total appropriation of an individual's property.

15.29 It would appear most likely that interference with a right to light would be classed as control rather than a deprivation of property. This is because there is no deprivation of the underlying property in the dominant tenement. The general position on the distinction between deprivation and control was examined by the Commission in *Banér v Sweden:*[40]

> 'Legislation of a general character affecting and redefining the rights of property owners cannot normally be assimilated to expropriation even if some aspect of the property right is thereby interfered with or even taken away. There are many examples in the Contracting States that the right to property is redefined as a result of legislative acts. Indeed, the wording of [A1P1] shows that general rules regulating the use of property are not to be considered as expropriation. The Commission finds support for this view in the national laws of many countries which make a clear distinction between, on the one hand, general legislation redefining the content of the property right and expropriation, on the other.'

15.30 This would support the proposition that interference with a right to light amounts to control rather than deprivation of possessions. Further, this position obtains some support from the domestic plain. In *JA Pye (Oxford) Ltd v United Kingdom*[41] the operation of the pre-Land Registration Act 2002 system of adverse possession was found to be incompatible with A1P1. This system allowed for the extinction of an owner's title to registered land by a prescriptive process of 12 years' adverse possession.

---

38   (1985) 44 DR 13; case subsequently subject to a friendly settlement: (1987) 52 DR 29.
39   See *S v UK 47 DR 274* at 279 and *Marckx v Belgium* (1979) 2 EHRR 330 at para 50.
40   (1989) 60 DR 128 at [5].
41   Application no 44302/02, 15 November 2005.

In *Oxfordshire County Council v Oxfordshire City Council*[42] the House of Lords distinguished *JA Pye* and held that the prescriptive acquisition of recreational rights for a village green amounted to a control on, rather than a deprivation of, proprietary rights. According to Lord Hoffmann, *JA Pye* was readily distinguishable because:

> 'The European Court stressed two matters: first, that the applicant's rights over the land were entirely extinguished and, secondly, that title was transferred by operation of law to another private individual. The first made it a "deprivation" and the second made it difficult to justify as a control of "the use of property" in the general interest. In the present case, first, the owner retains his title to the land and his right to use it in any way which does not prevent its use by the inhabitants for recreation and, secondly, the system of registration in the [Commons Registration Act 1965] was introduced to preserve open spaces in the public interest.'

15.31 By analogy with this situation, the acquisition of a statutory right to interfere with rights to light would seem more comparable with a control on the use of property than a deprivation. The owner of the dominant tenement retains his title to that land. The reason why the distinction is important is because, generally, a control on the use of property will be easier to justify and the lack of compensation will be less important.

15.32 The right to compensation is not expressly provided for by A1P1. As noted by the Commission, 'the Convention does not provide for an automatic right to compensation for the consequences of legislation'.[43] However, the existence of compensation is a factor in striking the 'fair balance' between public interest and private rights, and may be significant depending on the nature and extent of the control.[44] The requisite fair balance will not be struck if the person concerned has had to bear an 'individual and excessive burden'.[45]

15.33 There remain exceptional cases where compensation may not be required, such as 'the unique context of German reunification'.[46] However, to date this is the only example of a deprivation of property with no award of compensation which the Strasbourg Court has held to be justified. The control of use of property without compensation was found to be a proportionate interference with A1P1 in *Gasus Dosier und Fördertechnik GmbH v The Netherlands*.[47] See also *R (on the application of Trailer & Marina (Leven) Limited) v Secretary of State for the Environment, Food and Rural Affairs*[48] where it was held that, provided the state could properly take the view that the benefit to the community outweighs the detriment to the individual, a fair balance will be struck, without any requirement to compensate the individual in a control of use case.

15.34 The availability of compensation for the appropriation of rights to light under s 237 of the 1990 Act may well be a sufficient justification for any interference by the local authority within the scope of that section.[49] This was one of the provisions in issue in the *Midtown* case, which Peter Smith J did not ultimately have to determine on a human rights basis.

---

42 [2006] 2 AC 674 at 700C, para 59.
43 *Pinnacle Meat Processors v United Kingdom* (1999) 27 EHRR CD 217.
44 See, eg, *Holy Monasteries v Greece* (1994) 20 EHRR 1.
45 See *JA Pye* at paras 46–47, 75.
46 See *Jahn v Germany* App nos 46720/99, 72203/01 and 72552/01, 30 June 2005, at paras 116–117, 125.
47 (1995) 20 EHRR 403.
48 [2005] 1 WLR 1267 at 1281G, para 58 per Neuberger LJ.
49 See **8.56**.

15.35 Where the 20-year prescription period has not elapsed, there may well be a basis for arguing that there is no breach of Art 1. This is because any interference with property rights may, by analogy with *Marcic*, be justified on the basis that a fair balance has been struck by the legislature between the rights of the individual and the state by a rule requiring the enjoyment of light for 20 years before any right can be asserted.

15.36 However, it is easy to conceive a hypothetical situation where there has been a serious interference by the Crown with the light enjoyed by a property owner, where light has been enjoyed for a period exceeding 20 years. Under current domestic law, the Crown could rely on its immunity from the application of s 3 of the Prescription Act 1832 to defeat any claimed acquisition of a right to light by prescription.[50] However, where there is no objective justification for the interference and no compensation, there may well be a breach of A1P1. It will be recalled that s 3 of HRA 1998 only applies where there is an incompatibility.[51] On the one hand, it could be argued that s 3 of the Prescription Act 1832 was capable of being interpreted without the aid of s 3 of HRA 1998 in a Convention-compatible manner. However, it might be counter-argued that the effect of s 4 of the Rights of Light Act 1959 prevented such a natural reading. In such circumstances, recourse would have to be had to s 3 of HRA 1998 (and ultimately, perhaps, also s 4) to try to remedy any potential incompatibility.

DISCRIMINATION AND ART 14

15.37 Finally, it is conceivable that Art 14 of the Convention could have a role to play in the interpretation of s 3 of the Prescription Act 1832. Article 14 provides that:

> 'The enjoyment of the rights and freedoms set forth in this Convention shall be secured without discrimination on any ground such as sex, race, colour, language, religion, political or other opinion, national or social origin, association with a national minority, property, birth or other status.'

15.38 The first point to note about Art 14 is that it is not a free-standing prohibition on discrimination.[52] It applies vis-à-vis the other Convention rights. In order for Art 14 to be engaged, the alleged interference must be within the ambit of one of the other Convention rights. This does not mean that there has to be a breach of one of those rights, but equally it does not mean that any link, however tenuous, will suffice. Rather, the more seriously and directly the discriminatory provision or conduct impinges upon the values underlying the particular substantive Article, the more readily will it be regarded as within the ambit of that Article, and vice versa.[53] Accordingly, it is possible that a serious interference with a right to light within the ambit of Art 8 or A1P1 could raise issues under Art 14 where the Crown relied on the non-application of s 3 of the Prescription Act 1832 to defeat a claimed right to light by prescription. This would be on the basis of the difference in treatment between an individual claiming against the Crown as opposed to against another land owner. As with the other human rights issues raised by rights to light, this question will have to await determination at a later date.

---

[50]   See **6.29**.

[51]   *Oxfordshire County Council v Oxford City Council* [2006] 2 AC 674.

[52]   In contrast to Art 1 of the Twelfth Protocol to the Convention, which guarantees the 'enjoyment of any right set forth by law' without discrimination. At the time of writing, the UK was not a signatory to the Twelfth Protocol.

[53]   See *Secretary of State for Work and Pensions v M* [2006] 2 AC 91 at 100G-H, para 14 per Lord Nicholls.

Chapter 16

THE HIGH HEDGES LEGISLATION

SUMMARY

16.1 This chapter considers the legislation governing 'high hedges'. This deals with hedges that affect adversely the reasonable enjoyment of domestic property, including gardens and yards. For this legislation to be engaged it is crucial to understand at the outset that the complainant must prove that the hedge in question (as defined by s 66 of the Anti-Social Behaviour Act 2003) is more than 2 m above ground level and it is that part of the hedge above that height which is a barrier to light or access of light and is the cause of the adverse effect on reasonable enjoyment of the complainant's domestic property.

16.2 This legislation is contained in Part 8 of the Anti-Social Behaviour Act 2003 ('the 2003 Act'). In addition, there are Regulations governing the appeal procedure under it: the High Hedges (Appeal) (England) Regulations 2005.[1] The 2003 Act applies in Wales and similar Appeal Regulations apply there.[2] The 2003 Act is set out in Appendix 1 of this book.

BACKGROUND TO THE LEGISLATION

16.3 It is important to understand that this legislation imposes different standards from the common law relating to rights of light and the remedies for infringement of this legislation are also different. This is because this legislation fills a gap in the common law, which has been seen in the earlier chapters of this book, does not protect light to gardens, etc, nor does it protect the benefit of amenity conferred by daylight, or sunlight, except in extreme cases of deprivation which amount to a private nuisance. Over a number of years there has been a movement to control high hedges, especially fast-growing evergreen ones, the main culprit being the Leyland and Lawson's Cypress. After a number of unsuccessful attempts by Parliament to control what has been seen as a menace in urban and suburban gardens by successive High Hedges Bills, the Government inserted what is now Part 8 of the 2003 Act into the Anti-Social Behaviour Bill.[3] This part of the 2003 Act came into force in Wales on 31 December 2004, and in England on 1 June 2005.[4]

---

[1] SI 2005/711.

[2] SI 2004/3240 (W 282).

[3] The legislative history is complex. After government consultation in 1999 and the production of a paper entitled 'High Hedge: possible solutions', two private Members' Bills were lost in the Commons in 2001. In the 2002–03 session, a Bill promoted by Stephen Pound MP (The High Hedges (No 2) Bill) reached the Report Stage in the Commons in July 2003 with all party support. For reasons which are not entirely clear this Bill was 'talked out' by small group of Conservative MPs (the leader being Christopher Chope MP) in early July 2003: *Hansard*, HC Deb, vol 408, cols 722, 1382, 1574. After pressure exerted on the Government in the House of Lords later in July and in October 2003 to bring some form of High Hedge legislation into the Anti-Social Behaviour ('ASB') Bill, in November 2003 the Government introduced the terms of the High

PRELIMINARIES

16.4   When considering whether or not a case falls within Part 8 of the 2003 Act, it is necessary to consider the following matters.

(1)   Whether the 2003 Act applies at all; see the following parts of this chapter for the relevant provisions.

(2)   Whether there are planning conditions affecting the hedge which is the subject of the complaint. The same question applies as to whether or not the hedge is within a conservation area.

(3)   Whether or not the hedge falls within the scope of a Tree Preservation Order.

(4)   Whether the hedge is a protected hedge under the Hedgerow Regulations 1997.[5]

(5)   Whether there are restrictive covenants, or other obligations affecting the hedge which appear on the register of the titles to the properties affected. These matters are not considered in this chapter and reference should be made to the appropriate specialist text books for further guidance on them.

(6)   Whether the matter in question is one to which the Access to Neighbouring Land Act 1992 applies.[6]

In this chapter reference to a 'hedge' is a reference to a high hedge as defined by s 66 of the 2003 Act. As discussed at **16.22**, where detailed consideration is given to the definition of a 'high hedge' in s 66, it is clear that the relevant 'hedge' may include evergreens which are not necessarily a hedge in the dictionary definition of the word. However, in order to avoid repetition in this chapter, the reference to a 'hedge' will be to the definition of a hedge in s 66, which may be different from the dictionary definition.

Hedges (No 2) Bill into the ASB Bill by way of a Government amendment in the House of Lords: *Hansard*, HL Deb, vol 651, cols 1122–1123; vol 653, cols 247–253; vol 654, col 620–636. Those amendments were agreed to. The terms of the ASB Bill as amended went to the Commons and the Lords' amendments, with the inclusion of the High Hedge provisions in what is now Part 8 of the 2003 Act, were made subject to a 'guillotine' on 17 November 2003: *Hansard*, HC Deb, vol 413, cols 501–513. The amendments were agreed to without debate on 17 November 2003 and the ASB Bill received the Royal Assent on 20 November 2003: *Hansard*, HC Deb, vol 413, cols 551–561 and 1037.

4   Commencement Orders: Wales, SI 2004/238 (W 281) and England, SI 2005/710.

5   SI 1997/1160. These Regulations (made under s 97 of the Environment Act 1995) apply to hedges falling within the definition in reg 3, which requires the hedge to have a continuous length of, or exceeding, 20 m and that hedge must be growing in or be adjacent to common land, or land used for agriculture, forestry, or for the breeding or keeping of horses, ponies, or donkeys, or protected land (as defined in the Regulations). Hedgerows falling within these Regulations are subject to a regime protecting them from removal, which in some cases will include cutting back. Further information on these Regulations is available from the Department for Food and Rural Affairs ('Defra') website (www.defra.gov.uk).

6   See the definition of 'basic preservation works' in s 1(4) which will allow A to enter B's land under an Access Order made by the court under that Act if A can satisfy the court that the threshold set out in s 1(2) has been crossed. (The works are reasonably necessary for the preservation of all or part of A's land and the works could not be carried out or would be more difficult to carry out without entry onto B's land.) See in particular s 1(4)(c) which allows entry for the purpose of 'the treatment, cutting back, felling, removal or replacement of any hedge, tree, shrub or other growing thing which is so comprised and which is, or is in danger of becoming, damaged, diseased, dangerous, insecurely rooted or dead'.

WHAT IS COVERED IN THIS CHAPTER?

16.5

(1)   A summary of the provisions of the 2003 Act, Part 8.

(2)   Detailed examination of:
    (a)   What property does the 2003 Act protect?[7]
    (b)   Who can use the 2003 Act?[8]
    (c)   What has to be proved to found a complaint under the 2003 Act?[9]
    (d)   What has to be the subject of the complaint?[10]
    (e)   What is a 'high hedge'?[11]
    (f)   How can a complaint be made?
    (g)   How are complaints dealt with?
    (h)   Appeals.
    (i)   Costs of applications under the 2003 Act and other matters such as enforcement.
    (j)   Conclusion.

WHAT PROPERTY DOES THE 2003 ACT PROTECT?

16.6   The definition in s 65 under the heading of 'Complaints' to which Part 8 applies, refers to the fact that a complaint can only be made by an owner or occupier of 'a domestic property'.

16.7   By s 67(1) 'domestic property' is defined as either 'a dwelling' or 'a garden or yard which is used and enjoyed wholly or mainly in connection with a dwelling'. Section 67(2) defines 'dwelling' as 'any building or part of a building occupied, or intended to be occupied, as a separate dwelling'.

16.8   It is clear from this definition that, quite apart from the concept of a dwelling, protection is given to gardens or yards which are used and enjoyed wholly or mainly in connection with a dwelling.

16.9   A dwelling is not defined in the 2003 Act, but is conventionally defined as a place of residence. Therefore, this will exclude commercial uses such as offices, shops, hotels and other places where there is no element of residence. An old peoples' home or a residential care home can be said to be a dwelling within the definition in s 67(2).[12] At first sight the word 'separate' suggests that there is also a requirement of private user, so communal use of the building would be outside the definition. It is suggested, however, that what is really meant by the use of the word 'separate' before 'dwelling' is that the building referred to (or the relevant part) is used for residential purposes, even if it is divided into separate residential units. Thus a block of flats or a subdivided house is within the definition. This is consistent with the purpose of the 2003 Act. In cases of

---

[7]   Sections 65(1), (2) and 67 of the 2003 Act.
[8]   Section 65(1), (2) and (5).
[9]   Sections 65(1), (2) and 67(3).
[10]   Sections 65(1), (2) and 66.
[11]   Section 66.
[12]   *Words & Phrases Judicially Defined* (1990 edn) defines 'dwelling' by reference to various statutes and cases. The emphasis is on a place where a person lives, and the *Shorter Oxford English Dictionary* defines the word as 'a place of residence'.

mixed use, such as a flat on the first floor of a building where there is commercial use on the ground floor such as a shop, it is suggested that the protection of the Act will only apply to the first floor of the building.[13] Protection under the 2003 Act will also apply to the garden or yard used by that flat owner. A single room can also qualify if used as a 'dwelling'.[14] There may also be cases where there is mixed use of a yard, some parts of which may be used for commercial purposes and other parts may be used in connection with a flat or house. Such a case would be covered by the words 'used and enjoyed . . . mainly in connection with a dwelling'. What is important is that the 2003 Act only protects the reasonable enjoyment of what might generally be called 'property which falls within a residential user'. In that context, it can be stated with some degree of certainty that a barn garage or greenhouse used in connection with a dwelling will also fall within the definition. It is made plain by s 67(3) that in the context of reasonable enjoyment of domestic property, reasonable enjoyment of the part of that property falls within the 2003 Act.

16.10   As appears at **16.21(3)** there is no restriction on the type of property or its use on which the high hedge is situated and which is the subject of the complaint.

WHO CAN USE THE 2003 ACT?

16.11   Section 65(1) makes it clear that it is only the owner or occupier of a domestic property (whether occupied or not) who can complain under Part 8 of the 2003 Act. 'Owners' and 'occupiers' are respectively defined by s 82 of the 2003 Act: see **16.20**. Section 65(2) makes it clear that the owner of a domestic property which is for the time being unoccupied, can make a complaint under the 2003 Act.[15] As suggested at **16.1**, in the context of the definition in s 67(2) of the 2003 Act, the word 'dwelling' in this context signifies a place of residence and denotes a place where a person lives, regarding and treating it as home.[16] As is also suggested above, the distinction is clearly drawn between residential user and commercial user. So the ability to use the 2003 Act depends on the ability of that person to prove not only the relevant ownership or occupation, but also that the property owned or occupied satisfies the definition in s 65.

16.12   It does not matter whether the domestic property was built or converted before or after the high hedge was planted or grew to a height in excess of 2 m so as to fall within the 2003 Act. So the development of land behind an old 'high hedge' may require its owner to cut it back once the new house is adversely affected by it is occupation. The same principle will apply to the owner of the new house who plants some Leyland and Lawson's Cypresses which when mature and over 2 m high will affect the 'old' house whose garden has been sold off for development.

16.13   Where the complainant is in occupation he must show that the reasonable enjoyment of that property is being adversely affected by the height of the high hedge situated on the other person's land: s 65(1)(b).

---

[13]   See the extensive use of the words 'let as a dwelling' in Acts such as the Protection from Eviction Act 1977, which has been held to protect premises where there is a mixed residential and business user; the flat above the shop being a very common example.

[14]   See **16.11** and *Uratemp Ventures Ltd v Collins* [2001] UKHL 43, [2002] 1 AC 301.

[15]   For the definition of 'dwelling', see *Words & Phrases Judicially Defined* (1990 edn and Supplement). It is suggested that in the context of this legislation (the policy of which is to avoid disputes between neighbours in residential properties) the word dwelling should have the residential meaning given to it in *Uratemp*.

[16]   See *Uratemp Ventures Ltd v Collins* [2001] UKHL 43 at [30]–[31] per Lord Millett.

16.14 If the property is unoccupied, the complainant must satisfy the requirement in s 65(2)(b) that the reasonable enjoyment of that property by a *prospective occupier* of it would be adversely affected by the height of the high hedge situated on land owned or occupied by another person. This assumes the complainant is in occupation. See also s 65(3).

16.15 The complainant must show that reasonable enjoyment of a domestic property is affected and, as s 67(3) establishes, this will include the reasonable enjoyment of a part of his property.

16.16 Future owners and occupiers can be parties to complaints under the 2003 Act if they acquire an interest in the relevant property after the complaint has been made: see s 65(5)(b). No doubt pre-contract inquiries will (and must) refer to any complaints made whether by or against the vendor.

16.17 The concept of reasonable enjoyment is important and imports the objective standard applicable in the law of private nuisance. Therefore, reasonable enjoyment may be affected where the complainant suffers not just interference with light or a view, but there may also be an adverse effect on the reasonable enjoyment of his property when he is suffering from worry, or depression or even an inability to receive TV signals, all caused by the effect of the high hedge.[17] The reasonable enjoyment of property can also be adversely affected because of the risk of falling trees or falling structures caused by the relevant high hedge.

16.18 There is a degree of objectivity in applying the test of whether reasonable enjoyment is being or would be adversely affected. Purely subjective considerations (which may be regarded as being too sensitive in the modern world where parties have to live in relatively close proximity) may not be held to be within the 2003 Act. So the fact that a small part of a garden is in the shade after 5 pm on a summer's day as a result of the neighbour's high hedge may not amount to grounds for a complaint. As will be seen below local authorities have power to reject trivial complaints: s 68(2)(b), see **16.31**.

16.19 Therefore, the question whether the reasonable enjoyment of the complainant's property being adversely affected by the height of the high hedge will be judged by an objective set of standards bringing into account all the relevant circumstances. Such circumstances may not just be simply whether or not the enjoyment of sunlight or daylight has been affected.

WHAT HAS TO BE PROVED TO FOUND A COMPLAINT UNDER THE 2003 ACT?

16.20 There are three essential elements.[18]

(1) That you are the owner or occupier of a 'domestic property' within s 65. (See **16.11** for a discussion of what is a 'domestic property'.) The definition of 'owner' or

---

[17]   To this extent the 2003 Act is a radical departure from the common law, where there cannot be a right to a view, in the absence of an enforceable covenant protecting it. In *Hunter v Canary Wharf* [1997] AC 655, the House of Lords rejected a claim in nuisance for the effect of the Canary Wharf Tower building on the reception of TV signals by properties in the area. It is important to note that the cause of the interference

'occupier' in s 82 should be looked at in each case. The owner will include trustees holding the land as owners. 'Occupier' means 'a person entitled to possession of the land by virtue of an estate or interest in it'. This will include tenants and possibly beneficiaries entitled to possession under a trust of land. But bare licensees will not be able to make a complaint under the 2003 Act as they have no estate or interest in the land. Mortgagees not in possession are not within the definition of 'owner'.

(2)　　That the domestic property satisfies the requirements of s 67, as discussed above, noting that it may be occupied or unoccupied.

(3)　　That the reasonable enjoyment of that property is being (or would prospectively)[19] be adversely affected by the height of a high hedge on land owned or occupied by another person. Note that because a high hedge must be at least 2 m high (see **16.21**) it is the height of the hedge above that measurement which must be the cause of the adverse effect on enjoyment.

WHAT HAS TO BE THE SUBJECT OF THE COMPLAINT?

16.21　There are four elements here.

(1)　　The reasonable enjoyment of a domestic property must be adversely affected.

(2)　　That such reasonable enjoyment is being, or in the case of a prospective occupier falling within s 65(3) would prospectively be, *adversely* affected. Note that damage by the roots of a high hedge is not included in the 2003 Act; s 65(4).

(3)　　The adverse effect must be *caused* by the height of a 'high hedge' which is a barrier to light or access: ss 65(1)(b) and 66. Crucially, the high hedge must be a barrier to light or access. Because of the definition of a high hedge and the 2 m height requirement, it is only that part of the hedge above 2 m from the ground which will be relevant for the purpose of causation: s 66(1)(b).

---

with reasonable enjoyment must be the height of the high hedge. So interference to reasonable enjoyment of a domestic property caused by buildings, or other things, will not be within the 2003 Act. See **16.23** for causation in more detail.

[18]　For the general guidance to local authorities from the Department of Communities and Local Government ('DCLG') see 'High Hedges Complaints: Prevention and Cure', referred to in this chapter as 'DCLG'. This is a very useful guide. Other related publications from the DCLG on this area of law are referred to at the end of this chapter. The Guide and the other publications are all available to view or download from the DCLG website, and as the paragraph numbers may vary from time to time as the publications are updated the website should be consulted first: see www.communities.gov.uk. There has been criticism of the DCLG's guidance to Councils in the House of Lords: see *Hansard*, HL Deb, cols 250–251 (1 March 2006).

[19]　The reference to interference with reasonable enjoyment in the present tense ('is being adversely affected') suggest that cases where the anticipated effect of a high hedge on such enjoyment (e g where that hedge is not going to be kept cut back to a defined height above 2 m when fully grown) may fall within the 2003 Act. Hedges consisting of Leyland and Lawson's Cypress are an example of this because of their fast-growing nature. So a case for a complaint depends on proving the adverse effect at the time of the complaint. This is an unfortunate limit on the scope of the legislation as there are cases where it is plain that from the planting of the hedge it will grow to be a nuisance and will fall within the 2003 Act when it is over 2 m high. It looks as if the neighbour will have to wait until it falls within s 65. But see **16.4** and the reference to the Access to Neighbouring Land Act 1992 where a hedge or tree which 'is in danger of becoming . . . dangerous' may fall within the scope of an Order under that Act. That Act does not just apply to evergreen or semi-evergreen hedges as defined by the 2003 Act.

Therefore, the question to ask is 'does the height of this high hedge obstruct light or access of light and thereby interfere with reasonable enjoyment of the complainant's property'? As stated above, the high hedge may interfere with a view and thereby interfere with the access of light. If that view is interfered with to an extent that the access of light is interfered with, then there may be a remedy under the 2003 Act. Thinning out the hedge may, of course, not always work.

(4) The high hedge must be on land owned or occupied by another person.[20] It does not, therefore, matter where the hedge is on the other person's land, and that hedge does not have to be in a private garden.[21] It does not matter where that high hedge is on the other person's land, provided it has the adverse effect on enjoyment within s 65(1)(b). It does not, therefore, have to be adjoining the complainant's land. The high hedge may be separated from the complainant's land by the land of a third party, or by a road, whether public or private, or even a railway line, or river, etc.

WHAT IS A 'HIGH HEDGE'?

16.22 The high hedge must satisfy the test in s 66 of the 2003 Act and, therefore, must be within the following three principles:

(1) It must be wholly or predominantly a line of two or more 'evergreens': s 66(1)(a).[22] 'Evergreen' means an evergreen tree or shrub or a semi-evergreen tree or shrub: s 66(3).

(2) The high hedge must rise to a height of more than 2 m above 'ground level': s 66(1)(b). Therefore, the width of the hedge or the existence of overhanging branches will not be included in the definition of height.

(3) So much of the high hedge as rises to a height of more than 2 m above ground level must be a barrier to light, or the access of light: s 66(1). This is the core part of the definition. It is important to note that s 66(2) specifically provides that gaps

---

[20] In some cases there may be a dispute about whether the hedge is on the land of A or B, and this issue will have to be resolved before A (the complainant) can proceed under the 2003 Act. In this context recourse will be had to the rules which establish the location of boundaries, and the 'hedge and ditch rule' may well apply; see *Alan Wibberley v Insley* [1999] 1 WLR 894. The rule is that a man forms his boundary by cutting the ditch on the furthest extremity of this land and throws the spoil onto his land and grows the hedge on the bank made by the spoil. In such a case the further bank of the ditch will be the boundary and not the hedge. So in claims under the 2003 Act the first question should be 'whose hedge is it anyway?'. If there is a dispute about ownership it is always prudent to resolve that first, preferably by agreement, before taking the chain saw to the hedge. Recent 'hedge war' cases have even led to the death of one of the disputing parties, so a cautious approach is important. The 2003 Act requires that all reasonable attempts be made to settle the matter before a complaint can be made to the local authority: see **16.28**.

[21] Attempts were made during the ill-fated passage of the High Hedges (No 2) Bill in June 2003 to exclude the terms of the protection afforded by the legislation to cases where privacy was in issue and in cases, eg, where the high hedge was on public open spaces, school property, or within cemeteries or burial grounds, in 'rural areas', National Parks, or hedges planted after the legislation commenced. The terms of the 2003 Act do not contain any such restrictions. Nor does it matter when the dwelling was built, or the high hedge planted: see **16.12**.

[22] 'Wholly or predominantly' suggests that in a case that a word 'predominantly' is relied on, there must be in the line of the hedge a majority in terms of area, or in the appearance of the hedge in terms of evergreens as defined by s 66(3). Mathematical precision may not be required but in terms of surface area, or number of hedge plants or trees, anything over 75% of the total as evergreens or semi-evergreens ought to satisfy the requirement to be met by the use of the word 'predominantly'. Note that the word 'majority' is not used.

may significantly affect the overall effect of the hedge as a barrier to light at heights more than 2 m above ground level. Therefore gaps in the hedge (at any height) may affect the ability of the hedge to form a barrier to light or access and such gaps will be taken into account at heights of more than 2 m above ground level: s 66(2).

16.23 There are a number of points to note about these three requirements.

(1) Is so much of the high hedge as rises to a height of more than 2 m above ground level a barrier to light, or access of light? It is suggested that the word 'light' here will include not only direct light but also sunlight and daylight and, therefore, the general civil law of light which takes into account direct light only, is not applicable on its own. The words 'or access' after 'light' in s 66(1) refer, it is suggested, to the word 'light'. The alternative is there because it is possible for a high hedge to be a barrier to the access of light (as opposed to just light) and an example of this would be where the hedge creates by its shape a barrier to light. This is why gaps or other features in the shape of the hedge may be significant: see s 66(2).

(2) The evergreens must be in a 'line'. This need not be a straight line, but some formation 'in line' must be identifiable. Therefore, sporadic planting will not be a 'line'.

(3) What is an evergreen as defined by s 66 (3) will depend on evidence. The suggested interpretation of evergreen is that an evergreen will be one which sports live foliage throughout the year and, therefore, beeches and hornbeams which may sport dead leaves in the winter will not be an evergreen. A 'semi-evergreen' is also capable of definition by horticultural experts. Evidence from institutions such as the Royal Horticultural Society may have to be called in order to prove the assertion that any given hedge is within the 2003 Act.

(4) The evergreen must be a tree or shrub: so ivy covering deciduous trees or shrubs will not be a high hedge even if over 2 m high.

(5) What is 'ground level' may sometimes be in dispute. It is suggested that the measurement of ground level should be from the ground where the hedge is growing. This will usually be on the hedge owner's side. It is also suggested that the natural level of the ground should be taken at the base of the trunks or stems of the trees or shrubs in the hedge. However, where a hedge has been planted on a mound, or in a raised bed or in containers raised above the ground, then the measurement should be from the natural ground area rather than from the base of the hedge alone.[23] As already observed, overhanging branches and other matters which do not add anything to height will not be taken into account. In some cases the lie of the land may affect the ability of the high hedge to act as a barrier to light. For example, a high hedge on B's land which is downhill from A's land will not be so likely to be a barrier to light as opposed to one where the land is rising from A's land to B's land.

(6) It is important to note, as already stated, that gaps may significantly affect the overall height of the hedge at heights of more than 2 m above ground level and therefore, must be taken into account; s 66(2).

---

[23]   See DCLG paras 4.1.5–4.1.6.

(7)   As already observed, 'reasonable enjoyment' denotes an objective standard albeit with some subjectivity and it is suggested also that the Law of Nuisance may prove to be a guide here.

(8)   It does not matter whether the construction or conversion of the domestic property pre- or ante-dates the high hedge.

Causation

16.24

(1)   It is the height of the high hedge (above 2 m) which must be the *cause* of the adverse effect on reasonable enjoyment. If that is not the case the hedge is not a high hedge within s 66(1). It is, therefore, crucial to appreciate at the first opportunity that it is the height of the high hedge which causes this adverse effect and that there are not other forces at work. It may well be that an evergreen hedge just over 2 m high is casting severe shade onto B's garden. But the cause of B's complaint is the effect of the hedge as a whole and not just the 100 cm above the 2 m height measurement. By s 65(4) of the 2003 Act the effect of the roots of a high hedge are capable of being the subject of a complaint and therefore, root damage is governed by the common law and not the 2003 Act. Your own buildings, walls, fences and trees, as well as those of your neighbours, must be taken into account as must the buildings, walls, fences or trees of the adjoining owner.

(2)   The diagrams below give two examples of how different combinations of hedges, trees and buildings will determine whether or not the 2003 Act applies.

Figure 16.1

16.25 In Figure 16.1 one barrier to light or its access is the evergreen hedge. But there are other factors at work. The single evergreen tree is not a high hedge because the definition requires a line of *two or more* evergreens. In this diagram other buildings would clearly be relevant to whether the reasonable enjoyment of the complainant's property is being adversely affected by those buildings, or by the hedge, or by the tree. There may an adverse effect on enjoyment caused by buildings, walls, fences and other structures and this must be taken into account. It may be in these circumstances that the high hedge is not the cause of the adverse effect on the reasonable enjoyment of the complainant's land. No doubt there will be cases where there will be argument about the 'effective cause' of the adverse effect on reasonable enjoyment, just as such arguments arise in tort cases.[24] Is it the high hedge, or something else? Compare the diagram below where it is clear that the evergreen high hedge with the trees (which are also evergreens) will be within the 2003 Act.

Figure 16.2

16.26 Even in Figure 16.2 which shows a mixed hedge, but falling within s 66(1)(a) (a line formed of 'predominantly' evergreens – see **16.22**), deciduous trees within that hedge can be cut down as they are part of the barrier to light. Therefore, in a case formed predominantly by a line of two or more evergreens, deciduous trees will be subject to a cut-back just as much as the evergreen trees. There are no other features in this case which could be said to cast doubt on the question of causation. In this example it is the height of the high hedge above 2 m which is the cause of the adverse effect on the reasonable enjoyment of C's property.

HOW CAN A COMPLAINT BE MADE?

16.27 This question is governed by s 68 of the 2003 Act and there are two main stages.

Stage 1

16.28 The complainant must take all reasonable steps to resolve the matter with the adjoining owner: see s 68(2) of the 2003 Act.[25] When the complaint is referred to it the local authority may suggest that the complainant takes further steps to resolve the complaint.[26] All attempts to settle the complaint should be recorded in writing with meetings fully minuted. Communications should be in writing, with any telephone conversations logged and noted. Otherwise there will be no evidence that the complainant has tried to resolve the matter. Hostile conversations through or over the offending hedge will not be enough. Reasonable steps only are required and if the owner of the offending hedge is away, or cannot be traced, or refuses to engage in discussions, those facts must be reported when the complaint is made to the local authority with

---

[24] The 'but for' test is usually applied in cases where causation is in issue: see *Galoo v Bright Grahame Murray* [1994] 1 WLR 1360 and the discussion of the 'effective cause' in contract and tort text books, e g *Treitel on the Law of Contracts, Winfield & Jolowicz on Tort*. In cases under the 2003 Act the question should be asked: 'but for the presence of the high hedge (being specifically that part of it 2 m above ground level) would the reasonable enjoyment of the complainant's property be adversely affected?'.

[25] DCLG paras 5.01–5.5.

[26] See DCLG para 5.30 which sets out guidance in this respect.

evidence such as returned letters. If the complaint arose before 1 June 2005, it will be necessary to show that a fresh approach to resolve the complaint has been made after 1 June 2005.[27]

Stage 2

16.29 Having exhausted all reasonable attempts to reach an agreed settlement of the matter, the complainant can complain to the local authority under s 68 of the 2003 Act. The complainant must do this by means of a complaint form. There must be a separate complaint form used for each owner affected, even if it is one long hedge. The prescribed form is given at Appendix 3. There is a fee for lodging the complaint with the local authority. In England, fees are set by each local authority and there is no maximum, no regulations having been made in England under s 68(7)(a). In Wales, the National Assembly has set the maximum fee for each complaint at £320 under s 68(7)(b).[28] The fee may be refunded in full or in part by the local authority under s 68(8) at its discretion. There are no specific criteria. It may be appropriate to exercise this power in cases of severe financial hardship, or where the high hedge is on land owned by the local authority.

16.30 At the end of these two stages it is important to appreciate that the local authority does not act as mediator when a complaint has been made. Each local authority will have determined which department should deal with the complaint under internal directions given by it. The full council is ultimately responsible for the exercise of the functions under the 2003 Act set out in this chapter.[29] See **16.32** for what should happen if the local authority is the respondent to the complaint.

HOW ARE COMPLAINTS DEALT WITH?

16.31 There are three stages to the complaints procedure.

Stage 1

16.32 The local authority may decide not to proceed with the complaint because either stage 1 at **16.28** has not been complied with (ie the complainant has failed to take all reasonable steps to resolve the matter under s 68(2)) or because the complaint is frivolous, or vexatious: see s 68(2b). It may indicate to the complainant that he should take further reasonable steps to resolve the matter, before the local authority will consider the complaint: see **16.28**.

16.33 If it is the local authority which owns the hedge, then it is suggested that the local authority should put the complaint in the hand of an independent group of officers not responsible for the local authority's land management: see DCLG paras 5.114–5.117.

---

[27] DCLG para 5.28.
[28] See SI 2004/3241 (W 283). It has emerged that there is some degree of variation in the fees charged. In some areas the local authorities charge nothing, or they give concessions to pensioners, whereas in others the fee is as high as £650 per complaint, with no concessions. The average in early 2006 appeared to be £300–£400 per complaint. See *Hansard*, vol 679, cols 859–861 (HL Questions, 9 March 2006).
[29] The local authority cannot delegate the handling of complaints about high hedges under the 2003 Act to the executive of that authority: see the Local Authorities (Functions and Responsibilities) (England) Regulations 2002, SI 2000/2853 as amended by SI 2001/2212, Sch 1, para 47A as inserted by SI 2005/714. See the guidance to local authorities in DCLG paras 3.7–3.9.

Stage 2

16.34 The local authority must consider the complaint under s 68(3). There is no statutory time-limit, but DCLG para 5.118 suggests that it should do so within a 12-week period.

What must the local authority take into account at this stage?

16.35 It is suggested that there are two principal matters.

(1) Whether the high hedge complained of is adversely affecting the complainant's reasonable enjoyment of domestic property specified. Note that the definition of a high hedge in s 66(1) means that the inquiry is limited to that part of the high hedge more than 2 m above ground level which is a barrier to light or access. As discussed at **16.24** causation is a vital issue.

(2) If the answer to the first question is yes, what action should be taken?

16.36 As part of the decision making process the council will:

(1) Assess all relevant circumstances. For example, this means taking into account the British Standard Code of Practice for Daylighting, BS8206 Part 2, and, if necessary, the BRE Guidelines (March 2004). However, it is noteworthy that in this instance the complaint may not only be about the effect of the high hedge on the enjoyment of the dwelling, but also to the garden or yard. Therefore, the rules which may be applicable to the reception of light within dwellings should be applied extremely carefully (if at all) to the garden or yard, etc: see DCLG paras 5.75–5.79. Other features in the landscape will have to be considered: see **16.24**.

(2) The local authority must take an objective approach and should strike a fair balance between the complainant and the other parties to the dispute.

(3) The local authority must not just look at the complainant's concerns. Other factors may be at stake, for example, what is the effect of the high hedge on the landscape, or on general amenity, or the privacy to the adjoining owner derived from the hedge in any state? (For example, historic and significant (in landscape terms) yew trees in a churchyard should not be sacrificed.)

(4) Comparables may be difficult to apply and it is suggested that each complaint must be dealt with on its own facts.

(5) The local authority should gather all the appropriate evidence and should ask for and require an exchange of representations and submissions from all parties affected: DCLG para 5.34–5.66.

(6) A site visit is in all cases desirable, if not a necessity.

(7) The local authority must bear in mind existing legal restrictions applying to the hedge such as Tree Preservation Orders, planning conditions, conservation areas, the Hedgerow Regulations 1997 and the needs to protect flora and fauna which live in the hedge, or derive a benefit from it. There may also be restrictive covenants to take into account, as suggested at the outset of this chapter: see **16.4**.

Stage 3

What action will the local authority take?

16.37

This is governed by s 68 of the 2003 Act. The council may either:

(1) issue a remedial notice under s 69 of the 2003 Act and send that with reasons to the complainant and every owner and occupier of the neighbouring land: s 68(4). In the context of the definition of 'occupier', see s 82 of the 2003 Act which includes a person entitled to possession of the land by virtue of an estate or interest in it. This will, therefore, include tenants and co-owners, but probably not bare licensees. In addition, the remedial notice must state the terms of the decision and why the local authority has made that decision with reasons: ss 68(4) and 69. See the form at Appendix 3; or

(2) decide not to proceed with the complaint and will notify the complainant and adjoining owners and occupiers: see s 68(5). This decision can be made in a case where, for example, the complaint fails to meet the threshold definition of a 'high hedge' in s 66: s 68(5)(a); or

(3) decide that either the high hedge is not adversely affecting the reasonable enjoyment of the complainant's property, or that no remedial notice is to be issued and notify the complainant and adjoining owners and occupiers accordingly, with reasons: s 68(5)(b). (For example, where either the balance of the evidence leads to the conclusion that the objective test of whether reasonable enjoyment is being adversely affected by the high hedge is not met, or where the high hedge is so important in the landscape that it should not be the subject of a remedial notice.)

What is a remedial notice?

16.38 This is defined by s 69 and a form is at Appendix 3. Note that a remedial notice must contain the following particulars under s 69(2).

(1) The nature of the complaint: s 69(2)(a).

(2) The finding that the complaint is made out: s 69(2)(b).

(3) That action to comply with the notice is required and on what terms and the consequences of a failure to comply with the notice: s 69(2)(c) and (d) and s 69(9), which defines the forms of action which can be ordered. Note the distinction between initial action and preventative action; the former is short term and the latter is long term.

(4) A timetable for compliance: s 69(6).[30] Remedial notices should avoid the need to do work during periods when birds nest – between March and August in any year. It is also suggested that seasonal factors and practicalities should be taken into account. It is usually better to lop at times of the year when sap is not rising and the opinions of experts must be obtained to ascertain the best time for work to be done. The general rule is that the period for compliance with a remedial notice will not usually be extended unless there are some exceptional circumstances: see

---

[30] Section 69 and DCLG para 6.13.

DCLG para 7.11. Therefore, the time should take into account normal seasonal circumstances, bearing in mind such factors as are set out above.

16.39 As is pointed out at (3) above a remedial notice may also contain directions to prevent the recurrence of the problem initiating the complaint and this is made plain by s 69(9) which defines 'remedial action' within the scope of remedial notice as:

'. . . action to remedy the adverse effect of the height of the hedge on the complainant's reasonable enjoyment of domestic property in respect of which the complaint was made; and

"Preventative action" means action to prevent the recurrence of the adverse effect.'

16.40 In this context, it is important to note that a remedial notice cannot order a reduction of the high hedge below 2 m or the removal of the hedge: see s 69(3). The latter point is important and has caused some people to express criticism of the 2003 Act in this context. In some cases removal may be the only effective remedy, but that is not allowed under the 2003 Act.

16.41 A dead tree or hedge is not specifically referred to in the 2003 Act. This has led to uncertainty as to what is to happen in such cases. At present the law is uncertain as to whether a high hedge will include a dead high hedge. In certain cases a dead tree or hedge may be in such a position or condition that it poses a threat to the enjoyment of land to such an extent that a private nuisance claim could be brought to require its removal. There may also be cases where an Order under the Access to Neighbouring Land Act 1992 might be required: see **16.4**.

16.42 It is equally important to note a remedial notice does *not* have to require the hedge to be cut down to a 2 m height. The question is 'at what height does the hedge cease to affect adversely the enjoyment of the complainant's property?'. This question may be capable of being answered in such a way so as to lead to the conclusion that the hedge can be cut down to a height in excess of 2 m and in that state it will cease to have the adverse effect on reasonable enjoyment it had previously.

What effect does a remedial notice have?

16.43 Once it is issued, it is registered as a Local Land Charge under the Local Land Charges Act 1975: see s 69(8). The remedial notice will take effect on the date specified in it. This must be at least 28 days after issue: s 69(4) and (5).

16.44 A remedial notice can be relaxed, or withdrawn under s 70. But as indicated at **16.38**, a local authority will not relax the period for compliance unless there are exceptional circumstances: DCLG para 7.11. The withdrawal of a remedial notice does not prevent the local authority from issuing a further notice in respect of the same hedge: s 70(4).

16.45 It is, therefore, important to note that the terms of a remedial notice will depend on the facts of each case and therefore, there is a degree of flexibility as to what a remedial notice can dictate in terms of both remedial and preventative action: see DCLG para 6.28 and following paragraph.

How should a local authority approach the question of issuing a remedial notice?

16.46 It is suggested that a local authority should step back and look at the hedge from both sides. It should strike a balance between the complainant and others affected and should consider matters such as:

(1) opening up gaps in the hedge to allow the access of light;

(2) crown lifting or crown reduction;

(3) whether the side effects of any remedial notice would have an adverse effect on the hedge such as the death of the hedge. But the fact that it might die would appear not to be a good reason for refusing to issue a remedial notice in an appropriate case;[31]

(4) the cost of any remedial notice;

(5) as suggested above, the legal restrictions which may be on the hedge such as tree preservation orders or a hedge within the Hedgerow Regulations; see **16.4(4)**; and

(6) how far ongoing maintenance is a reasonable burden on the owner of the hedge and therefore, preventative action should take this into account.

APPEALS

16.47 These are governed by s 71 of the 2003 Act.

16.48 It is open to any party (ie either the complainant or the adjoining owner – or any of them if more than one) to appeal to the appeal authority against either the issue of a remedial notice, or the withdrawal or the relaxation of a remedial notice.

16.49 There is no appeal against the refusal of a local authority to proceed with a complaint under s 68(2). This covers cases where no reasonable attempts to settle have been made, or where the complaint is frivolous, or vexatious.

16.50 The persons who can appeal are either the complainant, or the adjoining owners or occupiers: s 71(2).

16.51 The appeal authority is the Secretary of State for the Department of the Environment, Food and Rural Affairs. In Wales the appeal authority is the National Assembly of Wales: s 71(7). In cases where the local authority has decided not to proceed with the complaint, the only remedy would appear to be that the complainant can go either to the local authority's Complaints Department, or to the Local

---

[31] Expert evidence as to the effect of cutting back will be important: see **16.38**. Some species of trees and shrubs are not likely to die as a result of being cut back. However, others can be badly affected by severe cutting back, and the timing of any work done under the notice may be crucial here. Ironically the chief 'villain' in the high hedge story is the Leyland and Lawson's Cypress which does not recover from cutting back into areas no longer sporting living growth. Compare Irish Yew and rhododendrons which generally make new growth from old wood.

Government Ombudsman or to seek judicial review of the local authority's decision not to proceed with the complaint under s 68(2): see s 71(3) and Civil Procedure Rules[32] ('CPR') Part 54 for judicial review.

16.52 An appeal must be brought within 28 days from the issue of the remedial notice or the notification of the decision, or at such later time as may be allowed: s 71(4).

16.53 The conduct of appeals is governed by s 72 and the Appeal Regulations applicable in England or Wales.[33]

16.54 The form to use is the appeal form provided by the planning inspectorate under reg 7.1 and the address can be found at DCLG para 8.27.

16.55 The grounds of the appeal must be as set out in regs 3, 4 and 5. This is a paper appeal only (DCLG para 8.45) and the Secretary of State's representative will notify in writing the outcome of the appeal under regs 9 and 10. The Secretary of State's representative can request further information under reg 11. There will invariably be a site limit, but no discussion of merits at that stage. A decision is set out with reasons under regs 12 and 13. Notification to the parties is governed by s 73(4).

16.56 The decision under appeal is binding on all parties under reg 14 and there is no further appeal. The remedy for a purpose dissatisfied with the outcome of appeal is likely to be that of judicial review under CPR Part 54.

16.57 Section 73(1) of the 2003 Act makes it clear that the appeal authority has full power to either allow or dismiss the appeal either in whole or in part. Section 73(2) gives the appeal authority power to:

(a)   quash the remedial notice or decision to which the appeal relates; or

(b)   to vary the remedial notice; or

(c)   to issue a remedial notice on behalf of the local authority where no remedial notice was issued.

16.58 Section 73(3) gives the appeal authority power to correct any error or misdescription in the remedial notice if satisfied that the correction will not cause injustice to the parties affected by the remedial notice. This caters for an error, for example, in the height of cutting down where numbers have been incorrectly copied in the remedial notice.

16.59 The compliance period in respect of a remedial notice affirmed or varied on appeal or a new notice runs from the date of the decision on the appeal; the latter is the operative date of the notice: s 73(5) and (7) and see also s 69(6).

16.60 Power to withdraw appeals is contained in s 73(6) and the compliance period in such a case will run from the date on which the appeal is withdrawn; the latter is the operative date of the notice: s 73(6) and (7) and see also s 69(6).

---

[32]   SI 1998/3132.
[33]   England, SI 2005/711; Wales, SI 2004/3240.

16.61 In cases under s 73(5) and (6) periods of time which have started to run under the 'old' notice are disregarded.

COSTS OF COMPLAINTS AND APPEALS

16.62 The general principle is that the costs of complaints will be borne by the local authority (subject to the fees charged offsetting those costs) and the costs of appeals will be borne by central government; in Wales the latter is the National Assembly. There are no fees for the lodging of an appeal.

16.63 A person seeking to use the relevant provisions of the 2003 Act should bear in mind the following potential costs at each stage:

(1)   The issue of a complaint form seeking a remedial notice requires payment of the appropriate fee. Reference is made at **16.29** to this. This is a refundable fee under s 68(8) on such terms as the local authority may determine.

(2)   Complainants should be aware that experts' fees will sometimes have to be incurred, particularly when setting out either the nature of the hedge (eg as to whether it falls within the 2003 Act) or the proper approach to be taken in cutting down the hedge to the necessary height.

(3)   There will also be the cost of appeals if legal expenses are incurred, for example, in drawing up the documents for the appeal. But there is no provision in this type of appeal for hostile costs orders. So each party bears its own costs whatever the outcome.

OTHER MATTERS: OFFENCES AND ENFORCEMENT

16.64

(1)   The local authority has power to enter neighbouring land to carry out its functions under the 2003 Act: s 74(1).

(2)   A person hearing the appeal has power of entry on neighbouring land: s 74(2).

(3)   In both cases 24 hours' notice is to be given. Identification is to be given. There is power in s 74 to attend with experts and take equipment (eg ladders) and take samples of the high hedge: s 74(4) and (5). Persons exercising the power of entry in cases of unoccupied land must secure it on leaving: s 74(6).

Offences

16.65

(1)   Obstructing the power of entry under s 74 attracts the maximum fine level 3 on the standard scale which is currently £1,000.

(2)   Failure to comply with a remedial notice under s 75(1) attracts the maximum fine
       level 3 on the standard scale which at present is £1,000. In this context the local
       authority will invariably seek informal action before enforcement: DCLG
       para 9.23.

Enforcement

16.66   In cases where the land is held under tenancies and leases, the local authority can
use the Public Health Act 1936, s 289 by virtue of the importation of that section under
s 76 of the 2003 Act. This means that the local authority can direct enforcement action
against the owner (the freeholder) even though it may be the occupier (the tenant) who
is primarily liable under the terms of the remedial notice. The local authority can
require compliance by the owner, even though under the terms of the lease, the tenant
will be liable to maintain the hedge. This means that the ultimate responsibility with a
remedial notice will be with the freehold owner: see DCLG para 9.6.

16.67   If owners or occupiers are untraceable the local authority may want to use its
powers to do the work itself under s 77 of the 2003 Act, although it is unable to charge
anyone if it cannot find them.

16.68   In the case of dissolved companies and estates without heirs it is understood that
the Treasury Solicitor will generally not undertake any management responsibility of
land which may vest in him as bona vacantia. However, that should not deflect attempts
to resolve the matter if the Treasury Solicitor is the owner of the land on which the high
hedge is situated. The Crown Estate (which will usually succeed to ownership of land on
a disclaimer of bona vacantia by the Treasury Solicitor) will assume responsibility for
high hedges on its land. By s 84(1) this part of the 2003 Act binds the Crown, so there is
no immunity for responsibility under the high hedges legislation considered in this
Chapter for land owned by HM The Queen in right of Her Crown, or in Her own right,
or in right of Her Duchy of Lancaster. Nor is there any exemption for land owned by
the Duchy of Cornwall, or land owned by government departments which is treated as
Crown land.

16.69   Before a prosecution for failure to comply with a remedial notice is undertaken,
the Crown Prosecution Service has to evaluate whether or not it is desirable to
undertake that prosecution under s 10 of the Prosecution of Offenders Act 1985: see
DCLG para 9.26. The factors applicable in making that decision under that Act are
beyond the scope of this book. Clearly minor infringements should not be prosecuted.

16.70   Where a person charged can prove that he did everything he could have done to
comply with a time-limit, there is a defence to the charge: see s 75(2) and 75(3) of the
2003 Act.

16.71   A failure to comply with a remedial notice within the time stated in it will include
the continuing failure to take preventative action: s 75(2)(b).

16.72   It is a defence if the party charged was not aware of the existence of the notice
because he was not sent a copy of the remedial notice, and does not have the 'deemed'
knowledge an owner would have under s 75(5) (as to which see below). See s 75(4) for
the extent of this defence. This defence can, therefore, apply to tenants and others in
occupation who are not owners, but who should have been served with a copy of the
remedial notice under s 68(4)(b). Clearly local authorities must be careful to ensure
service on all occupiers as well as owners and to keep a record of service.

16.73 There is, however, no defence of lack of knowledge available to the owner of the land on which the hedge is situated, if the remedial notice is registered as a Local Land Charge: s 75(5). Constructive notice (which is normally implied by s 198 of the Law of Property Act 1925) is expressly disregarded by s 75(6).

16.74 The court has power to take steps to secure direct compliance under s 75(7) and (8) where the breach is continuing and the accused can carry out the work. Failure to obey this order will attract a further fine on level 3 on the standard scale (currently £1,000) under s 75(9) of the 2003 Act. A further fine at one-twentieth of the level fine for each day of non-compliance may be imposed: s 75(10).

16.75 The local authority can take action directly and carry out the work to implement the remedial notice under s 77 of the 2003 Act. The local authority can recover the expense of doing this and charge it as a Local Land Charge: s 77(3).

16.76 The local authority has power of entry under s 77 and can also take materials on to the neighbouring land in order to carry out the work and the terms on which it can do this are set out in s 77(5)–(8).

16.77 Obstruction to the exercise of powers by a local authority under this section carries a maximum fine on level 3 of the standard scale which is currently £1,000.

16.78 The service of documents including service by electronic form under the 2003 Act is governed by ss 80 and 81 of the 2003 Act.

16.79 As mentioned in **16.37**, by s 84, this part of the 2003 Act binds the Crown, but the Crown is not criminally liable for any breach. The position of the Crown here is in contrast to the common law applicable to light where the Crown at present has immunity to claims to rights of light: see Chapter 11 and Chapter 15 as to the Human Rights Act implications of this immunity.

16.80 Section 83 of the 2003 Act gives the relevant English or Welsh bodies the power to amend ss 65 and 66 by regulation in order to extend the scope of complaints relating to high hedges and to amend the definition of a 'high hedge'.

CONCLUSION

16.81 In advising under the 2003 Act it is suggested that the following questions can be asked and serve as a useful checklist.

(1) Is it a 'high hedge'? (Note problems over what is an 'evergreen' and with ground levels.)

(2) Who owns it?

(3) Does the height of the high hedge above 2 m from ground level affect the reasonable enjoyment of a 'domestic property'? Is this the cause of the interference with reasonable enjoyment, or are there other causes, such as buildings, walls, deciduous trees, or hedges which are not high hedges?

(4)   Has a reasonable attempt been made to resolve the dispute and is there a proper record of this?

(5)   What practical issues will arise if the hedge is to be cut down to any height above 2 m?

(6)   Has the matter been considered from the point of view of the hedge owner?

(7)   Are there restrictions (planning, covenants, etc) which may make it difficult or impossible to use the 2003 Act?

(8)   Is there any other way in which the dispute can be resolved, for example, by some form of mediation, bearing in mind the need to preserve goodwill between neighbours?

16.82 Further questions will have to be asked in complex cases. Here are some examples.

(1)   A single hedge may have many neighbouring properties affected in different ways and therefore, there may be more than one complaint. Each complaint must be separate.

(2)   Alternatively, there may be many hedges with one complainant.

(3)   There may be many hedges, some of which are and some of which are not infringing.
       Consider the cumulative impact of such a situation.

(4)   What about the 'many-sided' hedge? In such cases there is one complainant but a number of respondents and all need to be participators and to be told what is happening and some of them may have to be served with remedial notices if appropriate.

16.83 In complex cases more than one remedial notice may be needed, for example, in the many-sided hedge case. And although cases cannot be formally linked, it is possible to address concerns by the local authority informing the complainant at a preliminary stage that there may need to be some form of informal linkage between the complaints and this is necessary at the stage when the local authority is considering whether it can accept the complaint: see DCLG paras 6.42–6.49.

16.84 The 2003 Act sets out a jurisdiction which is unique and which is not linked to the common law of light. It is suggested that this jurisdiction will avoid unnecessary litigation and the presence of a compulsory requirement that attempts be made to settle the problem is an important feature of the 2003 Act. The procedure is not cumbersome and should be implemented with the minimum of difficulty.

16.85 Further reading is contained on the DCLG website[34] and the following materials are worthy of consideration:
       Over the Garden Hedge.
       High Hedges Complaints: Prevention and Cure.
       High Hedges: Complaining to the Council.

---

[34]   www.communities.gov.uk.

High Hedges: Appealing against the Council's decision.
The Right Hedge for You.

Appendix 3 contains the relevant letters, forms, notes and decision letters and these are reproduced with Crown copyright consent.

Appendix 1

STATUTES

PRESCRIPTION ACT 1832 (2 & 3 WILL 4 C 71)

Sections 2–9

[. . .]

2 In claims of rights of way or other easement the periods to be twenty years and forty years

No claim which may be lawfully made at the common law, by custom, prescription, or grant, to any way or other easement, or to any watercourse, or the use of any water, to be enjoyed or derived upon, over, or from any land or water of our said lord the King . . . or being parcel of the duchy of Lancaster or of the duchy of Cornwall, or being the property of any ecclesiastical or lay person, or body corporate, when such way or other matter as herein last before mentioned shall have been actually enjoyed by any person claiming right thereto without interruption for the full period of twenty years, shall be defeated or destroyed by showing only that such way or other matter was first enjoyed at any time prior to such period of twenty years, but nevertheless such claim may be defeated in any other way by which the same is now liable to be defeated; and where such way or other matter as herein last before mentioned shall have been so enjoyed as aforesaid for the full period of forty years, the right thereto shall be deemed absolute and indefeasible, unless it shall appear that the same was enjoyed by some consent or agreement expressly given or made for that purpose by deed or writing.

NOTE

As amended by the Statute Law Revision (No 2) Act 1888; the Statute Law Revision Act 1890.

3 Right to the use of light enjoyed for twenty years indefeasible, unless shown to have been by consent

When the access and use of light to and for any dwelling house, workshop, or other building shall have been actually enjoyed therewith for the full period of twenty years without interruption, the right thereto shall be deemed absolute and indefeasible, any local usage or custom to the contrary notwithstanding, unless it shall appear that the same was enjoyed by some consent or agreement expressly made or given for that purpose by deed or writing.

NOTE

As amended by the Statute Law Revision (No 2) Act 1888.

4 Before mentioned periods to be deemed those next before suits for claiming to which such periods relate – What shall constitute an interruption

Each of the respective periods of years herein-before mentioned shall be deemed and taken to be the period next before some suit or action wherein the claim or matter to which such period may relate shall have been or shall be brought into question; and no act or other matter shall be deemed to be an interruption, within the meaning of this statute, unless the same shall have been or shall be submitted to or acquiesced in for one year after the period interrupted shall have had or shall have notice therefore, and of the person making or authorizing the same to be made.

NOTE

As amended by the Statute Law Revision (No 2) Act 1888.

5 In actions on the case the claimant may allege his right generally, as at present. In pleas to trespass and other pleadings, etc, the period mentioned in this Act may be alleged; and exceptions, etc, to be replied to specially

In all actions upon the case and other pleadings, wherein the party claiming may now by law allege his right generally, without averring the existence of such right from time immemorial, such general allegation shall still be deemed sufficient, and if the same shall be denied, all and every the matters in this Act mentioned and provided, which shall be applicable to the case, shall be admissible in evidence to sustain or rebut such allegation; and in all pleadings to actions of trespass, and in all other pleadings wherein before the passing of this Act it would have been necessary to allege the right to have existed from time immemorial, it shall be sufficient to allege the enjoyment thereof as of right by the occupiers of the tenement in respect whereof the same is claimed for and during such of the periods mentioned in this Act as may be applicable to the case, and without claiming in the name or right of the owner of the fee, as is now usually done; and if the other party shall intend to rely on any proviso, exception, incapacity, disability, contract, agreement, or other matter herein-before mentioned, or on any cause or matter of fact or of law not inconsistent with the simple fact of enjoyment, the same shall be specially alleged and set forth in answer to the allegation of the party claiming, and shall not be received in evidence on any general traverse or denial of such allegation.

NOTE

As amended by the Statute Law Revision (No 2) Act 1888.

6 Restricting the presumption to be allowed in support of claims herein provided for

In the several cases mentioned in and provided for by this Act, no presumption shall be allowed or made in favour or support of any claim, upon proof of the exercise or enjoyment of the right or matter claimed for any less period of time or number of years than for such period or number mentioned in this Act as may be applicable to the case and to the nature of the claim.

NOTE

As amended by the Statute Law Revision (No 2) Act 1888.

7 Proviso for infants, etc

Provided also, that the time during which any person otherwise capable of resisting any claim to any of the matters before mentioned shall have been or shall be infant, idiot, non compos mentis, feme covert, or tenant for life, or during which any action or suit shall have been pending, and which shall have been diligently prosecuted, until abated by the death of any party or parties thereto, shall be excluded in the computation of the periods herein-before mentioned, except only in cases where the right or claim is hereby declared to be absolute and indefeasible.

8 What time to be excluded in computing the term of forty years appointed by this Act

Provided always, that when any land or water upon, over or from which any such way or other convenient watercourse or use of water shall have been or shall be enjoyed or derived hath been or shall be held under or by virtue of any term of life, or any term of years exceeding three years from the granting thereof, the time of the enjoyment of any such way or other matter as herein last before mentioned, during the continuance of such term, shall be excluded in the computation of the said period of forty years, in case the claim shall within three years next after the end or sooner determination of such term be resisted by any period entitled to any reversion expectant on the determination thereof.

NOTE

As amended by the Statute Law Revision (No 2) Act 1888.

9 Extent of Act

This Act shall not extend to Scotland.

NOTE

As amended by the Statute Law Revision (No 2) Act 1888.

[. . .]

LAW OF PROPERTY ACT 1925 (1925 C 20)

Sections 1, 12, 52–54, 62, 187

PART I
GENERAL PRINCIPLES AS TO LEGAL ESTATES, EQUITABLE

Interests and Powers

1 Legal estates and equitable interests

(1)   The only estates in land which are capable of subsisting or of being conveyed or created at law are—

(a)   An estate in fee simple absolute in possession,
(b)   A term of years absolute.

(2)   The only interests or charges in or over land which are capable of subsisting or of being conveyed or created at law are—

(a)   An easement, right, or privilege in or over land for an interest equivalent to an estate in fee simple absolute in possession or a term of years absolute,

[. . .]

12 Limitation and Prescription Acts

Nothing in this Part of this Act affects the operation of any statute, or of the general law for the limitation of actions or proceedings relating to land or with reference to the acquisition of easements or rights over or in respect of land.

[. . .]

52 Conveyances to be by deed

(1)   All conveyances of land or of any interest therein are void for the purpose of conveying or creating a legal estate unless made by deed.

(2)   This section does not apply to—

- (a)   assents by a personal representative,
- (b)   disclaimers made in accordance with sections 178 to 180 or sections 315 to 319 of the Insolvency Act 1986, or not required to be evidenced in writing,
- (c)   surrenders by operation of law, including surrenders which may, by law, be effected without writing,
- (d)   leases or tenancies or other assurances not required by law to be made in writing,
- (e)   receipts other than those falling within section 115 below,
- (f)   vesting orders of the court or other competent authority,
- (g)   conveyances taking effect by operation of law.

NOTES

As amended by the Insolvency Act 1986, s 439(2), Sch 14; the Law of Property (Miscellaneous Provisions) Act 1989, s 1(8), Sch 1, para 2, except in relation to instruments delivered as deeds before 31 July 1990.

53 Instruments required to be in writing

(1)   Subject to the provisions hereinafter contained with respect to the creation of interests in land by parol—

- (a)   no interest in land can be created or disposed of except by writing signed by the person creating or conveying the same, or by his agent thereunto lawfully authorised in writing, or by will, or by operation of law,
- (b)   a declaration of trust respecting any land or any interest therein must be manifested and proved by some writing signed by some person who is able to declare such trust or by his will,
- (c)   a disposition of an equitable interest or trust subsisting at the time of the disposition, must be in writing signed by the person disposing of the same, or by his agent thereunto lawfully authorised in writing or by will.

(2)   This section does not affect the creation or operation of resulting, implied or constructive trusts.

54 Creation of interests in land by parol

(1)   All interests in land created by parol and not put in writing and signed by the persons so creating the same, or by their agents thereunto lawfully authorised in writing, have, notwithstanding any consideration having been given for the same, the force and effect of interests at will only.

(2)   Nothing in the foregoing provisions of this Part of this Act shall affect the creation by parol of leases taking effect in possession for a term not exceeding three years

(whether or not the lessee is given power to extend the term) at the best rent which can be reasonably obtained without taking a fine.

[. . .]

56 Persons taking who are not parties and as to indentures

(1) A person may take an immediate or other interest in land or other property, or the benefit of any condition, right of entry, covenant or agreement over or respecting land or other property, although he may not be named as a party to the conveyance or other instrument.

(2) A deed between parties, to effect its objects, has the effect of an indenture though not indented or expressed to be an indenture.

[. . .]

62 General words implied in conveyances

(1)   A conveyance of land shall be deemed to include and shall by virtue of this Act operate to convey, with the land, all buildings, erections, fixtures, commons, hedges, ditches, fences, ways, waters, watercourses, liberties, privileges, easements, rights, and advantages whatsoever, appertaining or reputed to appertain to the land, or any part thereof, or, at the time of conveyance, demised, occupied, or enjoyed with or reputed or known as part or parcel of or appurtenant to the land or any part thereof.

(2)   A conveyance of land, having houses or other buildings thereon, shall be deemed to include and shall by virtue of this Act operate to convey, with the land, houses, or other buildings, all outhouses, erections, fixtures, cellars, areas, courts, courtyards, cisterns, sewers, gutters, drains, ways, passages, lights, watercourses, liberties, privileges, easements, rights, and advantages whatsoever, appertaining or reputed to appertain to the land, houses, or other buildings conveyed, or any of them, or any part thereof, or, at the time of conveyance, demised, occupied, or enjoyed with, or reputed or known as part or parcel of or appurtenant to, the land, houses, other buildings conveyed, or any of them, or any part thereof.

[. . .]

(4)   This section applies only if and as far as a contrary intention is not expressed in the conveyance, and has effect subject to the terms of the conveyance and to the provisions therein contained.

(5)   This section shall not be construed as giving to any person a better title to any property, right, or thing in this section mentioned than the title which the conveyance gives to him to the land or manor expressed to be conveyed, or as conveying to him any property, right, or thing in this section mentioned, further or otherwise than as the same could have been conveyed to him by the conveying parties.

(6)   This section applies to conveyances made after the thirty-first day of December, eighteen hundred and eighty-one.

[. . .]

78 Benefit of covenants relating to land

(1) A covenant relating to any land of the covenantee shall be deemed to be made with the covenantee and his successors in title and the persons deriving title under him or them, and shall have effect as if such successors and other persons were expressed.

For the purposes of this subsection in connexion with covenants restrictive of the user of land 'successors in title' shall be deemed to include the owners and occupiers for the time being of the land of the covenantee intended to be benefited.

(2) This section applies to covenants made after the commencement of this Act, but the repeal of section fifty-eight of the Conveyancing Act 1881 does not affect the operation of covenants to which that section applied.

79 Burden of covenants relating to land

(1) A covenant relating to any land of a covenantor or capable of being bound by him, shall, unless a contrary intention is expressed, be deemed to be made by the covenantor on behalf of himself his successors in title and the persons deriving title under him or them, and, subject as aforesaid, shall have effect as if such successors and other persons were expressed.

This subsection extends to a covenant to do some act relating to the land, notwithstanding that the subject-matter may not be in existence when the covenant is made.

(2) For the purposes of this section in connexion with covenants restrictive of the user of land 'successors in title' shall be deemed to include the owners and occupiers for the time being of such land.

(3) This section applies only to covenants made after the commencement of this Act.

[. . .]

187 Legal easements

(1) Where an easement, right or privilege for a legal estate is created, it shall enure for the benefit of the land to which it is intended to be annexed.

(2) Nothing in this Act affects the right of a person to acquire, hold or exercise an easement, right or privilege over or in relation to land for a legal estate in common with any other person, or the power of creating or conveying such an easement right or privilege.

[. . .]

RIGHTS OF LIGHT ACT 1959 (1959 C 56)

1 (Repealed by the SL(R) Act 1974.)

2 Registration of notice in lieu of obstruction of access of light

(1) For the purpose of preventing the access and use of light from being taken to be enjoyed without interruption, any person who is an owner of land (in this and the next following section referred to as the 'servient land') over which light passes to a dwelling-house, workshop or other building (in this and the next following section

referred to as the 'the dominant building') may apply to the local authority in whose area the dominant building is situated for the registration of a notice under this section.

(2)   An application for the registration of a notice under this section shall be in the prescribed form and shall—

(a)   identify the servient land and the dominant building in the prescribed manner, and

(b)   state that the registration of a notice in pursuance of the application is intended to be equivalent to the obstruction of the access of light to the dominant building across the servient land which would be caused by the erection, in such position on the servient land as may be specified in the application, of an opaque structure of such dimensions (including, if the application so states, unlimited height) as may be so specified.

(3)   Any such application shall be accompanied by one or other of the following certificates issued by the Lands Tribunal, that is to say—

(a)   a certificate certifying that adequate notice of the proposed application has been given to all persons who, in the circumstances existing at the time when the certificate is issued, appear to the Lands Tribunal to be persons likely to be affected by the registration of a notice in pursuance of the application,

(b)   a certificate certifying that, in the opinion of the Lands Tribunal, the case is one of exceptional urgency, and that accordingly a notice should be registered forthwith as a temporary notice for such period as may be specified in the certificate.

(4)   Where application is duly made to a local authority for the registration of a notice under this section, it shall be the duty of that authority to register the notice in the appropriate local land charges register, and—

(a)   any notice so registered under this section shall be a local land charge, but

(b)   section 5(1) and (2) and section 10 of the Local Land Charges Act 1975 shall not apply in relation thereto.

(5)   Provision shall be made by rules under section three of the Lands Tribunal Act 1949 for regulating proceedings before the Lands Tribunal with respect to the issue of certificates for the purposes of this section, and, subject to the approval of the Treasury, the fees chargeable in respect of those proceedings; and, without prejudice to the generality of subsection (6) of that section, any such rules made for the purposes of this section shall include provision—

(a)   for requiring applicants for certificates under paragraph (a) of subsection (3) of this section to give such notices, whether by way of advertisement or otherwise, and to produce such documents and provide such information, as may be determined by or under the rules,

(b)   for determining the period to be specified in a certificate issued under paragraph (b) of subsection (3) of this section, and

(c)   in connection with any certificate issued under the said paragraph (b), for enabling a further certificate to be issued in accordance (subject to the necessary modifications) with paragraph (a) of subsection (3) of this section.

NOTE

As amended by the Local Land Charges Act 1975, s 17(2), Sch 1.

3 Effect of registered notice and proceedings relating thereto

(1)   Where, in pursuance of an application made in accordance with the last preceding section, a notice is registered thereunder, then, for the purpose of determining whether any person is entitled (by virtue of the Prescription Act 1832, or otherwise) to a right to the access of light to the dominant building across the servient land, the access of light to that building across that land shall be treated as obstructed to the same extent, and with the like consequences, as if an opaque structure, of the dimensions specified in the application,—

   (a)   had, on the date of registration of the notice, been erected in the position on the servient land specified in the application, and had been so erected by the person who made the application, and

   (b)   had remained in that position during the period for which the notice has effect and had been removed at the end of that period.

(2)   For the purposes of this section a notice registered under the last preceding section shall be taken to have effect until either—

   (a)   the registration is cancelled, or

   (b)   the period of one year beginning with the date of registration of the notice expires, or

   (c)   in the case of a notice registered in pursuance of an application accompanied by a certificate issued under paragraph (b) of subsection (3) of the last preceding section, the period specified in the certificate expires without such a further certificate as is mentioned in paragraph (c) of subsection (5) of that section having before the end of that period been lodged with the local authority,

and shall cease to have effect on the occurrence of any one of those events.

(3)   Subject to the following provisions of this section, any person who, if such a structure as is mentioned in subsection (1) of this section had been erected as therein mentioned, would have had a right of action in any court in respect of that structure, on the grounds that he was entitled to a right to the access of light to the dominant building across the servient land, and that the said right was infringed by that structure, shall have the like right of action in that court in respect of the registration of a notice under the last preceding section:

Provided that an action shall not be begun by virtue of this subsection after the notice in question has ceased to have effect.

(4)   Where, at any time during the period for which a notice registered under the last preceding section has effect, the circumstances are such that, if the access of light to the dominant building had been enjoyed continuously from a date one year earlier than the date on which the enjoyment thereof in fact began, a person would have had a right of action in any court by virtue of the last preceding subsection in respect of the registration of the notice, that person shall have the like right of action in that court by virtue of this subsection in respect of the registration of the notice.

(5)   The remedies available to the plaintiff in an action brought by virtue of subsection (3) or subsection (4) of this section (apart from any order as to costs) shall be such declaration as the court may consider appropriate in the circumstances, and an order directing the registration of the notice to be cancelled or varied, as the court may determine.

(6) For the purposes of section four of the Prescription Act 1832 (under which a period of enjoyment of any of the rights to which that Act applies is not to be treated as interrupted except by a matter submitted to or acquiesced in for one year after notice thereof)—

(a) as from the date of registration of a notice under the last preceding section, all persons interested in the dominant building or any part thereof shall be deemed to have notice of the registration thereof and of the person on whose application it was registered,

(b) until such time as an action is brought by virtue of subsection (3) or subsection (4) of this section in respect of the registration of a notice under the last preceding section, all persons interested in the dominant building or any part thereof shall be deemed to acquiesce in the obstruction which, in accordance with subsection (1) of this section, is to be treated as resulting from the registration of the notice,

(c) as from the date on which such action is brought, no person shall be treated as submitting to or acquiescing in that obstruction,

Provided that, if in any such action, the court decides against the claim of the plaintiff, the court may direct that the preceding provisions of this subsection shall apply in relation to the notice as if that action had not been brought.

4 Application to Crown land

(1) Subject to the next following subsection, this Act shall apply in relation to land in which there is a Crown or Duchy interest as it applies in relation to land in which there is no such interest.

(2) Section three of the Prescription Act 1832, as modified by the preceding provisions of this Act, shall not by virtue of this section be construed as applying to any land to which (by reason that there is a Crown or Duchy interest therein) that section would not apply apart from this Act.

(3) In this section 'Crown or Duchy interest' means an interest belonging to Her Majesty in right of the Crown or of the Duchy of Lancaster, or belonging to the Duchy of Cornwall, or belonging to a government department, or held in trust for Her Majesty for the purposes of a government department.

5 Power to make rules

(1) (Repealed).

(2) Any rules made under section 14 of the Local Land Charges Act 1975 for the purposes of section 2 of this Act shall (without prejudice to the inclusion therein of other provisions as to cancelling or varying the registration of notices or agreements) include provision for giving effect to any order of the court under subsection (5) of section three of this Act.

NOTE

As amended by the Local Land Charges Act 1975, ss 17(2), 19(1), Schs 1, 2.

6 (Repealed by the Northern Ireland Constitution Act 1973, s 41(1), Sch 6, Pt I.)

7 Interpretation

(1) In this Act, except in so far as the context otherwise requires, the following expressions have the meanings hereby assigned to them respectively, that is to say:—

'action' includes a counterclaim, and any reference to the plaintiff in an action shall be construed accordingly,

'local authority', in relation to land in a district or a London borough, means the council of the district or borough, and, in relation to land in the City of London, means the Common Council of the City,

'owner', in relation to any land, means a person who is the estate owner in respect of the fee simple thereof, or is entitled to a tenancy thereof (within the meaning of the Landlord and Tenant Act 1954) for a term of years certain of which, at the time in question, not less than seven years remain unexpired, or is a mortgagee in possession (within the meaning of the Law of Property Act 1925) where the interest mortgaged is either the fee simple of the land or such a tenancy thereof,

'prescribed' means prescribed by rules made by virtue of subsection (6) of section fifteen of the Land Charges Act 1925 as applied by section five of this Act.

(2) References in this Act to any enactment shall, except where the context otherwise requires, be construed as references to that enactment as amended by or under any other enactment.

NOTE

As amended by the Local Land Charges Act 1975, s 17(2), Sch 1.

8 Short title, commencement and extent

(1) This Act may be cited as the Rights of Light Act 1959.

(2) This Act, except sections one and six thereof, shall come into operation at the end of the period of three months beginning with the day on which it is passed.

(3) This Act shall not extend to Scotland.

(4) This Act shall not extend to Northern Ireland.

NOTE

As amended by the Northern Ireland Constitution Act 1973, s 41(1), Sch 6, Pt I.

[. . .]

LOCAL LAND CHARGES ACT 1975 (1975 C 76)

Sections 1, 3–5, 8–11

Definition of local land charges

1 Local land charges

(1) A charge or other matter affecting land is a local land charge if it falls within any of the following descriptions and is not one of the matters set out in section 2 below:—

[. . .]

Local land charges registers, registration and related matters

3 Registering authorities, local land charges registers, and indexes

(1)   Each of the following local authorities—

    (a)   the council of any district,
    (aa)   a Welsh county council,
    (ab)   a county borough council,
    (b)   the council of any London borough, and
    (c)   the Common Council of the City of London,

shall be a registered authority for the purposes of this Act.

(2)   There shall continue to be kept for the area of each registering authority—

    (a)   a local land charges register, and
    (b)   an index whereby all entries made in that register can readily be traced,

and as from the commencement of this Act the register and index kept for the area of a registering authority shall be kept by that authority.

(3)   Neither a local land charges register nor an index such as is mentioned in subsection (2)(b) above need be kept in documentary form.

(4)   For the purposes of this Act the area of the Common Council of the City of London includes the Inner Temple and the Middle Temple.

NOTE

As amended by the Local Government (Wales) Act 1994, s 66(6), Sch 16, para 49; the Local Government (Miscellaneous Provisions) Act 1982, s 34(a).

4 The appropriate local land charges register

In this Act, unless the context otherwise requires, 'the appropriate local land charges register', in relation to any land or to a local land charge, means the local land charges register for the area in which the land or, as the case may be, the land affected by the charge is situated or, if the land in question is situated in two or more areas for which local land charges registers are kept, each of the local land charges registers kept for those areas respectively.

NOTE

As amended by the Interpretation Act 1978, s 25(1), Sch 3.

5 Registration

(1)   Subject to subsection (6) below, where the originating authority as respects a local land charge are the registering authority, it shall be their duty to register it in the appropriate local land charges register.

(2)   Subject to subsection (6) below, where the originating authority as respects a local land charge are not the registering authority, it shall be the duty of the originating authority to apply to the registering authority for its registration in the appropriate local land charges register and upon any such application being made it shall be the duty of the registering authority to register the charge accordingly.

(3)   The registration in a local land charges register of a local land charge, or of any matter which when registered becomes a local land charge, shall be carried out by reference to the land affected or such part of it as is situated in the area for which the register is kept.

(4)   In this Act, 'the originating authority', as respects a local land charge, means the Minister of the Crown, government department, local authority or other person by whom the charge is brought into existence or by whom, on its coming into existence, the charge is enforceable; and for this purpose—

(a)   where a matter that is a local land charge consists of or is embodied in, or is otherwise given effect by, an order, scheme or other instrument made or confirmed by a Minister of the Crown or government department on the application of another authority the charge shall be treated as brought into existence by that other authority, and

(b)   a local land charge brought into existence by a Minister of the Crown or government department on an appeal from a decision or determination of another authority or in the exercise of powers ordinarily exercisable by another authority shall be treated as brought into existence by that other authority.

(5)   The registration of a local land charge may be cancelled pursuant to an order of the court.

(6)   Where a charge or other matter is registrable in a local land charges register and before the commencement of this Act was also registrable in a register kept under the Land Charges Act 1972, then, if before the commencement of this Act it was registered in a register kept under that Act, there shall be no duty to register it, or to apply for its registration, under this Act and section 10 below shall not apply in relation to it.

[. . .]

Searches

8 Personal searches

(1)   Any person may search in any local land charges register on paying the prescribed fee.

(1A)   If a local land charges register is kept otherwise than in documentary form, the entitlement of a person to search in it is satisfied if the registering authority makes the portion of it which he wishes to examine available for inspection in visible and legible form.

(2)   Without prejudice to subsections (1) and (1A) above, a registering authority may provide facilities for enabling persons entitled to search in the authority's local land charges register to see photographic or other images of copies of any portion of the register which they may wish to examine.

NOTE

As amended by the Local Government (Miscellaneous Provisions) Act 1982, s 34(b); the Local Government (Miscellaneous Provisions) Act 1982, s 34(c).

9 Official searches

(1)   Where any person requires an official search of the appropriate local land charges register to be made in respect of any land, he may make a requisition in that behalf to the registering authority.

(2)   A requisition under this section must be in writing, and for the purposes of serving any such requisition on the Common Council of the City of London section 231(1) of the Local Government Act 1972 shall apply in relation to that Council as it applies in relation to a local authority within the meaning of that Act.

(3)   In relation to England, the fee (if any) specified by a registering authority under section 13A below shall be payable, in such manner as the authority may specify, in respect of any requisition made under this section to that authority.

(3A)   In relation to Wales, the prescribed fee (if any) shall be payable in the prescribed manner in respect of any requisition made under this section.

(4)   Where a requisition is made to a registering authority under this section and the fee (if any) payable in respect of it is paid in accordance with subsection (3) or (3A) above, the registering authority shall thereupon make the search required and shall issue an official certificate setting out the result of the search.

NOTE

As prospectively amended by the Local Government and Housing Act 1989, ss 158, 194, Sch 12, Pt II; as amended by the Constitutional Reform Act 2005, s 15(1), Sch 4, Pt 1, paras 82, 84(1), (2), (3)(a), (b).

Compensation for non-registration or defective official search certificate

10 Compensation for non-registration or defective official search certificate

(1)   Failure to register a local land charge in the appropriate local land charges register shall not affect the enforceability of the charge but where a person has purchased any land affected by a local land charge, then—

(a)   in a case where a material personal search of the appropriate local land charges register was made in respect of the land in question before the relevant time, if at the time of the search the charge was in existence but not registered in that register, or

(aa)   in a case where the appropriate local land charges register is kept otherwise than in documentary form and a material personal search of that register was made in respect of the land in question before the relevant time, if the entitlement to search in that register conferred by section 8 above was not satisfied as mentioned in subsection (1A) of that section, or

(b)   in a case where a material official search of the appropriate local land charges register was made in respect of the land in question before the relevant time, if the charge was in existence at the time of the search but (whether registered or not) was not shown by the official search certificate as registered in that register,

the purchaser shall (subject to section 11(1) below) be entitled to compensation for any loss suffered by him in consequence.

(2)   At any time when rules made under this Act make provision for local land charges registers to be divided into parts then, for the purposes subsection (1) above—

(a)   a search (whether personal or official) of a part or parts only of any such register shall not constitute a search of that register in relation to any local land charge registrable in a part of the register not searched, and

(b)   a charge shall not be taken to be registered in the appropriate local land charges register unless registered in the appropriate part of the register.

(3)   For the purposes of this section—

(a)   a person purchases land where, for valuable consideration, he acquires any interest in land or the proceeds of sale of land, and this includes cases where he acquires as lessee or mortgagee and shall be treated as including cases where an interest is conveyed or assigned at his direction to another person,

(b)   the relevant time—

(i)   where the acquisition of the interest in question was preceded by a contract for its acquisition, other than a qualified liability contract, is the time when that contract was made,

(ii)   in any other case, is the time when the purchaser acquired the interest in question or, if he acquired it under a disposition which took effect only when registered in the register of title kept under the Land Registration Act 2002, the time when that disposition was made; and for the purposes of sub-paragraph (i) above, a qualified liability contract is a contract containing a term the effect of which is to make the liability of the purchaser dependent upon, or avoidable by reference to, the outcome of a search for local land charges affecting the land to be purchased.

(c)   a personal search is material if, but only if—

(i)   it is made after the commencement of this Act, and

(ii)   it is made by or on behalf of the purchaser or, before the relevant time, the purchaser or his agent has knowledge of the result of it,

(d)   an official search is material if, but only if—

(i)   it is made after the commencement of this Act, and

(ii)   it is requisitioned by or on behalf of the purchaser or, before the relevant time, the purchaser or his agent has knowledge of the contents of the official search certificate.

(4)   Any compensation for loss under this section shall be paid by the registering authority in whose area the land affected is situated; and where the purchaser has incurred expenditure for the purpose of obtaining compensation under this section, the amount of the compensation shall include the amount of the expenditure reasonably incurred by him for that purpose (so far as that expenditure would not otherwise fall to be treated as loss for which he is entitled to compensation under this section).

[. . .]

NOTE

As amended by the Local Government (Miscellaneous Provisions) Act 1982, s 34(d); the Land Registration Act 2002, s 133, Sch 11, para 13.

11 Mortgages, trusts for sale and settled land

(1)   Where there appear to be grounds for a claim under section 10 above in respect of an interest that is subject to a mortgage—

(a)   the claim may be made by any mortgagee of the interest as if he were the person entitled to that interest but without prejudice to the making of a claim by that person,

(b)   no compensation shall be payable under that section in respect of the interest of the mortgagee (as distinct from the interest which is subject to the mortgage),

(c)   any compensation payable under that section in respect of the interest that is subject to the mortgage shall be paid to the mortgagee or, if there is more than one mortgagee, to the first mortgagee and shall in either case be applied by him as if it were proceeds of sale.

(2)   Where an interest is subject to a trust of land any compensation payable in respect of it under section 10 above shall be dealt with as if it were proceeds of sale arising under the trust.

(3)   Where an interest is settled land for the purposes of the Settled Land Act 1925 any compensation payable in respect of it under section 10 above shall be treated as capital money arising under that Act.

NOTE

As amended by the Trusts of Land and Appointment of Trustees Act 1996, s 25(1), Sch 3, para 14.

[. . .]

SUPREME COURT ACT 1981 (1981 C 54)

Sections 37(1), (2), 50

PART II
JURISDICTION

37 Powers of High Court with respect to injunctions and receivers

(1) The High Court may by order (whether interlocutory or final) grant an injunction or appoint a receiver in all cases in which it appears to the court to be just and convenient to do so.

(2) Any such order may be made either unconditionally or on such terms and conditions as the court thinks just.

[. . .]

50 Power to award damages as well as, or in substitution for, injunction or specific performance

Where the Court of Appeal or the High Court has jurisdiction to entertain an application for an injunction or specific performance, it may award damages in addition to, or in substitution for, an injunction or specific performance.

[. . .]

TOWN AND COUNTRY PLANNING ACT 1990 (1990 C 8)

237 Power to override easements and other rights

(1) Subject to subsection (3), the erection, construction or carrying out or maintenance of any building or work on land which has been acquired or appropriated by a local authority for planning purposes (whether done by the local authority or by a person deriving title under them) is authorised by virtue of this section if it is done in accordance with planning permission, notwithstanding that it involves–

    (a)   interference with an interest or right to which this section applies, or

    (b)   a breach of a restriction as to the user of land arising by virtue of a contract.

(2) Subject to subsection (3), the interests and rights to which this section applies are any easement, liberty, privilege, right or advantage annexed to land and adversely affecting other land, including any natural right to support.

(3) Nothing in this section shall authorise interference with any right of way or right of laying down, erecting, continuing or maintaining apparatus on, under or over land which is–

    (a)   a right vested in or belonging to statutory undertakers for the purpose of the carrying on of their undertaking, or

    (b)   a right conferred by or in accordance with the electronic communications code on the operator of an electronic communications code network.

(4) In respect of any interference or breach in pursuance of subsection (1), compensation–

    (a)   shall be payable under section 63 or 68 of the Lands Clauses Consolidation Act 1845 or under section 7 or 10 of the Compulsory Purchase Act 1965, and

    (b)   shall be assessed in the same manner and subject to the same rules as in the case of other compensation under those sections in respect of injurious affection where–

        (i)   the compensation is to be estimated in connection with a purchase under those Acts, or

        (ii)   the injury arises from the execution of works on land acquired under those Acts.

(5) Where a person deriving title under the local authority by whom the land in question was acquired or appropriated–

    (a)   is liable to pay compensation by virtue of subsection (4), and

    (b)   fails to discharge that liability,

the liability shall be enforceable against the local authority.

(6) Nothing in subsection (5) shall be construed as affecting any agreement between the local authority and any other person for indemnifying the local authority against any liability under that subsection.

(7) Nothing in this section shall be construed as authorising any act or omission on the part of any person which is actionable at the suit of any person on any grounds other than such an interference or breach as is mentioned in subsection (1).

NOTES

As amended by the Communications Act 2003, s 406(1), Sch 17, para 103(1)(b), (2)(a), (b).

[. . .]

PARTY WALL ETC ACT 1996 (1996 C 40)

Section 9

[. . .]

9 Easements

Nothing in this Act shall—

(a) authorise any interference with an easement of light or other easements in or relating to a party wall, or

(b) prejudicially affect any right of any person to preserve or restore any right or other thing in or connected with a party wall in case of the party wall being pulled down or rebuilt.

[. . .]

LAND REGISTRATION ACT 2002 (2002 C 9)

Sections 11, 12, 27, 32, 34, 35, 36, Sch 1, paras 3, 6, Sch 3, paras 2, 3, Sch 12, paras 8, 9, 10

Effect of first registration

[. . .]

11 Freehold estates

(1) This section is concerned with the registration of a person under this Chapter as the proprietor of a freehold estate.

(2) Registration with absolute title has the effect described in subsections (3) to (5).

(3) The estate is vested in the proprietor together with all interests subsisting for the benefit of the estate.

(4) The estate is vested in the proprietor subject only to the following interests affecting the estate at the time of registration–

(a) interests which are the subject of an entry in the register in relation to the estate,

(b) unregistered interests which fall within any of the paragraphs of Schedule 1, and

(c) interests acquired under the Limitation Act 1980 (c 58) of which the proprietor has notice.

(5) If the proprietor is not entitled to the estate for his own benefit, or not entitled solely for his own benefit, then, as between himself and the persons beneficially entitled to the estate, the estate is vested in him subject to such of their interests as he has notice of.

(6) Registration with qualified title has the same effect as registration with absolute title, except that it does not affect the enforcement of any estate, right or interest which appears from the register to be excepted from the effect of registration.

(7) Registration with possessory title has the same effect as registration with absolute title, except that it does not affect the enforcement of any estate, right or interest adverse to, or in derogation of, the proprietor's title subsisting at the time of registration or then capable of arising.

12 Leasehold estates

(1) This section is concerned with the registration of a person under this Chapter as the proprietor of a leasehold estate.

(2) Registration with absolute title has the effect described in subsections (3) to (5).

(3) The estate is vested in the proprietor together with all interests subsisting for the benefit of the estate.

(4) The estate is vested subject only to the following interests affecting the estate at the time of registration–

   (a)   implied and express covenants, obligations and liabilities incident to the estate,
   (b)   interests which are the subject of an entry in the register in relation to the estate,
   (c)   unregistered interests which fall within any of the paragraphs of Schedule 1, and
   (d)   interests acquired under the Limitation Act 1980 (c 58) of which the proprietor has notice.

(5) If the proprietor is not entitled to the estate for his own benefit, or not entitled solely for his own benefit, then, as between himself and the persons beneficially entitled to the estate, the estate is vested in him subject to such of their interests as he has notice of.

(6) Registration with good leasehold title has the same effect as registration with absolute title, except that it does not affect the enforcement of any estate, right or interest affecting, or in derogation of, the title of the lessor to grant the lease.

(7) Registration with qualified title has the same effect as registration with absolute title except that it does not affect the enforcement of any estate, right or interest which appears from the register to be excepted from the effect of registration.

(8) Registration with possessory title has the same effect as registration with absolute title, except that it does not affect the enforcement of any estate, right or interest adverse to, or in derogation of, the proprietor's title subsisting at the time of registration or then capable of arising.

[. . .]

Registrable dispositions

27 Dispositions required to be registered

(1) If a disposition of a registered estate or registered charge is required to be completed by registration, it does not operate at law until the relevant registration requirements are met.

(2) In the case of a registered estate, the following are the dispositions which are required to be completed by registration–

(a)　a transfer,

(b)　where the registered estate is an estate in land, the grant of a term of years absolute–

(i)　for a term of more than seven years from the date of the grant,

(ii)　to take effect in possession after the end of the period of three months beginning with the date of the grant,

(iii)　under which the right to possession is discontinuous,

(iv)　in pursuance of Part 5 of the Housing Act 1985 (c 68) (the right to buy), or

(v)　in circumstances where section 171A of that Act applies (disposal by landlord which leads to a person no longer being a secure tenant),

(c)　where the registered estate is a franchise or manor, the grant of a lease,

(d)　the express grant or reservation of an interest of a kind falling within section 1(2)(a) of the Law of Property Act 1925 (c 20), other than one which is capable of being registered under the Commons Registration Act 1965 (c 64) [Part 1 of the Commons Act 2006],

(e)　the express grant or reservation of an interest of a kind falling within section 1(2)(b) or (e) of the Law of Property Act 1925, and

(f)　the grant of a legal charge.

(3) In the case of a registered charge, the following are the dispositions which are required to be completed by registration–

(a)　a transfer, and

(b)　the grant of a sub-charge.

(4) Schedule 2 to this Act (which deals with the relevant registration requirements) has effect.

(5) This section applies to dispositions by operation of law as it applies to other dispositions, but with the exception of the following–

(a)　a transfer on the death or bankruptcy of an individual proprietor,

(b)　a transfer on the dissolution of a corporate proprietor, and

(c)　the creation of a legal charge which is a local land charge.

(6) Rules may make provision about applications to the registrar for the purpose of meeting registration requirements under this section.

(7) In subsection (2)(d), the reference to express grant does not include grant as a result of the operation of section 62 of the Law of Property Act 1925 (c 20).

NOTES

As prospectively amended by the Commons Act 2006, s 52, Sch 5, para 8(1), (2).

[. . .]

PART 4
NOTICES AND RESTRICTIONS

Notices

32 Nature and effect

(1) A notice is an entry in the register in respect of the burden of an interest affecting a registered estate or charge.

(2) The entry of a notice is to be made in relation to the registered estate or charge affected by the interest concerned.

(3) The fact that an interest is the subject of a notice does not necessarily mean that the interest is valid, but does mean that the priority of the interest, if valid, is protected for the purposes of sections 29 and 30.

[. . .]

34 Entry on application

(1) A person who claims to be entitled to the benefit of an interest affecting a registered estate or charge may, if the interest is not excluded by section 33, apply to the registrar for the entry in the register of a notice in respect of the interest.

(2) Subject to rules, an application under this section may be for–

    (a)   an agreed notice, or
    (b)   a unilateral notice.

(3) The registrar may only approve an application for an agreed notice if–

    (a)   the applicant is the relevant registered proprietor, or a person entitled to be registered as such proprietor,
    (b)   the relevant registered proprietor, or a person entitled to be registered as such proprietor, consents to the entry of the notice, or
    (c)   the registrar is satisfied as to the validity of the applicant's claim.

(4) In subsection (3), references to the relevant registered proprietor are to the proprietor of the registered estate or charge affected by the interest to which the application relates.

35 Unilateral notices

(1) If the registrar enters a notice in the register in pursuance of an application under section 34(2)(b) ('a unilateral notice'), he must give notice of the entry to–

    (a)   the proprietor of the registered estate or charge to which it relates, and
    (b)   such other persons as rules may provide.

(2) A unilateral notice must–

    (a)   indicate that it is such a notice, and
    (b)   identify who is the beneficiary of the notice.

(3) The person shown in the register as the beneficiary of a unilateral notice, or such other person as rules may provide, may apply to the registrar for the removal of the notice from the register.

36 Cancellation of unilateral notices

(1) A person may apply to the registrar for the cancellation of a unilateral notice if he is–

(a)   the registered proprietor of the estate or charge to which the notice relates, or

(b)   a person entitled to be registered as the proprietor of that estate or charge.

(2) Where an application is made under subsection (1), the registrar must give the beneficiary of the notice notice of the application and of the effect of subsection (3).

(3) If the beneficiary of the notice does not exercise his right to object to the application before the end of such period as rules may provide, the registrar must cancel the notice.

(4) In this section–

'beneficiary', in relation to a unilateral notice, means the person shown in the register as the beneficiary of the notice, or such other person as rules may provide,

'unilateral notice' means a notice entered in the register in pursuance of an application under section 34(2)(b).

[. . .]

38 Registrable dispositions

Where a person is entered in the register as the proprietor of an interest under a disposition falling within section 27(2)(b) to (e), the registrar must also enter a notice in the register in respect of that interest.

Schedule 1
Unregistered interests which override first registration

[. . .]

Easements and profits a prendre

3

A legal easement or profit a prendre.

[. . .]

Local land charges

6

A local land charge.

Schedule 3
Unregistered interests which override registered dispositions

Interests of persons in actual occupation

[. . .]

2

An interest belonging at the time of the disposition to a person in actual occupation, so far as relating to land of which he is in actual occupation, except for–

- (a) an interest under a settlement under the Settled Land Act 1925 (c 18),
- (b) an interest of a person of whom inquiry was made before the disposition and who failed to disclose the right when he could reasonably have been expected to do so,
- (c) an interest–
  - (i) which belongs to a person whose occupation would not have been obvious on a reasonably careful inspection of the land at the time of the disposition, and
  - (ii) of which the person to whom the disposition is made does not have actual knowledge at that time;
- (d) a leasehold estate in land granted to take effect in possession after the end of the period of three months beginning with the date of the grant and which has not taken effect in possession at the time of the disposition.

Easements and profits a prendre

3

(1) A legal easement or profit a prendre, except for an easement, or a profit a prendre which is not registered under the Commons Registration Act 1965 (c 64) [Part 1 of the Commons Act 2006], which at the time of the disposition–

- (a) is not within the actual knowledge of the person to whom the disposition is made, and
- (b) would not have been obvious on a reasonably careful inspection of the land over which the easement or profit is exercisable.

(2) The exception in sub-paragraph (1) does not apply if the person entitled to the easement or profit proves that it has been exercised in the period of one year ending with the day of the disposition.

NOTES

As prospectively amended by the Commons Act 2006, s 52, Sch 5, para 8(1), (4).

Schedule 12
Transition

Former overriding interests

[. . .]

8

Schedule 3 has effect with the insertion after paragraph 2 of–

'2A

(1) An interest which, immediately before the coming into force of this Schedule, was an overriding interest under section 70(1)(g) of the Land Registration Act 1925 by virtue of a person's receipt of rents and profits, except

for an interest of a person of whom inquiry was made before the disposition and who failed to disclose the right when he could reasonably have been expected to do so.

(2) Sub-paragraph (1) does not apply to an interest if at any time since the coming into force of this Schedule it has been an interest which, had the Land Registration Act 1925 (c 21) continued in force, would not have been an overriding interest under section 70(1)(g) of that Act by virtue of a person's receipt of rents and profits.'

9

(1) This paragraph applies to an easement or profit a prendre which was an overriding interest in relation to a registered estate immediately before the coming into force of Schedule 3, but which would not fall within paragraph 3 of that Schedule if created after the coming into force of that Schedule.

(2) In relation to an interest to which this paragraph applies, Schedule 3 has effect as if the interest were not excluded from paragraph 3.

10

For the period of three years beginning with the day on which Schedule 3 comes into force, paragraph 3 of the Schedule has effect with the omission of the exception.

[. . .]

ANTI-SOCIAL BEHAVIOUR ACT 2003 (2003 C 38)

Sections 65–84

PART 8
HIGH HEDGES

Introductory

65 Complaints to which this Part applies

(1) This Part applies to a complaint which–

(a)   is made for the purposes of this Part by an owner or occupier of a domestic property, and

(b)   alleges that his reasonable enjoyment of that property is being adversely affected by the height of a high hedge situated on land owned or occupied by another person.

(2) This Part also applies to a complaint which–

(a)   is made for the purposes of this Part by an owner of a domestic property that is for the time being unoccupied, and

(b)   alleges that the reasonable enjoyment of that property by a prospective occupier of that property would be adversely affected by the height of a high hedge situated on land owned or occupied by another person,

as it applies to a complaint falling within subsection (1).

(3) In relation to a complaint falling within subsection (2), references in sections 68 and 69 to the effect of the height of a high hedge on the complainant's reasonable enjoyment of a domestic property shall be read as references to the effect that it would have on the reasonable enjoyment of that property by a prospective occupier of the property.

(4) This Part does not apply to complaints about the effect of the roots of a high hedge.

(5) In this Part, in relation to a complaint–

'complainant' means–

    (a)   a person by whom the complaint is made, or

    (b)   if every person who made the complaint ceases to be an owner or occupier of the domestic property specified in the complaint, any other person who is for the time being an owner or occupier of that property,

and references to the complainant include references to one or more of the complainants,

'the neighbouring land' means the land on which the high hedge is situated, and

'the relevant authority' means the local authority in whose area that land is situated.

66 High hedges

(1) In this Part 'high hedge' means so much of a barrier to light or access as–

    (a)   is formed wholly or predominantly by a line of two or more evergreens, and

    (b)   rises to a height of more than two metres above ground level.

(2) For the purposes of subsection (1) a line of evergreens is not to be regarded as forming a barrier to light or access if the existence of gaps significantly affects its overall effect as such a barrier at heights of more than two metres above ground level.

(3) In this section 'evergreen' means an evergreen tree or shrub or a semi-evergreen tree or shrub.

67 Domestic property

(1) In this Part 'domestic property' means–

    (a)   a dwelling, or

    (b)   a garden or yard which is used and enjoyed wholly or mainly in connection with a dwelling.

(2) In subsection (1) 'dwelling' means any building or part of a building occupied, or intended to be occupied, as a separate dwelling.

(3) A reference in this Part to a person's reasonable enjoyment of domestic property includes a reference to his reasonable enjoyment of a part of the property.

Complaints procedure

68 Procedure for dealing with complaints

(1) This section has effect where a complaint to which this Part applies–

    (a)   is made to the relevant authority, and

    (b)   is accompanied by such fee (if any) as the authority may determine.

(2) If the authority consider–

(a)   that the complainant has not taken all reasonable steps to resolve the matters complained of without proceeding by way of such a complaint to the authority, or

(b)   that the complaint is frivolous or vexatious,

the authority may decide that the complaint should not be proceeded with.

(3) If the authority do not so decide, they must decide–

(a)   whether the height of the high hedge specified in the complaint is adversely affecting the complainant's reasonable enjoyment of the domestic property so specified, and

(b)   if so, what action (if any) should be taken in relation to that hedge, in pursuance of a remedial notice under section 69, with a view to remedying the adverse effect or preventing its recurrence.

(4) If the authority decide under subsection (3) that action should be taken as mentioned in paragraph (b) of that subsection, they must as soon as is reasonably practicable–

(a)   issue a remedial notice under section 69 implementing their decision,

(b)   send a copy of that notice to the following persons, namely–

　　(i)   every complainant, and

　　(ii)   every owner and every occupier of the neighbouring land, and

(c)   notify each of those persons of the reasons for their decision.

(5) If the authority–

(a)   decide that the complaint should not be proceeded with, or

(b)   decide either or both of the issues specified in subsection (3) otherwise than in the complainant's favour, they must as soon as is reasonably practicable notify the appropriate person or persons of any such decision and of their reasons for it.

(6) For the purposes of subsection (5)–

(a)   every complainant is an appropriate person in relation to a decision falling within paragraph (a) or (b) of that subsection, and

(b)   every owner and every occupier of the neighbouring land is an appropriate person in relation to a decision falling within paragraph (b) of that subsection.

(7) A fee determined under subsection (1)(b) must not exceed the amount prescribed in regulations made–

(a)   in relation to complaints relating to hedges situated in England, by the Secretary of State, and

(b)   in relation to complaints relating to hedges situated in Wales, by the National Assembly for Wales.

(8) A fee received by a local authority by virtue of subsection (1)(b) may be refunded by them in such circumstances and to such extent as they may determine.

69 Remedial notices

(1) For the purposes of this Part a remedial notice is a notice–

(a)   issued by the relevant authority in respect of a complaint to which this Part applies, and

(b)   stating the matters mentioned in subsection (2).

(2) Those matters are–

(a)   that a complaint has been made to the authority under this Part about a high hedge specified in the notice which is situated on land so specified,

(b)   that the authority have decided that the height of that hedge is adversely affecting the complainant's reasonable enjoyment of the domestic property specified in the notice,

(c)   the initial action that must be taken in relation to that hedge before the end of the compliance period,

(d)   any preventative action that they consider must be taken in relation to that hedge at times following the end of that period while the hedge remains on the land, and

(e)   the consequences under sections 75 and 77 of a failure to comply with the notice.

(3) The action specified in a remedial notice is not to require or involve–

(a)   a reduction in the height of the hedge to less than two metres above ground level, or

(b)   the removal of the hedge.

(4) A remedial notice shall take effect on its operative date.

(5) 'The operative date' of a remedial notice is such date (falling at least 28 days after that on which the notice is issued) as is specified in the notice as the date on which it is to take effect.

(6) 'The compliance period' in the case of a remedial notice is such reasonable period as is specified in the notice for the purposes of subsection (2)(c) as the period within which the action so specified is to be taken; and that period shall begin with the operative date of the notice.

(7) Subsections (4) to (6) have effect in relation to a remedial notice subject to–

(a)   the exercise of any power of the relevant authority under section 70, and

(b)   the operation of sections 71 to 73 in relation to the notice.

(8) While a remedial notice has effect, the notice–

(a)   shall be a local land charge, and

(b)   shall be binding on every person who is for the time being an owner or occupier of the land specified in the notice as the land where the hedge in question is situated.

(9) In this Part–

'initial action' means remedial action or preventative action, or both,

'remedial action' means action to remedy the adverse effect of the height of the hedge on the complainant's reasonable enjoyment of the domestic property in respect of which the complaint was made, and

'preventative action' means action to prevent the recurrence of the adverse effect.

70 Withdrawal or relaxation of requirements of remedial notices

(1) The relevant authority may–

(a)   withdraw a remedial notice issued by them, or

(b)   waive or relax a requirement of a remedial notice so issued.

(2) The powers conferred by this section are exercisable both before and after a remedial notice has taken effect.

(3) Where the relevant authority exercise the powers conferred by this section, they must give notice of what they have done to–

(a) every complainant, and
(b) every owner and every occupier of the neighbouring land.

(4) The withdrawal of a remedial notice does not affect the power of the relevant authority to issue a further remedial notice in respect of the same hedge.

71 Appeals against remedial notices and other decisions of relevant authorities

(1) Where the relevant authority–

(a) issue a remedial notice,
(b) withdraw such a notice, or
(c) waive or relax the requirements of such a notice,

each of the persons falling within subsection (2) may appeal to the appeal authority against the issue or withdrawal of the notice or (as the case may be) the waiver or relaxation of its requirements.

(2) Those persons are–

(a) every person who is a complainant in relation to the complaint by reference to which the notice was given, and
(b) every person who is an owner or occupier of the neighbouring land.

(3) Where the relevant authority decide either or both of the issues specified in section 68(3) otherwise than in the complainant's favour, the complainant may appeal to the appeal authority against the decision.

(4) An appeal under this section must be made before–

(a) the end of the period of 28 days beginning with the relevant date, or
(b) such later time as the appeal authority may allow.

(5) In subsection (4) 'the relevant date'–

(a) in the case of an appeal against the issue of a remedial notice, means the date on which the notice was issued, and
(b) in the case of any other appeal under this section, means the date of the notification given by the relevant authority under section 68 or 70 of the decision in question.

(6) Where an appeal is duly made under subsection (1), the notice or (as the case may be) withdrawal, waiver or relaxation in question shall not have effect pending the final determination or withdrawal of the appeal.

(7) In this Part 'the appeal authority' means–

(a) in relation to appeals relating to hedges situated in England, the Secretary of State, and
(b) in relation to appeals relating to hedges situated in Wales, the National Assembly for Wales.

72 Appeals procedure

(1) The appeal authority may by regulations make provision with respect to–

- (a) the procedure which is to be followed in connection with appeals to that authority under section 71, and
- (b) other matters consequential on or connected with such appeals.

(2) Regulations under this section may, in particular, make provision–

- (a) specifying the grounds on which appeals may be made,
- (b) prescribing the manner in which appeals are to be made,
- (c) requiring persons making appeals to send copies of such documents as may be prescribed to such persons as may be prescribed,
- (d) requiring local authorities against whose decisions appeals are made to send to the appeal authority such documents as may be prescribed,
- (e) specifying, where a local authority are required by virtue of paragraph (d) to send the appeal authority a statement indicating the submissions which they propose to put forward on the appeal, the matters to be included in such a statement,
- (f) prescribing the period within which a requirement imposed by the regulations is to be complied with,
- (g) enabling such a period to be extended by the appeal authority,
- (h) for a decision on an appeal to be binding on persons falling within section 71(2) in addition to the person by whom the appeal was made,
- (i) for incidental or ancillary matters, including the awarding of costs.

(3) Where an appeal is made to the appeal authority under section 71 the appeal authority may appoint a person to hear and determine the appeal on its behalf.

(4) The appeal authority may require such a person to exercise on its behalf any functions which–

- (a) are conferred on the appeal authority in connection with such an appeal by section 71 or 73 or by regulations under this section, and
- (b) are specified in that person's appointment,

and references to the appeal authority in section 71 or 73 or in any regulations under this section shall be construed accordingly.

(5) The appeal authority may pay a person appointed under subsection (3) such remuneration as it may determine.

(6) Regulations under this section may provide for any provision of Schedule 20 to the Environment Act 1995 (c 25) (delegation of appellate functions) to apply in relation to a person appointed under subsection (3) with such modifications (if any) as may be prescribed.

(7) In this section, 'prescribed' means prescribed by regulations made by the appeal authority.

73 Determination or withdrawal of appeals

(1) On an appeal under section 71 the appeal authority may allow or dismiss the appeal, either in whole or in part.

(2) Where the appeal authority decides to allow such an appeal to any extent, it may do such of the following as it considers appropriate–

(a) quash a remedial notice or decision to which the appeal relates,
(b) vary the requirements of such a notice, or
(c) in a case where no remedial notice has been issued, issue on behalf of the relevant authority a remedial notice that could have been issued by the relevant authority on the complaint in question.

(3) On an appeal under section 71 relating to a remedial notice, the appeal authority may also correct any defect, error or misdescription in the notice if it is satisfied that the correction will not cause injustice to any person falling within section 71(2).

(4) Once the appeal authority has made its decision on an appeal under section 71, it must, as soon as is reasonably practicable–

(a) give a notification of the decision, and
(b) if the decision is to issue a remedial notice or to vary or correct the requirements of such a notice, send copies of the notice as issued, varied or corrected,

to every person falling within section 71(2) and to the relevant authority.

(5) Where, in consequence of the appeal authority's decision on an appeal, a remedial notice is upheld or varied or corrected, the operative date of the notice shall be–

(a) the date of the appeal authority's decision, or
(b) such later date as may be specified in its decision.

(6) Where the person making an appeal under section 71 against a remedial notice withdraws his appeal, the operative date of the notice shall be the date on which the appeal is withdrawn.

(7) In any case falling within subsection (5) or (6), the compliance period for the notice shall accordingly run from the date which is its operative date by virtue of that subsection (and any period which may have started to run from a date preceding that on which the appeal was made shall accordingly be disregarded).

Powers of entry

74 Powers of entry for the purposes of complaints and appeals

(1) Where, under this Part, a complaint has been made or a remedial notice has been issued, a person authorised by the relevant authority may enter the neighbouring land in order to obtain information required by the relevant authority for the purpose of determining–

(a) whether this Part applies to the complaint,
(b) whether to issue or withdraw a remedial notice,
(c) whether to waive or relax a requirement of a remedial notice,
(d) whether a requirement of a remedial notice has been complied with.

(2) Where an appeal has been made under section 71, a person authorised–

(a) by the appeal authority, or
(b) by a person appointed to determine appeals on its behalf,

may enter the neighbouring land in order to obtain information required by the appeal authority, or by the person so appointed, for the purpose of determining an appeal under this Part.

(3) A person shall not enter land in the exercise of a power conferred by this section unless at least 24 hours' notice of the intended entry has been given to every occupier of the land.

(4) A person authorised under this section to enter land–

    (a)   shall, if so required, produce evidence of his authority before entering, and

    (b)   shall produce such evidence if required to do so at any time while he remains on the land.

(5) A person who enters land in the exercise of a power conferred by this section may–

    (a)   take with him such other persons as may be necessary,

    (b)   take with him equipment and materials needed in order to obtain the information required,

    (c)   take samples of any trees or shrubs that appear to him to form part of a high hedge.

(6) If, in the exercise of a power conferred by this section, a person enters land which is unoccupied or from which all of the persons occupying the land are temporarily absent, he must on his departure leave it as effectively secured against unauthorised entry as he found it.

(7) A person who intentionally obstructs a person acting in the exercise of the powers under this section is guilty of an offence and shall be liable, on summary conviction, to a fine not exceeding level 3 on the standard scale.

Enforcement powers etc

75 Offences

(1) Where–

    (a)   a remedial notice requires the taking of any action, and

    (b)   that action is not taken in accordance with that notice within the compliance period or (as the case may be) by the subsequent time by which it is required to be taken,

every person who, at a relevant time, is an owner or occupier of the neighbouring land is guilty of an offence and shall be liable, on summary conviction, to a fine not exceeding level 3 on the standard scale.

(2) In subsection (1) 'relevant time'–

    (a)   in relation to action required to be taken before the end of the compliance period, means a time after the end of that period and before the action is taken, and

    (b)   in relation to any preventative action which is required to be taken after the end of that period, means a time after that at which the action is required to be taken but before it is taken.

(3) In proceedings against a person for an offence under subsection (1) it shall be a defence for him to show that he did everything he could be expected to do to secure compliance with the notice.

(4) In any such proceedings against a person, it shall also be a defence for him to show, in a case in which he–

(a)   is not a person to whom a copy of the remedial notice was sent in accordance with a provision of this Part, and

(b)   is not assumed under subsection (5) to have had knowledge of the notice at the time of the alleged offence,

that he was not aware of the existence of the notice at that time.

(5) A person shall be assumed to have had knowledge of a remedial notice at any time if at that time–

(a)   he was an owner of the neighbouring land, and

(b)   the notice was at that time registered as a local land charge.

(6) Section 198 of the Law of Property Act 1925 (c 20) (constructive notice) shall be disregarded for the purposes of this section.

(7) Where a person is convicted of an offence under subsection (1) and it appears to the court–

(a)   that a failure to comply with the remedial notice is continuing, and

(b)   that it is within that person's power to secure compliance with the notice,

the court may, in addition to or instead of imposing a punishment, order him to take the steps specified in the order for securing compliance with the notice.

(8) An order under subsection (7) must require those steps to be taken within such reasonable period as may be fixed by the order.

(9) Where a person fails without reasonable excuse to comply with an order under subsection (7) he is guilty of an offence and shall be liable, on summary conviction, to a fine not exceeding level 3 on the standard scale.

(10) Where a person continues after conviction of an offence under subsection (9) (or of an offence under this subsection) to fail, without reasonable excuse, to take steps which he has been ordered to take under subsection (7), he is guilty of a further offence and shall be liable, on summary conviction, to a fine not exceeding one-twentieth of that level for each day on which the failure has so continued.

76 Power to require occupier to permit action to be taken by owner

Section 289 of the Public Health Act 1936 (c 49) (power of court to require occupier to permit work to be done by owner) shall apply with any necessary modifications for the purpose of giving an owner of land to which a remedial notice relates the right, as against all other persons interested in the land, to comply with the notice.

77 Action by relevant authority

(1) This section applies where–

(a)   a remedial notice requires the taking of any action, and

(b)   that action is not taken in accordance with that notice within the compliance period or (as the case may be) after the end of that period when it is required to be taken by the notice.

(2) Where this section applies–

(a)   a person authorised by the relevant authority may enter the neighbouring land and take the required action, and

(b)   the relevant authority may recover any expenses reasonably incurred by that person in doing so from any person who is an owner or occupier of the land.

(3) Expenses recoverable under this section shall be a local land charge and binding on successive owners of the land and on successive occupiers of it.

(4) Where expenses are recoverable under this section from two or more persons, those persons shall be jointly and severally liable for the expenses.

(5) A person shall not enter land in the exercise of a power conferred by this section unless at least 7 days' notice of the intended entry has been given to every occupier of the land.

(6) A person authorised under this section to enter land–

(a)   shall, if so required, produce evidence of his authority before entering, and
(b)   shall produce such evidence if required to do so at any time while he remains on the land.

(7) A person who enters land in the exercise of a power conferred by this section may–

(a)   use a vehicle to enter the land,
(b)   take with him such other persons as may be necessary,
(c)   take with him equipment and materials needed for the purpose of taking the required action.

(8) If, in the exercise of a power conferred by this section, a person enters land which is unoccupied or from which all of the persons occupying the land are temporarily absent, he must on his departure leave it as effectively secured against unauthorised entry as he found it.

(9) A person who wilfully obstructs a person acting in the exercise of powers under this section to enter land and take action on that land is guilty of an offence and shall be liable, on summary conviction, to a fine not exceeding level 3 on the standard scale.

78 Offences committed by bodies corporate

(1) Where an offence under this Part committed by a body corporate is proved to have been committed with the consent or connivance of, or to be attributable to any neglect on the part of–

(a)   a director, manager, secretary or other similar officer of the body corporate, or
(b)   any person who was purporting to act in any such capacity,

he, as well as the body corporate, shall be guilty of that offence and be liable to be proceeded against and punished accordingly.

(2) Where the affairs of a body corporate are managed by its members, subsection (1) applies in relation to the acts and defaults of a member in connection with his functions of management as if he were a director of the body corporate.

Supplementary

79 Service of documents

(1) A notification or other document required to be given or sent to a person by virtue of this Part shall be taken to be duly given or sent to him if served in accordance with the following provisions of this section.

(2) Such a document may be served–

    (a)   by delivering it to the person in question,

    (b)   by leaving it at his proper address, or

    (c)   by sending it by post to him at that address.

(3) Such a document may–

    (a)   in the case of a body corporate, be served on the secretary or clerk of that body,

    (b)   in the case of a partnership, be served on a partner or a person having the control or management of the partnership business.

(4) For the purposes of this section and of section 7 of the Interpretation Act 1978 (c 30) (service of documents by post) in its application to this section, a person's proper address shall be his last known address, except that–

    (a)   in the case of a body corporate or their secretary or clerk, it shall be the address of the registered or principal office of that body, and

    (b)   in the case of a partnership or person having the control or the management of the partnership business, it shall be the principal office of the partnership.

(5) For the purposes of subsection (4) the principal office of–

    (a)   a company registered outside the United Kingdom, or

    (b)   a partnership carrying on business outside the United Kingdom,

shall be their principal office within the United Kingdom.

(6) If a person has specified an address in the United Kingdom other than his proper address within the meaning of subsection (4) as the one at which he or someone on his behalf will accept documents of a particular description, that address shall also be treated for the purposes of this section and section 7 of the Interpretation Act 1978 as his proper address in connection with the service on him of a document of that description.

(7) Where–

    (a)   by virtue of this Part a document is required to be given or sent to a person who is an owner or occupier of any land, and

    (b)   the name or address of that person cannot be ascertained after reasonable inquiry,

the document may be served either by leaving it in the hands of a person who is or appears to be resident or employed on the land or by leaving it conspicuously affixed to some building or object on the land.

80 Documents in electronic form

(1) A requirement of this Part–

    (a)   to send a copy of a remedial notice to a person, or

    (b)   to notify a person under section 68(4) of the reasons for the issue of a remedial notice,

is not capable of being satisfied by transmitting the copy or notification electronically or by making it available on a web-site.

(2) The delivery of any other document to a person (the 'recipient') may be effected for the purposes of section 79(2)(a)–

(a)   by transmitting it electronically, or

(b)   by making it available on a web-site,

but only if it is transmitted or made available in accordance with subsection (3) or (5).

(3) A document is transmitted electronically in accordance with this subsection if–

(a)   the recipient has agreed that documents may be delivered to him by being transmitted to an electronic address and in an electronic form specified by him for that purpose, and

(b)   the document is a document to which that agreement applies and is transmitted to that address in that form.

(4) A document which is transmitted in accordance with subsection (3) by means of an electronic communications network shall, unless the contrary is proved, be treated as having been delivered at 9 a.m. on the working day immediately following the day on which it is transmitted.

(5) A document is made available on a web-site in accordance with this subsection if–

(a)   the recipient has agreed that documents may be delivered to him by being made available on a web-site,

(b)   the document is a document to which that agreement applies and is made available on a web-site,

(c)   the recipient is notified, in a manner agreed by him, of–

(i)   the presence of the document on the web-site,

(ii)   the address of the web-site, and

(iii)   the place on the web-site where the document may be accessed.

(6) A document made available on a web-site in accordance with subsection (5) shall, unless the contrary is proved, be treated as having been delivered at 9a.m. on the working day immediately following the day on which the recipient is notified in accordance with subsection (5)(c).

(7) In this section–

'electronic address' includes any number or address used for the purposes of receiving electronic communications,

'electronic communication' means an electronic communication within the meaning of the Electronic Communications Act 2000 (c 7) the processing of which on receipt is intended to produce writing,

'electronic communications network' means an electronic communications network within the meaning of the Communications Act 2003 (c 21),

'electronically' means in the form of an electronic communication,

'working day' means a day which is not a Saturday or a Sunday, Christmas Day, Good Friday or a bank holiday in England and Wales under the Banking and Financial Dealings Act 1971 (c 80).

81 Power to make further provision about documents in electronic form

(1) Regulations may amend section 80 by modifying the circumstances in which, and the conditions subject to which, the delivery of a document for the purposes of section 79(2)(a) may be effected by–

(a)   transmitting the document electronically, or

(b)   making the document available on a web-site.

(2) Regulations may also amend section 80 by modifying the day on which and the time at which documents which are transmitted electronically or made available on a web-site in accordance with that section are to be treated as having been delivered.

(3) Regulations under this section may make such consequential amendments of this Part as the person making the regulations considers appropriate.

(4) The power to make such regulations shall be exercisable–

(a) in relation to documents relating to complaints about hedges situated in England, by the Secretary of State, and

(b) in relation to documents relating to complaints about hedges situated in Wales, by the National Assembly for Wales.

(5) In this section 'electronically' has the meaning given in section 80.

82 Interpretation

In this Part–

'the appeal authority' has the meaning given by section 71(7),
'complaint' shall be construed in accordance with section 65,
'complainant' has the meaning given by section 65(5),
'the compliance period' has the meaning given by section 69(6),
'domestic property' has the meaning given by section 67,
'high hedge' has the meaning given by section 66,
'local authority', in relation to England, means–

(a) a district council,

(b) a county council for a county in which there are no districts,

(c) a London borough council, or

(d) the Common Council of the City of London,

and, in relation to Wales, means a county council or a county borough council,
'the neighbouring land' has the meaning given by section 65(5),
'occupier', in relation to any land, means a person entitled to possession of the land by virtue of an estate or interest in it,
'the operative date' shall be construed in accordance with sections 69(5) and 73(5) and (6),
'owner', in relation to any land, means a person (other than a mortgagee not in possession) who, whether in his own right or as trustee for any person–

(a) is entitled to receive the rack rent of the land, or

(b) where the land is not let at a rack rent, would be so entitled if it were so let,

'preventative action' has the meaning given by section 69(9),
'the relevant authority' has the meaning given by section 65(5),
'remedial notice' shall be construed in accordance with section 69(1),
'remedial action' has the meaning given by section 69(9).

83 Power to amend sections 65 and 66

(1) Regulations may do one or both of the following–

(a) amend section 65 for the purpose of extending the scope of complaints relating to high hedges to which this Part applies, and

(b) amend section 66 (definition of 'high hedge').

(2) The power to make such regulations shall be exercisable–

    (a)   in relation to complaints about hedges situated in England, by the Secretary of State, and

    (b)   in relation to complaints about hedges situated in Wales, by the National Assembly for Wales.

(3) Regulations under this section may make such consequential amendments of this Part as the person making the regulations considers appropriate.

84 Crown application

(1) This Part and any provision made under it bind the Crown.

(2) This section does not impose criminal liability on the Crown.

(3) Subsection (2) does not affect the criminal liability of persons in the service of the Crown.

Appendix 2

STATUTORY INSTRUMENTS

LOCAL LAND CHARGES RULES 1977
SI 1977/985

Rules 1–16, Sch 1

(as amended by the Local Land Charges (Amendment) Rules 1995, SI 1995/260)

[These rules are reproduced here only insofar as they affect applications under the Rights of Light Act 1959, s 2.]

1 Title and commencement

These Rules may be cited as the Local Land Charges Rules 1977 and shall come into operation on 1st August 1977.

2 Interpretation

(1)   The Interpretation Act 1889 shall apply to the interpretation of these Rules as it applies to the interpretation of an Act of Parliament.

(2)   In these Rules, unless the context otherwise requires—

'the Act' means the Local Land Charges Act 1975,
'charge' means a local land charge or a matter which is registrable in a local land charges register,
'description' in relation to a charge means a description which is sufficient to indicate—

    (a)   the nature of any agreement, certificate, notice, order, resolution, scheme or other instrument or document (not being a statute or an instrument embodying statutory provisions) which comprises the charge or in connection with which the charge came into existence,

    (b)   where apparent from the instrument or document, the date on which the charge came into existence,

    (c)   any statutory provision (other than section 1(1)(e) of the Act or a provision specified in the part of Schedule 2 appropriate for the charge) under or by virtue of which the charge is a local land charge or registrable, or which comprises the charge,

[. . .]

'register' means local land charges register,

[. . .]

(3)   In these Rules, unless the context otherwise requires, a rule or schedule referred to by number means the rule or schedule so numbered in these Rules and a form designated by letter means the form so designated in Schedule 1.

(4)   In these Rules, unless the context otherwise requires, a reference to an enactment is a reference to that enactment as amended, extended or applied by or under any other enactment.

3 Parts of the Register

The register shall continue to be divided into parts, for the registration of different types of charge, as follows—

[. . .]

Part 11, for charges falling within section 2(4) of the Rights of Light Act 1959 ('light obstruction notices'),

[. . .]

4 Application for registration

(1)   Without prejudice to rule 10(1) below, an application to a registering authority for registration of a charge shall be in writing and shall contain a description of the charge and any other particulars necessary to enable the registering authority to register the charge in accordance with these Rules.

(2)   An application for registration may be sent by post to, or left at the office of, the registering authority.

5 Delivery of applications

(1)   For the purposes of section 10(5) of the Act, it shall be regarded as practicable for a registering authority to register a charge on the day on which the application for registration is delivered or treated in accordance with paragraph (2) below as having been delivered.

(2)   An application for registration delivered between the time when the office of the registering authority closes and the time when it next opens shall be treated as having been delivered immediately after that interval.

6 Registration

(1)   Every charge shall be registered by reference to the land in the area of the registering authority affected by the charge, in such a manner as to show the situation and extent of that land.

(2)   Subject to rule 7, the registration of a charge shall be effected by entering in the part of the register appropriate for that charge the particulars specified in Schedule 2 in relation to that part.

7 Use of existing registers

Where the particulars of a planning charge or other charge which are required by these Rules to be entered in the register have been entered in another record maintained and kept open for public inspection in pursuance of a statutory obligation, it shall be a sufficient compliance with that requirement to enter in the register a reference whereby the particulars in that other record can readily be traced.

8 Amendment and cancellation of registrations

(1)   Without prejudice to any other provisions of these Rules . . .

(a)   where a registered charge has been varied or modified or any registration is incorrect, the registering authority shall amend the registration accordingly,

(b)   where a registered charge has been disclosed, ceased to have effect or ceased to be a charge, the registering authority shall cancel the registration.

[. . .]

10 Light obstruction notices

(1)   An application under section 2(2) of the Rights of Light Act 1959 for registration of a light obstruction notice shall be in Form A and shall be accompanied by the certificate of the Lands Tribunal relating to the notice.

(2)   On receiving the application and the certificate the registering authority shall file them and register the notice in accordance with rule 6.

(3)   Where, after a temporary certificate has been filed and before the period for which it operates has expired a definitive certificate is lodged with the registering authority, they shall file the definitive certificate with the application and amend the registration accordingly.

(4)   On receiving an office copy of a judgment or order directing the registration of a light obstruction notice to be varied or cancelled, the registering authority shall file the office copy with the application for that registration and shall amend or cancel the registration accordingly.

(5)   The person on whose application the notice was registered, or any owner of the servient land or part of it who is a successor in title to that person, may within a year from the date of registration apply in Form B for—

(a)   amendment of the registered particulars of the position or dimensions of the structure to which registration is intended to be equivalent, so as to reduce its height or length or to increase its distance from the dominant building, or

(b)   cancellation of the registration,

and on receiving any such application the registering authority shall file it and amend or cancel the registration accordingly.

(6)   Without prejudice to the preceding paragraphs of this rule, the registering authority shall cancel the registration of a notice—

(a)   where in relation to the notice a temporary certificate has been filed and no definitive certificate has been filed, on the expiration of the period of operation specified in the temporary certificate,

(b)   in any other case, on the expiration of 21 years from the date of registration,

and thereupon any document relating to the notice and filed pursuant to these Rules shall be taken off the file.

(7)   In this rule 'definitive certificate' means a certificate issued by the Lands Tribunal under section 2(3)(a) of the Rights of Light Act 1959 and 'temporary certificate' means a certificate so issued under section 2(3)(b) of that Act; 'dominant building' and 'servient land' have the meanings assigned to them by section 2(1) of that Act; and 'owner' has the meaning assigned to it by section 7(1) of that Act.

11 Searches

(1)   A person who wishes to make a personal search shall, if so requested by the registering authority, state his name and address and indicate the parcel of land in respect of which he wishes to search.

(2)   Subject to Rule 16 (requisition and issue of official search certificates by electronic means) a requisition for an official search of the register and the official search certificate shall be in Form C.

(3)   A separate personal search or (as the case may be) a separate requisition for an official search shall be made in respect of each parcel of land against which a search is required, except where for the purpose of a single transaction the search is required in respect of two or more parcels of land which have a common boundary or are separated only by a road, railway, river, stream or canal.

(4)   Subject to Rule 16 (requisition and issue of official search certificates by electronic means) an official search certificate shall, where there are subsisting registrations, be accompanied by a schedule substantially in accordance with Schedule 2 (or such numbered parts of it as may be appropriate) showing the particulars of the registrations.

NOTE

As amended by Local Land Charges (Amendment) Rules 1995, SI 1995/260, r 2.

12 Office copies

On the written request of any person, and on payment of the prescribed fee, the registering authority shall supply an office copy of any registration or any document, map or plan deposited with or filed by that authority in connection with a registration.

13 Use of forms

Subject to Rule 16 (requisition and issue of official search certificates by electronic means) except for the purposes of schedules accompanying official search certificates in accordance with rule 11(4) above, no forms other than those supplied by Her Majesty's Stationery Office or, until the Lord Chancellor otherwise directs, clear and legible facsimiles of such forms may be used for the purposes of these Rules.

NOTE

As amended by Local Land Charges (Amendment) Rules 1978, SI 1978/1638, r 3 and by Local Land Charges (Amendment) Rules 1995, SI 1995/260, r 2.

14 Fees

The fees specified in Schedule 3 shall be payable under the Act and every fee shall be paid in advance.

15 Transitional provisions

(1)   Any application or requisition which—

    (a)   was sent to the registering authority before 1st August 1977,
    (b)   was not dealt with by the registering authority before that date,
    (c)   could have been made under these Rules if they had been in force,

shall be treated as an application or requisition under these Rules and shall be dealt with by the registering authority accordingly.

(2)   As respects registrations subsisting on 31st July 1977, registering authorities shall not be bound to register or to disclose by an official certificate of search or otherwise any particulars the registration or disclosure of which could not be required by or under the Rules applicable on that date to such registrations.

(3)   Notwithstanding the provisions of these Rules, the forms prescribed by the rules applicable on 31st July 1977 to charges may, until the Lord Chancellor otherwise directs, be used, with such adaptations as may be appropriate, for the purposes of these Rules.

16 Requisition and issue of office search certificates by electronic means

(1)   A requisition for an official search of the register may be made by electronic means, notwithstanding section 231(1) of the Local Government Act 1972 (service of documents on local authorities), where the local authority to whom it is made consents to the use of those means.

(2)   An official search certificate may be issued by electronic means where the person requiring the search consents to the use of those means.

(3)   Where a requisition is made under paragraph (1), or a certificate issued under paragraph (2), all the information that would otherwise be required by these Rules to be set out in Form C shall be transmitted electronically together with—

(a)   in the case of a requisition, the name of the person making the requisition or his solicitor, or

(b)   in the case of a certificate, the name and office of the person certifying the search and the name of the registering authority.

(4)   The signatures otherwise required by these Rules shall not be transmitted.

NOTE

As inserted by Local Land Charges (Amendment) Rules 1995, SI 1995/260, r 3.

[. . .]

Schedule 1
Forms

Part 11 of local land charges register: light obstruction notices

Rights of Light Act 1959, section 2(4)

SCHEDULE 1

FORMS

Form A

APPLICATION FOR REGISTRATION OF
A LIGHT OBSTRUCTION NOTICE

¹Delete inapplicable words.

²Insert description of servient land.

³Insert description of dominant building (wherever practicable, a map or plan of the building should be attached).

I, ... of ...., being the freehold owner *or* the tenant of a term of years of which over 7 years remain unexpired *or* the mortgagee in possession¹ of ....

....

....

....²,

which is shown on the plan attached hereto, hereby apply to the

....Council for registration of this notice under section 2 of the Rights of Light Act 1959 against the building known as ....

....

....

....³

⁴Delete inappropriate words.

⁵Delete "of unlimited height" if inappropriate and insert description of height and other dimensions.

Registration of this notice is intended to be equivalent to the obstruction of the access of light to the said building across my land which would be caused by the erection of an opaque structure on all the boundaries of my land *or* in the position on my land marked on the attached plan⁴ and of unlimited height

or ....

....

....

....

....⁵

Signed ....

Date ....

Form B

APPLICATION TO AMEND OR CANCEL A LIGHT OBSTRUCTION NOTICE WITH STATUTORY DECLARATION

Application

¹Delete inapplicable words.

I, ... of ...., being the owner of the interest described below in the land known as ....

²Delete and insert as appropriate.

....

hereby apply for the amendment *or* the cancellation¹ of the light obstruction notice registered on my application *or* on the application of ....

³If an amendment is required, give particulars; if a cancellation, delete sentence.

of .... ²

The amendment³ which I require is ....

....

....

⁴Give names and addresses of persons indicated; if there are no such persons, delete sentence.

The consent to this application by the following persons, being persons who would be entitled to apply for the registration of a light obstruction notice, is attached: ....

....

....⁴

Signed ....

Date ....

Statutory Declaration

¹Delete inapplicable words.

I, ... of ...., solemnly and sincerely declare that:—

²Insert description of servient land.

(*a*) I am the freehold owner *or* the tenant for a term of years of which over 7 years remain unexpired *or* the mortgagee in possession¹ of ....

....

.... ²,

³Delete and insert as appropriate.

(*b*) the light obstruction notice referred to above was registered on my application *or* on the application of ....

....

⁴Insert if appropriate "apart from the persons named above."

of .... ³,

(*c*) there are no other persons who would be entitled to apply for the registration of a light obstruction notice ....

....⁴

And I make this solemn declaration, conscientiously believing the same to be true, by virtue of the Statutory Declarations Act 1835. Declared by the said ....

at .... this   day of

.... before me ....

A Commissioner for Oaths *or* a practising solicitor.

Form C

REQUISITION FOR SEARCH AND OFFICIAL CERTIFICATE OF SEARCH

Requisition for Search

Official number ....

Name of registering authority ....

[1]Delete if
inappropriate.

An official search is required in [[Part   of][1] the register of local land charges kept by the above-named registering authority for subsisting registration against the land [defined in the attached plan and][2] described below:

[2]Delete if
inappropriate.

....

....

....

....

Signature of applicant ....

or his solicitor

Date ....

Official Certificate of Search

[3]Delete inappropriate
words.

It is hereby certified that the search requested above reveals no subsisting registration *or* the registrations described in the Schedule hereto[3] up to and including the date of this certificate.

[4]Insert name of
registering authority.

Signed ....

On behalf of ....[4]

Date ....

Description of charge	Description of dominant building	Name and address of applicant and short description of his interest in servient land	Position and dimension of structure to which registration equivalent	Date of temporary Lands Tribunal certificate (if any) and of its expiration	Date of definitive Lands Tribunal certificate	List of documents filed	Date of registration
1	2	3	4	5	6	7	8

[Author's note: see rule 3]

Schedule 3
Fees

[Not reproduced.]

LANDS TRIBUNAL RULES 1996
SI 1996/1022

Rules 1, 2, 21–24, 30, 34, 35, 38, Sch 1

PART I
PRELIMINARY

1 Citation and commencement

These Rules may be cited as the Lands Tribunal Rules 1996 and shall come into force on May 1, 1996.

2 Interpretation

(1)   In these Rules—

'the Act' means the Lands Tribunal Act 1949,

[. . .]

'appeal' means an appeal against a determination of any question by an authority in respect of whose decision an appeal lies to the Lands Tribunal,
'authority' means the person or body in respect of whose decision an appeal is brought,

[. . .]

'party' in relation to an appeal, means the appellant, the authority and any person who has served notice of intention to respond in accordance with rule 7,
'the President' means the President of the Lands Tribunal, or the member appointed under section 2(3) of the Act to act for the time being as deputy for the President,
'proceedings' means proceedings before the Lands Tribunal,

[. . .]

'the registrar' means the registrar of the Lands Tribunal or, as respects any powers or functions of the registrar, an officer of the Lands Tribunal authorised by the Lord Chancellor, after consulting the Lord Chief Justice, to exercise those powers or functions,
'the Tribunal' means the member or members of the Lands Tribunal selected under section 3(2) of the Act to deal with a case,

[. . .]

(1A) The Lord Chief Justice may nominate a judicial office holder (as defined in section 109(4) of the Constitutional Reform Act 2005) to exercise his functions referred to in the definition of 'the registrar' in paragraph (1).

(2)   In these Rules, a form referred to by number alone means the form so numbered in Schedule 1 to these Rules.

NOTE

As amended by the Lands Tribunal (Amendment) Rules 1997, SI 1997/1965, r 3; by the Lord Chancellor (Transfer of Functions and Supplementary Provisions) Order 2006, SI 2006/680, art 2, Sch 1, para 54(1)-(3).

[. . .]

PART VI
APPLICATIONS UNDER SECTION 2 OF THE RIGHTS OF LIGHT ACT 1959

21 Form of application

(1)   An application for a certificate of the Lands Tribunal under section 2 of the Rights of Light Act 1959 shall be in Form 1.

(2)   An application under paragraph (1) shall be accompanied by two copies of the application which the applicant proposes to make to the local authority in whose area the dominant building is situated.

22 Publicity

(1)   Upon receipt of an application the registrar shall determine what notices are to be given, whether by advertisement or otherwise, to persons who appear to have an interest in the dominant building referred to in rule 21(2).

(2)   For the purpose of paragraph (1), the registrar shall require the applicant to provide any documents or information which it is within his power to provide.

(3)   The notices that the registrar determines shall be given under this rule shall be given by the applicant who shall notify the registrar in writing once this has been done setting out full particulars of the steps he has taken.

23 Issue of temporary certificate

(1)   Where the Tribunal is satisfied that exceptional urgency requires the immediate registration of a temporary notice in the register of local land charges, it shall issue a temporary certificate in Form 2.

(2)   A temporary certificate shall not last longer than six months.

24 Issue of definitive certificates

The Tribunal shall issue a certificate in Form 3 or, where a temporary certificate has been issued under rule 23, in Form 4, once it is satisfied that the notices which the registrar has determined shall be given under rule 22 have been duly given.

[. . .]

30 Consolidation of proceedings

(1)   Where two or more notices of appeal, references or applications have been made which—

(a)   are in respect of the same land or buildings, or

(b)   relate to different interests in the same land or buildings, or

(c)   raise the same issues,

the President or the Tribunal may, on his or its own motion or on the application of a party to the proceedings, order that the appeals, references or applications be consolidated or heard together.

(2)   An order may be made with respect to some only of the matters to which the appeals, references or applications relate.

[. . .]

34 Powers to order discovery, etc.

(1)   The Tribunal, or subject to any directions given by the Tribunal, the registrar may, on the application of any party to the proceedings or of its or his own motion, order any party—

(a)   to deliver to the registrar any document or information which the Tribunal may require and which it is in the power of the party to deliver,

(b)   to afford to every other party to the proceedings an opportunity to inspect those documents (or copies of them) and to take copies,

(c)   to deliver to the registrar an affidavit or make a list stating whether any document or class of document specified or described in the order or application is, or has at any time been in his possession, custody or power and stating when he parted with it,

(d)   to deliver to the registrar a statement in the form of a pleading setting out further and better particulars of the grounds on which he intends to rely and any relevant facts or contentions,

(e)   to answer interrogatories on affidavit relating to any matter at issue between the applicant and the other party,

(f)   to deliver to the registrar a statement of agreed facts, facts in dispute and the issue or issues to be tried by the Tribunal, or

(g)   to deliver to the registrar witness statements or proofs of evidence.

(2)   Where an order is made under paragraph (1) the Tribunal or registrar may give directions as to the time within which any document is to be sent to the registrar (being at least 14 days from the date of the direction) and the parties to whom copies of the document are to be sent.

(3)   Rule 38 shall apply to this rule as appropriate both in relation to applications and where the registrar acts of his own motion.

35 Extension of time

(1)   The time appointed by or under these Rules for doing any act or taking any steps in connection with any proceedings may be extended on application to the registrar under rule 38.

(2)   The registrar may extend the time limit on such terms as he thinks fit and may order an extension even if the application is not made until after the time limit has expired.

[. . .]

38 Interlocutory applications

(1)   Except where these Rules make other provision or the President otherwise orders, an application for directions of an interlocutory nature in connection with any proceedings shall be made to the registrar.

(2)   The application shall be made in writing and shall state the title of the proceedings, and the grounds upon which the application is made.

(3)   If the application is made with the consent of all parties, it shall be accompanied by consents signed by or on behalf of the parties.

(4)   If the application is not made with the consent of every party the applicant shall serve a copy of the proposed application on every other party before it is made and the application shall state that this has been done.

(5)   A party who objects to an application may, within 7 days of service of a copy on him, send written notice of his objection to the registrar.

(6)   Before making an order on an application the registrar shall consider all the objections that he has received and may allow any party who wishes to appear before him the opportunity to do so.

(7)   In dealing with an application the registrar shall have regard to the convenience of all the parties and the desirability of limiting so far as practicable the costs of the proceedings and shall inform the parties in writing of his decision.

(8)   The registrar may refer the application to the President for a decision and he shall do so if requested by the applicant or a party objecting to the application.

(9)   A party may appeal to the President from a decision of the registrar under this rule by giving written notice to the registrar within 7 days of service of the notice of decision or such further time as the registrar may allow.

(10)   An appeal under paragraph (9) shall not act as a stay of proceedings unless the President so orders.

(11)   Where an application under this rule is made—

   (a)   with respect to a case that has been included by the President in a class or group of cases under section 3(2) of the Act, or
   (b)   with respect to a case for which a member or members of the Lands Tribunal has or have been selected,

the powers and duties of the President under this rule may be exercised and discharged in relation to the application by any member or members of the Lands Tribunal authorised by the President for that purpose.

[. . .]

Schedule 1

Form 1

Application for Certificate under section 2 of the Rights of Light Act 1959

To:—

The Registrar,
Lands Tribunal.

I/We

of

being [owner(s)] [tenant(s) for a term of years certain expiring in 19   ]

[mortgagee(s) in possession] of (*here describe the servient land*]

apply to the Lands Tribunal for the issue of a certificate that adequate publicity has been given to my/our proposed application for the registration in the register of local land charges of the

Council of a notice under section 2 of the Rights of Light Act 1959.

I/We attach two copies of the proposed application.

[I/We also apply for the issue of a certificate authorising the registration forthwith of the proposed notice as a temporary notice. The case is one of exceptional urgency because (*here insert reasons*)

To the best of my/our knowledge persons likely to be affected by the registration of the notice are (*here insert names and addresses of all persons in occupation of the dominant building or having a proprietary interest in it*)

All communications regarding this application should be addressed to me/us at the address shown above [*or* to my/our solicitor/agent of].

Dated

Signed

Form 2

Temporary Certificate for Registration of a Notice under section 2 of the Rights of Light Act 1959

I hereby certify that for reasons of exceptional urgency a temporary notice may be registered by (*name of applicant*)

forthwith against the building specified in the attached Form of Application for the registration of a notice under section 2 of the Rights of Light Act 1959.

A notice registered under the said application shall not have effect after the effluxion of   months from the date of registration unless before the expiration of that period a further certificate of this Tribunal has been lodged with the registering authority stating that due publicity has been given to the proposed registration.

Dated

Signed

Registrar

Lands Tribunal

Form 3

Certificate for Registration of a Notice under section 2 of the Rights of Light Act 1959

I certify that adequate notice of the proposed application by (*name of applicant*)
          a copy of which is attached to this certificate, to register a notice under section 2 of the Rights of Light Act 1959 against (*description of dominant building as specified in*

the application)   has been given to all persons who, in the circumstances existing at the present time, appear to the Lands Tribunal to be persons likely to be affected by the registration of such a notice.

Dated

Signed

Registrar

Lands Tribunal

Form 4

Certificate for Registration of a Notice under section 2 of the Rights of Light Act 1959 following Registration of a Temporary Notice

I certify that adequate notice of the proposed application by (*name of applicant*)   to register a notice under section 2 of the Rights of Light Act 1959 against (*description of dominant building as specified in the application*)   has been given to all person who, in the circumstances existing at the present time, appear to the Lands Tribunal to be persons likely to be affected by the registration of such a notice.

A temporary certificate authorising the registration of a temporary notice was issued by the Lands Tribunal on 19 . . . .

Dated

Signed

Registrar

Lands Tribunal

LAND REGISTRATION RULES 2003
SI 2003/1417

Rules 36, 73, 74, 76, 197

[. . .]

36 First registration–note as to rights of light and air

On first registration, if it appears to the registrar that an agreement prevents the acquisition of rights of light or air for the benefit of the registered estate, he may make an entry in the property register of that estate.

[. . .]

73 Application for register entries for express appurtenant rights over unregistered land

(1) A proprietor of a registered estate who claims the benefit of a legal easement or profit a prendre which has been expressly granted over an unregistered legal estate may apply for it to be registered as appurtenant to his estate.

(2) The application must be accompanied by the grant and evidence of the grantor's title to the unregistered estate.

(3) In paragraph (1) the reference to express grant does not include a grant as a result of the operation of section 62 of the Law of Property Act 1925.

74 Application for register entries for implied or prescriptive appurtenant rights

(1) A proprietor of a registered estate who claims the benefit of a legal easement or profit a prendre, which has been acquired otherwise than by express grant, may apply for it to be registered as appurtenant to his estate.

(2) The application must be accompanied by evidence to satisfy the registrar that the right subsists as a legal estate appurtenant to the applicant's registered estate.

(3) In paragraph (1) the reference to an acquisition otherwise than by express grant includes acquired as a result of the operation of section 62 of the Law of Property Act 1925.

[. . .]

76 Note as to rights of light or air

If it appears to the registrar that an agreement prevents the acquisition of rights of light or air for the benefit of the registered estate, he may make an entry in the property register of that estate.

[. . .]

PART 15
GENERAL PROVISIONS

Notices and addresses for service

197 Content of notice

(1) Every notice given by the registrar must–

- (a) fix the time within which the recipient is to take any action required by the notice,
- (b) state what the consequence will be of a failure to take such action as is required by the notice within the time fixed,
- (c) state the manner in which any reply to the notice must be given and the address to which it must be sent.

(2) Except where otherwise provided by these rules, the time fixed by the notice will be the period ending at 12 noon on the fifteenth business day after the date of issue of the notice.

[. . .]

Appendix 3

OTHER MATERIALS

MATERIALS ON THE CUSTOM OF LONDON

Hilary Term 30 Geo. 2.
Plummer versus Bentham.[1]
Saturday, 12th February 1757.
If a custom of the city of London be put in issue,
it is triable by the mayor and aldermen,
certified at the bar of the court, *ore tenùs*,
by the mouth of their recorder.

THE recorder of *London (Sir William Moreton)* came to the bar, and CERTIFIED TWO *customs* of that city ORE TENUS.

Mr. *Williams* moved (when Sir *William Moreton* was down at the bar,) that the *recorder of London* might return two writs of *certiorari* directed to the lord mayor and aldermen of *London*, to certify two of the customs of their city.

And then Mr. *Williams* opened the case, *viz.* That it was an action of trespass on the case brought by the plaintiff against the defendant, for *obstructing his ancient lights*, by a *new erection or building* which the defendant had raised against them: to which the defendant had (by leave) pleaded two justifications, both of them under the custom of the city of *London*. One of them was, that there is an ancient custom in the city of *London*, 'That if any person has a messusage or house in the city of *London*, adjoining or contiguous to another MESSUAGE OR HOUSE, or to the ancient *foundations of one* in the said city, which former house has *ancient lights or windows* fronting, opposite to, or over such other adjoining or contiguous MESSUAGE OR HOUSE, or ancient *foundation of one*; such *other* person, *owner of the* LATTER *messuage or house or ancient* foundation of one, may well and lawfully *exalt* such his *messuage or house*, or *rebuild upon the ancient foundations* of such his adjacent or contiguous MESSUAGE OR HOUSE any *new messuage or house*, to ANY HEIGHT *that he shall please, against and opposite to the said ancient lights and windows* of such first mentioned neighbouring messuage or house to which his *messuage or house* or ancient foundations of a *messuage or house* are so contiguous or adjoining; and *thereby darken and obscure* such ancient lights and windows of such first-mentioned neighbouring house, having such ancient lights and windows: unless there has been some writing, instrument, or record of an agreement or restriction to the contrary.'

On this plea issue was joined: and a *certiorari* issued, directed to the mayor and aldermen of the city of *London*, to certify 'whether they have or have not such a custom.'

The second plea, issue, and *certiorari*, were the same with the first, only with this difference or rather *extension* of the custom pleaded; *viz.* 'That the owner of any

---

[1]   (1757) 1 Burr 248, 97 ER 297.

ERECTION OR BUILDING, or the ancient foundation of any ERECTION OR BUILDING, might well and lawfully exalt such ERECTION OR BUILDING, or erect and build thereon a new ERECTION OR BUILDING to any height that he pleases, &c.' and so on as in the former plea: only that the former plea confined the claim of the privilege to *messuages* or *houses*; which this latter plea extends to *all erections or buildings.*'

Sir *William Moreton* Knt. recorder of *London*, accordingly *certified* ORE TENUS, by command of the lord mayor and aldermen, (after having recited the pleadings and *certiorari*), 'That there *is* such a custom as is alleged in the *former* plea: but that there is NO such custom as is alleged in the latter plea.'

The recorder then delivered in both the writs of *certiorari*, with *written copies* of the respective returns annexed; though he had delivered them *ore tenùs* at the bar: (which, he told me, was usual.) The returns were worded as follows: *viz*. The execution of this writ appears in a certain certificate by us the mayor and aldermen of the said city of *London*, made by the recorder of the said city at the day and place within contained, according to the custom of the said city, by word of mouth, as is within commanded.

Note—See the first case in Sir H. Calthrop's Reports (prettily reported and worth reading;) where the question was very like the present, and the determination agreeable to the certificate as to this first plea.

The Answer of Marshe Dickinson *Esq. the mayor, and of the aldermen of the said city.*

We the said mayor and aldermen of the said city, by Sir *William Moreton* Knt. Recorder of the said city, by word of mouth of the said recorder, according to the said custom of the said city, do, in obedience to the said annexed writ, humbly certify, that there is now had, and from the time whereof the memory of man is not to the contrary there hath been had and received such ancient and laudable custom in the said city used and approved; to wit, 'That if any one hath a messuage or house in the said city, near or contiguous and adjoining to *another ancient* MESSUAGE OR HOUSE, or to the ancient *foundation or another ancient* MESSUAGE OR HOUSE in the said city, *of another person his neighbour* there: and the windows or lights of *such messuage or house* are looking fronting or situate towards, upon, over, or against the said *other* ancient MESSUAGE OR HOUSE, or ancient *foundation* of such other ancient MESSUAGE OR HOUSE of such *other person his neighbour*, so being near, adjacent, contiguous, or adjoining, *although* such messuage or house, and the lights and windows thereof be or were *ancient*, YET such *other person his neighbour*, being the owner of such other MESSUAGE OR HOUSE or ancient *foundations* so being near, adjacent or adjoining, by and according to the custom of the said city in the same city for all the time aforesaid used and approved, *well and lawfully may*, might and hath used, at his will and pleasure, his *said other* MESSUAGE OR HOUSE so being near, adjacent or adjoining, by building *to exalt or erect*; or, of new, upon the ancient *foundations* of such *other* MESSUAGE OR HOUSE so being near, adjacent or adjoining, *to build and erect a new messuage or house* to SUCH HEIGHT AS THE SAID OWNER SHALL PLEASE, *against* and *opposite* to the said *lights and windows* near or contiguous to such OTHER MESSUAGE OR HOUSE, and by means thereof TO OBSCURE AND DARKEN such windows or lights: unless there be or hath been some writing, instrument or record of an agreement or restriction to the contrary thereof in that behalf.'

The return to the other writ of *certiorari* was in the same form, and to the very same effect as to the custom certified by the former; and repeated the return to the former *certiorari in totidem verbis*, very nearly: but it went on further, with a *negation* of the existence of any such custom as the defendant had alleged in his *second* justification. The additional part was as follows.

And that in the said city of *London* there is not now or ever was any *such* custom, 'That if any one hath a messuage or house in the said city, near or contiguous and adjoining to an ERECTION *or* BUILDING, or to the ancient foundations of an ERECTION *or* BUILDING in the said city, of another person his neighbour there; and the windows or lights of such messuage or house are looking fronting or situate towards, upon, over, or against such ERECTION *or* BUILDING, or the ancient foundations of such ERECTION *or* BUILDING of such other person his neighbour so being near, adjacent, contiguous or adjoining; although such messuage or house and the lights and windows thereof be or were ancient, yet such other person his neighbour, being the owner of such ERECTION *or* BUILDING, *or ancient* foundations of such ERECTION *or* BUILDING so being near, adjacent or adjoining, by and according to the custom of the said city in the same city for all the time aforesaid used and approved, well and lawfully may, might, and hath used, at his will and pleasure, his said ERECTION *or* BUILDING so being adjacent or adjoining, by building to *exalt and erect*; or, of new, upon the ancient foundations of the said ERECTION OR BUILDING so being near, adjacent or adjoining to build and erect a *new erection or building* to SUCH HEIGHT *as the owner shall please* against and opposite to the said lights and windows of such messuage or house, and by means thereof to obscure and darken such windows or lights.'

The Court ordered the certiorari to be filed, and the *return* RECORDED.

Note—Nothing of this kind has actually happened for many years past (not even since *H*. the sixth's reign,) in *this* Court; (though it has in the Court of Chancery.) And a consultation was had in the city concerning the sort of gown which it was proper for the recorder to put on, to make his *ore tenùs* return: in which consultation it was determined that it ought to be the purple cloth robe, faced with black velvet: and not his scarlet gown, his black silk one, nor the common bar-gown.

REPORT OF THE COMMITTEE ON THE LAW RELATING TO RIGHTS OF LIGHT

(extract)

To the Right Honourable the Viscount KILMUIR,

Lord High Chancellor of Great Britain.

MY LORD,

We were appointed on the 29th March, 1957, to advise you whether legislation is desirable—

(1)   to amend the law relating to rights of light in relation to war-damaged sites or sites whose development was prevented or impeded by reason of restrictions or controls imposed during or after the late war; and

(2)   to preserve rights of light acquired or in process of acquisition by buildings which subsequently suffered war damage.

2   At an early stage in our deliberations we became aware that planning legislation of recent decades has altered to a very significant degree the position of owners of land or buildings over which rights of light may be acquired. The impact of these changes in the law of light, which does not hitherto appear to have been widely appreciated, is universal and not confined to war-damaged sites or sites prejudiced in their development as a result of the war. We therefore sought an extension of our terms of reference which would enable us to consider the wider problems which arise, and were invited by you in December, 1957, to consider also—

'Whether any alterations are desirable in the law and practice relating to the means whereby the acquisition of rights of light over any land may be prevented.'

3   We held seven meetings and were assisted by written and oral evidence from the various persons and bodies whose names are set out in the Appendix to this Report. We express our thanks and appreciation to all of them.

The practical extent of the problem

4   It is evident that the value of a site can be greatly reduced if, by lapse of time, neighbouring buildings acquire rights of light over it. If the opportunities of acquiring such rights are afforded by circumstances outside the control of the owner, as in war, or if factors not of his choosing prevent him from protecting himself against the acquisition of such rights, the owner has *prima facie* a moral claim to relief. Owners of sites of the classes defined in our terms of reference fall within this category. But legislation for hard cases may easily make bad law. Hence, before examining possible forms of relief, we have thought it necessary to satisfy ourselves that the need for a remedy in the cases to which our enquiry relates is a real one. Not only has a decade now passed since the end of the war, during which much destroyed property has been rebuilt, but it has also been suggested to us that present day planning legislation leaves so little room for the operation of the old established law on rights of light that the need for measures in support of such rights has disappeared.

5   The evidence we have received, particularly from the Royal Institution of Chartered Surveyors and the Law Society, convinces us that there remain to this day numbers of sites, empty since before the war or damaged in the war, on which the erection of buildings will before long be seriously hampered by adverse rights of light. Indeed in some cases which were brought to our notice adverse rights have already accrued. Difficulties are likely to be experienced primarily in densely built-up areas, amongst which the City of London and such towns as Bristol and Manchester may prove to be particularly affected. It is impossible to estimate the number of properties involved, but we are satisfied on the evidence before us that the potential loss in individual cases is so substantial that it would call for a remedy even if the total numbers proved to be few.

6   It is true that planning legislation has had a considerable impact on rights of light, but it has not superseded the ordinary law. We have been given examples where legal rights to light over a site could prevent the erection of buildings for which planning permission would be readily granted. The standards of daylighting applied by local planning authorities, whether evolved by the authorities themselves or based on the guidance about daylighting given in the advisory handbook on the Redevelopment of Central Areas issued by the Ministry of Town and Country Planning in 1946, may not in all circumstances recommend a flow of light equal to that which the owner of a building can claim at law; and there may well be instances where even the complete obstruction of light would not conflict with high standards of town planning.

We have accordingly reached the conclusion that there is a real practical problem calling for a remedy.

The right to light

7   In order to ascertain the exact nature of the problems facing owners and occupiers of war-damaged and vacant sites, it may perhaps be useful briefly to summarize the present law in relation to the right of light. This right is not a natural right of property, but an easement; it cannot appertain to open land, nor even to buildings as such, but

only to apertures in buildings, and it exists only in those cases in which it has been acquired by one or other of the means which the law recognises for the acquisition of easements.

8   An easement must be an advantage to a dominant tenement and a burden on a servient tenement. It may be acquired either by express or implied grant or by long enjoyment. There are three ways in which long enjoyment can create an easement, *viz.*, by prescription at common law, under the doctrine of lost grant, and by prescription under the Prescription Act, 1832. We are not concerned with cases of express or implied grant, and prescription at common law is in this sphere of no practical significance. Rights of light can be acquired under the doctrine of lost grant, but such cases are rare. In practice, the normal mode of acquiring an easement of light is under the Prescription Act, 1832.

Prescription Act, 1832, section 3

9   The easement of light is treated separately from all other easements by section 3 of the Act, which is as follows:

'When the access and use of light to and for any dwelling house, workshop, or other building shall have been actually enjoyed therewith for the full period of twenty years without interruption, the right thereto shall be deemed absolute and indefeasible, any local usage or custom to the contrary notwithstanding, unless it shall appear that the same was enjoyed by some consent or agreement expressly made or given for that purpose by deed or writing'.

10   Section 3 must be read with section 4, which provides that any period specified in the Act is to be the period 'next before some suit or action wherein the claim or matter to which such period may relate shall . . . be brought into question.' and that nothing 'should be deemed to be an interruption . . . unless the same shall . . . be submitted to or acquiesced in for one year after the party interrupted shall . . . have notice thereof . . .'. It follows that, since an interruption lasting less than a year does not stop the running of time, an easement of light can be acquired under the Act by actual enjoyment (not under a written consent) for nineteen years and one day. But since this period must immediately precede action brought, the right under the Act may still be lost by one year's interruption occurring at any time later than the original period of nineteen years and a day. Hence the statutory right is, strictly speaking, inchoate in every case in which it has not been brought in issue in an action. On the other hand, where there has been enjoyment for upwards of nineteen years, followed by an interruption for more than one year but not for long enough to lead to the inference that the right has been abandoned, the court would be inclined to uphold the right under the doctrine of lost grant. This, we think, is the only practical relevance of that doctrine to the subject of our inquiry.

The right to light is a negative easement

11   An easement may be either positive or negative. A positive easement entitles the dominant owner to do something upon the land of the servient owner; in terms of pleading, a positive easement affords to the dominant owner a defence to the servient owner's action for trespass. A negative easement merely entitles the dominant owner to restrain the servient owner from doing on the servient land something which interferes with the enjoyment of the easement; in terms of pleading, a negative easement gives the dominant owner an action for nuisance against a servient owner who fails to observe it.

12   This distinction has important practical consequences. A person who is in process of acquiring a positive easement (eg a right of way) by long enjoyment must throughout the prescriptive period go on the servient tenement as a trespasser. It is only when time has fully run that he acquires the positive easement and so is protected by the defence which it affords. At all earlier times the servient owner can sue successfully for trespass; he will normally obtain an injunction which will effectively interrupt the running of time. But a period who is in process of acquiring a negative easement (eg a right to light) by long enjoyment never trespasses on the servient tenement at all; he merely enjoys the access of light to his holding across the servient tenement. There is no process of law by which the owner of the prospective servient tenement can compel the prospective dominant owner to interrupt his enjoyment, and so protect the prospective servient tenement against the acquisition of a negative easement. In some cases, no doubt, the prospective dominant owner can be persuaded to accept a deed or written agreement granting him consent for the passage of light over the grantor's premises; if so, time will not run at all, because of the concluding words of section 3 of the Prescription Act. But the prospective servient owner's only weapon in negotiation for such an agreement is to threaten physically to interrupt the access of light to his neighbour's building; and, if the threat does not succeed, his only remedy is actually to bring about such an interruption.

Interruption of the access of light: planning legislation

13   Of course, if the owner of the servient tenement can erect buildings on his land before the dominant owner's right to light has accrued, he does not need to take prior preventive action. But, for various reasons it is not always practicable or desirable to do so at the time when it becomes necessary or expedient to interrupt the flow of light to the dominant tenement. The conventional remedy has therefore been to erect a screen on the prospective servient tenement. The cost of doing so has been some check upon frivolous interruptions; nevertheless the remedy is a crude one and its results are unsightly.

14   The conventional remedy has, however, ceased to exist as of right. Early in the war which started on 3rd September, 1939, controls were imposed on building operations and on the use of timber and other materials, which in practice made it impossible to erect a screen. Those difficulties were, no doubt, of a transient kind. But from 1st July, 1948, there has been a permanent change, in that it has been necessary, under the Town and Country Planning Act, 1947, to obtain planning permission for all development, a term which is so defined as to include the erection of a screen. We have been informed of cases in which a planning authority has refused permission for a screen. In some cases development of this kind has been allowed on appeal by the Minister of Housing and Local Government who, we are informed, in reaching his decision took account of the fact that the object of erecting the screen was to prevent the acquisition of a right of light. Nevertheless, the present position is unsatisfactory. On the one hand, we do not think that Parliament can have intended, in enacting the Town and Country Planning Act, 1947, to make precarious the time-honoured remedy of erecting a screen to interrupt the access of light and so prevent the acquisition of an easement. On the other hand, a screen erected for such a purpose is at best unsightly, uses up labour and materials which might with advantage be put to more productive purposes, and, since it is in no one's interest to spend money on its maintenance once it has stood for a year, it is calculated to deteriorate progressively. We do not think that in these days the planning authorities or the Minister should be expected to permit such an affront. It appears to us to be desirable to devise a scheme by which a statutory notice may be given having the like legal effect as the actual erection of a screen. That is to say, the giving of the notice

should be treated as an interruption of the access of light both for the purposes of the Prescription Act, 1832, and at common law.

[. . .]

War damage to the dominant tenement

19   So far in this Report we have been concerned mainly with the position of servient owners needing protection against adverse rights of light. But we were also invited to consider whether a dominant owner, namely the owner of a building which had acquired rights of light or was in process of doing so, should be protected against any loss of his rights which might otherwise result from its subsequent destruction. In our opinion no such protection is necessary. A subsisting right to light is lost only by express release or abandonment. Abandonment is a matter of inference and intention, and it is manifest that a person whose building is demolished by the enemy does not *ipso facto* abandon his right to light. He may have difficulty in proving exactly what his rights were, if there are no plans or drawings of the old building; but no change in the law could supply that deficiency. The time will, no doubt, come when the owner's prolonged failure to rebuild could induce the court to infer that he has abandoned his right; but in considering the question of abandonment we do not think that the court would hold it against him that he failed to rebuild while building restrictions were in force.

20   Different considerations apply to buildings which have been demolished while they were in the process of acquiring rights of light, for destruction of the building will have put an end to the running of time. In our opinion it would not be right now to revive such embryonic rights; they might never have matured even if the building had survived. Furthermore as rights of light must be claimed in respect of specific apertures in buildings, legislation to revive such rights would probably be neither useful nor effective. For it is improbable that the exact extent of the former rights could now be established, or, if it could, that the old building would be replaced by one whose windows and dimensions would enable the former rights to be reclaimed.

General conclusions

21   Our general conclusions therefore are—

(i)   that the present system, by which a prospective servient owner can protect his land only by the erection of a screen, is unsatisfactory, and that he should be enabled instead to serve a statutory notice having the like effect (paragraphs 13 and 14);

(ii)   that in computing the period of prescription under section 3 of the Act of 1832, and in applying the doctrine of lost grant in cases of light, some allowance ought to be made, in favour of the prospective servient owner, for the period during which there were serious restrictions on building operations (paragraphs 15 to 17);

(iii)   that it is not desirable to legislate for the preservation of rights of light acquired by buildings which later suffered war damage or of rights in process of acquisition by such buildings (paragraphs 19 and 20).

We now turn to consider the best means to give effect to our general conclusions.

Statutory notice in lieu of screen

22   The erection of a screen was a troublesome and expensive matter, but once it was erected there was little doubt that all those concerned to know of the interruption did know of it. Any system of registration in lieu of physical obstruction must not, in our view, be so easy or cheap as to encourage notices that are frivolous or worse, and it must contain full safeguards that all interested parties do in fact know of the notice.

23   We recommend that, by registering a statutory notice against a prospective dominant building, the prospective servient owner should be able to bring about the like legal consequences as at present flow from the erection of a screen. The consequences of a registration which remains on the register for the requisite period (as suggested in the next paragraph) should be that there will be a break in the running of time for the purposes of acquiring an easement of light under the Prescription Act, 1832, and that in proceedings at common law the fact that the notice has been registered and has not been removed from the register is to be taken into account by the court in considering whether an easement of light has been acquired by prescription at common law or under the doctrine of lost grant, or whether an easement already existing has been abandoned. The notice should adequately identify the servient owner's site, reference being made in appropriate cases to a plan attached to the notice; and registration should be treated as a notional obstruction of the light of the dominant building by a screen, erected on the boundaries of that site, either of unlimited height or of such limited height as the notice may specify.

Registration of notice

24   The notice should be registered, provisionally in the first place, in the register of local land charges and should take effect (subject as mentioned below) as if the access of light from the neighbouring property had been interrupted on the date of the registration. Unless the notice is taken off the register, as explained in paragraph 31 below, the notional obstruction should be treated as having begun at the date of registration. After the notice has been registered for one year, the obstruction should be treated as having been submitted to or acquiesced in for one year after registration by all persons interested in the property against which the registration is made.

25   We suggest one year as an appropriate period of notional obstruction, because that is the minimum period required under section 4 of the Prescription Act to effect a break in the running of the period of prescription. No building in fact exists on the servient owner's site and the fiction of its existence should not be maintained for longer than is necessary. If the notional obstruction endures for one year, the servient owner will have twenty years before the period of prescription has run against him once more, which should be ample time to carry out his building projects. It follows, of course, that the notice should remain on the register for twenty years from the date of registration.

26   The registration should, in our opinion, be in a local land charges register and not in one of the central registers, because it is essential that the charge should be registered against potentially dominant premises identified by their site and that the register should be open to inspection by all interested parties. These requirements are partially satisfied in the case of the Land Registry where charges on registered land are entered, but not in the case of the central Land Charges Register which deals with unregistered land and operates by reference to names of owners and not by reference to a map. On the other hand the system of registration in local land charges registers fulfils all the requirements.

Notification of registration

27   As the notional interruption of the access of light will start on the date of provisional registration, it is necessary that notice should in fact be given to all interested persons who are likely to be affected by it and that it should be given within so short a time after that registration as to give them plenty of time in which to challenge the notional interruption before it has subsisted for a year. For a notice acquiesced in for a year will be fatal to any claims under the Prescription act, 1832, by persons interested in the property against which the notice is registered.

28   The giving of notice should be too widespread rather than too chary and cannot, in our opinion, be left without judicial supervision to the person serving the statutory notice. A somewhat similar need has for a generation existed in respect of notice of proceedings under subsection (1) of section 84 of the Law of Property Act, 1925, for the modification or removal by the Lands Tribunal of a covenant restrictive of the use of land. In the Lands Tribunal the procedure, governed by Rule 21 of the Lands Tribunal Rules, 1956, is that the Registrar arranges before the hearing for the necessary notices to be given, subject to reference to the President in cases of difficulty. This is, we understand, a simple and informal procedure and is in most cases carried through by correspondence. The notices are given to any neighbours who are near enough to be likely to be affected, and public notices are given in the local newspapers and by being posted on the site affected by the restrictions which it is sought to modify or remove. We suggest that a similar procedure should be adopted and that the judicial supervision of the notices should be vested in the Lands Tribunal. It will be a matter of internal organisation how far these cases are dealt with by a member of the Tribunal or by the Registrar; but we should expect them normally to be in the hands of the Registrar, at least when the system is fully under way.

29   Having provisionally registered his notice, the prospective servient owner would next apply to the Lands Tribunal for directions. He would attach a copy of his notice (including the identification of his own site) and a plan indicating clearly the property against which the notice has been registered. The Tribunal would then issue directions as to service, designed to ensure that all persons whose interests in the properties concerned are likely to be affected will receive due notice of the proposed notional obstruction. As soon as the tribunal has been satisfied that its directions as to service have been carried out, it would issue a certificate to that effect, and on the filing of this certificate in the register of local land charges the provisional notice would become definitive with effect from the date of original registration.

30   In order to ensure that all interested persons receive notice quickly, leaving them plenty of time to assert their rights before a year has expired, we also recommend that the provisional notice should cease to have any validity unless the Lands Tribunal's certificate is filed by the end of three months from the date of provisional registration. There should be provision for an extension of the time limit by order of the court, provided application for the order is made within the three months, but no power of extension should be conferred upon the Lands Tribunal.

Variation or cancellation of registration

31   A person who receives a notice given under the directions of the Lands Tribunal, or who otherwise learns of the registration, and who claims to be entitled to object to the notional obstruction, should be free to bring an action for a declaration that the obstruction infringes his rights and for an injunction against its continuance. The court should be given power in such an action to make any order that it sees fit for the

variation or cancellation of the entries in the register of local land charges. It would be of assistance to the parties concerned if rules of court could also provide a more summary method of taking the court's opinion on the right of the person serving the statutory notice to interrupt the flow of light to his neighbour's premises. In a simple case application might, for instance, be made to the Chancery Division of the High Court by originating motion for a declaration as to the parties' rights, a simple and expeditious form of proceeding. We do not contemplate that the Lands Tribunal should receive or consider any objections that may be made to the notional obstructions: such objections will normally raise questions of title, which are a matter for the court. The Lands Tribunal's only functions would be to ensure that the notices receive all necessary publicity among persons likely to be interested and to issue its certificate within the prescribed time.

[. . .]

Summary of recommendations

37   Our recommendations may be summarised as follows—

(i)   A prospective servient owner should be able to bring about the consequences which at present flow from the erection of a screen by registering a statutory notice against a prospective dominant building (paras 14 and 23).

(ii)   The statutory notice should have the same effect as a screen erected on the boundary of the servient owner's land and maintained there for one year (paras 23 to 25).

(iii)   The statutory notice should be registered in a register of local land charges and the registration published under directions to be given by the Lands Tribunal. Registration should cease to have effect unless the Lands Tribunal certifies within three months (or such extended period as the court may allow) from the original date of registration that it has been duly publicised (paras 26 to 30).

(iv)   Objections to the notional obstruction should be raised by proceedings in the court, which should have power to make any order it sees fit for the variation or cancellation of the restriction (para 31).

(v)   The twenty year period for the prescriptive acquisition of rights of light under the Prescription Act, 1832, should be extended to 27 years for the purposes of any action either asserting a claim to rights of light and started after the date of publication of this Report and before the 31st December, 1962, or brought in respect of an actual or notional interruption effected between those dates (paras 33 and 34).

(vi)   We do not recommend any legislation for the preservation of rights of light acquired by buildings which later suffered war damage or of rights in process of acquisition by such buildings (paras 19 and 20).

CHARLES HARMAN, *Chairman*,

GUY BISCOE,

PERCY V. BURNETT,

JOHN CATLOW,

J. C. CRAIG,

ARTHUR J. DRIVER,

G. H. NEWSOM.

K. M. NEWMAN, *Secretary*,

12th May, 1958.

HIGH HEDGES: PRESCRIBED FORMS AND PRECEDENTS

This Appendix offers examples of forms and letters for use in dealing with complaints about high hedges. Councils are not required to follow them. Where they do, it must be stressed that Councils should adapt the wording to the individual circumstances of the particular case.

In addition, these letters will need to be adapted if sent by email. Rather than sending copies of leaflets Councils might refer to relevant web addresses. The following are all available on the DCLG website at www.communities.gov.uk/index.asp?id=1127822:

- Over the garden hedge
- High hedges: complaining to the Council
- High hedges: appealing against the Council's decision

The complaint form, and accompanying guidance notes on its completion, should be available on the Council's website.

First contact

To be sent to the enquirer/potential complainant

Complaint about a high hedge

Thank you for your [letter/email/telephone call] of [date] indicating that you wish to make a formal complaint about your neighbour's hedge, under Part 8 of the Anti-social Behaviour Act 2003.

The Council can only intervene once you have tried and exhausted all other avenues for resolving your hedge dispute. I am enclosing a copy of the leaflet *Over the garden hedge* which sets out some steps that you should consider trying.

The Council's role is to act as an independent and impartial adjudicator in those cases which people cannot settle for themselves. We cannot, therefore, negotiate or mediate between you and your neighbour. [But I am sending details of the local community mediation service who might be able to help.]

If you cannot agree a solution with your neighbour, let me know and I will send further information about the procedure for making a formal complaint. You should, however, bear in mind that the Council can reject a complaint if we think someone has not done everything they reasonably could to negotiate a solution to their hedge problems. So if you don't follow the advice in the leaflet, you will need to explain why not.

Complaint form: Cover letter

To be sent to the complainant

Complaint about a high hedge

Thank you for your [letter/email/telephone call] of [date] indicating that you wish to make a formal complaint about your neighbour's hedge, under Part 8 of the Anti-social Behaviour Act 2003. You said that you had discussed the problem with your neighbour but had been unable to agree a solution.

I enclose our complaints form together with some guidance notes to help you complete it. Before filling it in, I recommend that you read the enclosed leaflet *High hedges: complaining to the Council.* It explains what complaints we can consider and how we will deal with them.

The leaflet also sets out what we expect you to have done to try to settle your hedge dispute. If you have not exhausted all the avenues mentioned, you should consider giving them a try. If you don't, you will need to explain why not. Otherwise, we might not proceed with your complaint.

The complaint form constitutes your statement of case as to why you consider the hedge is adversely affecting the reasonable enjoyment of your domestic property. It will be an important document in the Council's consideration of the complaint, as well as in any subsequent appeal against our decision. In setting out your grounds of complaint, therefore, you should describe fully the problems caused by the hedge, their severity and the impact on you. Please also send us any supporting information that you want us to take into account.

Please return the completed form to me at the above address. You must also send a copy to the owner and occupier of the land where the hedge is situated. [These are the people listed in sections 5.4 and 5.5 of the form.]

When we receive your formal complaint, we will run some checks to make sure that it meets the requirements set out in Part 8 of the Anti-social Behaviour Act 2003 and that we can, therefore, deal with it.

If we cannot proceed with the complaint, we will tell you why not. Otherwise, we will acknowledge that we have received it and explain what happens next.

Complaint form: High hedges

[Not reproduced here. A version is available to download at the DCLG website 'http://www.communities.gov.uk/index.asp?id=1127885'.]

Guidance notes for completing the complaint form

General notes

These guidance notes are to help you fill in the form to make a complaint about a neighbouring high hedge. You should also read the leaflet *High hedges: complaining to the Council.*

Consideration of your complaint will be delayed if you do not complete the form properly or do not provide the information requested.

If you are still unsure how to answer any of the questions, please contact [x department] on [y telephone number] or [z email address].

You can obtain translations and large print versions of this guidance and the form through the Council.

Section 1: Attempts to resolve the complaint

Please keep the descriptions brief but say how you made the approach (eg face to face, phone, letter) and what the result was.

Example 1

- 12 March 2005 – phoned neighbour [Mr Bloggs of 12 High Street] to ask if we could discuss hedge. Met on 19 March but we couldn't agree a solution;
- 15 April – mediators visited;
- 29 April – met neighbours [Mr Bloggs] and mediators. But still couldn't find an answer we were both happy with;
- 14 May – wrote to inform neighbours [Mr Bloggs] would be complaining to Council.

Example 2

- 12 March 2005 – wrote to neighbours [Mr Bloggs of 12 High Street] to ask if we could discuss hedge. 2 weeks later still no reply;
- 9 April – wrote to ask if would speak to mediator. 2 weeks later still no reply;
- 7 May – wrote to inform neighbours [Mr Bloggs] would be complaining to Council.

Example 3

- 12 March 2005 – saw neighbours [Mr Bloggs of 12 High Street] in their garden and asked if we could discuss hedge. Neighbours [Mr Bloggs] came round on 19 March. Saw the effect of the hedge for themselves. Sympathetic but unwilling to reduce the hedge as much as we wanted;
- Neighbours [Mr Bloggs] willing to try mediation but discovered that neighbour mediation not available in our area. We live too far from the nearest service;
- 23 April – saw neighbours [Mr Bloggs] again and told them that, if we couldn't agree a solution, we would make a formal complaint to Council. Left it for a couple of weeks then confirmed in writing that we would be going ahead with the complaint.

It is not necessary to send copies of all correspondence with your neighbour about the hedge – especially if the dispute is a long-running one. You need only provide evidence of your latest attempts to settle it.

Section 2: Criteria for making a complaint

Who can complain

Q2.6   You must be the owner **or** occupier of the property affected by a high hedge in order to make a formal complaint to the Council.

If you do not own the property (eg because you are a tenant or a leaseholder), you can still make a complaint. But you should let the owner (eg landlord or management company) know what you are doing.

Q2.7   The property does not have to be wholly residential but must include separate living accommodation otherwise we cannot consider the complaint.

Section 3: Grounds of complaint

It will help if you provide as much information as you can but keep it factual. Remember that a copy of this form will be sent to the person who owns the property where the hedge is growing, and to the person who lives there if they are different people.

Concentrate on the hedge and the disadvantages you experience because of its height.

We cannot consider problems that are not connected with the height of the hedge. For example, if the roots of the hedge are pushing up a path.

Nor can we consider things that are not directly about the hedge in question. For example, that other people keep their hedges trimmed to a lower height; or that the worry is making you ill.

Please also provide a photo of the hedge and a plan showing the location of the hedge and surrounding properties.

When drawing your plan, please look at the example below and make sure that you:

- Mark and name surrounding roads.
- Sketch in buildings, including adjoining properties. Add house numbers or names.
- Mark clearly the position of the hedge and how far it extends.

If you are complaining about the hedge blocking light, please also show on your plan:

- Which way is north.
- The position of windows that are affected by the hedge (e g whether they are located on the front, side or rear of the house).
- Relevant measurements (e g size of garden, distance between the hedge and any windows affected).

All measurements must be in metres (m).

[Insert example of typical plan]

Please include copies of any professional reports that you may have had prepared and of any other documents that you want the Council to take into account.

Section 4: Previous complaints to the Council

We only need to know about formal complaints, made under the high hedges Part of the Anti-social Behaviour Act 2003. You don't need to tell us about telephone calls or other informal contact with the Council about your hedge problems.

Section 5: Who's who/The parties

We need all these names and addresses because there are some documents that we are required, by law, to send to the owner **and** occupier of the land on which the hedge grows. These include our decision on the complaint.

Q5.1   Even if someone else is submitting the complaint on your behalf, it is important that we have your contact details.

Tick the 'Yes' box if you prefer to be contacted by e-mail. We cannot send documents to you electronically unless you agree.

Q5.2   You need to complete this section only if the complainant does not live in the property affected by the hedge. We need this information because we will have to get in touch with, the occupier to arrange to visit the property so that we can see for ourselves the effect of the hedge.

Q5.3   Complete this section if you are a professional adviser, relative, friend or other representative.

You will be our main contact on all matters relating to this complaint. We will direct all queries and correspondence to you. Please bear this in mind.

If you tick the 'Yes' box, we will conduct all business relating to this complaint by e-mail. But we cannot send documents to you electronically unless you agree.

Q5.4   This will normally be the person you have talked to when you tried to agree a solution to your hedge problems.

If the site where the hedge is growing does not have a postal address, use the box to describe as clearly as possible where it is, e g 'Land to rear of 12 to 18 High Street' or 'Park adjoining Tower Road'.

We need this information because we will have to contact these people for their comments, and to arrange to visit the site where the hedge is growing.

Q5.5   If you are in any doubt about who owns the property where the hedge is situated, you can check with the Land Registry. The relevant form (313) is on their website (www.landregistry.gov.uk) or can be obtained from the Local Office. The current fee for this service is [£4], if you know the full postal address of the property.

Alternatively, Land Register Online (at www.landregisteronline.gov.uk) provides easy access to details of registered properties in England. Copies of title plans and registers held in electronic format can be downloaded in PDF format for [£2] each. The register includes ownership details.

Section 6: Supporting documents

Please make sure you have ticked all the relevant boxes.

If you have ticked the last box, please list these documents by date and title (e g January 2005 – surveyor's report). This will help us to check that we have got everything.

If you are submitting this form by email but will be posting supporting documents to us separately, put a reference number or title on them (e g hedge complaint, Joe Bloggs, 12 High Street) so that we can match them up with your complaint.

Section 7: Sending the complaint

If you have to pay a fee, you should make out your cheque to [insert name] Council.

Complaint rejection: Invalid complaint

To be sent to the complainant

COMPLAINT ABOUT A HIGH HEDGE SITUATED AT [ADDRESS]

REFERENCE NUMBER [XXX]

I refer to your complaint of [date] about the high hedge situated at [address].

I am sorry to tell you that, under the terms of Part 8 of the Anti-social Behaviour Act 2003, the Council is unable to deal with your complaint and so will be taking no further action on it.

The reasons for our decision are as follows:

[explain why the requirements of the Act are not met – for example:

- your complaint is about a single tree. Under the Act, we can deal only with complaints about hedges that are made up of a line of 2 or more trees or shrubs;
- your complaint is about [species of tree or shrub] which are deciduous. Under the Act, we can deal only with complaints about hedges that are predominantly evergreen or semi-evergreen;
- your grounds of complaint are about the effect of the roots of the hedge. The Act states specifically that the Council cannot deal with such matters. We can only consider complaints related to the height of the hedge.]

I am returning the fee that accompanied your complaint.

If you would like further information about our decision, please contact [name and contact details of case officer], quoting the reference number given above.

There is no specific right of appeal if you disagree with our decision. But if you consider the Council has not applied the legislation properly or has treated you unfairly, you should write to the Council's complaints officer [name and contact details]. Alternatively, you may apply to the High Court to challenge the decision by judicial review. If you are considering applying for judicial review, you are advised to seek specialist legal help. Community Legal Service (CLS) [insert local contact details] can help you to find the right legal advice.

Complaint rejection: Insufficient efforts to resolve by negotiation

To be sent to the complainant

COMPLAINT ABOUT A HIGH HEDGE SITUATED AT [ADDRESS]

REFERENCE NUMBER [XXX]

I refer to your complaint of [date] about the high hedge situated at [address].

We have considered your complaint but have decided that we cannot take any further action on it for the following reasons:

[SET OUT REASONS – FOR EXAMPLE, you have not taken all reasonable steps to resolve the matter for yourselves.]

In particular, the Council consider that you should [set out what steps they should take to try to settle the dispute – for example:

- make a fresh approach to your neighbour as it is over [x] months since you last raised the issue with them;
- write to your neighbour if you are nervous about speaking to them. It is not enough to say that they are unapproachable;
- ask your neighbour to consider talking to independent mediators.]

Further advice on settling your hedge dispute is in the enclosed leaflet *Over the garden hedge*. [I am also sending details of the local community mediation service who can help you and your neighbour find a way forward.]

[INSERT COUNCIL POLICY ON FEES. FOR EXAMPLE, *it is the Council's policy not to refund fees in these circumstances.* OR *If these further steps lead to an agreed solution with your neighbour, you should write to us to reclaim your fee.*]

If, despite taking these further steps, you still cannot agree a solution with your neighbour, let me know. I will then advise you whether we can re-activate this complaint or whether you will need to submit a fresh one [with the relevant fee].

If you would like further information about our decision, please contact [name and contact details of case officer], quoting the reference number given above.

There is no specific right of appeal if you disagree with our decision. But if you consider the Council has not applied the legislation properly or has treated you unfairly, you should write to the Council's complaints officer [name and contact details]. Alternatively, you may apply to the High Court to challenge the decision by judicial review. If you are considering applying for judicial review, you are advised to seek specialist legal help. Community Legal Service (CLS) [insert local contact details] can help you to find the right legal advice.

Complaint rejection: Frivolous or vexatious

To be sent to the complainant

COMPLAINT ABOUT A HIGH HEDGE SITUATED AT [ADDRESS]

REFERENCE NUMBER [XXX]

I refer to your complaint of [date] about the high hedge situated at [address].

We have considered your complaint but have decided that we cannot take any further action on it for the following reasons:

[SET OUT REASONS – FOR EXAMPLE, the complaint is considered frivolous/vexatious.]

[EXPLAIN REASONS – FOR EXAMPLE, you previously complained about the hedge on [date] and were notified on [date] that the Council had decided that the hedge was not adversely affecting your reasonable enjoyment of your property. [This decision was upheld following an appeal to the Planning Inspectorate.] Your latest complaint indicates there has, subsequently, been no significant change in circumstances which would affect the Council's earlier decision.]

If you would like further information about our decision, please contact [name and contact details of case officer], quoting the reference number given above.

There is no specific right of appeal if you disagree with our decision. But if you consider the Council has not applied the legislation properly or has treated you unfairly, you should write to the Council's complaints officer [name and contact details]. Alternatively, you may apply to the High Court to challenge the decision by judicial review. If you are considering applying for judicial review, you are advised to seek specialist legal help. Community Legal Service (CLS) [insert local contact details] can help you to find the right legal advice.

Acknowledgement of complaint

To be sent to the complainant

COMPLAINT ABOUT A HIGH HEDGE SITUATED AT [ADDRESS]

REFERENCE NUMBER [XXX]

I acknowledge receipt of your complaint about a neighbouring high hedge, made under Part 8 of the Anti-social Behaviour Act 2003. We received your complaint and fee of £[amount] on [date].

Your complaint has been given the reference number: [insert].

It is being dealt with by [name, address and other contact details of the case officer].

Please contact this officer, quoting the reference number given above, if you have any questions about your complaint or our procedures. In particular, please let us know immediately of any relevant change in your circumstances. For example, if you cease to own or occupy the property affected by the hedge. Or if your neighbour agrees to reduce the hedge to a height that solves the problem.

We are satisfied, from the information you have provided, that your complaint meets the requirements set out in Part 8 of the Anti-social Behaviour Act 2003 and so is one that we can deal with.

We will be writing to the owner and occupier of the land where the hedge is situated to notify them that the Council are considering a complaint about their hedge. We will also invite them to comment on the points you have raised in your complaint and to provide any further information that they want us to take into account.

[SET OUT ANY ARRANGEMENTS FOR CONSULTING OTHER INTERESTED PARTIES. FOR EXAMPLE:

We will also be seeking the views of the occupiers of the properties at [addresses]. As the hedge in question also neighbours these properties, they could potentially be affected by the Council's decision on your complaint.

OR

As the trees in the hedge are protected under the Town and Country Planning Act 1990, it is the Council's policy to write to the Parish Council and local residents asking for their comments on your complaint.]

We will send you copies of all the comments that we receive so that you know what information and views we will be considering as we make a decision on your complaint.

When we have gathered all the written information and evidence, we will be in touch again to arrange a suitable date for an officer of the Council to visit the site. The purpose of the visit is to enable the officer to see the hedge and surroundings at first hand, to help us assess the comments that you and others have provided. The officer is not there to negotiate or mediate between you and your neighbour.

You will probably need to attend the visit as the officer will need to gain entry to your property. But please bear in mind that, although the Council officer might wish to ask questions to clarify factual points, they will not be able to discuss the merits of the case with either party. We will also be contacting the owner or occupier of the land where the hedge is situated so that the officer can view both sides of the hedge.

Under the Act, the Council is required to decide two things:

- whether the hedge, because of its height, is adversely affecting your reasonable enjoyment of your property; and
- if so, what action (if any) should be taken to remedy the situation or prevent it from recurring.

In reaching their decision, the Council will take account of all relevant factors and will seek to strike a balance between the competing interests of you and your neighbour, as well as the interests of the wider community.

We aim to issue a decision on your complaint within [number] weeks from the date of the site visit. We will send a copy of our decision, and the reasons for it, to you, [your agent,] the owner and occupier of the land where the hedge is situated [and anyone else who sends us comments on your complaint].

Notification of complaint: Occupier of the land where the hedge is situated

To be sent to the occupier of the property where the hedge is situated

COMPLAINT ABOUT A HIGH HEDGE SITUATED AT [ADDRESS]

REFERENCE NUMBER [XXX]

We have received the enclosed complaint, made under Part 8 of the Anti-social Behaviour Act 2003, that a hedge on your property is adversely affecting your neighbour at [address]. I understand your neighbour has discussed this with you previously but you have been unable to agree a solution.

I also enclose a copy of the leaflet *High hedges: complaining to the Council* which explains how the Council deals with such complaints.

The complaint has been given the reference number: [insert].

It is being dealt with by [name, address and other contact details of the case officer].

Please contact this officer, quoting the reference number given above, if you have any questions about the complaint or our procedures. In particular, please let us know immediately of any change in your circumstances. For example, if you cease to [own or] occupy the property where the hedge is situated. Or if you agree to reduce the hedge to a height that solves the problem.

To help us consider this complaint further, please complete the enclosed questionnaire and return it to me by [date]. You are also invited to send us any comments you might have on the points raised in the complaint and to provide any further information that you want us to take into account. This should reach us no later than [date].

You should send a copy of the questionnaire and other papers to the person who has made the complaint [and to the owner of your property], at the same time as you submit them to the Council. You might wish to bear this in mind in framing your comments. The complainant's name and address are on the complaints form. Please send us confirmation that you have done this.

[Set out any arrangements for consulting other interested parties. For example:

We will also be seeking the views of the occupiers of the properties at [addresses]. As the hedge in question also neighbours these properties, they could potentially be affected by the Council's decision on your complaint.

OR

As the trees in the hedge are protected under the Town and Country Planning Act 1990, it is the Council's policy to write to the Parish Council and local residents asking for their comments on your complaint.

We will send you copies of all the comments that we receive so that you know what information and views we will be considering as we make a decision on the complaint.]

When we have gathered all the written information and evidence, we will be in touch again to arrange a suitable date for an officer of the Council to visit the site. The purpose of the visit is to enable the officer to see the hedge and surroundings at first hand, to help us assess the comments that you and [your neighbour/others] have provided. The officer is not there to negotiate or mediate between you and your neighbour.

You will probably need to attend the visit as the officer will need to gain entry to your property. But please bear in mind that, although the Council officer might wish to ask questions to clarify factual points, they will not be able to discuss the merits of the case with either party. We will also be contacting the complainant so that the officer can view both sides of the hedge.

Under the Act, the Council is required to decide two things:

- whether the hedge, because of its height, is adversely affecting the complainant's reasonable enjoyment of their property; and
- if so, what action (if any) should be taken to remedy the situation or prevent it from recurring.

In reaching their decision, the Council will take account of all relevant factors and will seek to strike a balance between the competing interests of you and your neighbour, as well as the interests of the wider community.

We aim to issue a decision on the complaint within [number] weeks from the date of the site visit. We will send a copy of our decision, and the reasons for it, to you, [the owner of your property,] the complainant [and anyone else who sends us comments on the complaint].

Questionnaire: To be completed by the occupier of the land where the hedge is situated

COMPLAINT ABOUT A HIGH HEDGE SITUATED AT [ADDRESS]

1. Your name and contact details

Name:

Telephone No. (daytime):

Email address:

Do you prefer to be contacted by email?

2. Contact details for the owner of the property (if different)

Name:

Address:

Telephone No. (daytime):

Email address:

3. Legal restrictions

As far as you know:

- Was the hedge planted under a condition attached to a planning permission?
- Does a condition attached to a planning permission specify that the hedge must be retained?
  - If you have answered YES to either of the above questions, what year was the permission given?
  - Please supply a copy.
- Is there a legal covenant that stipulates the size or type of hedge that can be grown (this will usually be spelt out in the deeds to the property)?
  - If you have answered YES, what are the terms of the covenant?
  - What year was it introduced?
  - Please supply a copy.
- Is the property a listed building?
- Is it located within a conservation area?
- Are any trees in the hedge protected by a tree preservation order?
- Have you seen any birds or bats nesting or roosting in the hedge?

4. Representations

Please delete as appropriate

I shall/shall not be sending comments on the complaint, or other information that I want the Council to take into account.

Notification of complaint: Owner of the land where the hedge is situated (if different to the occupier)

To be sent to the owner of the property where the hedge is situated. This letter should be issued as soon as the relevant contact details are provided to the Council – either on the complaint form or the occupier's questionnaire.

COMPLAINT ABOUT A HIGH HEDGE SITUATED AT [ADDRESS]

REFERENCE NUMBER [XXX]

I enclose a copy of a letter sent to [name and address of the occupier of the land where the hedge is situated] notifying them that the Council has received a complaint about a hedge on the property. I understand that you own the land in question and so have an interest in this matter.

To help us consider this complaint further, you are invited to send us any comments you might have on the points raised in the complaint and to provide any further information that you want us to take into account. This should reach us no later than [date]. [Please also let us have answers to any items of the questionnaire that the occupier of the property has been unable to deal with.]

You should send a copy of these papers to the person who has made the complaint and to the occupier of your property, at the same time as you submit them to the Council. You might wish to bear this in mind in framing your comments. The complainant's name and address is on the complaints form. Please send us confirmation that you have done this.

We will send you a copy of our decision, and the reasons for it, in due course.

Decision letter: No remedial action (illustrates short decision letter for use where case report is appended to the decision)

To be sent to the complainant and every owner and occupier of the land where the hedge is situated

COMPLAINT ABOUT A HIGH HEDGE LOCATED AT [ADDRESS]

REFERENCE NUMBER [XXX]

I refer to the complaint, made under Part 8 of the Anti-social Behaviour Act 2003, about the high hedge situated at [site address/description]. The complaint alleged that the hedge is adversely affecting the enjoyment of the domestic property at [address]. In particular, it was alleged that the hedge [summarise main grounds of complaint].

The Council have taken into account:

- representations and other information submitted by the complainant and by the [owner/occupier] of the land where the hedge is situated;
- [representations received from [number] other interested parties;]
- the contribution that the hedge makes to the character and amenity of the area. [We have paid special attention to the fact that the hedge is situated in a conservation area/the trees in the hedge are protected by a tree preservation order.]

An officer of the Council visited the site on [date].

Main Considerations and Conclusion

I enclose a copy of the case report which summarises the representations and other information before the Council and explains how we have assessed and weighed the various issues raised by the complaint.

The Council's role in these cases is to seek to strike a balance between the competing rights of neighbours to enjoy their respective properties and the rights of the community in general, and thereby to formulate a proportionate response to the complaint.

As the report indicates, the main considerations in this case are whether the problems complained of are sufficiently serious to justify action being taken in relation to the hedge, bearing in mind the effect such action would have on the property where the hedge is situated and on the wider area. [DEAL CONCISELY WITH THE MAIN ISSUES. THESE WILL NORMALLY RELATE TO THE DEGREE OF HARM CAUSED BY THE HEDGE AND WHETHER THIS IS OUTWEIGHED BY ITS AMENITY VALUE TO BOTH THE HEDGE OWNER AND THE WIDER COMMUNITY. FOR EXAMPLE:

The report notes that the hedge is obstructing light to some windows in the complainant's property. The impact, at present, is not severe and would be remedied by the hedge being lightly trimmed. Other problems identified, such as litter from the hedge, are considered to be inconvenient and of little significance. On the other hand, the hedges defining the separation between the dwellings in this street are a characteristic feature of the conservation area. If the size of the hedge were to be reduced, it would have an adverse effect on the appearance of the neighbourhood and on the amenity of other residents. On balance, the Council believe that the harm caused by the hedge is outweighed by other factors and that no remedial action is justified.]

Formal Decision

For the reasons given [above/in the case report], the Council have decided that [the height of the hedge in question is not adversely affecting the complainant's reasonable enjoyment of their property/no action should be taken in relation to the hedge to remedy its adverse effect or to prevent its recurrence].

If you would like further information about our decision, please contact [name and contact details of case officer], quoting the reference number given above.

Right of Appeal

The complainant, [name], can appeal to the Planning Inspectorate against the Council's decision. Further information is in the leaflet *High hedges: appealing against the Council's decision*, a copy of which is enclosed. An appeal must be submitted to the Planning Inspectorate, on their official form, within 28 days from the date of this letter. The form is available on the Planning Inspectorate website at www.planning-inspectorate.gov.uk or from:

High Hedges Appeals Team
Planning Inspectorate
Regus House
Room 2/15
1 Friary
Temple Quay
Bristol BS1 6EA

Telephone: 0117 344 5687.

The complainant can appeal on either of the following grounds:

- that, contrary to the decision of the Council, the hedge in question is adversely affecting the complainant's reasonable enjoyment of their property; and/or
- that the adverse effect warrants action being taken in relation to the hedge.

Advice

[Offer practical advice on how the hedge might be managed so that it does not cause problems in the future. For example:

It is recommended that the hedge is trimmed annually to maintain it at, or around, its current height of [4] metres, in order to preserve the contribution it makes to the character of the conservation area and prevent any adverse effect on the reasonable enjoyment of the complainant's property.]

I am sending this letter to the complainant and the owner and occupier of the land where the hedge is situated. [Copies also go to other interested parties who commented on the complaint].

Decision letter: Remedial action (illustrates longer decision letter for use where there is no separate case report)

To be sent to the complainant and every owner and occupier of the land where the hedge is situated

COMPLAINT ABOUT A HIGH HEDGE LOCATED AT [ADDRESS]

REFERENCE NUMBER [XXX]

I refer to the complaint, made under Part 8 of the Anti-social Behaviour Act 2003, about the high hedge situated at [site address/description]. The complaint alleged that the hedge is adversely affecting the enjoyment of the domestic property at [address].

The Council gathered evidence and information in relation to the complaint by inviting the [owner/occupier] of the land where the hedge is situated to submit a statement [and by consulting selected organisations that appeared to the Council to have an interest in the matter]. In addition, an officer of the Council visited the site on [date].

This letter summarises the evidence and information gathered by the Council and explains how we have assessed and weighed the various issues raised by the complaint.

The Hedge and its Surroundings

[Brief description of the hedge and its setting. Include the height and length of the hedge and general species content; assessment of its growth habit and condition (e g gaps); evidence (if any) of past management; its position in relation to the complainant's property, with relevant measurements, and in relation to other features on the land where it is growing (e g the hedge owner's house). Other relevant factors might include orientation, size of gardens, any differences in levels between the two properties, other trees and vegetation. In addition, describe the general character of the area and any special features (e g conservation area).]

Relevant Policies or Legislation

[Draw attention to any policies, or legal restrictions, that apply and could be material to the Council's consideration of the complaint. These provide evidence of the community/public interest in the matter. They might include local landscape character assessments, planning policies, existence of a tree preservation order or a planning condition.]

Case for the Complainant

[Summarise the material points from the complaint form and other information submitted. For example:

The hedge is too large in view of its proximity to the small bungalow at [address] and the limited extent of the rear gardens. The dense shade it casts makes it necessary to use artificial lights within the bungalow during the daytime throughout the year. The hedge also blocks out the sky and creates a depressing living environment. In the garden, it suppresses plant growth. It also sheds copious amounts of needles throughout the year which create hazardous conditions if not cleared continually.]

Case for the Owner/Occupier of the Land where the Hedge is Situated

[Summarise the material points from the statement and other information submitted. For example:

If the hedge were reduced to the height that the complainant wants, it would affect the privacy enjoyed by the occupiers of [address] and would probably kill the hedge. It helps to stop noise and smoke from the complainant's barbecue parties. An offer was made to the complainant allowing them to trim the hedge at their expense. The cost involved in reducing the size of the hedge is beyond the means of the occupiers of [address].]

Case for Other Interested Parties/Results of Consultation

[State the nature of any representations received and summarise the material points. For example:

The Council received a petition signed by 10 residents of [name of street/address]. They supported the complainant's case but, as their properties do not neighbour the land where the hedge is situated, none experience problems with it.]

Main Considerations

[Set out the role of the Council and the main issues to be considered. For example:

The Council's role in these cases is to seek to strike a balance between the competing rights of neighbours to enjoy their respective properties and the rights of the community in general, and thereby to formulate a proportionate response to the complaint.

The main considerations in this case are whether the problems complained of are sufficiently serious to justify action being taken in relation to the hedge, bearing in mind the effect such action would have on the property where the hedge is situated and on the wider area.]

Appraisal of the Evidence

[Drawing on the advice in Chapter 5: *Assessing and Weighing the Evidence*, assess the harm caused by the hedge with specific reference to the material points in the complainant's case. Weigh against this the amenity value of the hedge to the hedge owner and the wider community, with specific reference to the material points identified in the earlier sections. For example:

Light obstruction

The Council followed the method in the BRE guidelines on 'Hedge height and light loss' for calculating what height a hedge should be in order not to cause an unreasonable obstruction of light to windows and gardens. The results showed that the hedge in question is 3 metres taller than the recommended height. This indicates it is having a significant impact on the complainant's property. This was reinforced by observations during the site visit. This was made at 11:00 am. At that time, the rear windows of the bungalow and a substantial portion of the garden were in dense shade cast by the hedge.

Visual amenity

The complainant's property is in a terrace of small bungalows with very limited rear gardens. There are few trees in the area. The hedge is out of keeping with this setting. Through its size and proximity to the complainant's bungalow and garden, the hedge dominates the scene and has a severe effect on the complainant's living conditions.

Plant growth, litter

Although many plants in the complainant's garden were straggly and in poor condition, it was impossible to assess whether this was due to the height of the hedge. The roots of it and other vegetation could dry out the soil. Under the high hedges legislation, the Council cannot take into account the effects of the roots of a hedge. In addition, the problem might be remedied by using alternative plants that are more suited to the prevailing conditions. During the site visit, there was little tree debris noted in the complainant's garden. Most came from other vegetation and the volume was sufficient to fill a single bag. This might be an inconvenience but, on its own, has no appreciable effect on the complainant's enjoyment of their property.

Privacy

There is no difference in level between the land where the hedge is situated and the complainant's property. Although reduction of the height of the hedge would mean less privacy for the property with the hedge than they now enjoy, a height of 2 metres would be enough to prevent overlooking and so provide a reasonable degree of privacy.

Noise, smoke

Although the perception might be that the hedge blocks noise and smoke, in practice it is ineffective as a barrier against such nuisances. Both noise and smoke will pass through or round a hedge. These are not, therefore good reasons for growing a large hedge.

Cost of remedial action

The Council note that cutting down the hedge is considered unaffordable. This is not, however, material to the question that the Council must determine – ie whether the hedge is adversely affecting the reasonable enjoyment of the complainant's property – and so has not been taken into account. Such expenses must be expected and accepted as part of the general maintenance of the property, with its trees, in the same way as maintenance of doors and windows and household wear and tear.

Health of the hedge

The hedge is vigorous and healthy. However, cutting the hedge down to the height recommended by the BRE guidelines on 'Hedge height and light loss' would involve a reduction of more than one-third of its current height. This could result in the destruction of the hedge and might restrict any action to be taken in relation to the hedge.]

Conclusion

[Summarise the material points emerging from the appraisal. For example:

The hedge is causing significant obstruction of daylight and sunlight to the complainant's bungalow. It is out of keeping with its setting and dominates the complainant's property, severely affecting living conditions and visual amenity. Other problems identified, such as litter from the hedge, are considered to be inconvenient and of little significance. Evidence suggests that the height of the hedge would need to be reduced by 4 metres in order to remedy the problems identified. Such a height would be sufficient to safeguard the privacy of the occupiers of [address] and would not, in the Council's view, adversely affect the enjoyment of that property or the general character and amenity of the neighbourhood. On balance, the Council believe that the harm caused by the hedge outweighs other factors and that remedial action is justified.

Such action would, however, involve a reduction of more than one-third of its current height, affecting the ability of the hedge to regenerate and possibly leading to its destruction. For this reason, the Council considers the reduction of the hedge should be carried out in stages over a period of years/less drastic reduction of the hedge is justified.]

Formal Decision

For the reasons given [above/in the case report], the Council have decided that the height of the hedge in question is adversely affecting the complainant's reasonable enjoyment of their property and hereby issue the enclosed remedial notice specifying the action that must be taken in relation to the hedge to remedy its adverse effect [and to prevent its recurrence].

Summary of Requirements of Remedial Notice

[SUMMARISE, IN PLAIN LANGUAGE, THE MAIN REQUIREMENTS OF THE REMEDIAL NOTICE SO THAT IT IS CLEAR WHAT ACTION NEEDS TO BE TAKEN. FOR EXAMPLE:

The remedial notice specifies that the hedge should be reduced [in stages] to a height of no more than [3] metres above ground level within [2 years] of the date of the notice – that is by [date]. Reduction to this height allows the hedge to grow between annual or more frequent trimming and still not cause significant problems.

After the above date, the hedge should be trimmed regularly to ensure that it never exceeds a height of [4] metres above ground level. The requirement to maintain the hedge at, or below, this height lasts until the hedge is removed or dies.]

Person Responsible for Taking Remedial Action

Under the Act, the owner or occupier of [address of the land where the hedge is situated] is obliged to carry out the works specified in the remedial notice, within any timescale set there. Failure to do so may result in prosecution and a fine.

The remedial notice does not give the complainant any right to intervene and take the necessary action themselves.

Right of Appeal

The complainant and everyone who is an owner or occupier of the land where the hedge is situated, that is [names], can appeal to the Planning Inspectorate against the issue of the remedial notice. Further information is in the leaflet *High hedges: appealing against the Council's decision*, a copy of which is enclosed. An appeal must be submitted to the Planning Inspectorate, on their official form, within 28 days from the date of this letter. The form is available on the Planning Inspectorate website at www.planning-inspectorate.gov.uk or from:

High Hedges Appeals Team
Planning Inspectorate
Regus House
Room 2/15
1 Friary
Temple Quay
Bristol BS1 6EA

Telephone: 0117 344 5687.

An appeal can be made on any one or more of the following grounds:

- that the action specified in the remedial notice falls short of what is needed to remedy the adverse effect of the hedge or to prevent it recurring;
- (that, contrary to the decision of the Council, the hedge in question is not adversely affecting the complainant's reasonable enjoyment of their property;
- that the action specified in the remedial notice exceeds what is reasonably necessary or appropriate to remedy the adverse effect of the hedge or to prevent it recurring;
- that not enough time has been allowed to carry out the works set out in the notice.

The remedial notice will be suspended while any appeal is being determined.

If you would like further information about our decision, please contact [name and contact details of case officer], quoting the reference number given above.

I am sending this letter to the complainant and the owner and occupier of the land where the hedge is situated. [Copies also go to other interested parties who commented on the complaint.]

Remedial notice

To be sent to the complainant and every owner and occupier of the land where the hedge is situated

Important – this notice affects the property at [address of the land where the hedge is situated]

Anti-social Behaviour Act 2003

Remedial notice

ISSUED BY: [Council name]

1. The notice

This Notice is issued by the Council under section 69 of the Anti-social Behaviour Act 2003 pursuant to a complaint about a high hedge situated at [address]. The Council has decided that the hedge in question is adversely affecting the reasonable enjoyment of the property at [complainant's address] and that action should be taken in relation to the hedge with a view to remedying the adverse effect [and preventing its recurrence].

2. The hedge to which the notice relates

[This will normally be the hedge, or part of it, that meets the legal definition and is the subject of the complaint.]

The hedge [in the rear garden] at [address] and marked red on the attached plan. *[complaint relates to whole hedge]*

OR

The portion of hedge [in the rear garden] at [address] marked red on the attached plan. The portion is [10] metres in length, measured from the end of the hedge that is closest to the house at this address. This point is marked X on the plan. *[complaint relates to part of a longer hedge, the rest of which is not a high hedge]*

AND

The [portion of] hedge is formed predominantly of [name e g cypress] trees [and shrubs].

3.   What action must be taken in relation to the hedge

Initial Action

The Council requires the following steps to be taken in relation to the hedge before the end of the period specified in paragraph 4 below: [SPECIFY THE ACTION NECESSARY TO REMEDY THE PROBLEMS CAUSED BY THE HEDGE, PLUS A GROWING MARGIN TO FORESTALL FURTHER PROBLEMS IN THE SHORT TERM. FOR EXAMPLE:

    (i)   reduce the hedge to a height not exceeding [3] metres above ground level.]

Preventative Action

Following the end of the period specified in paragraph 4 below, the Council requires the following steps to be taken in relation to the hedge: [SPECIFY THE LONG-TERM MANAGEMENT OF THE HEDGE NECESSARY TO PREVENT PROBLEMS RECURRING. FOR EXAMPLE:

    (i)   maintain the hedge so that at no time does it exceed a height of [4] metres above ground level.]

Informative

[Offer practical advice on implementing the requirements in the Notice. For example:

It is recommended that the hedge is cut back annually to a height of [3] metres. This allows room for the hedge to re-grow between annual trimmings and still not exceed a height of [4] metres.

As set out above, the hedge should be reduced in stages. Please contact the Council to discuss and agree a suitable timetable for these works.

All works should be carried out in accordance with good arboricultural practice/BS 3998: ''Recommendations for Tree Work'.

It is recommended that skilled contractors are employed to carry out this specialist work. For a list of approved contractors to carry out works on trees and hedges, see the Arboricultural Association's website at www.trees.org.uk.

In taking the action specified in this Notice, special care should be taken not to disturb wild animals that are protected by the Wildlife and Countryside Act 1981. This includes birds and bats that nest or roost in trees.]

4.   Time for compliance

The initial action [steps (x) to (y)] specified in paragraph 3 above to be complied with in full within [8] months of the date specified in paragraph 5 of this Notice.

[NOTE: SPECIFY A 'PERIOD' OF TIME; UNDER THE ACT, THE NOTICE CANNOT FIX A DATE FOR COMPLETION.]

5.   When this notice takes effect

This Notice takes effect on [specify date, not less than 28 days after the date of issue].

6. Failure to comply with the notice

Failure by any person who, at the relevant time, is an owner or occupier of the land where the [portion of] hedge specified in paragraph 2 above is situated:

     a.   to take action in accordance with steps [(x) to (y) – the initial action] specified in paragraph 3 above within the period specified in paragraph 4; or

     b.   to take action in accordance with steps [(c) to (d) – preventative action] specified in paragraph 3 above by any time stated there;

may result in prosecution in the Magistrates Court with a fine of up to £1,000. The Council also has power, in these circumstances, to enter the land where the hedge is situated and carry out the specified works. The Council may use these powers whether or not a prosecution is brought. The costs of such works will be recovered from the owner or occupier of the land.

Dated:

Signed: [Council's authorised officer] on behalf of

[Council's name and address]

Remedial notice: Specifying the action

Initial Action

Reduction to a single height along the whole of its length

     (i)   reduce the hedge to a height not exceeding [3] metres above ground level.

Reduction to a single height in stages

     (i)   reduce the hedge to a height not exceeding [6] metres above ground level;

     (ii)   [9] months after the completion of step (i), further reduce the hedge to a height not exceeding [4.5] metres above ground level.

Reduction to a single height along part of its length

The following example might apply where only the section of the hedge nearest the windows of the complainant's property is to be reduced.

     (i)   reduce the hedge to a height not exceeding [3] metres above ground level for a length of [8] metres, [measured from/centred on] the point where the hedge is closest to the windows of the house at [complainant's address]. This point is marked X on the attached plan.

The following might apply where only a section of a longer hedge affects the complainant's property.

     (i)   reduce the section of hedge that adjoins the (complainant's) property at [address] to a height not exceeding [3] metres above ground level;

OR

     (i)   reduce to a height not exceeding [3] metres above ground level the section of hedge measuring 20 metres in length from the point where the boundaries of the properties at [addresses – complainant's and site of the hedge] meet. This point is marked X on the plan.

Lift the crowns of trees in the hedge

(i)   lift the crowns of the trees/shrubs in the hedge to a height of [4] metres above ground level.

Retain selected trees in the hedge

(i)   reduce the hedge, other than the trees identified below, to a height not exceeding [3] metres above ground level;

(ii)   no action is to be taken in relation to 1 x [rowan] tree and 1 x [oak] tree circled black on the attached plan.

Preventative Action

Maintain at a single height along the whole of its length

THE FOLLOWING FORMULA LEAVES THE DETAILS OF THE MANAGEMENT REGIME FOR THE OWNER OR OCCUPIER OF THE LAND WHERE THE HEDGE IS SITUATED TO DECIDE. THEY MIGHT COMPLY WITH THE TERMS OF THE NOTICE BY ANNUAL PRUNING TO A HEIGHT THAT ALLOWS THE HEDGE TO RE-GROW BETWEEN CUTS. ALTERNATIVELY, THEY MIGHT CARRY OUT MORE FREQUENT LIGHT TRIMMING TO ACHIEVE THE SAME EFFECT.

(i)   maintain the hedge so that at no time does it exceed a height of [4] metres.

The example below would require the owner or occupier of the land where the hedge is situated to carry out annual pruning to a height that allows the hedge to re-grow between cuts. The margin allowed for re-growth would vary according to the species of trees/shrubs in the hedge.

(i)   at any time that the hedge reaches a height of [4] metres above ground level, reduce it to a height not exceeding [3] metres above ground level.

Maintain at a single height along part of its length

(i)   maintain the section of hedge to which the initial action specified above relates so that at no time does it exceed a height of [4] metres above ground level.

Maintain hedge at a reduced height whilst retaining selected trees

(i)   maintain the hedge so that – other than the trees identified above – at no time does it exceed a height of [4] metres above ground level.

INDEX

References are to paragraph numbers.